DESCUBRE 1

Lengua y cultura del mundo hispánico

Testing Program

ISBN: 978-1-68004-517-8

1 2 3 4 5 6 7 8 9 PP 21 20 19 18 17 16

Table of Contents

Introduction

Descubre Testing Program

The **Descubre nivel 1** Testing Program contains quizzes for each **Contextos** section and **Estructura** grammar point, six tests for each lesson, two versions of a cumulative final exam, oral testing suggestions, optional testing sections, and scripts for the listening activities. All components of the printed Testing Program are available on the Instructor side of the Supersite in RTF.

Vocabulary and Grammar Quizzes

The **Descubre nivel 1** Testing Program offers two Quizzes for each lesson's **Contextos** section and every grammar point in **Estructura.** Each **Quiz A** uses discrete answer formats, such as multiple-choice, fill-in-the-blanks, matching, and completing charts, while **Quiz B** uses more open-ended formats, such as asking students to write sentences using prompts or respond to a topic in paragraph format. There is no listening comprehension section on the **Quizzes.** Each quiz is one to two pages in length and is based on a 20-point scale. These quizzes are ideal for spot-checking student comprehension of lesson vocabulary or a specific grammar topic. They can be completed in 5–10 minutes.

The Lesson Tests

The lesson tests consist of three different sets of testing materials per lesson, with two versions per set. **Tests** A and B are three pages long; they contain open-ended questions requiring students to write sentences and paragraphs, as well as discrete-answer activities. Versions A and B are interchangeable, for purposes of administering make-up tests.

Tests C and **D** are briefer and also interchangeable. **Tests A, B, C,** and **D** have been updated and edited to simplify the instructions to students.

Tests E and **F** are a third interchangeable pair that test students' mastery of lesson vocabulary and grammar. This pair uses discrete answer formats, such as matching, multiple-choice, and fill-in-the-blanks. **Tests E** and **F** can be assigned on the Supersite and are graded by computer. All of the **Tests** contain a listening comprehension section.

Each **Test** begins with a listening section that focuses on the grammar, vocabulary, and theme of the lesson. For this section, you may either read from the script in the Testing Program or play the recording on the Testing Program MP3s, available on the Supersite and on the Teacher's Resource DVD. For **Tests A** and **B** and **Tests E** and **F**, the recordings consist of narrations presented in a variety of formats, such as commercials, radio broadcasts, voicemail messages, television broadcasts, and descriptive monologues. The accompanying exercises focus on global comprehension and, where appropriate, students' ability to understand key details. You should therefore prompt students to read the items in the listening comprehension section before playing the audio or reading the script aloud. For **Tests C** and **D**, students must listen to and answer personalized questions, which are designed to incorporate the lesson's theme and vocabulary while prompting students to respond using the new grammar structures.

After the listening section, you will find test activities that check students' knowledge of the corresponding lesson's active vocabulary and grammar structures. For **Tests A** and **B**, activities combine open-ended questions with discrete answer items. Formats include, but are not limited to, art-based activities, personalized questions, sentence completion, and cloze paragraphs. For **Tests C** and **D**, primarily open-ended formats are used, and for **Tests E** and **F**, discrete answer items are used.

All tests incorporate a reading section. Readings are presented as various forms of realia, such as advertisements, articles, or personal correspondence. Each reading is accompanied by a set of questions designed to test students' overall comprehension of the text.

Tests A, B, C, and **D** end with a writing activity that emphasizes personalized communication and self-expression. Students are asked to produce a brief writing sample designed to elicit the vocabulary and grammar of the corresponding textbook lesson within a realistic context.

Tests A, B, E, and **F** are three pages each and are based on a 100-point scale. They are designed to take about 25–30 minutes. **Tests C** and **D** are two pages each and are based on a 50-point scale. They should take students about 15–20 minutes. Point values for each test section are provided in parentheses at the end of each direction line.

The Cumulative Final Exams

The final exams follow the same general organization as **Tests A** and **B**. Each **Exam** begins with a listening comprehension section, continues with achievement- and proficiency-oriented vocabulary and grammar checks, and ends with a reading activity and a personalized writing task. The exams are cumulative and comprehensive, encompassing the main vocabulary fields, key grammar points, and principal language functions covered in the corresponding textbook lessons. Scripts for the listening passages are located in the same separate section of this Testing Program as the scripts for the **Tests**.

Like **Tests A** and **B**, each **Exam** is based on a 100-point scale. Point values for each activity are provided in parentheses at the end of each direction line. The exams are six pages each and are designed to take 40–50 minutes.

The Optional Test Sections

For instructors who wish to evaluate students in areas outside the scope of the **Tests** and **Exams,** five optional sections are provided for each set of tests and exams. Four brief activities separately review the **Fotonovela** video, the **Panorama** textbook section, the **Panorama cultural** video, and the **Flash cultura** video. In addition, an alternate listening section is provided for **Tests A** and **B** and **Exams A** and **B**, in which students answer personalized questions instead of listening to a narration and completing a comprehension exercise. Each activity should take 5–7 minutes.

The Testing Program MP3s and Test Files

The Testing Program includes the quizzes, tests, exams, audioscripts, optional test sections, and answer key in RTF, as well as the audio recordings for the tests and exams in MP3 files.

The Oral Testing Suggestions

Suggestions for oral tests are offered for groups of three lessons. The suggestions consist of two options: personalized questions and situational role-plays. As is standard for proficiency-oriented assessments, the situations are given in English so as not to reveal to students the Spanish vocabulary fields and structures they are intended to elicit. The questions, on the other hand, are provided in Spanish to allow you to use them readily without time-consuming advance preparation.

Some Suggestions for Use

While the materials in the quizzes, tests, and exams reflect the content of the corresponding lessons in the **Descubre nivel 1** Student Text, you may have emphasized certain vocabulary topics, grammar points, or textbook sections more than others. It is therefore strongly recommended that you look over each test or exam before you administer it, to ensure that it reflects the vocabulary, grammar, and language skills you have stressed in class. Additionally, you should feel free to modify any test or exam by adding an optional test section or adapting an existing activity so that the testing material meets the guidelines of "testing what you teach." The editable RTF Test Files on the Supersite are a useful tool for this purpose.

You can alleviate many students' test anxieties by telling them in advance how many points are assigned to each section and what sorts of activities they will see. You may even provide them with a few sample test items. If, for example, you are going to be administering **Test A** for **Lección 1**, you may want to show students items from **Test B**.

When administering the listening sections of the tests or exams, it is a good idea to begin by going over the direction lines with students so that they are comfortable with the instructions and the content of what they are going to hear. You might also want to give them a moment to look over any listening-based items they will have to complete and let them know if they will hear the narration or questions once or twice. If you read from the scripts yourself instead of playing the Testing Program MP3s, it is recommended that you read each selection twice at a normal speed, without emphasizing or pausing to isolate specific words or expressions.

Like many instructors nationwide, you may want to evaluate your students' oral communication skills at the end of each semester or quarter. For ideas and information, see the Oral Testing Suggestions section in this Testing Program.

*The **Descubre** Authors and the Vista Higher Learning Editorial Staff*

Oral Testing Suggestions

As you begin each oral test, remind students that you are testing their ability to understand and produce acceptable Spanish, so they must give you as complete an answer as possible. It is strongly recommended that you establish a tone in which the test takes on, as much as possible, the ambience of natural communication, rather than that of an interrogation or artificial exchange in which the instructor asks all the questions and students answer them. To put students at ease, start with small talk in Spanish, using familiar questions such as **¿Cómo estás?** and commenting on the weather or time of day. During the test, it is also a good idea to give students verbal or gestural feedback about the messages they convey, including reactions, comments, signs of agreement or disagreement, or transitions in the form of conversational fillers. Finally, as you end the test, it is recommended that you bring students to closure and put them at ease by asking them simple, personalized questions.

If the oral test revolves around a situation, you can have two students interact, or you can play the role of one of the characters. To build students' confidence and comfort levels, you might want to begin the interaction so that students have some language to react to.

Many evaluation tools or rubrics exist for the grading of oral tests. The following is a simplified rubric, which you should feel free to adjust to reflect the type of task that students are asked to perform, the elements that you have stressed in your classes, and your own beliefs about language learning.

Oral Testing Rubric

Fluency	1	2	3	4	5	**24–25**	Excellent (A)
Pronunciation	1	2	3	4	5	**21–23**	Very Good (B)
Vocabulary	1	2	3	4	5	**18–20**	Average (C)
Structure	1	2	3	4	5	**15–17**	Below Average (D)
Comprehensibility	1	2	3	4	5	**Below 15**	Unacceptable (F)

Oral Testing Suggestions for *Lecciones 1–3*

Preguntas

- ¿Cómo te llamas?
- ¿Cómo estás?
- ¿De dónde eres?
- ¿Cuántos años tienes?
- ¿Dónde vive tu familia?
- ¿Dónde vives tú?
- ¿Cuál es tu (número de) teléfono?
- ¿Tienes una familia grande?
- ¿Tienes hermanos? ¿Cuántos?
- ¿Tienes novio/a (esposo/a)? ¿Cómo es?
- ¿Cómo son tus padres? ¿Cómo se llaman?
- ¿Qué tienes que hacer hoy?
- ¿Qué tienes ganas de hacer esta noche?
- ¿Qué clases tomas?
- ¿Qué hay en tu mochila?
- ¿Trabajas? ¿Dónde?

Situación

You run into a Spanish-speaking friend at your university or college. Greet your friend, talk about the classes you are taking (what they are, the days of the week and/or time of day they take place) and what the professors are like. Then say goodbye.

Oral Testing Suggestions for *Lecciones 4–6*

Preguntas

- ¿Cómo pasaste tus ratos libres el fin de semana pasado?
- ¿Qué hiciste anoche?
- ¿Qué vas a hacer el fin de semana que viene?
- ¿Qué quieres hacer esta noche?
- ¿Adónde vas esta tarde después de la clase?
- Cuando estás de vacaciones, ¿qué haces?
- ¿Qué lugares bonitos conoces para ir de vacaciones?
- ¿Piensas ir de vacaciones este verano? ¿Adónde? ¿Por qué?
- ¿Sales mucho? ¿Cuándo sales? ¿Con quién(es)?
- ¿Sabes hablar otras lenguas? ¿Cuáles?
- ¿Dónde te gusta ir cuando hace buen tiempo? ¿Por qué?
- ¿Qué te gusta hacer cuando llueve/nieva?
- ¿Qué están haciendo tus compañeros/as de clase ahora mismo?
- ¿Qué están haciendo tus amigos/as en este momento?
- ¿Cuáles son tus colores favoritos?
- ¿Qué ropa llevas en el invierno? ¿En el verano?

Situación

You are in a store looking for some new clothes to wear to a party. Interact with the sales clerk. Find out how much at least three articles of clothing cost, and buy at least one item.

Oral Testing Suggestions for *Lecciones 7–9*

Preguntas

- ¿Cómo es tu rutina diaria? Por ejemplo, ¿a qué hora te levantas?
- ¿A qué hora te acostaste anoche? ¿Dormiste bien?
- ¿Cómo te sientes cuando tomas un examen? ¿Y cuando hablas en español?
- ¿Te interesan más las ciencias o las humanidades? ¿Por qué?
- ¿Quién fue tu maestro/a favorito/a el semestre/trimestre pasado? ¿Por qué?
- ¿Qué te molesta más de esta universidad? ¿Qué cosas te encantan?
- ¿Cuáles son tus comidas y bebidas favoritas? ¿Por qué?
- ¿Cuáles son los mejores restaurantes que conoces? ¿Y los peores? ¿Por qué? ¿Vas mucho a comer a estos restaurantes?
- ¿Fuiste a una fiesta el fin de semana pasado? ¿Adónde? ¿Con quién(es)?
- ¿Tuviste que trabajar el sábado pasado? ¿Dónde? ¿Qué hiciste?
- ¿Les das regalos a tus amigos/as (hijos/as) (padres)? ¿Cuándo y por qué?
- ¿Cuándo es tu cumpleaños? ¿Qué te regalaron tus amigos y tu familia el año pasado?

Situación

You are in a café or a restaurant. Interact with the server to order something to eat and drink.

Nombre ______________________ Fecha ______________________

CONTEXTOS Lección 1

Quiz A

1 Seleccionar Select the item that does not belong. (5 x 1 pt. each = 5 pts.)

1. a. ¿Qué tal?
   b. ¿De dónde eres?
   c. ¿Cómo estás?
   d. ¿Qué hay de nuevo?
2. a. Chau.
   b. Nos vemos.
   c. Igualmente.
   d. Adiós.
3. a. Hola, me llamo Ángel.
   b. Soy el señor Carvajal.
   c. Saludos a Fabiana.
   d. ¿Cómo se llama usted?
4. a. Encantado.
   b. Bien, gracias. ¿Y tú?
   c. No muy bien.
   d. Regular.
5. a. Le presento a David González.
   b. Ésta es Teresa.
   c. Te presento a Federico.
   d. No hay de qué.

2 Emparejar Match the questions and responses. One answer will not be used. (5 x 1 pt. each = 5 pts.)

______ 1. ¿De dónde es usted?
______ 2. ¿Cómo te llamas?
______ 3. ¿Qué hay de nuevo?
______ 4. ¿Cómo estás?
______ 5. ¿Cómo se llama usted?

a. Nada.
b. Me llamo Juanita.
c. Muy bien.
d. Lo siento.
e. De Argentina.
f. Soy la señora Cruz.

Quizzes

Quizzes

Nombre ______________________ Fecha ______________________

3 Conversaciones Fill in the blanks with the appropriate words. (5 x 1 pt. each = 5 pts.)

1. —__________ días, señor López. ¿Cómo __________ usted?

   —Bien, gracias. ¿Y __________?

2. —Fernando, ¿de __________ eres?

   —__________ de Colombia.

4 Completar Complete the conversation. (5 x 1 pt. each = 5 pts.)

ELENA Buenas tardes.

FELIPE (1) ______________________.

ELENA Me llamo Elena, ¿y tú?

FELIPE (2) ______________________.

ELENA (3) ______________________.

FELIPE El gusto es mío.

ELENA (4) ¿______________________?

FELIPE Soy de Nicaragua. (5) ¿______________________?

ELENA De España.

Nombre ______________________________ Fecha ____________________

CONTEXTOS

Lección 1

Quiz B

1 Ordenar Order the questions and statements from 1 to 6. (6 x 1 pt. each = 6 pts.)

_____ a. Soy de Nicaragua.

_____ b. Bien, gracias. Soy Felipe.

_____ c. Igualmente. ¿De dónde eres tú, Elena?

_____ d. Buenas tardes. Me llamo Elena. ¿Cómo estás?

_____ e. Mucho gusto, Felipe.

_____ f. Soy de España, ¿y tú?

2 Conversación Write a formal conversation between two people who are sitting next to each other at a business meeting. (6 x 1 pt. each = 6 pts.)

SR. DÁVILA **Buenas tardes, señor Garcia.**

SR. GARCÍA (1) ____________________, ____________________.

(2) ¿____?

SR. DÁVILA (3) ____________________. ¿____________________?

SR. GARCÍA (4) ____.

SR. DÁVILA (5) ____.

SR. GARCÍA (6) ____.

3 Escribir Write a conversation between two students who are meeting for the first time. Have them greet each other, ask each other how they are doing, ask each other where they are from, introduce a third person, and say goodbye. (5 pts. for vocabulary + 3 pts. for dialogue accuracy = 8 pts.)

____

____

____

____

____

____

____

____

____

Quizzes

Nombre ______________________ Fecha ______________________

ESTRUCTURA 1.1 — Lección 1

Quiz A

1 Artículos Write the definite article (**el, la, los, las**) for each word. If both masculine and feminine articles are possible, write both. (4 x 1 pt. each = 4 pts.)

1. ____________ estudiante
2. ____________ comunidades
3. ____________ día
4. ____________ chicos

2 Más artículos Write the indefinite article (**un, una, unos, unas**) for each word. If both masculine and feminine articles are possible, write both. (4 x 1 pt. each = 4 pts.)

1. ____________ autobús
2. ____________ foto
3. ____________ turistas
4. ____________ números

3 Clasificar Sort the words from the box into the appropriate categories. Include the definite article (**el, la, los, las**) for each word. If both masculine and feminine articles are possible, write both. (6 x 1 pt. each = 6 pts.)

diario escuelas hombres joven mapas país

People	Places	Objects
____________	____________	____________
____________	____________	____________

4 Plural Write the plural form of each word and article. (6 x 1 pt. each = 6 pts.)

1. un cuaderno ____________________
2. la lección ____________________
3. una mujer ____________________
4. el programa ____________________
5. la conductora ____________________
6. el lápiz ____________________

ESTRUCTURA 1.1 Lección 1

Quiz B

1 Clasificar For each category, write three Spanish words you learned in this lesson. Include the definite article. (8 x 1 pt. each = 8 pts.)

People	Objects
______________	______________
______________	______________
______________	______________
______________	______________

2 Asociaciones Choose six items and provide an associated word or phrase for each one. Include definite articles. Follow the model. (6 x 1 pt. each = 6 pts.)

modelo

math class **el número**

1. Mexican ______________
2. DVD ______________
3. group of travelers ______________
4. people who teach ______________
5. Chile ______________
6. words and definitions ______________
7. 24 hours ______________
8. taking notes in class ______________
9. packing before a trip ______________
10. people who study ______________

3 En la escuela List six people or things that you see in school every day. Include the indefinite article for each word. (6 x 1 pt. each = 6 pts.)

1. ______________
2. ______________
3. ______________
4. ______________
5. ______________
6. ______________

Quizzes

ESTRUCTURA 1.2 Lección 1

Quiz A

1 Números Write the numbers as words. (5 x 1 pt. each = 5 pts.)

a. 11 __________

b. 30 __________

c. 22 __________

d. 9 __________

e. 16 __________

2 ¿Cierto o falso? Indicate whether each statement is **cierto** (*true*) or **falso** (*false*). Remember that **más** means *plus*, **menos** means *minus*, and **son** means *equals*. (6 x 1 pt. each = 6 pts.)

____________________ 1. Seis más quince son veintiuno.

____________________ 2. Dieciocho menos catorce son once.

____________________ 3. Veinticinco menos doce son trece.

____________________ 4. Siete más siete son cinco.

____________________ 5. Treinta menos seis son veinticuatro.

____________________ 6. Diez más nueve son veintiuno.

3 Matemáticas Complete the math problems by filling in the missing numbers. Write the numbers as words. (5 x 1 pt. each = 5 pts.)

1. ________________ – 14 = 9
2. 17 + 12 = ________________
3. ________________ – 5 = 8
4. 20 – 20 = ________________
5. 1 + 13 = ________________

4 Completar Fill in the blanks. (4 x 1 pt. each = 4 pts.)

1. —¿____________ chicas hay en la clase?

   —____________ doce chicas.

2. —¿Hay ____________ diccionario aquí (*here*)?

   —Aquí no hay, pero (*but*) en la biblioteca (*library*) hay ____________ [6] diccionarios.

Nombre ______________________ Fecha ______________________

ESTRUCTURA 1.2 — Lección 1

Quiz B

Quizzes

1 Matemáticas Write six math problems. Use **más** for *plus*, **menos** for *minus*, and **son** for *equals*. (6 x 1 pt. each = 6 pts.)

modelo

Dos más diecisiete son diecinueve.

1. ______________________ 4. ______________________
2. ______________________ 5. ______________________
3. ______________________ 6. ______________________

2 ¿Qué hay? Answer the questions about your school using complete sentences. (7 x 1 pt. each = 7 pts.)

1. ¿Cuántos profesores de español hay?
____
2. ¿Cuántas fotos hay en la clase de español?
____
3. ¿Cuántas clases de español hay?
____
4. ¿Hay computadoras en la biblioteca (*library*)?
____
5. ¿Cuántos mapas hay en la clase de español?
____
6. ¿Hay autobuses?
____
7. ¿Cuántos chicos hay en la clase de español? ¿Y chicas?
____

3 En la clase ideal Write seven sentences about the people and objects found in an ideal Spanish class. (7 x 1 pt. each = 7 pts.)

En la clase ideal, hay ______________________

____

____

____

____

____

____

Nombre ______________________ Fecha ______________________

ESTRUCTURA 1.3 — Lección 1

Quiz A

1 Pronombres Match the nouns in Column A to the subject pronouns in Column B. One subject pronoun will not be used. (5 x 1 pt. each = 5 pts.)

A	B
______ 1. el joven	a. nosotros
______ 2. Armando y yo	b. ellos
______ 3. Natalia	c. ella
______ 4. los turistas	d. él
______ 5. Fernanda y Lucía	e. nosotras
	f. ellas

2 Verbos Complete the chart. (4 x 1 pt. each = 4 pts.)

Infinitivo	(1)
yo	(2)
tú	eres
usted	(3)
nosotros/as	(4)
ellos	son

Nombre ______________________________ Fecha ____________________

Quizzes

3 Completar Fill in the blanks. (5 x 1 pt. each = 5 pts.)

1. —¿_____________ es ella?

   —¿Ella? Se llama Laura.

2. —¿______________________ de la capital?

   —Sí. Yo ______________________ de Madrid.

3. —¿De ______________________ son ustedes?

   —______________________ de Panamá.

4 Oraciones Write complete sentences using the information provided. Make any necessary changes. (6 x 1 pt. each = 6 pts.)

modelo

nosotros / ser / turista

Nosotros somos turistas.

1. Carmen / ser / profesora de arte

   ____

2. ¿tú / ser / Canadá?

   ____

3. ustedes / ser / España

   ____

4. maletas / ser / pasajero

   ____

5. ¿de / quién / ser / lápices?

   ____

6. yo / ser / estudiante

   ____

Quizzes

Nombre ______________________ Fecha ______________________

ESTRUCTURA 1.3 Lección 1

Quiz B

1 Oraciones Write sentences using one element from each column. Make any necessary changes. (6 x 1 pt. each = 6 pts.)

Alberto y yo		**estudiante**
ustedes		**Canadá**
tú		**pasajero/a**
las maletas	**ser**	**España**
ella		**profesor(a) de arte**
los lápices		**el señor Sánchez**

1. ______________________
2. ______________________
3. ______________________
4. ______________________
5. ______________________
6. ______________________

2 Preguntas Answer these questions about your Spanish class using complete sentences. (4 x 1 pt. each = 4 pts.)

1. ¿Eres estudiante o profesor(a)? ______________________
2. ¿Quién es el/la profesor(a)? ______________________
3. ¿De dónde es el/la profesor(a)? ______________________
4. ¿De quiénes son los cuadernos? ______________________

3 Escribir Write a short e-mail to a new student in your Spanish class. Say hello, introduce yourself, state where you are from, and ask where he/she is from. Mention who your Spanish teacher is and that you'll see him/her tomorrow. (6 pts. for grammar + 4 pts. for style and creativity = 10 pts.)

____

____

____

____

____

____

Nombre ______________________ Fecha ______________________

ESTRUCTURA 1.4 Lección 1

Quiz A

1 La hora Select the correct option. (4 x 1 pt. each = 4 pts.)

1. 12:30
   a. Son las doce y cuarto.
   b. Es el mediodía.
   c. Son las doce y media.

2. 8:15
   a. Son las ocho y quince.
   b. Es la una y cuarto.
   c. Son las nueve menos cuarto.

3. 4:04
   a. Son las cuatro menos cuatro.
   b. Son las cuatro y cuatro.
   c. Son las cuatro y cuarto.

4. 1:55
   a. Es la una menos cinco.
   b. Son las dos menos cinco.
   c. Son las dos menos quince.

2 ¿Qué hora es? Write the times using complete sentences. Follow the model. (7 x 1 pt. each = 7 pts.)

modelo

3:00 p.m.

Son las tres de la tarde.

a. 11:15 a.m. ______________________

b. 9:45 p.m. ______________________

c. 12:35 p.m. ______________________

d. 12:00 a.m. ______________________

e. 6:30 a.m. ______________________

f. 7:23 p.m. ______________________

g. 10:10 a.m. ______________________

Quizzes

Nombre ____________________ Fecha ____________________

3 Preguntas Answer the questions using the times given in parentheses. Use complete sentences and write the numbers as words. (6 x 1.5 pt. each = 9 pts.)

1. ¿A qué hora es la clase de historia? (2:20)

   ____

2. ¿Qué hora es? (1:00)

   ____

3. ¿A qué hora es el programa? (8:50)

   ____

4. ¿A qué hora es la prueba (*quiz*)? (1:15)

   ____

5. ¿Qué hora es? (5:30)

   ____

6. ¿A qué hora es la clase de español? (11:45)

   ____

Nombre ______________________ Fecha ______________

ESTRUCTURA 1.4 Lección 1

Quiz B

1 Oraciones Write complete sentences that indicate what time the events take place. (4 x 1 pt. each = 4 pts.)

modelo

La clase de español...

La clase de español es a las tres de la tarde.

1. El almuerzo (*lunch*) ______________________
2. La primera (*first*) clase del día ______________________
3. Mi (*My*) programa de televisión favorito ______________________
4. La película (*movie*) ______________________

2 Clases Choose three subjects from the box and write what time each class begins. Follow the model. (3 x 2 pts. each = 6 pts)

ciencias (*science*) español historia matemáticas inglés (*English*)

modelo

La clase de **historia**

La clase de historia es a las ocho de la mañana.

1. la clase de ______________________

   ____
2. la clase de ______________________

   ____
3. la clase de ______________________

   ____

3 Escribir Write a conversation between two students. Have them greet each other, ask each other how they are doing, ask and tell what time Spanish class is, ask and tell what time it is, and say goodbye. (6 pts. for grammar + 4 pts. for style and creativity = 10 pts.)

____

____

____

____

____

____

Quizzes

Nombre ______________________ Fecha ______________________

CONTEXTOS

Lección 2

Quiz A

1 Emparejar Match the subjects in Column A to the topics in Column B. One item in Column B will not be used. (5 x 1 pt. each = 5 pts.)

A

______ 1. la economía
______ 2. la literatura
______ 3. las matemáticas
______ 4. la geografía
______ 5. el arte

B

a. países y capitales
b. Picasso, Dalí
c. *Don Quijote*, Shakespeare
d. Beethoven, Chopin
e. Wall Street
f. triángulos y rectángulos

2 Calendario Complete the chart with the missing days of the week. (4 x 1 pt. each = 4 pts.)

	martes		jueves			domingo

3 ¿Lógico o ilógico? Indicate whether each statement is **lógico (L)** or **ilógico (I)**. (7 x 1 pt. each = 7 pts.)

______ 1. Hay tiza y unos borradores en la pizarra.
______ 2. En el estadio hay libros.
______ 3. Hay una pluma en el escritorio.
______ 4. El inglés y el español son clases de lenguas.
______ 5. Hay una papelera en la mesa del profesor.
______ 6. Hoy es miércoles. Mañana es martes.
______ 7. Hay tareas, libros y ventanas en mi (my) mochila.

4 Completar Fill in the blanks with the appropriate words from the box. Three words will not be used. (4 x 1 pt. each = 4 pts.)

examen	física	horario	humanidades	prueba	reloj	semana

—Oye, mañana hay una (1) ________________ de ciencias, ¿no?

—¿De ciencias? ¿En qué clase? ¿Biología o (*or*) (2) ________________?

—En la clase de biología.

—¡Ah, sí! Hay una de biología mañana y también (*also*) hay un (3) ______________ de computación.

—¡Oh, no! Es una (4) ________________ difícil (*difficult*).

Nombre ______________________ Fecha ______________________

CONTEXTOS Lección 2

Quiz B

1 Asociaciones Write two words or phrases associated with each item. Do not repeat words. (10 x 0.5 pt. each = 5 pts.)

modelo

la clase **los estudiantes, la pizarra**

1. las ciencias ______________ ______________
2. la biblioteca ______________ ______________
3. la mochila ______________ ______________
4. el reloj ______________ ______________
5. la calculadora ______________ ______________

2 Horario Complete the chart with information about 3 classes you are taking. (12 x 0.5 pt. each = 6 pts.)

Materia	Hora	Días	Profesor(a)

3 Escribir Write six sentences about your favorite class. Include the name of the class, what day and time it is, who the teacher is, and how many students there are. (6 pts. for grammar + 3 pts. for style and creativity = 9 pts.)

Mi clase favorita es… ______________________

Nombre ______________________ Fecha ______________________

ESTRUCTURA 2.1 Lección 2

Quiz A

Quizzes

1 Verbos Select the correct conjugation for each pronoun. (4 x 1 pt. each = 4 pts.)

1. él
   a. esperamos
   b. espero
   c. espera
   d. esperas

2. nosotras
   a. preguntan
   b. preguntamos
   c. pregunto
   d. pregunta

3. tú
   a. cenas
   b. cenan
   c. cena
   d. ceno

4. ustedes
   a. llevo
   b. llevan
   c. llevas
   d. llevamos

2 Emparejar Match the sentences. Two items in Column B will not be used. (4 x 1 pt. each = 4 pts.)

A	B
______ 1. Trabajas mucho.	a. Me gusta la literatura.
______ 2. Tomo una clase de arte.	b. Te gusta la sociología.
______ 3. Busco un libro.	c. No te gusta descansar.
______ 4. Estudias contabilidad.	d. Me gusta dibujar.
	e. Te gustan las matemáticas.
	f. No me gusta viajar.

Nombre ____________________ Fecha ____________________

3 Oraciones Write sentences using the information provided. Make any necessary changes. (6 x 1 pt. each = 6 pts.)

modelo

nosotros / desear / bailar

Nosotros deseamos bailar.

1. ellas / enseñar / administración de empresas
____
2. yo / necesitar / preparar / la tarea
____
3. Héctor y yo / comprar / libros / en la librería
____
4. (mí) / gustar / bailar / los sábados
____
5. Enrique / desear / escuchar música
____
6. ¿(ti) / gustar / la psicología?
____

4 Completar Fill in the blanks with the present tense form of the appropriate verbs. (8 x 0.75 pt. each = 6 pts.)

Tomás, Patricia y yo somos estudiantes; nosotros (1) ____________________ (regresar / estudiar) en la escuela. Tomás y Patricia (2) ____________________ (necesitar / enseñar) llegar a la escuela a las siete y media. Patricia (3) ____________________ (tomar / llevar) una clase de inglés y Tomás (4) ____________________ (cantar / trabajar) en la clase de música. Mi primera (*first*) clase es a las ocho de la mañana. A las siete, yo (5) ____________________ (desayunar / bailar) y (6) ____________________ (buscar / mirar) televisión. Me (7) ____________________ (conversar / gustar) los programas de ciencias y de animales. Y a ti, ¿te gusta (8) ____________________ (dibujar / mirar) programas educativos (*educational*)?

Quizzes

ESTRUCTURA 2.1 Lección 2

Quiz B

1 Oraciones Write sentences using the partial information provided. Follow the model. (4 x 1 pt. each = 4 pts.)

modelo

¿? / desear / ¿? / Costa Rica

Ricardo y yo deseamos viajar a Costa Rica.

1. Héctor y yo / comprar / ¿? / en / ¿?
2. tú / esperar / ¿?
3. ¿? / necesitar / ¿? / la tarea
4. usted / ¿? / bailar / ¿?

2 Preguntas Answer the questions using complete sentences. (4 x 1 pt. each = 4 pts.)

1. ¿Te gusta cantar? ¿Cantas bien?
2. ¿Deseas viajar a países extranjeros?
3. ¿Miras televisión?
4. ¿Qué programas de televisión te gustan?

Nombre ______________________ Fecha ______________________

Quizzes

3 Oraciones Write sentences using one element from each column. Make any necessary changes. (6 x 1 pt. each = 6 pts.)

mí **ti**	**(no) gustar**	**la clase de español** **escuchar música** **los exámenes** **bailar y cantar** **las computadoras** **el arte** **estudiar periodismo**

modelo

A ti no te gusta estudiar periodismo.

1. ______________________
2. ______________________
3. ______________________
4. ______________________
5. ______________________
6. ______________________

4 Un día normal Write a paragraph about a typical school day. Include what time you eat breakfast, what time you get to school, how you get to class, etc. Include at least four **-ar** verbs and two uses of **gustar**. (3 pts. for grammar + 3 pts. for style and creativity = 6 pts.)

____

Quizzes

Nombre ______________________ Fecha ______________

ESTRUCTURA 2.2 Lección 2

Quiz A

1 Emparejar Match the questions and responses. Three items in Column B will not be used. (6 x 1 pt. each = 6 pts.)

A	B
______ 1. ¿Quiénes desean descansar?	a. Viajan a México.
______ 2. ¿Cuál es la palabra correcta?	b. ¡Sí! Estudio español e italiano.
______ 3. ¿Te gustan las lenguas extranjeras?	c. Sí, te gusta cantar.
______ 4. Cantas en la clase de música, ¿no?	d. No, yo camino.
______ 5. ¿Adónde viajan los turistas?	e. Felipe y Ángel desean descansar.
______ 6. Usted no toma el autobús, ¿verdad?	f. La palabra correcta es *clase*.
	g. No, no deseo descansar.
	h. Sí, canto mucho en la clase.
	i. No desean viajar a México.

2 Completar Fill in the blanks with the appropriate words from the box. Four words will not be used. (4 x 1 pt. each = 4 pts.)

cómo	**dónde**
cuál	**por qué**
cuánto	**qué**
de dónde	**verdad**

1. —Alberto, ¿______________________ eres?

   —Soy de Lima.

2. —¿______________________ es un profesor?

   —Es una persona que enseña en una escuela o universidad.

3. —Ustedes viajan a la República Dominicana, ¿______________________?

   —No, viajamos a Puerto Rico.

4. —¿______________________ hay tres laboratorios?

   —Hay tres porque muchos estudiantes estudian química.

3 Contestar Answer questions 1 and 2 affirmatively and questions 3 and 4 negatively. Use complete sentences. (4 x 1 pt. each = 4 pts.)

1. ¿Tomas seis clases este (*this*) semestre?
   ____
2. Ustedes no necesitan estudiar el sábado, ¿verdad?
   ____
3. ¿Enseña a las diez el señor Ortiz?
   ____
4. ¿Miran la televisión Samuel y Lourdes?
   ____

4 El libro Complete the conversation with appropriate questions. (6 x 1 pt. each = 6 pts.)

JULIO Hola, Fabiana. (1) ______________________________

FABIANA Hola, Julio. Busco un libro.

JULIO (2) ______________________________

FABIANA El libro se llama *Cien años de soledad.*

JULIO (3) ______________________________

FABIANA Busco el libro porque necesito estudiar para (*for*) el examen de literatura.

JULIO (4) ______________________________

FABIANA Sí, el examen es mañana.

JULIO (5) ______________________________

FABIANA Es a las cuatro.

JULIO (6) ______________________________

FABIANA No, el profesor Méndez no enseña la clase. La profesora es la señora Hoyos. Por favor, ¡ayúdame (*help me*) a buscar el libro!

Quizzes

Nombre ______________________ Fecha ______________________

ESTRUCTURA 2.2 — Lección 2

Quiz B

1 Completar Finish writing the questions and then write logical answers. (3 x 2 pts. each = 6 pts.)

modelo

¿A qué hora terminan...?

¿A qué hora terminan las clases?

Las clases terminan a las tres y media.

1. ¿Quiénes... los sábados?

2. ¿... en la clase de inglés?

3. ¿Por qué deseas...?

2 Preguntas Write questions using five of the words from the box. (5 x 1 pt. each = 5 pts.)

¿Cómo?	**¿Qué?**	**¿Dónde?**	**¿Cuándo?**
¿Cuántos/as?	**¿Cuál(es)?**	**¿Quién(es)?**	**¿Por qué?**

1.
2.
3.
4.
5.

3 Entrevista Imagine you are interviewing someone who works at your school. Write five questions you would ask him/her and then five answers he/she would give. Use **usted** in your questions.
(5 pts. for grammar + 4 pts. for style and creativity = 9 pts.)

Nombre ______________________ Fecha ______________________

ESTRUCTURA 2.3 Lección 2

Quizzes

Quiz A

1 Completar Fill in the blanks with the appropriate forms of **estar**. (5 x 1 pt. each = 5 pts.)

1. Paulina y Esteban ______________ en el estadio, ¿no?
2. Yo ______________ en casa.
3. Hola, Mónica. ¿Cómo ______________?
4. Usted ______________ en la librería.
5. Nosotros ______________ enfermos.

2 ¿Lógico o ilógico? Indicate whether each statement is **lógico** (**L**) or **ilógico** (**I**). (5 x 1 pt. each = 5 pts.)

______ 1. Nueva York está encima de Los Ángeles.

______ 2. Las plumas están sobre el escritorio.

______ 3. La cafetería está al lado de la residencia estudiantil.

______ 4. México está a la izquierda de los Estados Unidos.

______ 5. Los pasajeros están debajo del autobús.

3 Oraciones Write sentences using the verb **estar** and the information provided. Make any necessary changes. (4 x 1 pt. each = 4 pts.)

modelo

la librería / allá

La librería está allá.

1. las mochilas / detrás de / las sillas ______________________________
2. la papelera / a la derecha de / el profesor ______________________________
3. ¿(tú) / entre / las ventanas / y / la puerta? ______________________________
4. nosotros / con / Ramiro ______________________________

4 *¿Ser* o *estar*? Fill in the blanks with the appropriate forms of **ser** or **estar**. (6 x 1 pt. each = 6 pts.)

Hola, me llamo Claudia. Yo (1) ______________ estudiante. (2) ______________ las dos y media de la tarde y mis (*my*) compañeros de clase y yo (3) ______________ en la clase de español. Mi amiga (*friend*) Sandra (4) ______________ de Honduras y habla español muy bien; por eso (*therefore*), ella no (5) ______________ en la clase. Hoy no escucho bien a la profesora porque (yo) (6) ______________ enferma. ¡Necesito descansar en casa!

Quizzes

Nombre ______________________ Fecha ______________________

ESTRUCTURA 2.3

Lección 2

Quiz B

1 ¿Dónde? Use **estar** to describe the location of each item or person. (5 x 1 pt. each = 5 pts.)

modelo

Las pruebas...

Las pruebas están sobre la mesa de la profesora.

1. La tiza… ______________________
2. El profesor Domínguez… ______________________
3. Los pasajeros… ______________________
4. Las ventanas… ______________________
5. Yo… ______________________

2 La escuela Write complete sentences indicating the locations of these places in your school. Use at least two prepositions of location for each place. (4 x 1.5 pts. each = 6 pts.)

modelo

laboratorio

El laboratorio está cerca del gimnasio y al lado del baño.

1. la cafetería

____

2. la biblioteca

____

3. el baño (*bathroom*) de los chicos

____

4. el gimnasio

____

3 El mensaje Write an e-mail to a friend using **ser** and **estar**. Say hello, ask how he/she is, say how you are, what time it is, what class you are in, who the teacher is, and where he/she is from. (5 pts. for grammar + 4 pts. for style and creativity = 9 pts.)

____

____

____

____

____

Nombre ______________________ Fecha ______________________

ESTRUCTURA 2.4 Lección 2

Quiz A

Quizzes

1 Números Write the numbers as words. (6 x 1 pt. each = 6 pts.)

a. 38 ______________________

b. 116 ______________________

c. 537 ______________________

d. 1.821 ______________________

e. 754.322 ______________________

f. 6.615.010 ______________________

2 Historia Match the historical events in Column A to the years in Column B. Two items in Column B will not be used. (4 x 1 pt. each = 4 pts.)

A

______ 1. Cristóbal Colón llega a las Américas.

______ 2. Termina la guerra (*war*) entre España y los Estados Unidos.

______ 3. Termina la presidencia de George W. Bush.

______ 4. Neil Armstrong camina en la Luna (*Moon*).

B

a. mil novecientos sesenta y nueve

b. mil cuatrocientos noventa y dos

c. dos mil noventa

d. mil novecientos noventa y ocho

e. dos mil nueve

f. mil ochocientos noventa y ocho

Quizzes

3 La serie Write the number that completes each series. (5 x 1 pt. each = 5 pts.)

1. noventa y siete, noventa y ocho, noventa y nueve, ______________________
2. trescientos mil, seiscientos mil, ______________________
3. cuatro mil, tres mil, dos mil, ______________________
4. ochenta y cinco, setenta y cinco, ______________________, cincuenta y cinco
5. cuatro millones, tres millones, dos millones, ______________________

4 Más números Fill in the blanks by writing the numbers in Spanish. (5 x 1 pt. each = 5 pts.)

1. —¿Cuántos estudiantes hay en la Universidad Nacional Autónoma de México?

   —¡Uf! Hay más o menos ______________________ (270.000) estudiantes.
2. —¿Hay muchos libros en la biblioteca?

   —Sí, hay ______________________ (1.120.461) libros.
3. —En mi escuela hay sólo (*only*) ______________________ (100) chicos.

   —¿Verdad? ¡En mi (*my*) escuela hay ______________________ (100) chicas!
4. —El examen de matemáticas es difícil (*difficult*).

   —¿Por qué?

   —Porque hay ______________________ (241) preguntas.

Nombre ______________________ Fecha ______________________

ESTRUCTURA 2.4 Lección 2

Quizzes

Quiz B

1 Matemáticas Write six math equations using numbers greater than 30. Use **más** for *plus*, **menos** for *minus*, and **son** for *equals*. Follow the model. (6 x 1 pt. each = 6 pts.)

modelo

Un millón menos cincuenta y cinco mil son novecientos cuarenta y cinco mil.

1. ______________________
2. ______________________
3. ______________________
4. ______________________
5. ______________________
6. ______________________

2 Mi escuela Answer these questions using complete sentences. (6 x 1 pt. each = 6 pts.)

1. ¿Cuántos profesores enseñan en la escuela?
____
2. ¿Cuántos estudiantes hay?
____
3. ¿Cuántos libros hay en la biblioteca?
____
4. ¿Cuántas chicas practican deportes (*sports*)? ¿Y chicos?
____
5. ¿Cuántos días de clase hay en un año (*year*)?
____
6. ¿Cuántas pruebas tomas en un año?
____

3 La escuela ideal Write four sentences describing the people, places, and objects that would be found in an ideal school. Use numbers greater than 30. (4 x 2 pts. each = 8 pts.)

En la escuela ideal hay... ______________________
____
____
____
____

Nombre ______________________________ Fecha ____________________

CONTEXTOS Lección 3

Quiz A

1 Seleccionar Select the item that does not belong. (4 x 1 pt. each = 4 pts.)

1. a. apellidos
   b. gemelas
   c. parientes
   d. hijastros
2. a. suegro
   b. yerno
   c. muchacho
   d. nuera
3. a. bisabuelo
   b. tío
   c. primo
   d. niño
4. a. cuñada
   b. ingeniera
   c. sobrina
   d. novia

2 Emparejar Match the definitions in Column A to the words in Column B. Three items from Column B will not be used. (5 x 1 pt. each = 5 pts.)

A	B
______ 1. la esposa de mi padre	a. yernos
______ 2. los padres de mi esposo	b. hermanastros
______ 3. la hija de mi tía	c. sobrina
______ 4. los hijos de mi madrastra	d. gente
______ 5. la hija de mi hermano	e. suegros
	f. prima
	g. madre
	h. hijastros

Nombre ______________________________ Fecha ____________________

3 Completar Fill in the blanks with words from the box. Three words will not be used. (6 x 1 pt. each = 6 pts.)

amigos	**gemelos**	**periodista**
artista	**gente**	**programador**
familia	**muchacho**	**novia**

1. El tío de Guillermo es ______________________. Le gustan las computadoras.
2. En mi ______________________ hay cuatro personas: mi madre, mi padre, mi hermano y yo.
3. Mi media hermana dibuja muy bien. Es ______________________.
4. Hay mucha ______________________ en el estadio. Hay un partido (*game*) importante.
5. Mi hermano espera trabajar en la televisión. Desea ser ______________________.
6. Alejandro y Álvaro, los hijos de mi tía, son idénticos. Ellos son ______________________.

4 Oraciones Fill in the blanks with the appropriate family-related words. (5 x 1 pt. each = 5 pts.)

1. El padre de mi padre es mi ______________________.
2. La abuela de mi madre es mi ______________________.
3. Mi ______________________ es el hijo de mis abuelos y el esposo de mi madre.
4. Mis hermanos son los ______________________ de mis abuelos.
5. La esposa del hermano de mi madre es mi ______________________.

Quizzes

Nombre ______________________ Fecha ______________

CONTEXTOS

Lección 3

Quiz B

1 Identificar Identify the people being described. (6 x 0.5 pt. each = 3 pts.)

modelo

Es el esposo de mi tía.
Es mi tío.
Mi hermana enseña en la universidad.
Es profesora.

1. Mi padre programa las computadoras.
____
2. Es el esposo de mi hermana.
____
3. Mi abuelo dibuja muy bien.
____
4. Mi madre trabaja en un hospital.
____
5. Es la esposa de mi hijo.
____
6. Son las hijas de mi padrastro, pero no de mi madre.
____

2 Preguntas Answer the questions using complete sentences. (4 x 1 pt. each = 4 pts.)

1. ¿Cuál es tu apellido?
____
2. ¿Cuántas personas hay en tu familia?
____
3. ¿Cómo se llaman tus padres? ¿Dónde trabajan?
____
4. ¿De dónde son tus abuelos? ¿Hablas mucho con ellos?
____

Nombre ______________________ Fecha ______________________

Quizzes

3 La familia Write four sentences describing the relationships between family members. Follow the model. (4 x 1 pt. each = 4 pts.)

modelo

Mis hermanos son los nietos de mi abuela.

1. ______________________
2. ______________________
3. ______________________
4. ______________________

4 Mi pariente favorito Write a description of your favorite relative. Include his/her name and relationship to you, where he/she is from, and where he/she works or studies. Also mention one thing he/she likes and one thing he/she dislikes. (6 pts. for grammar + 3 pts. for style and creativity = 9 pts.)

Nombre ______________________ Fecha ______________________

ESTRUCTURA 3.1 Lección 3

Quiz A

Quizzes

1 Opuestos Write an adjective with the opposite meaning. (5 x 1 pt. each = 5 pts.)

1. alto ______________
2. difícil ______________
3. malo ______________
4. grande ______________
5. viejo ______________

2 Nacionalidades Rewrite the sentences using adjectives of nationality. (6 x 1 pt. each = 6 pts.)

modelo

Emiliano es de Italia.

Es italiano.

1. Olivia es de Argentina.

   ____

2. El profesor es de Alemania.

   ____

3. Carlos y yo somos de Canadá.

   ____

4. La turista es de Costa Rica.

   ____

5. Los ingenieros son de España.

   ____

6. Margaret y Anne son de Inglaterra.

   ____

Nombre ______________________ Fecha ______________________

3 Oraciones Write sentences using the information provided. Make any necessary changes. (4 x 1 pt. each = 4 pts.)

modelo

mi novio / ser / inteligente / y / guapo

Mi novio es inteligente y guapo.

1. la mujer / pelirrojo / enseñar / periodismo
____

2. las mochilas / ser / blanco / y / azul
____

3. ¿los turistas / japonés / esperar / el autobús?
____

4. ustedes / tomar / mucho / pruebas / en la clase de español
____

4 Completar Fill in the blanks with the appropriate form of the correct adjectives. (5 x 1 pt. each = 5 pts.)

Mi madre es muy (1) __________ (trabajador / rubio): es artista y también enseña en una universidad. A los estudiantes les gusta mi madre porque es una profesora (2) __________ (bueno / antipático), pero ella da (*gives*) exámenes muy (3) __________ (bonito / difícil). Este semestre enseña dos clases de arte (4) __________ (delgado / chino). Mi madre es una (5) __________ (grande / mismo) mujer, ¿verdad?

Quizzes

Nombre ______________________ Fecha ______________________

Quizzes

ESTRUCTURA 3.1 — Lección 3

Quiz B

1 Completar Fill in the blanks with adjectives. Do not repeat words. (6 x 1 pt. each = 6 pts.)

Me gusta mucho la escuela. Tengo muchos amigos y ellos son (1) ______________.

Mis profesores son (2) ______________; explican bien las materias. En la biblioteca hay

(3) ______________ libros. La cafetería es (4) ______________, pero la comida está

(5) ______________. Lo que (*What*) no me gusta nada es el gimnasio. Es muy (6) ____________.

2 Oraciones Write sentences using one element from each column. (5 x 1 pt. each = 5 pts.)

la escuela **mis amigos y yo** **los profesores** **tú** **los estudiantes** **ustedes** **las clases**	**ser**	**canadiense** **fácil** **feo** **francés** **moreno** **cubano** **trabajador** **viejo**

1. ____
2. ____
3. ____
4. ____
5. ____

3 Preguntas Answer the questions using complete sentences. (3 x 1 pt. each = 3 pts.)

1. ¿Cómo eres? ______________________________
2. ¿Cómo son tus amigos/as? ______________________________
3. ¿Te gustan las clases? ¿Por qué? ______________________________

4 Mi amigo/a Write a description of one of your friends. Include his/her name and nationality, and describe his/her appearance and personality. (3 pts. for grammar + 3 pts. for style and creativity = 6 pts.)

____

____

____

____

____

Nombre ______________________________ Fecha ____________________

ESTRUCTURA 3.2 — Lección 3

Quiz A

1 Posesivos Fill in the blanks with the appropriate possessive adjectives. (5 x 1 pt. each = 5 pts.)

1. ______________________ (*Your,* fam.) libros están en la mesa.
2. Es ______________________ (*their*) nieto.
3. ______________________ (*Our*) abuelos son simpáticos.
4. Es ______________________ (*my*) primo.
5. ______________________ (*His*) tíos son de Perú.

2 Completar Select the correct option. (5 x 1 pt. each = 5 pts.)

Me llamo Miguel. Tengo un hermano gemelo, Mateo. (1) (Nuestro, Mi, Su) hermano y yo estudiamos en la misma escuela. Somos altos, morenos y simpáticos, pero (2) (nuestra, nuestros, mis) madre dice (*says*) que Mateo es más responsable. ¡No es verdad! Cuando yo camino a (3) (tus, sus, mis) clases, los amigos de Mateo quieren (*want*) conversar conmigo (*with me*). (4) (Su, Sus, Tus) amigos son simpáticos, ¡pero no me gusta llegar tarde a clase! Y tú, ¿tienes problemas con (5) (tus, nuestros, mis) hermanos?

3 Oraciones Write sentences using the information provided. Make any necessary changes.
(5 x 1 pt. each = 5 pts.)

modelo

los estudiantes / preparar / su / ensayo

Los estudiantes preparan sus ensayos.

1. yo / llevar / mi / papeles / a / la clase

____

2. Gustavo y yo / terminar / nuestro / tareas

____

3. tú / comprar / tu / calculadora / en / la librería

____

4. ¿ustedes / hablar / con / su / abuela?

____

5. Ana / estudiar / para (*for*) / su / exámenes

____

4 ¿De quién es? Rewrite the sentences using possessive adjectives. Follow the model.
(5 x 1 pt. each = 5 pts.)

modelo

Yo tengo libros de matemáticas.

Son mis libros.

1. El profesor tiene tiza.

____

2. Tú tienes mochilas.

____

3. Los turistas tienen mapa.

____

4. Usted tiene cuadernos.

____

5. Nosotros tenemos papelera.

____

Nombre ______________________ Fecha ______________________

ESTRUCTURA 3.2 Lección 3

Quiz B

1 Oraciones Complete the sentences with possessive adjectives and words from each box. (6 x 1 pt. each = 6 pts.)

buscar	**llevar**	**abuelo**	**papeles**
comprar	**preparar**	**cuadernos**	**pluma**
estudiar para (*for*)	**terminar**	**exámenes**	**profesores**
hablar con		**mapa**	**tareas**

modelo

Yo **llevo mis tareas a clase.**

1. Los turistas ______________________
2. Tú ______________________
3. Ustedes ______________________
4. Gustavo y yo ______________________
5. Yo ______________________
6. Ana ______________________

2 Preguntas Answer the questions using possessive adjectives. (4 x 1 pt. each = 4 pts.)

1. ¿Dónde compras tus libros? ______________________
2. ¿Cómo se llama tu mejor (*best*) amigo/a? ______________________
3. ¿Cómo son los padres de tu amigo/a? ______________________
4. ¿Qué música escuchan tú y tus amigos? ______________________

3 Escribir Write a description of the likes and dislikes you share with a family member or friend. Use at least five possessive adjectives. (5 pts. for grammar + 5 pts. for style and creativity = 10 pts.)

Quizzes

Nombre ______________________________ Fecha ______________________

ESTRUCTURA 3.3 — Lección 3

Quiz A

1 Conjugar Complete the chart with the correct verb forms. (6 x 0.5 pt. each = 3 pts.)

Infinitive	yo	tú	nosotros/as	ellos/ellas
comprender	(1)	comprendes	(2)	(3)
(4)	vivo	(5)	vivimos	(6)

2 Escoger Select the appropriate verbs. (6 x 1 pt. each = 6 pts.)

1. Tú ______________ el almuerzo (*lunch*) con tus amigos.
   a. comparten
   b. compartes
   c. comparte
   d. compartimos
2. Usted ______________ los viernes.
   a. corro
   b. corres
   c. corre
   d. corren
3. Nuestro abuelo ______________ en una casa muy bonita.
   a. vive
   b. vives
   c. vivimos
   d. vivo
4. Los turistas ______________ sus experiencias.
   a. describes
   b. describen
   c. describo
   d. describimos
5. Tomás y yo ______________ unos libros.
   a. leemos
   b. leo
   c. lee
   d. lees
6. Ustedes ______________ estudiar ciencias.
   a. decido
   b. decides
   c. decide
   d. deciden

Nombre ______________________ Fecha ______________________

3 Oraciones Write sentences using the information provided. Make any necessary changes. (5 x 1 pt. each = 5 pts.)

modelo

los profesores / vivir / lejos / escuela

Los profesores viven lejos de la escuela.

1. Ángel / abrir / puerta / laboratorio

____

2. mi cuñada y yo / decidir / leer / libros / interesante

____

3. ustedes / aprender / hablar / español

____

4. yo / correr / estadio / domingos

____

5. tú / asistir / clase / historia

____

4 Completar Fill in the blanks with the correct form of the appropriate verbs. (6 x 1 pt. each = 6 pts.)

abrir	**beber**	**deber**
aprender	**comer**	**escribir**
asistir	**creer**	**recibir**

¿Cómo son los sábados con mi familia? Los sábados, todos nosotros (1) ______________ a una clase de yoga a las siete y media. Mi madre es buena en yoga, pero mi padre (2) ______________ practicar más. A las nueve, desayunamos en casa. Mis padres (3) ______________ té (*tea*) japonés y mi hermana y yo (4) ______________ bananas y cereales. Luego mi hermana y sus amigas escuchan música y yo (5) ______________ en mi diario. Y tú,¿(6) ______________ que (*that*) es importante compartir actividades con tu familia?

Quizzes

Nombre ______________________________ Fecha ______________________

Quizzes

ESTRUCTURA 3.3 — Lección 3

Quiz B

1 Ordenar Order the events from 1 to 6. (6 x 0.5 pt. each = 3 pts.)

______ a. Mis amigos y yo comemos al mediodía en la cafetería de la escuela.

______ b. Asisto a la clase de español.

______ c. Como el desayuno (*breakfast*) en casa.

______ d. Corro cerca de mi casa.

______ e. Abro la puerta de la escuela y camino a mi primera clase.

______ f. Leo un libro en la biblioteca y regreso a casa.

2 Completar Use **-er** and **-ir** verbs to fill in the blanks. Do not repeat verbs. (5 x 1 pt. each = 5 pts.)

1. Tomás y yo ________________________ unos libros.
2. Usted ________________________ los viernes.
3. Nuestros primos ________________________ practicar yoga.
4. Tú ________________________ unos cuadernos.
5. Yo ________________________ la escuela.

3 Preguntas Answer the questions using **-er** and **-ir** verbs. Use complete sentences. (3 x 1 pt. each = 3 pts.)

1. ¿Con qué personas de tu familia vives? ¿Dónde viven ustedes?

____

2. ¿Recibes muchos mensajes electrónicos (*e-mails*)?

____

3. ¿Escriben tus amigos en un diario o un blog?

____

4 Escribir Write six sentences describing what you and your friends do in a typical week. Use at least six **-er** and **-ir** verbs. (6 pts. for grammar + 3 pts. for style and creativity = 9 pts.)

____

____

____

____

____

____

ESTRUCTURA 3.4 Lección 3

Quiz A

1 Conjugar Complete the chart with the correct verb forms. (4 x 0.5 pt. each = 2 pts.)

Infinitive	yo	nosotros	ustedes
(1)	tengo	tenemos	(2)
venir	(3)	(4)	vienen

2 Emparejar Match the sentences. Three items in Column B will not be used. (6 x 1 pt. each = 6 pts.)

A	B
______ 1. El señor Beltrán es viejo.	a. No tenemos hambre.
______ 2. Es la una de la mañana.	b. Tiene ochenta años.
______ 3. No deseo llegar tarde (*late*).	c. Tengo miedo.
______ 4. Ustedes están en el Polo Norte.	d. Tienes ganas de comer.
______ 5. Es el mediodía.	e. No tiene razón.
______ 6. Marcos escribe *20 + 7 = 26.*	f. Tienes sueño.
	g. Tenemos cuidado.
	h. Tengo mucha prisa.
	i. Tienen mucho frío.

Nombre ______________________________ Fecha ______________________

Quizzes

3 Completar Fill in the blanks with the correct forms of **tener** or **venir**. (6 x 1 pt. each = 6 pts.) (5 x 1 pt. each = 5 pts.)

1. Mañana hay un examen y yo ________________________ que estudiar.
2. Tere y Amalia ________________________ al estadio para practicar el tenis.
3. Iván y yo ________________________ a clase para aprender.
4. Los profesores ________________________ razón; la educación es muy importante.
5. No deseas descansar porque no ________________________ sueño.
6. Usted ________________________ al mediodía, ¿no?

4 Oraciones Write sentences using the information provided and the correct form of **tener** or **venir**. Make any necessary changes. (6 x 1 pt. each = 6 pts.)

modelo

mis amigos / en autobús / de la biblioteca

Mis amigos vienen en autobús de la biblioteca.

1. yo / de / Italia
   ____
2. nuestros primos / 10:00 p.m.
   ____
3. tú / miedo / la película (*movie*) de horror
   ____
4. nosotras / ganas / mirar / televisión
   ____
5. usted / mucho / sed
   ____
6. Er. esto / decidir / a la casa?
   ____

Nombre ______________________ Fecha ______________________

ESTRUCTURA 3.4 Lección 3

Quizzes

Quiz B

1 Oraciones Complete each sentence with a logical ending. (6 x 1 pt. each = 6 pts.)

modelo

Cuando los estudiantes no tienen razón…

Cuando los estudiantes no tienen razón, el profesor explica la información.

1. Cuando tengo miedo...
____
2. Cuando Ernesto tiene ganas de mirar la televisión...
____
3. Cuando la profesora Hernández viene a la clase...
____
4. Cuando mis amigos y yo tenemos hambre...
____
5. Cuando tienes mucho sueño...
____
6. Cuando mis abuelos vienen a mi casa...
____

2 Preguntas Answer the questions using complete sentences. (5 x 1 pt. each = 5 pts.)

1. ¿Cuántos años tienes? ______________________
2. ¿Cuántos años tiene tu padre? ¿Y tu madre? ______________________
3. ¿Qué tienen que hacer (*to do*) tus padres mañana? ______________________
4. ¿Cuándo vienes a la clase de español? ______________________
5. ¿Qué tienen ganas de hacer hoy tú y tus amigos? ______________________

3 Escribir Write a paragraph about a family member, describing his/her relationship to you, when he/she comes to your house, how old he/she is, one obligation he/she has this weekend, and what he/she feels like doing this Saturday. (6 pts. for grammar + 3 pts. for style and creativity = 9 pts.)

____

____

____

____

Nombre ______________________ Fecha ______________________

CONTEXTOS Lección 4

Quiz A

1 Clasificar Sort the words from the box into the appropriate categories. (6 x 1 pt. each = 6 pts.)

esquí	**escribir**	**gimnasio**	**jugar videojuegos**	**restaurante**	**vóleibol**

Lugares	**Pasatiempos**	**Deportes**
______________	______________	______________
______________	______________	______________

2 Deportes Identify each sport using vocabulary from the lesson. Follow the model. (4 x 1 pt. each = 4 pts.)

modelo

club + ball = **el golf**

1. ball + racket + net = ______________
2. bat + ball = ______________
3. swimming suit + cap + goggles = ______________
4. bicycle + helmet = ______________

3 Emparejar Match the actions in Column A to the places in Column B. (5 x 1 pt. each = 5 pts.)

A	**B**
______ 1. comer con amigos	a. el museo
______ 2. ver películas	b. la piscina
______ 3. ir de excursión	c. el cine
______ 4. practicar la natación	d. las montañas
______ 5. ver obras (*works*) de Picasso, Dalí y Miró	e. el restaurante

4 Completar Fill in the blanks with words from the box. One word will not be used. (5 x 1 pt. each = 5 pts.)

equipo	**jugador**	**parque**	**partidos**	**pasatiempo**	**videojuegos**

1. Ver películas es mi ______________ favorito.
2. Alejandro está en el ______________ de fútbol americano de la escuela.
3. Cuando podemos (*we can*), Gloria y yo asistimos a los ______________ de los Yankees.
4. ¿Te gusta jugar ______________ en tus ratos libres?
5. Daniel y Felipe pasean en bicicleta por el ______________.

Nombre ____________________ Fecha ____________________

CONTEXTOS Lección 4

Quiz B

1 Identificar Identify the place where these activities can occur. Follow the model. (5 x 1 pt. each = 5 pts.)

modelo

Vemos una película.

Es un cine.

1. Hay mucho tráfico.

____

2. Practicamos el baloncesto.

____

3. Cenamos.

____

4. Bebemos un chocolate caliente (*hot*).

____

5. Admiramos el arte.

____

2 Preguntas Answer the questions using complete sentences. (5 x 1 pt. each = 5 pts.)

1. ¿Cuál es tu deporte favorito?____________________

____

2. ¿Qué otras (*other*) actividades te gustan? Nombra por lo menos (*at least*) dos.____________________

____

3. ¿Cuáles son los pasatiempos favoritos de tus padres?____________________

____

4. ¿Adónde te gusta ir con tus amigos/as?____________________

____

5. ¿Qué te gusta hacer (*to do*) los fines de semana?____________________

____

Nombre ______________________ Fecha ______________

Quizzes

3 Preguntar Use verbs from the box to write what you do in these places. Follow the model. (4 x 1 pt. each = 4 pts.)

beber	**correr**	**escribir**	**mirar**	**patinar**	**tomar**
caminar	**escalar**	**leer**	**nadar**	**practicar**	**visitar**

modelo

¿Qué haces (*do you do*) cuando estás en una piscina?

Nado y tomo el sol.

¿Qué haces cuando estás en...

1. un parque?
____
2. un gimnasio?
____
3. una montaña?
____
4. una plaza?
____

4 Escribir Write an e-mail to your parents telling them what activities four of your friends enjoy, and where these activities occur. (3 pts. for grammar + 3 pts. for style and creativity = 6 pts.)

____

Nombre ______________________________ Fecha ______________________

ESTRUCTURA 4.1 Lección 4

Quiz A

1 Completar Fill in the blanks with the appropriate forms of **ir**. (6 x 0.5 pt. each = 3 pts.)

1. El sábado tío Luis y tía Tere ______________________ de excursión a las montañas.
2. Mi hermana Perla ______________________ con unas amigas al cine.
3. Ustedes ______________________ a un restaurante muy elegante.
4. Tú ______________________ a casa de tu amigo Manuel.
5. Nosotros ______________________ al centro.
6. Yo ______________________ a un partido de fútbol americano con mi hermano mayor.

2 ¿Adónde van? Write sentences with the verb **ir** using the information provided. (6 x 1 pt. each = 6 pts.)

modelo

usted / el partido de fútbol

Usted va al partido de fútbol.

1. yo / la biblioteca
____
2. nosotros / la piscina
____
3. mis primas / el gimnasio
____
4. tú / de excursión
____
5. ustedes / el parque municipal
____
6. Alejandro / el museo de ciencias
____

Quizzes

Nombre ______________________ Fecha ______________

3 Mañana Rewrite the sentences using **ir a** + [*infinitive*] to say that these people will do the same activities again tomorrow. Follow the model. (5 x 1 pt. each = 5 pts.)

modelo

Ustedes pasean por el centro.

Van a pasear por el centro mañana también.

1. Rosa patina en línea.

 ____

2. Nosotros vemos una película.

 ____

3. Tú andas en patineta.

 ____

4. Yo leo un mensaje electrónico.

 ____

5. Mis abuelos escriben una carta.

 ____

4 Oraciones Write sentences using the information provided. (4 x 1.5 pts. each = 6 pts.)

modelo

nosotros / ir / practicar / deportes

Nosotros vamos a practicar deportes.

1. yo / ir / nadar / piscina

 ____

2. Carmela y yo / ir / caminar / plaza

 ____

3. Fernando / ir / parque / cuatro de la tarde

 ____

4. doña Inés y don Mario / ir / comer / café Alameda

 ____

ESTRUCTURA 4.1 Lección 4

Quiz B

1 Situaciones Write where you and your friends go in these situations. (5 x 1 pt. each = 5 pts.)

1. Cuando tengo hambre...
____
2. Si deseamos ir de excursión...
____
3. Cuando mi mejor amigo/a necesita estudiar...
____
4. Si mis amigos/as tienen dinero...
____
5. Cuando cenamos juntos (*together*)...
____

2 Oraciones Choose five people from the box and write what they do at the times indicated. Follow the model and use a different activity for each person. (5 x 1 pt. each = 5 pts.)

mis abuelos	mi hermano/a	mi padre
mis primos	mi mejor amigo/a	mi profesor(a)

modelo

Los lunes **mi madre va al gimnasio.**

1. Los lunes ______________________________
2. Los jueves por la tarde ______________________________
3. Los viernes por la noche ______________________________
4. Los sábados por la mañana ______________________________
5. Los domingos ______________________________

3 Entrevista Write at least four sentences using the construction **ir a** + [*infinitive*] to describe what you and your friends plan on doing next weekend. (6 pts. for grammar + 4 pts. for style and creativity = 10 pts.)

____
____
____
____
____
____

Nombre ______________________________ Fecha ______________________

ESTRUCTURA 4.2 — Lección 4

Quiz A

1 Verbos Complete the chart with the correct verb forms. (8 x 0.5 pt. each = 4 pts.)

Infinitivo	tú	nosotras	ellos
contar	(1)	contamos	(2)
(3)	juegas	(4)	juegan
mostrar	(5)	mostramos	(6)
(7)	empiezas	(8)	empiezan

2 Elegir Fill in the blanks with the correct form of the appropriate verbs. (5 x 1 pt. each = 5 pts.)

1. Javier ________________________ (entender / dormir) las reglas (*rules*) del fútbol.
2. ¿A qué hora ______________________ (recordar / querer) almorzar tú?
3. Mañana comienzo a ____________________ (jugar / almorzar) al tenis con el equipo de mi escuela.
4. Si ustedes ______________________ (perder / cerrar) muchos partidos, no van a ser campeones (*champions*).
5. Ignacio y yo ______________________ (encontrar / recordar) que mañana es el partido.

3 Oraciones Write sentences using the information provided. Make any necessary changes. (5 x 1 pt. each = 5 pts.)

modelo

nuestro equipo / siempre perder / los partidos importantes

Nuestro equipo siempre pierde los partidos importantes.

1. Omar y Antonio / almorzar / restaurante japonés

   ____

2. usted / no poder / ver la película / porque / no encontrar / el cine.

   ____

3. ¿cerrar / ellas / las ventanas?

   ____

4. yo / volver / casa / seis de la tarde

   ____

5. nosotras / dormir / ocho horas

   ____

Nombre ____________________ Fecha ____________________

4 Completar Fill in the blanks with the correct form of the appropriate verb. Do not repeat verbs. Four verbs will not be used. (6 x 1 pt. each = 6 pts.)

cerrar	**perder**
dormir	**poder**
empezar	**preferir**
jugar	**querer**
pensar	**volver**

Mañana (1) ________________ una serie importante de partidos de vóleibol. Los jugadores de nuestro equipo no (2) ______________ dormir bien porque sólo (3) ______________ en los partidos. Pero si nosotros (4) _________________ ganar, tenemos que practicar mucho y también descansar. Por mi parte, yo (5) ________________ almorzar, dormir una siesta y luego practicar con el equipo. Y tú, ¿(6) _________________ al vóleibol con tus amigos?

Quizzes

Nombre ______________________ Fecha ______________________

ESTRUCTURA 4.2 Lección 4

Quiz B

1 Situaciones Use the verbs from the box to write a sentence for each situation. Follow the model and use a different verb in each sentence. (6 x 1 pt. each = 6 pts.)

almorzar	comenzar	jugar	poder	querer
cerrar	dorimir	pensar	preferir	volver

modelo

Óscar toma el autobús el viernes.

Piensa en sus planes para el fin de semana.

1. Los jugadores llegan al estadio.
____
2. Tú caminas por la plaza.
____
3. Ustedes están en el parque.
____
4. Son las diez de la mañana y termina la clase de química.
____
5. Ana Sofía y yo estamos en el cine.
____
6. Hoy no tengo que estudiar.
____

2 Preguntas Answer the questions using complete sentences. (5 x 1 pt. each = 5 pts.)

1. ¿A qué hora empiezan tus clases? ______________________
2. ¿Prefieres estudiar en casa o en la biblioteca? ______________________
3. ¿Dónde almuerzan tú y tus amigos? ______________________
4. ¿Cuántas horas duermes cada *(each)* noche? ______________________
5. ¿Juegas algún (*any*) deporte? ¿Dónde? ______________________

3 Entrevista Write a paragraph about what you typically do on Saturday afternoons, and mention two things you and your friends want to do this Saturday. Use at least six different **e:ie** and **o:ue** stem-changing verbs. (6 pts. for grammar + 3 pts. for style and creativity = 9 pts.)

____

____

____

____

Nombre ____________________ Fecha ____________________

ESTRUCTURA 4.3 Lección 4

Quiz A

1 Verbos Select the correct verb form. (4 x 1 pt. each = 4 pts.)

1. ella
   a. consiguen
   b. consigo
   c. conseguimos
   d. consigue
2. nosotros
   a. repite
   b. repetimos
   c. repito
   d. repiten
3. tú
   a. dices
   b. dicen
   c. decimos
   d. dice
4. ustedes
   a. pedimos
   b. piden
   c. pide
   d. pido

2 Emparejar Match the locations in Column A to the actions in Column B. Two items from Column B will not be used. (5 x 1 pt. each = 5 pts.)

A	B
______ 1. el cine	a. Sigo al guía (*guide*).
______ 2. el estadio	b. Repiten los verbos.
______ 3. el museo	c. Pido muchos favores.
______ 4. el restaurante	d. Consiguen ver una buena película.
______ 5. la clase de francés	e. Ana dice que va a ganar.
	f. Pedimos pizza.
	g. Consigues novelas.

Nombre ______________________ Fecha ______________________

Quizzes

3 Preguntas Answer the questions affirmatively, using complete sentences. (6 x 1 pt. each = 6 pts.)

1. ¿Piden ayuda (*help*) Verónica y Carlos?

   ____

2. ¿Dices que quieres ver una película?

   ____

3. ¿Ustedes consiguen videojuegos en el centro?

   ____

4. ¿Sigue una dieta Mateo?

   ____

5. ¿Repetimos las actividades?

   ____

6. ¿Piden muchos favores tú y tus amigos?

   ____

4 Completar Fill in the blanks with the correct form of the appropriate verb. Use each verb once. (5 x 1 pt. each = 5 pts.)

conseguir decir pedir repetir seguir

Mi amigo (1) ____________________ que la clase de italiano es súper difícil. Cuando él (2) ______________ ayuda con su tarea, yo siempre (*always*) (3) ______________ la misma cosa: "Es cuestión (*matter*) de tener disciplina". Debe ir a clase preparado, estudiar una o dos horas al día y hablar con el profesor si no entiende la materia. Si mi amigo (4) ____________________ mis consejos (*advice*), va a (5) ____________________ lo que quiere: ¡una A!

Nombre ______________________ Fecha ______________________

ESTRUCTURA 4.3 Lección 4

Quizzes

Quiz B

1 Ordenar Andrés is going to the movies. Order the events from 1 to 8. (8 x 0.5 pt. each = 4 pts.)

______ a. Digo que prefiero las películas de ciencia ficción.

______ b. Encuentro a mi amiga Noelia delante del cine.

______ c. El señor de la ventanilla (*ticket window*) no me escucha; repito la orden.

______ d. Empieza la película.

______ e. Compramos unas sodas porque tenemos mucha sed.

______ f. Noelia dice que le gustan las películas románticas.

______ g. Seguimos a la sala y buscamos asientos (*seats*).

______ h. Consigo dos entradas (*tickets*) para *Amor en el espacio*.

2 Preguntas Answer the questions using complete sentences. (6 x 1 pt. each = 6 pts.)

1. ¿Dónde consigues libros? ______________________
2. Cuando comes en tu restaurante favorito, ¿qué pides? ______________________
3. ¿Siempre (*Always*) dicen la verdad tú y tus amigos? ______________________
4. ¿Quién en tu familia siempre consigue lo que (*what*) quiere? ______________________
____
5. ¿Repiten tus padres siempre las mismas recomendaciones? ¿Cuáles? ______________________
____
6. ¿Sigues las recomendaciones de tus padres? ¿Por qué? ______________________
____

3 Escribir Write five sentences using the verbs from the box to describe what happens in your Spanish class. Use each verb at least once. (5 pts. for grammar + 5 pts. for style and creativity = 10 pts.)

conseguir	**decir**	**pedir**	**repetir**	**seguir**

____

____

____

____

____

____

Nombre ______________________________ Fecha ______________________

ESTRUCTURA 4.4 Lección 4

Quiz A

1 Completar Fill in the blanks with the **yo** form of the verbs in parentheses. (5 x 1 pt. each = 5 pts.)

1. ______________________ (Poner) los libros en la mesa.
2. ______________________ (Traer) la mochila a clase.
3. ______________________ (Oír) la música de los vecinos (*neighbors*).
4. ______________________ (Hacer) la tarea.
5. ______________________ (Suponer) que vamos a perder.

2 Conversaciones Fill in the blanks with the appropriate words from the box. Four words will not be used. (4 x 1 pt. each = 4 pts.)

a	buceamos	con	de	hacemos	para	poner	suponer

1. —¿Qué hacen ustedes los fines de semana?
   —Nosotros ______________________. Nos gusta mucho el océano.
2. —¿Sales ______________________ Puerto Rico?
   —Sí, mañana viajo. Quiero estar con mi familia en el Caribe.
3. —Voy a ______________________ la televisión.
   —Ahora no, por favor. Tengo sueño y quiero dormir.
4. —Luis es el novio de Teresa, ¿verdad?
   —Sí, ella sale ______________________ él.

3 Los domingos Fill in the blanks with the correct form of the appropriate verbs. (7 x 1 pt. each = 7 pts.)

Me gustan los domingos. Por la mañana, vamos a la iglesia y (1) ______________ (oír / poner) el sermón. Al mediodía, (2)______________(decir / salir) de la iglesia y venimos a este (*this*) parque. Mis tíos vienen a almorzar con nosotros. Mi tía Gloria (3) ___________ (traer / ver) unos sándwiches y, como me gusta la música, yo (4) ______________ (traer / hacer) una radio. No (5) ______________ (hacer / poner) la música con mucho volumen. Más tarde (*Later*), yo (6) ____________ (salir / ver) con mis amigos al cine y (7) ___________ (decir / ver) una película.

4 Oraciones Write sentences using the information provided. Make any necessary changes. (4 x 1 pt. each = 4 pts.)

modelo

México / salir / nosotros / para

Nosotros salimos para México.

1. no / bien / yo / oír
2. ver / en / televisión / partido / de / usted / tenis / la / el
3. de / amigos / la / instrucciones / mis / oír / las / profesora
4. mentiras / decir / no / yo

Nombre ______________________________ Fecha ______________________

ESTRUCTURA 4.4 Lección 4

Quizzes

Quiz B

1 Oraciones Complete the sentences using the verbs from the box. Use each verb once. (6 x 1 pt. each = 6 pts.)

decir	hacer	oír	salir	traer	ver

1. Los fines de semana, yo ______________________________
2. Ustedes no ______________________________
3. Esta noche Julio va a ______________________________
4. ¿Hoy yo ______________________________
5. En sus ratos libres, ellas ______________________________
6. Si tengo tiempo, ______________________________

2 Preguntas Answer the questions using complete sentences. (4 x 1 pt. each = 4 pts.)

1. ¿A qué hora sales de la casa los lunes?
____
2. ¿Dónde ves películas?
____
3. Cuando quieres bailar, ¿qué música pones?
____
4. ¿Qué traes a la escuela?
____

3 Escribir Write a description of an ideal Saturday. Mention what you do, where you go, and with whom, using at least five verbs from the box. (5 pts. for grammar + 5 pts. for style and creativity = 10 pts.)

almorzar	salir	hacer	traer
oír	poner	ver	volver

____
____
____
____
____
____
____
____

Nombre ______________________ Fecha ______________

Quizzes

CONTEXTOS Lección 5

Quiz A

1 Seleccionar Select the item that does not belong. (5 x 1 pt. each = 5 pts.)

1. a. avión
   b. agente de viajes
   c. motocicleta
   d. auto
2. a. viento
   b. décimo
   c. octavo
   d. tercero
3. a. la huésped
   b. el ascensor
   c. el botones
   d. el viajero
4. a. estar de vacaciones
   b. ir de vacaciones
   c. estar nublado
   d. hacer un viaje
5. a. otoño
   b. primavera
   c. mes
   d. invierno
6. a. llover
   b. acampar
   c. jugar a las cartas
   d. pescar

2 ¿Lógico o ilógico? Indicate whether each statement is **lógico** (**L**) or **ilógico** (**I**). (5 x 1 pt. each = 5 pts.)

______ 1. Una habitación doble puede tener dos camas.

______ 2. Hago un viaje al campo porque me gusta ir de compras.

______ 3. Doña Isabel es vieja y no camina bien; por eso (*therefore*) vive en la planta baja.

______ 4. Si quieres ver el paisaje, debes reservar una habitación en el séptimo piso.

______ 5. Tengo miedo de los animales y hoy pienso montar a caballo.

3 Oraciones Select the correct option. (5 x 1 pt. each = 5 pts.)

1. Hoy esperamos la ______________________ (llegada / salida) de mi tío, quien viene de Venezuela.
2. El verano es la ______________________ (novena / tercera) estación del año.
3. Vamos a la playa porque nos gusta el ______________________ (mar / empleado).
4. Quiero recordar siempre estas vacaciones. Voy a ________________ (llevar equipaje / sacar fotos).
5. Ahora ______________________ (hace fresco / está nevando). No quiero salir del hotel.

4 Completar Fill in the blanks with the appropriate words. (4 x 1 pt. each = 4 pts.)

1. El ______________________ es el documento que necesito para viajar a otro país.
2. Enero es el ______________________ mes del año.
3. Mi hermana viaja de Miami a Puerto Rico. Puede ir en avión o en ______________________.
4. Un pasaje de Nueva York a Chicago y otra vez (*again*) a Nueva York es un pasaje de __________.

Nombre ______________________ Fecha ______________________

Quizzes

CONTEXTOS — Lección 5

Quiz B

1 Oraciones Complete the sentences. (6 x 1 pt. each = 6 pts.)

1. Cuando hace calor, mis amigos y yo…
____
2. En la primavera…
____
3. El botones…
____
4. Ustedes van a la agencia de viajes porque...
____
5. Si nieva...
____
6. Cuando estoy de vacaciones, ...
____

2 Preguntas Answer the questions using complete sentences. (4 x 1 pt. each = 4 pts.)

1. ¿Cuál es la fecha de hoy?
____
2. ¿Qué estación es? ¿Te gusta? ¿Por qué?
____
3. ¿Prefieres la playa o el campo? ¿Por qué?
____
4. ¿Viajan mucho tú y tu familia? ¿Adónde? ¿Cómo prefieren viajar?
____

3 En el hotel Write a conversation between a hotel receptionist and a guest arriving at the hotel. Include references to the weather and the date, the guest's room and luggage, two nearby activities, and ways to get there. (6 pts. for grammar + 4 pts. for style and creativity = 10 pts.)

____
____
____
____
____
____

Nombre ________________________________ Fecha ____________________

ESTRUCTURA 5.1 Lección 5

Quiz A

1 Opuestos Write an adjective with the opposite meaning. (4 x 1 pt. each = 4 pts.)

1. cerrado ____________________
2. alegre ____________________
3. ordenado ____________________
4. sucio ____________________

2 Emparejar Match the sentence parts. Three items from Column B will not be used. (6 x 1 pt. each = 6 pts.)

A

______ 1. Cuando los estudiantes tienen problemas, los profesores...

______ 2. Cuando estoy de vacaciones...

______ 3. Cuando mi prima ve películas como (*like*) *Titanic*...

______ 4. Cuando Sonia tiene muchos exámenes...

______ 5. Cuando los aviones no salen a tiempo (*on time*), los viajeros...

______ 6. Cuando no tenemos razón, ...

B

a. está triste.

b. están preocupados.

c. estamos equivocadas.

d. está nerviosa.

e. están cómodos.

f. están enojados.

g. estoy de mal humor.

h. estamos desordenados.

i. estoy contenta.

Nombre ______________________ Fecha ______________________

3 Completar Write the appropriate form of **estar** in the first blank of each sentence, and an appropriate adjective in the second. (6 x 1 pt. each = 6 pts.)

1. —Esta película no es interesante. Nosotras ______________________

   un poco ______________________.

2. —¿Son novios Ángela y Miguel?

   —Sí, ella ______________________ ______________________ de él.

3. —Ahora mismo salimos para el aeropuerto. José, ¿tú ______________________

   ______________________?

4. —¡No entiendo nada (*anything*) en la clase de física! Siempre ______________________

   ______________________.

5. —Ahora las ventanas ______________________ ______________________, pero debemos cerrarlas

   (*close them*) porque hace mucho viento.

6. —Después de (*After*) estar en el avión quince horas, usted debe ______________________

   muy ______________________.

   —Sí, deseo descansar en el hotel.

4 Oraciones Write sentences with the verb **estar** using the information provided. Make any necessary changes. (4 x 1 pt. each = 4 pts.)

modelo

Sara y María / listo

Sara y María están listas.

1. los viajeros / de buen humor

   ____

2. Tomás y yo / preocupado / la situación en el aeropuerto

   ____

3. mi sobrina / avergonzado

   ____

4. ¿tú / seguro de / que / querer / ser / médico?

   ____

Quizzes

Nombre ______________________ Fecha ______________

ESTRUCTURA 5.1 Lección 5

Quiz B

1 Situaciones Complete the sentences using **estar** with adjectives. (5 x 1 pt. each = 5 pts.)

1. Cuando estoy de vacaciones...
____
2. Cuando mis amigos y yo tenemos muchos exámenes...
____
3. Cuando los estudiantes llegan tarde (*late*), ...
____
4. Cuando ustedes no tienen razón, ...
____
5. Cuando la viajera espera muchas horas en el aeropuerto...
____

2 Completar Fill in the blanks to create sentences that make sense. Do not repeat any words. (3 x 2 pts. each = 6 pts.)

1. Quiero ______________ porque hoy estoy ______________.
2. Hoy mis amigos van a ______________ porque están ______________.
3. Mi madre siempre (*always*) está ______________ porque ______________.

3 Más oraciones Write three original sentences similar to those in the previous activity. Do not repeat any adjectives. (6 pts. for grammar + 3 pts. for style and creativity = 9 pts.)

____

ESTRUCTURA 5.2 Lección 5

Quiz A

1 Verbos Write the present progressive form of each verb. Follow the model. (5 x 1 pt. each = 5 pts.)

modelo

leer

(ella) **está leyendo.**

1. jugar
   (ellas) ______
2. vivir
   (tú) ______
3. poder
   (yo) ______
4. aprender
   (nosotros) ______
5. ir
   (él) ______

2 Emparejar Match the descriptions in Column A to the locations in Column B. Two items from Column B will not be used. (4 x 1 pt. each = 4 pts.)

A	B
______ 1. Están trayendo las maletas.	a. la aduana
______ 2. Estamos comprando los pasajes.	b. la agencia de viajes
______ 3. Están cerrando los libros.	c. la playa
______ 4. Estamos mostrando los pasaportes.	d. la clase
	e. el mar
	f. la habitación de hotel

Nombre ______________________________ Fecha ____________________

3 Completar Marta is on vacation with her family. Fill in the blanks with the present progressive form of the verbs. (6 x 1 pt. each = 6 pts.)

Mi familia y yo (1) ____________ (pasar) las vacaciones en la República Dominicana, en la playa Bávaro de Punta Cana. Yo (2) ____________ (escribir) unas postales a mis amigos. Mi madre (3) ____________ (bucear) y mi padre (4) ____________ (pescar) en un barco. Mis hermanos Julio y Enrique (5) ____________ (leer) unos libros aquí en la playa. Y tú, ¿qué (6) ____________ (hacer)?

4 Completar Fill in the blanks with the present progressive form of verbs from the box. Use each verb only once. (5 x 1 pt. each = 5 pts.)

abrir	**dormir**	**pedir**	**viajar**
buscar	**llevar**	**tomar**	

1. —¿Qué haces, Juan?

   —____________________ mis llaves.
2. Los turistas ____________________ fotos con sus cámaras digitales.
3. Tú ____________________ porque estás muy cansado.
4. Tenemos hambre. ____________________ una pizza.
5. —El botones ____________________ las ventanas de la habitación.

   —Pero ¿por qué? ¡Hace mucho frío!

Nombre ______________________ Fecha ______________________

ESTRUCTURA 5.2 — Lección 5

Quizzes

Quiz B

1 Lugares Use the present progressive to say what the people are doing in each location. (6 x 1 pt. each = 6 pts.)

modelo

la habitación (ustedes)

Ustedes están mirando televisión en la habitación.

1. el avión (mi familia y yo) ______________________
2. el aeropuerto (los viajeros) ______________________
3. la clase de español (yo) ______________________
4. el hotel (usted) ______________________
5. la agencia de viajes (Lucía y Beto) ______________________
6. el parque (tú) ______________________

2 Preguntas Answer the questions using complete sentences. (4 x 1 pt. each = 4 pts.)

1. ¿Qué estás haciendo tú?
____
2. ¿Qué están haciendo tus padres?
____
3. ¿Qué está haciendo el/la profesor(a)?
____
4. ¿Qué está haciendo tu mejor (*best*) amigo/a?
____

3 Famosos Imagine that you are a Hollywood reporter. Write an e-mail to your boss, using the present progressive to describe what six celebrities are doing. (6 pts. for grammar + 4 pts. for style and creativity = 10 pts.)

____

____

____

____

____

____

____

Nombre ______________________________ Fecha ____________________

ESTRUCTURA 5.3 Lección 5

Quiz A

1 Emparejar Match the sentences in Column A to the descriptions in Column B. Three items from Column B will not be used. (5 x 1 pt. each = 5 pts.)

A	B
______ 1. Tenemos que salir ahora mismo.	a. Está ocupado.
______ 2. Carmen no viene a trabajar por una semana.	b. Estamos listos.
______ 3. El señor Gómez tiene mucho trabajo.	c. Es nerviosa.
______ 4. Mi profesor de historia tiene 25 años.	d. Están verdes.
______ 5. No debes comer las peras (*pears*) ahora.	e. Está mala.
	f. Somos seguros.
	g. Es joven.
	h. Son verdes.

2 Escoger Select the correct option. (6 x 1 pt. each = 6 pts.)

1. Mi esposo ________________________ (está / es) muy alto.
2. Tú ________________________ (eres / estás) puertorriqueño.
3. Yo ________________________ (estoy / soy) aburrida, porque esta clase ________________________ (está / es) aburrida.
4. El concierto de rock ________________________ (está / es) en el estadio.
5. Mis amigos Olivia y Eduardo ____________________ (son / están) enamorados.

3 Completar Carolina is on vacation with her friends. Fill in the blanks with the correct forms of **ser** or **estar**. (12 x 0.75 pt. each = 9 pts.)

Mis compañeros de clase y yo (1) ________________ de Michigan y ahora estamos en Costa Rica con la escuela. Nosotros (2) ________________ muy buenos estudiantes, y (3) ________________ cansados porque (4) ________________ muy trabajadores y tenemos muchos exámenes. ¡Necesitamos descansar! Nuestro hotel (5) ________________ bonito y todas las decoraciones (6) ________________ de coral. Tiene habitaciones cómodas y (7) ________________ muy limpias. Pero mis amigas Rebeca y Daniela (8) ________________ enojadas porque su habitación (9) ________________ en la planta baja y no pueden ver el mar. Mañana (10) ________________ domingo y regresamos a casa. Mis padres (11) ________________ preocupados porque (12) ________________ nevando mucho en Michigan.

Nombre ______________________ Fecha ______________________

ESTRUCTURA 5.3 Lección 5

Quizzes

Quiz B

1 Describir Fill in the blanks with appropriate adjectives. (4 x 1.5 pts. each = 6 pts.)

1. Mi madre es ______________ y ______________ y siempre (*always*) está ______________.
2. Mi padre es ______________ y ______________ y siempre está ______________.
3. Yo soy ______________ y ______________ y siempre estoy ______________.
4. Mis amigos son ______________ y ______________ y siempre están ______________.

2 Oraciones Use **ser** or **estar** to complete the sentences. (3 x 2 pts. each = 6 pts.)

1. El próximo (*next*) examen de español...
____
2. El/La profesor(a) de español...
____
3. Ahora mismo...
____

3 Escribir Write a paragraph about someone you admire using the questions in the box as a guide. (5 pts. for grammar + 3 pts. for style and creativity = 8 pts.)

¿Cómo es?	**¿Cuál es su profesión?**	**¿Dónde está?**
¿Cómo está?	**¿De dónde es?**	**¿Qué está haciendo?**

____
____
____
____
____
____
____

Nombre ______________________ Fecha ______________________

ESTRUCTURA 5.4 — Lección 5

Quiz A

1 Conversaciones Select the correct answer. (5 x 1 pt. each = 5 pts.)

1. —¿Quién toma fotos?
   —Margarita _______ toma.
   a. las
   b. los
   c. la
2. —David, ¿estás usando la computadora?
   —No, ahora no. _______ más tarde (*later on*).
   a. Lo voy a usar
   b. Voy a usarla
   c. No voy a usarla
3. —Quiero ver el hotel donde vamos a quedarnos (*stay*).
   —Lo siento, no _______ ahora.
   a. me puedes ver
   b. puedes vernos
   c. lo puedes ver
4. —¿Nos entienden ustedes?
   —Sí, ______.
   a. te entienden
   b. nos entienden
   c. los entendemos
5. —¿Dónde está Ana leyendo el libro?
   —______ al lado de la piscina.
   a. La estoy leyendo
   b. Está leyéndolo
   c. Estás leyéndolo

2 Oraciones Rewrite each sentence, replacing the direct object noun with the appropriate direct object pronoun. Follow the model. (5 x 1 pt. each = 5 pts.)

modelo

Juan lleva la maleta.

Juan la lleva.

1. Ustedes buscan el hotel.
2. Anabela está mirando su programa favorito.
3. No veo a mi familia.
4. Debemos llamar a nuestros tíos.
5. Vamos a comprar unas maletas grandes.

3 Más oraciones Rewrite the sentences without changing their meaning. Follow the model.
(4 x 1 pt. each = 4 pts.)

modelo

Nos va a ver el martes.

Va a vernos el martes.

1. Tengo que hacerlas mañana.
____
2. Te puedo llevar al aeropuerto.
____
3. Lo estoy aprendiendo.
____
4. Van a visitarnos hoy.
____

4 Preguntas Answer the questions negatively, using complete sentences and direct object pronouns.
(6 x 1 pt. each = 6 pts.)

1. ¿Me estás llamando?
____
2. ¿Confirma la reservación la agente de viajes?
____
3. ¿Nos espera el botones?
____
4. ¿Van a traer los pasajes?
____
5. ¿Te vienen a visitar tus abuelos?
____
6. ¿Quieren hacer un viaje Lola y Ricardo?
____

Nombre ______________________ Fecha ______________

ESTRUCTURA 5.4 Lección 5

Quiz B

1 Definiciones Write definitions for the words, using direct object pronouns. (4 x 2 pts. each = 8 pts.)

modelo

computadora

La usamos para buscar información en Internet. La usamos cuando estudiamos. La necesitamos cuando escribimos composiciones. Son de plástico y metal.

1. llave ______________________
2. calculadora ______________________
3. maletas ______________________
4. pasaporte ______________________

2 Preguntas Answer the questions using direct object pronouns. Use complete sentences. (4 x 1 pt. each = 4 pts.)

1. ¿Te llaman mucho tus amigos/as?
2. ¿Vas a visitar a tus padres este año? ¿Cuándo?
3. ¿Tus profesores los entienden a ti y a tus amigos? ¿Por qué?
4. ¿Estás escribiendo la respuesta?

3 Escribir Write a description of someone you know who is very different from you. Contrast what you do with what he/she does. Use at least five direct object pronouns. (5 pts. for grammar + 3 pts. for style and creativity = 8 pts.)

Quizzes

Nombre ______________________ Fecha ______________________

CONTEXTOS Lección 6

Quiz A

1 Clasificar Sort the words from the box into the appropriate categories. (6 x 0.5 pt. each = 3 pts.)

abrigo	guantes	impermeable	sandalias	sombrero	traje de baño

A. Llueve y hace fresco.	B. Hace mucho calor.	C. Hace frío.
____________	____________	____________
____________	____________	____________

2 Seleccionar Choose the item that does not belong. (7 x 1 pt. each = 7 pts.)

1. a. hermoso
   b. elegante
   c. morado
   d. caro
2. a. hacer juego
   b. regatear
   c. gastar
   d. pagar
3. a. suéter
   b. calcetines
   c. chaqueta
   d. cartera
4. a. almacén
   b. mercado
   c. tienda
   d. dependiente
5. a. tarjeta de crédito
   b. rebaja
   c. efectivo
   d. dinero
6. a. cada
   b. caja
   c. vendedora
   d. clienta
7. a. blusa
   b. falda
   c. corbata
   d. vestido

3 Asociaciones Write the color(s) you associate with each item. (5 x 1 pt. each = 5 pts.)

modelo

el dólar estadounidense **verde**

1. el elefante Dumbo ______________________
2. una pelota de baloncesto ______________________
3. el chocolate ______________________
4. la mermelada de uva (*grape jelly*) ______________________
5. la noche ______________________

4 Completar Fill in the blanks with words from the box. Four items will not be used. (5 x 1 pt. each = 5 pts.)

anaranjado	**pantalones cortos**	**precio fijo**
barata	**regalo**	**ricas**
caras	**par**	**vendedor**

1. En el verano uso ______________________.
2. Juanita busca un ______________________ de sandalias.
3. Mis primas tienen mucho dinero. Son ______________________.
4. Cuando hay una rebaja, la ropa es ______________________.
5. Si hay un ______________________, no puedes regatear.

Nombre ______________________ Fecha ______________________

Quizzes

CONTEXTOS

Lección 6

Quiz B

1 Categorías Write what people wear in each situation. Include the indefinite article, and do not repeat any items. (8 x 0.5 pt. each = 4 pts.)

A. unas vacaciones en Cancún

____

____

B. una excursión en Alaska

____

____

C. una boda (*wedding*)

____

____

D. una fiesta (*party*) de jóvenes en tu ciudad

____

____

2 Preguntas Answer the questions using complete sentences. (6 x 1 pt. each = 6 pts.)

1. ¿Tus amigos prefieren usar ropa elegante o casual? ______________________
2. ¿Es posible regatear en alguna (*any*) tienda de tu comunidad? ______________________
3. ¿Dónde venden ropa barata en tu ciudad? ¿Y ropa cara? ______________________
4. ¿Qué ropa lleva tu padre o tu madre para trabajar? ______________________
5. ¿Cuál es tu almacén o tienda favorito/a? ¿Qué venden allí? ______________________
6. ¿Cuánto crees que gastas en ropa anualmente (*annually*)? ______________________

3 Escribir Write a paragraph describing what you and your Spanish teacher are wearing today. Specify colors and include adjectives. (6 pts. for grammar + 4 pts. for style and creativity = 10 pts.)

____

Nombre ______________________ Fecha ______________________

Quizzes

ESTRUCTURA 6.1 Lección 6

Quiz A

1 Escoger Select the correct option. (4 x 1 pt. each = 4 pts.)

1. Mi hermana _______ bailar salsa.
   a. sabe b. conoce
2. ¿_______ tú el monumento la Mitad del Mundo?
   a. Sabes b. Conoces
3. Raúl y yo _______ al profesor de matemáticas.
   a. sabemos b. conocemos
4. Ustedes _______ dónde está nuestra casa, ¿verdad?
   a. saben b. conocen

2 Oraciones Fill in the blanks with the correct form of **saber** or **conocer**. (6 x 1 pt. each = 6 pts.)

1. Ellas ______________________ Cuba muy bien porque viven allí.
2. Yo no ______________________ la película *Los abrazos rotos*.
3. —¿______________________ (tú) cuándo es el examen?
   —No tengo idea.
4. Nosotros ______________________ el número de teléfono de Zulema.
5. ¿______________________ tú a mi tío Ramón?
6. Ustedes ______________________ esquiar bien porque toman clases de esquí.

3 Completar Complete the paragraph with the correct form of **saber** or **conocer**. (6 x 1 pt. each = 6 pts.)

Hay una chica muy interesante en mi escuela. Yo (1) ____________ cómo se llama: Valentina. Es un nombre bonito, ¿no? Quiero (2) ____________ más de ella, pero soy muy tímido (*shy*). Voy a llamar a mi amigo Julio; él (3) ____________ a casi (*almost*) todas las personas de mi escuela. Pero si Julio no (4) ____________ quién es ella, mañana después de la clase voy a escribirle un mensaje a Valentina. Pienso darle un poema de Bécquer. Tú (5) ____________ los poemas de Bécquer, ¿no? Son muy románticos. También puedo invitarla a salir conmigo; yo (6) ____________ un café muy bueno que se llama La Rana.

4 Preguntas Fill in the blanks with the correct form of the appropriate verbs from the box. Use each verb once. Then complete the responses. Two verbs will not be used. (4 x 1 pt. each = 4 pts.)

conducir	conocer	ofrecer	parecer	saber	traducir

1. ¿Tus amigos ______________________ estar contentos hoy?
   Sí, ____.
2. ¿Tú ______________________ personalmente (*personally*) a una persona famosa?
   No, ____.
3. ¿Tus padres ______________________ un automóvil feo?
   No, ____.
4. ¿______________________ ustedes del inglés al español?
   Sí, ____.

Nombre ______________________ Fecha ______________________

ESTRUCTURA 6.1 Lección 6

Quizzes

Quiz B

1 Preguntas Fill in the blanks with the correct form of **saber** or **conocer**. Then provide responses, using complete sentences. (5 x 1 pt. each = 5 pts.)

1. ¿________________ bailar tus amigos y tú?
   ____
2. ¿Ustedes ________________ un buen lugar para bailar en su ciudad?
   ____
3. En tu familia, ¿quién no ________________ cantar bien?
   ____
4. ¿Tus hermanos ________________ cómo se llaman tus profesores?
   ____
5. ¿________________ tú personalmente (*personally*) a una persona famosa?
   ____

2 Combinar Write sentences using one element from each column. Make any necessary changes. (4 x 1 pt. each = 4 pts.)

yo **la profesora Sandoval** **ustedes** **tú** **mis amigos y yo**	**(no) conocer** **(no) saber**	**nosotros/as** **el profesor de historia** **jugar bien al golf** **mucha gente simpática**

1. ____
   ____
2. ____
   ____
3. ____
   ____
4. ____
   ____

Nombre ______________________ Fecha ______________________

3 Responder Answer the questions using complete sentences. (4 x 1 pt. each = 4 pts.)

1. ¿Traduces bien del inglés al español?
____
2. ¿Qué lugares interesantes conoces?
____
3. ¿Qué automóvil conduce tu padre? ¿Conduce bien o mal?
____
4. ¿Cómo parecen estar tus amigos/as hoy?
____

4 Escribir Write eight sentences describing someone you know. Use the questions in the box as a guide. (4 pts. for grammar + 3 pts. for style and creativity = 7 pts.)

¿Quién es? ¿Cómo es?	**¿Por qué lo/la conoces bien?**
¿Qué sabes de él/ella?	**¿Qué sabe hacer bien él/ella?**

modelo

Mi amigo Ignacio vive cerca de mi apartamento. Sé mucho de Ignacio; su color favorito es...

____

Nombre ____________________ Fecha ____________________

ESTRUCTURA 6.2 Lección 6

Quizzes

Quiz A

1 Completar Fill in the blanks with indirect object pronouns. (6 x 1 pt. each = 6 pts.)

modelo

Ellos no __me__ quieren pagar a mí.

1. Penélope ____________________ muestra sus fotos a mí.
2. A ustedes ____________________ explican el problema.
3. ¿Quién ____________________ presta el libro de historia a José?
4. A ti ____________________ compro un suéter bonito.
5. Yo ____________________ voy a dar mis composiciones a mis profesores.
6. ¿____________________ vas a traer el documento a Ramón y a mí?

2 Preguntas Answer the questions with affirmative sentences. (4 x 1 pt. each = 4 pts.)

1. ¿Te ofrecen el trabajo?
____
2. ¿Carlos les describe la tarea a Ana y a ti?
____
3. ¿Nos puedes vender la computadora?
____
4. ¿A usted le están explicando la verdad?
____

3 Oraciones Write sentences using the information provided. Use indirect object pronouns and the present indicative. Make any necessary changes. (4 x 1 pt. each = 4 pts.)

modelo

yo / no / decir / mentiras / a / mi / amigos

No les digo mentiras a mis amigos.

1. yo / pedir / dinero / a / ti
____
2. la vendedora / mostrar / mucho / chaquetas / a / Laura / y / a / mí
____
3. ¿quién / pagar / los estudios / a / Manuel?
____
4. nosotros / pensar / comprar / regalos / a / nuestro / madres
____

Nombre ______________________________ Fecha ____________________

4 Una fiesta Fill in the blanks with the appropriate indirect object pronouns. (8 x 0.75 pt. each = 6 pts.)

Hola, Ana Milena:

(1) ___________ voy a contar un secreto (a ti): mi cuñada y yo (2) ___________ estamos preparando a mi esposo una fiesta sorpresa (*surprise party*). Tú tienes mucha experiencia en dar fiestas, ¿verdad? Si nos puedes dar unas ideas a mi cuñada y (3) ___________, estoy segura de que va a ser fabulosa. El cumpleaños de Esteban es el 5 de diciembre. Para ese día, mi amiga Yolanda (4) ___________ va a prestar su casa. Tiene una casa enorme en el centro de la ciudad. Está bien para sesenta invitados (*guests*), ¿no? También pensamos contratar (*hire*) a un grupo musical. ¿(5) ___________ debemos pagar un depósito a los músicos? Bueno, ¿(6) ___________ puedes contestar las preguntas hoy, por favor? Es que esta semana (7) ___________ quiero mandar (*send*) las invitaciones a los invitados.

Tu amiga,
Carolina

P.D.: (8) ___________ voy a dar un regalo muy especial a Esteban: ¡un automóvil nuevo!

Nombre ______________________ Fecha ______________________

Quizzes

ESTRUCTURA 6.2 Lección 6

Quiz B

1 Preguntas Answer the questions using complete sentences. (5 x 1 pt. each = 5 pts.)

1. Carlos te explica mi problema, ¿verdad? ______________________
2. ¿Quieres venderme la computadora? ______________________
3. ¿Qué les va a mostrar la vendedora a los clientes? ______________________
4. ¿Nos está mirando la profesora? ______________________
5. ¿Por qué usted no le ofrece el trabajo a Carolina? ______________________

2 Combinar Write sentences using one element from each column. Use indirect object pronouns and the present indicative. Make any necessary changes. Follow the model. (6 x 1 pt. each = 6 pts.)

modelo

yo / dar / dinero / novio/a

Yo le doy dinero a mi novio.

mis tíos/as	**comprar**	**problemas**	**nosotros/as**
yo	**dar**	**zapatos**	**mí**
usted	**escribir**	**composición**	**novio/a**
el/la vendedor(a)	**pedir**	**dinero**	**ti**
tú	**prestar**	**regalos**	**el/la profesor(a)**
nosotros/as	**vender**	**ayuda (*help*)**	**Victor**
ustedes		**¿?**	**cliente/a**

1. ______________________
2. ______________________
3. ______________________
4. ______________________
5. ______________________
6. ______________________

3 Escribir Write five sentences about your plans for gift-giving this year. Use **ir a** + [*infinitive*] and four different indirect object pronouns. (5 pts. for grammar + 4 pts. for style and creativity = 9 pts.)

____

____

____

____

ESTRUCTURA 6.3 Lección 6

Quiz A

1 Verbos Complete the chart with the correct preterite forms. (8 x 0.5 pt. each = 4 pts.)

yo	usted	nosotros	ellas
leí	leyó	(1)	(2)
(3)	comenzó	comenzamos	comenzaron
(4)	aprendió	(5)	aprendieron
abrí	(6)	abrimos	(7)
(8)	buscó	buscamos	buscaron

2 Escoger Fill in the blanks with the preterite form of the appropriate verb. (5 x 1 pt. each = 5 pts.)

1. Ustedes ____________________ la explosión anteayer. (gastar, oír)
2. ¿____________________ tú a la clase de inglés? (asistir, decidir)
3. Anoche Lucía ____________________ una película interesante. (ver, jugar)
4. El viernes pasado yo ____________________ cincuenta dólares por una corbata. (creer, pagar)
5. Ayer Felipe y yo ____________________ en un restaurante cubano. (salir, almorzar)

3 Completar Fill in the blanks with the appropriate form (present, preterite, or infinitive) of the verb in parentheses. (5 x 1 pt. each = 5 pts.)

1. Hoy vamos a ____________________ una composición. (escribir)
2. De repente, ____________________ a llover y corrí a la casa. (empezar)
3. Ellos ____________________ en Cuba desde 2002 hasta 2007. (vivir)
4. No debemos ____________________ el auto. (vender)
5. Todos los días, Eduardo ____________________ al fútbol con sus amigos. (jugar)

Nombre ______________________ Fecha ______________________

4 Conversación Fill in the blanks with the correct preterite or present tense form of the appropriate verb from the box. Two verbs will not be used. (8 x 0.75 pt. each = 6 pts.)

acabar	**comer**	**decidir**	**llevar**	**salir**
bailar	**comprar**	**esperar**	**pasar**	**volver**

ANDRÉS Sofía, ¡cuánto tiempo! ¿Ya (1) ____________________ (tú) de Guatemala?

SOFÍA Hola, Andrés. Sí, (2) ____________________de llegar del aeropuerto. Pasé unas vacaciones maravillosas, pero ahora estoy muy cansada por el viaje. Fue (*It was*) terrible.

ANDRÉS ¿Qué (3) ____________________? ¿Llegaste tarde (*late*) al aeropuerto?

SOFÍA No, mi esposo y yo (4) ____________________del hotel muy temprano (*early*). Además, el taxista que nos (5) ____________________al aeropuerto condujo (*drove*) muy rápido. Pero en el aeropuerto había (*there were*) mucha gente. Nosotros (6) ____________________ desde las siete de la mañana hasta la una de la tarde. Por fin, a la una, salió el avión.

ANDRÉS Uf, ¡seis horas en el aeropuerto! ¡Qué mala suerte! Ahora, cuéntame (*tell me*), ¿me (7) ____________________ la camiseta que te pedí?

SOFÍA No, yo (8) ____________________ comprarte esto: es una réplica de las ruinas en Tikal.

ANDRÉS ¡Qué bonita!

Quizzes

Nombre ______________________ Fecha ______________

ESTRUCTURA 6.3 Lección 6

Quiz B

1 Completar Complete the conversation using the preterite and direct object pronouns. Invent any necessary information. (4 x 1 pt. each = 4 pts.)

modelo

ANDRÉS Hola, Eva. ¿Buscaste los libros en la biblioteca?
EVA **Hola, Andrés. Sí, los busqué.**

ANDRÉS ¿Ya abrieron la nueva librería? ¿Qué encontraste allí?
EVA (1) ______________________
ANDRÉS ¿Y compraste el periódico? ¿Cuánto te costó? ¿Cómo pagaste?
EVA (2) ______________________
ANDRÉS ¿Le llevaste mi tarea a la profesora de inglés? ¿Escribió mi nota (*grade*) en el papel?
EVA (3) ______________________
ANDRÉS ¿Viste a Juan y a Héctor? ¿De qué hablaron ustedes?
EVA (4) ______________________

2 Combinar Write sentences using one element from each column. Make any necessary changes. (6 x 1 pt. each = 6 pts.)

yo	**comer en un restaurante**	**el mes pasado**
el profesor Cortínez	**empezar un libro interesante**	**anteayer**
nosotros/as	**volver a la escuela primaria**	**anoche**
mis amigos/as	**comprar ropa**	**el año pasado**
ustedes	**salir a bailar**	**una vez**
tú	**leer el periódico**	**desde… hasta…**
¿?	**llegar tarde (*late*) a clase**	**ayer**
	ver una película de terror	**¿?**

1. ______________________
2. ______________________
3. ______________________
4. ______________________
5. ______________________
6. ______________________

3 Escribir On a separate piece of paper, write an e-mail to a friend, describing three things you did last week, two things you and your friends did last weekend, and one thing you are going to do next week. (6 pts. for grammar + 4 pts. for style and creativity = 10 pts.)

Nombre ______________________ Fecha ______________________

ESTRUCTURA 6.4 Lección 6

Quizzes

Quiz A

1 Transformar Make the singular sentences plural and the plural sentences singular. Follow the model. (5 x 1 pt. each = 5 pts.)

modelo

Aquella revista es de Marco.

Aquellas revistas son de Elena.

1. Estas faldas elegantes están de moda.
____
2. ¿Compraste aquel traje marrón?
____
3. Estos sombreros cuestan cuarenta dólares.
____
4. Pienso comprar aquellas camisas verdes.
____
5. Esa vendedora está organizando los zapatos.
____

2 Completar Fill in the blanks with the appropriate demonstrative pronouns. (5 x 1 pt. each = 5 pts.)

1. Esa revista es aburrida. Prefiero ____________ (*this one*).
2. ¡Hay muchas gangas aquí! Voy a comprar estas botas y también ____________ (*those over there*).
3. No me gustan esos museos. ¿Por qué no visitamos ____________ (*this one*)?
4. Yo trabajo en este restaurante y Joaquín trabaja en ____________ (*that one*).
5. Primero vamos a este almacén y luego vamos a ____________ (*that one over there*).

Nombre ____________________ Fecha ____________________

3 Escoger Select the appropriate demonstrative word and then write the correct form to complete each conversation. (4 x 1.5 pts. each = 6 pts.)

1. —Me gustan los abrigos que están cerca de la caja.
   —¿________________ abrigos que están allí? (este, ese)
2. (*con una llave en la mano*) —Señora, ________________ es la llave de su habitación. (este, aquel)
   —Gracias. Es la habitación número 512, ¿no?
3. —Perdón, ¿dónde está la biblioteca?
   —Tienes que caminar un poco. ¿Ves ________________ puerta que está allá (*over there*), detrás de la cafetería? (este, aquel)
4. —¿Sabes qué? Los jugadores de este equipo hacen trabajo voluntario con niños pobres.
   —________________ es muy interesante. (este, eso)

4 Oraciones Write sentences with the information provided. Use the preterite and make any necessary changes. (4 x 1 pt. each = 4 pts.)

modelo

¿comprar / (tú) / este / falda / morado?

¿Compraste esta falda morada?

1. yo / llevar / este / reloj / la semana pasada
   ____
2. ¿cuándo / encontrar / (tú) / ese / corbata?
   ____
3. ayer / nosotros / oír / este / música / en la fiesta
   ____
4. Juanjo / venderle / aquel / libros / a Raquel.
   ____

Nombre ______________________ Fecha ______________________

ESTRUCTURA 6.4 Lección 6

Quiz B

Quizzes

1 Completar Fill in the blanks with the appropriate demonstrative words. (4 x 1.5 pts. each = 6 pts.)

1. —Perdón, ¿dónde está la tienda Mucha Moda?
   —Tienes que caminar un poco. ¿Ves ______________________ puerta roja que está allá (*over there*), al lado del café Moderno?
2. —Me gusta el cinturón que está cerca de la ventana.
   —¿______________________ que está allí?
3. (*con un CD en la mano*) —Hijo, si te vuelvo a ver (*see you again*) con ______________________ música, no puedes salir más con tus amigos.
   —¡Pero papá! ¡Es mi grupo favorito!
4. —Quiero reservar una noche en el hotel Flamingo.
   —Lo siento, señor. ______________________ habitaciones ya no están disponibles (*available*).

2 Preguntas Imagine you are shopping with a friend. Respond to your friend's questions with complete sentences using demonstrative pronouns. (4 x 1 pt. each = 4 pts.)

1. ¿Por qué quieres comprar esos zapatos rosados y no estos marrones?
   ____
2. ¿Nos está hablando aquella vendedora?
   ____
3. ¿Quién te prestó esa tarjeta de crédito?
   ____
4. ¿Por qué te gustan aquellos pantalones?
   ____

3 Escribir Write six sentences with demonstrative adjectives that describe the people and objects in your classroom. (6 pts. for grammar + 4 pts. for style and creativity = 10 pts.)

modelo

Aquella chica se llama Nuria.

____

____

____

____

____

____

____

Nombre ______________________________ Fecha ____________________

CONTEXTOS Lección 7

Quiz A

1 Seleccionar Select the item that does not belong. (5 x 1 pt. each = 5 pts.)

1. a. espejo b. champú c. maquillaje d. crema de afeitar
2. a. bañarse b. ducharse c. lavarse d. ponerse
3. a. inodoro b. ducha c. lavado d. pantuflas
4. a. despertador b. levantarse c. jabón d. despertarse
5. a. entonces b. manos c. cara d. pelo

2 Ordenar Order the events from 1 to 5. (5 x 1 pt. each = 5 pts.)

______ a. Aarón se despierta a las siete, pero no se levanta hasta las siete y cuarto.

______ b. Se pone la ropa y come el desayuno (*breakfast*).

______ c. Va al baño y se ducha; luego se afeita.

______ d. Antes de vestirse, se cepilla el pelo.

______ e. Se cepilla los dientes, se pone los zapatos y por último sale para sus clases.

3 ¿Lógico o ilógico? Indicate whether each statement is **lógico** (**L**) or **ilógico** (**I**). (5 x 1 pt. each = 5 pts.)

______ 1. Después de bañarse, Alfredo necesita un despertador.

______ 2. Valentina se levanta, se viste y por último se ducha.

______ 3. La niña se lava el pelo con champú.

______ 4. Antes de comer, los chicos se ponen las manos.

______ 5. La señora Bustamante se lava la cara y luego se maquilla.

4 Analogías Complete the analogies. Follow the model. (5 x 1 pt. each = 5 pts.)

modelo

lavado : lavarse :: ducha : **ducharse**

1. levantarse : acostarse :: despertarse : ________________________
2. cepillarse los dientes : pasta de dientes :: lavarse las manos : ________________________
3. acostarse : dormirse :: despertarse : ________________________
4. crema de afeitar : afeitarse :: ropa : ________________________
5. por la noche : por la mañana :: después de : ________________________

Nombre ______________________ Fecha ______________________

CONTEXTOS Lección 7

Quiz B

1 Asociaciones Using vocabulary from the lesson, write one word you associate with each item. Do not repeat words. (7 x 1 pt. each = 7 pts.)

1. bañarse ______________________
2. el despertador ______________________
3. el lavabo ______________________
4. el champú ______________________
5. la ropa ______________________
6. la cara ______________________
7. cepillarse ______________________

2 Oraciones ilógicas Edit the sentences so they make sense. Follow the model. (6 x 1 pt. each = 6 pts.)

modelo

Raquel se maquilla con la pasta de dientes.

Raquel se maquilla con el maquillaje.

1. La niña se lava el pelo con pantuflas.
____
2. Después de bañarse, Alfredo necesita un despertador.
____
3. Valentina se levanta, se viste y por último se ducha.
____
4. Antes de acostarse, Adrián se cepilla los dientes y se duerme.
____
5. Antes de comer, los chicos se ponen las manos.
____
6. La señora Bustamante se afeita la cara y se maquilla el pelo.
____

3 Escribir Describe the morning routine of someone you know using at least six words from the box. (4 pts. for grammar + 3 pts. for style and creativity = 7 pts.)

antes (de)	**luego**	**por último se cepilla**	**se ducha**	**se pone**
después (de)	**por la mañana**	**se despierta**	**se levanta**	

____
____
____
____
____
____

Nombre ________________________ Fecha ________________

ESTRUCTURA 7.1 Lección 7

Quiz A

1 ¿Reflexivo o no? Choose the correct answer. (4 x 1 pt. each = 4 pts.)

1. Rafael _______ por la mañana.
   a. se afeita
   b. afeita
2. Todos los domingos mi padre _______ el auto.
   a. se lava
   b. lava
3. Mi hermana tiene que _______ los platos.
   a. secarse
   b. secar
4. Voy a _______ un vestido elegante.
   a. poner
   b. ponerme

2 Completar Fill in the blanks with the correct form of the verbs in parentheses. (5 x 1 pt. each = 5 pts.)

1. Emiliano ________________________ los zapatos. (quitarse)
2. Los señores Guzmán ________________________ por sus hijos. (preocuparse)
3. ¿Tú ________________________ del nombre del profesor? (acordarse)
4. Después de bañarme, (yo) ________________________ con la toalla. (secarse)
5. Antes de salir, nosotras ________________________ la cara. (maquillarse)

3 Oraciones Write sentences using the information provided. Make any necessary changes. (5 x 1 pt. each = 5 pts.)

modelo

nosotros / preocuparse / trabajo

Nos preocupamos por el trabajo.

1. Miguel / enojarse / novia.
2. María Elena y yo / dormirse / a las once.
3. antes de / dormirse / ustedes / cepillarse / dientes
4. ¿(tú) / ducharse / o / bañarse?
5. yo / ponerse / triste / cuando / tener que / irse / de la casa de / mi abuela

Quizzes

4 Una rutina Fill in the blanks with the correct form of the verbs in the box. Do not use the same verb more than once. Four verbs will not be used. (8 x 0.75 pt. each = 6 pts.)

afeitarse	**leer**	**salir**
lavarse	**quitarse**	**ducharse**
quedarse	**despertarse**	**ponerse**
cepillarse	**mirar**	**sentarse**

En mi casa, todos los sábados comienzan de la misma forma. Mis padres (1) ____________ a las nueve. Mi madre va al baño y (2) ______________, pero mi padre (3) _____________ en la cama y (4) ________________ la televisión un rato. Después de salir del baño, mi madre prepara el café. Entonces mi padre (5) ________________ la cara, pero no (6) ____________ porque le gusta tener barba (*beard*). Nosotros tres (7) _____________ en la mesa, tomamos café y hablamos de los planes para el día. Después de (8) ____________ el pelo, me visto y salgo para la casa de un amigo.

Nombre ______________________________ Fecha ______________

ESTRUCTURA 7.1 — Lección 7

Quiz B

1 La rutina de Rafael Rafael's routine is the same every morning. Fill in the blanks with the correct form of an appropriate verb and then place the events in order, numbering them from 1 to 5. (9 x 1 pt. each = 9 pts.)

_______ a. Rafael ____________________ a las siete, pero no se levanta hasta las siete y cuarto.

_______ b. Se pone la ropa y come el desayuno (*breakfast*).

_______ c. Va al baño y se ducha; luego ____________________ la barba (*beard*).

_______ d. Antes de vestirse, ____________________ el pelo.

_______ e. Se cepilla los dientes, ____________________ los zapatos y por último sale para sus clases.

2 Oraciones Write sentences using one element from each column. Use reflexive verbs and do not repeat any verbs. Follow the model. (4 x 1 pt. each = 4 pts.)

los lunes por la mañana	**mi madre**	**acostarse**
los viernes por la noche	**yo**	**cepillarse**
los fines de semana	**mis amigos y yo**	**dormirse**
¿?	**¿?**	**¿?**

modelo

Los viernes por la noche mis hermanos se acuestan tarde.

1. ____
2. ____
3. ____
4. ____

3 Escribir Describe what you do on a typical Sunday using six reflexive verbs. (4 pts. for grammar + 3 pts. for style and creativity = 7 pts.)

____

____

____

____

____

____

____

Nombre ____________________ Fecha ____________________

ESTRUCTURA 7.2

Lección 7

Quizzes

Quiz A

1 Escoger Choose the correct word. (4 x 1 pt. each = 4 pts.)

1. Raquel trabaja 40 horas a la semana y Yolanda _______. Son trabajadoras.
   a. tampoco
   b. también
2. No hay _______ restaurante chino en esta ciudad.
   a. algún
   b. ningún
3. ¿Hay _______ que quieres saber?
   a. algo
   b. alguien
4. No sé nadar; por eso (*that's why*) yo _______ voy a la piscina.
   a. jamás
   b. nada

2 Completar Fill in the blanks with words from the box. Two words will not be used. (6 x 1 pt. each = 6 pts.)

algo	algunas	nada	ningún	nunca	pero	siempre	tampoco

Penélope:

Busqué por toda la casa y no encontré (1) ______________________ despertador.
(2) ______________________ encontré (3) ______________________ en el baño; el champú y tu toalla amarilla deben estar en tu maleta. Bueno, tengo que salir ahora al supermercado para comprar (4) ______________________ cosas, (5) ______________________ te voy a llamar por la noche para ver si ya encontraste (6) ____________________.

Un abrazo,

César

Quizzes

3 Conversaciones Complete each conversation with the correct form of the appropriate words. (4 x 1 pt. each = 4 pts.)

1. —¿Cuántos estudiantes vienen a la clase?
   —Hoy no viene ________________________. (alguien / ninguno)
2. —¿Está enojada Lourdes?
   —Lourdes no está enojada, ________________________ triste. (pero / sino)
3. —Quiero ducharme. ¿Tienes champú y jabón?
   —No, no tengo ________________________ champú ________________________ jabón. (pero, sino / ni, ni)
4. —¿Hay ________________________ almacén bueno en este centro comercial?
   —No, no hay ________________________ almacén bueno, pero hay uno muy barato. (alguno, ninguno / algo, tampoco)

4 Transformar Write sentences with the opposite meaning by changing the indefinite or negative word. Follow the model. (6 x 1 pt. each = 6 pts.)

modelo

No me afeito tampoco.

Me afeito también.

1. Yo también me siento bien.
   ____
2. Siempre me llama alguien.
   ____
3. Hay algunas películas interesantes en el cine.
   ____
4. No hay nada bonito en los almacenes.
   ____
5. No tengo ganas de ir de compras ni de ir al cine.
   ____
6. No veo a nadie jamás.
   ____

Nombre ______________________ Fecha ______________

ESTRUCTURA 7.2 Lección 7

Quizzes

Quiz B

1 Transformar Write sentences with the opposite meaning by changing the indefinite or negative word. Follow the model. (6 x 1 pt. each = 6 pts.)

modelo

No me afeito tampoco.

Me afeito también.

1. Veo a alguien también.
____
2. Siempre hay algo bonito en los almacenes.
____
3. Tengo ganas de ir de compras o de ir al cine.
____
4. No hay ninguna película interesante en el cine.
____
5. Yo tampoco quiero hacer nada.
____
6. No me llama nadie nunca.
____

2 Oraciones Complete the sentences. (5 x 1 pt. each = 5 pts.)

1. Los fines de semana mis amigos jamás ______________.
2. Mi madre es ______________, pero ______________.
3. Tengo algunas ______________, pero no tengo ningún ______________.
4. Mi familia siempre ______________ algún ______________.
5. Hoy no quiero ______________ sino ______________.

3 Escribir Use six indefinite or negative words or expressions to describe what your campus has and does not have. (6 pts. for grammar + 3 pts. for style and creativity = 9 pts.)

____
____
____
____
____
____

Nombre ______________________________ Fecha ______________________

ESTRUCTURA 7.3 — Lección 7

Quiz A

1 Verbos Complete the chart with the correct preterite forms. (4 x 1 pt. each = 4 pts.)

Infinitivo	ser/ir
yo	(1)
tú	fuiste
usted	(2)
nosotros	(3)
ellas	(4)

2 Emparejar Match the questions in Column A to the responses in Column B. Then write the infinitive (**ser** or **ir**) of the verb used in each question. Three items from Column B will not be used. (6 x 1 pt. each = 6 pts.)

A

______ 1. ¿Adónde fuiste anoche? ______________

______ 2. ¿Quiénes más fueron? ______________

______ 3. ¿Fue Carlos también? ______________

______ 4. ¿Cómo fue la comida (*food*)? ______________

______ 5. ¿Adónde fueron después de comer? ______________

______ 6. ¿Fue divertido? (*entertaining*) ______________

B

a. Fuimos novios.

b. No, fue un poco aburrido.

c. Fueron estupendas.

d. Fuimos a las ocho.

e. Fui a un restaurante japonés.

f. Fue maravillosa, pero cara.

g. Fuimos al cine.

h. Francisco y Verónica fueron.

i. No, él no fue.

Nombre ______________________ Fecha ______________________

3 Oracciones Write sentences using the information provided. Use the preterite and make any necessary changes. (4 x 1 pt. each = 4 pts.)

modelo

¿adónde / ir / (usted) / vacaciones?

¿Adónde fue usted de vacaciones?

1. anteayer / Danilo / ir / playa

____

2. ¿cómo / ser / tus vacaciones / Perú?

____

3. yo / ser / presidente / club de ciencias

____

4. ustedes / no ir / clase / el viernes pasado

____

4 Transformar Rewrite the sentences using the preterite. (6 x 1 pt. each = 6 pts.)

1. Usted es muy inteligente.

____

2. Mario y yo vamos al cine.

____

3. ¿Vas a trabajar?

____

4. Somos estudiantes de la escuela secundaria.

____

5. ¿Cómo son las películas de terror?

____

6. Voy al parque para jugar al tenis.

____

Quizzes

Nombre ______________________ Fecha ______________

ESTRUCTURA 7.3 Lección 7

Quiz B

1 Conversación Read Raquel's questions and provide Teresa's responses. Indicate the infinitive (**ser** or **ir**) of the verb you used in each answer. (6 x 1 pt. each = 6 pts.)

RAQUEL ¿Adónde fuiste anoche?
TERESA (1) ______________________
Infinitivo: __________

RAQUEL ¿Quiénes más fueron? ¿Fue Enrique también?
TERESA (2) ______________________
Infinitivo: __________

RAQUEL ¿Cómo fue la comida (*food*)?
TERESA (3) ______________________
Infinitivo: __________

RAQUEL ¿Adónde fueron ustedes después de comer?
TERESA (4) ______________________
Infinitivo: __________

RAQUEL ¿Fue divertido (*entertaining*)? Y Enrique, ¿qué hizo allí?
TERESA (5) ______________________
Infinitivo: __________

RAQUEL ¿Con Paulina? Enrique y Paulina fueron novios, ¿verdad?
TERESA (6) ______________________
Infinitivo: __________

2 Preguntas Answer the questions using complete sentences. (5 x 1 pt. each = 5 pts.)

1. ¿Fuiste a la clase de español ayer?
____
2. ¿Adónde fueron tus amigos y tú el fin de semana pasado?
____
3. ¿Fueron a trabajar hoy tus padres? ¿A qué hora se fueron de la casa?
____
4. ¿Quién fue tu profesor(a) favorito/a en la escuela primaria?
____
5. ¿Cuál fue el último examen que tomaste? ¿Cómo fue?
____

3 Escribir On a separate piece of paper, write a paragraph about your last vacation. Describe where you went, what you did, who went with you, whether it was expensive or inexpensive, and if you enjoyed it. (6 pts. for grammar + 3 pts. for style and creativity = 9 pts.)

Nombre ______________________ Fecha ______________________

ESTRUCTURA 7.4 Lección 7

Quizzes

Quiz A

1 Escoger Select the correct answer. (5 x 1 pt. each = 5 pts.)

1. Daniela y yo vamos a las montañas.
   a. No nos queda nada.
   b. Nos encanta esquiar.
   c. Nos aburren los paisajes.

2. Ellas no quieren ir al museo.
   a. Les aburre el arte.
   b. Les importan los cuadros (*paintings*) de Picasso.
   c. Les molesta conducir.

3. La señorita Ríos trabaja en una agencia de viajes.
   a. Le molesta el turismo.
   b. Le interesa conocer otros países.
   c. Le faltan dos maletas.

4. Usted tiene que ir al banco (*bank*).
   a. Le faltan cincuenta dólares.
   b. Le interesa viajar.
   c. Le queda la chaqueta.

5. El señor García es profesor.
   a. No le importa la cultura inca.
   b. Le molestan las computadoras.
   c. Le fascina enseñar filosofía.

2 Completar Fill in the blanks with the correct present tense form of the verbs in parentheses. Include the indirect object pronoun. (5 x 1 pt. each = 5 pts.)

1. A Ernesto y a Alejandro ______________________ el golf. (fascinar)
2. A la señora Robles ______________________ las ruinas de Machu Picchu. (interesar)
3. A ustedes ______________________ cantar y bailar. (aburrir)
4. A mí ______________________ la educación. (importar)
5. A nosotros ______________________ ducharnos con agua fría. (molestar)

Nombre ____________________ Fecha ____________________

3 Oraciones Write sentences using the information provided. Use the preterite or the present tense as indicated and make any necessary changes. (4 x 1 pt. each = 4 pts.)

1. (a ti) / molestar / despertarse / temprano (presente)

   ____

2. (a José) / quedar / bien / zapatos / anaranjado (pretérito)

   ____

3. ¿(a ustedes) / encantar / sus vacaciones / playa? (pretérito)

   ____

4. (a Carlos y a mí) / aburrir / clases de sociología (presente)

   ____

4 En el cine Complete the paragraph with the appropriate word(s). (6 x 1 pt. each = 6 pts.)

Ayer mis amigos Esteban, Ana, Olivia y yo fuimos al cine a ver la nueva película de Javier Bardem. A mí me (1) ________________ la película porque Javier es uno de mis actores favoritos. Pero a (2) ________________ le (3) ________________; él empezó a dormirse al final. A Ana y (4) ________________ Olivia les molestaron las escenas (*scenes*) violentas. Si tengo que criticar algo de la película, digo que le faltaron más escenas con Javier, pero entiendo que (5) ________________ director le importó más el argumento (*plot*). Y a (6) ________________, ¿te interesan las películas extranjeras?

Nombre ______________________________ Fecha ____________________

ESTRUCTURA 7.4 Lección 7

Quiz B

Quizzes

1 Oraciones Write sentences using the verbs in parentheses. Follow the model. (4 x 1 pt. each = 4 pts.)

modelo

La señorita Ríos trabaja en una agencia de viajes. (interesar)

A la señorita Ríos le interesa conocer otros países.

1. Ellas no quieren ir al museo. (aburrir)
   ____
2. El señor García es profesor. (encantar)
   ____
3. Daniela y yo vamos a las montañas. (fascinar)
   ____
4. Usted tiene que ir al banco (*bank*). (faltar)
   ____

2 Combinar Write sentences using one element from each column. Make any necessary changes. (4 x 1 pt. each = 4 pts.)

yo	**aburrir**	**acostarse temprano**
mis amigos y yo	**fascinar**	**cien dólares**
el profesor Morales	**interesar**	**los zapatos italianos**
tú	**molestar**	**cantar y bailar**
Piedad y Juana	**quedar**	**mucho dinero**
ustedes		**la música pop**

modelo

A ti te fascina la música pop.

1. ____
2. ____
3. ____
4. ____

Nombre ______________________ Fecha ______________________

Quizzes

3 La escuela Write two sentences describing what you love about your school, one sentence describing what bothers you about it, and one sentence describing what your school lacks. (4 x 1 pt. each = 4 pts.)

(encantar)

1. ______________________

2. ______________________

(molestar)

3. ______________________

(faltar)

4. ______________________

4 Escribir Use verbs like **gustar** to describe your likes and dislikes and those of your friends. Include what likes and dislikes you have in common. (5 pts. for grammar + 3 pts. for style and creativity = 8 pts.)

modelo

A mí me aburre...

A mis amigos les importan...

A nosotros nos encanta...

____

Nombre ______________________ Fecha ______________________

CONTEXTOS

Lección 8

Quiz A

1 Clasificar Sort the words from the box into the appropriate categories. Follow the model. (8 x 0.5 pt. each = 4 pts.)

arroz con pollo	**entremeses**	**refresco**
café con leche	**espárragos**	**sándwich de jamón**
cereales	**huevos**	**uvas**

La cena	El almuerzo	El desayuno
entremeses		

2 Seleccionar Select the item that does not belong. (6 x 1 pt. each = 6 pts.)

1. a. arvejas
   b. champiñones
   c. frijoles
   d. entremeses
2. a. pavo
   b. camarones
   c. salmón
   d. atún
3. a. jugo
   b. aceite
   c. vino
   d. té
4. a. naranja
   b. maíz
   c. manzana
   d. pera
5. a. chuleta de cerdo
   b. melocotón
   c. camarero
   d. zanahoria
6. a. lechuga
   b. queso
   c. yogur
   d. leche

Quizzes

Nombre ______________________________ Fecha ______________________

3 ¿Lógico o ilógico? Indicate whether each statement is **lógico** (**L**) or **ilógico** (**I**). (6 x 1 pt. each = 6 pts.)

______ 1. Tengo sed; voy a beber un jugo de pimienta.

______ 2. Normalmente, las salchichas son de carne, de pollo o de cerdo.

______ 3. Comemos la ensalada con mantequilla.

______ 4. Generalmente, el dueño de un restaurante no sirve los platos.

______ 5. El limón es una verdura.

______ 6. Si quieres merendar, puedes comer una fruta.

4 Completar Fill in the blanks with the correct form of the words from the box. Four words will not be used. (4 x 1 pt. each = 4 pts.)

frijoles	**menú**	**pollo**	**saber**
langosta	**probar**	**recomendar**	**sabroso/a**

1. —Y tu amiga Cristina, ¿come ________________________?

   —No, a ella no le gustan nada los mariscos.

2. —No conozco este restaurante. ¿Usted me puede recomendar un plato principal?

   —Sí. Debe ________________________ el bistec con cebolla. Es muy ________________________.

3. —¿Te gusta la sopa?

   —Mmm… sí. ________________________ mucho a ajo.

Nombre ____________________ Fecha ____________________

CONTEXTOS

Lección 8

Quizzes

Quiz B

1 Oraciones ilógicas Edit the sentences so they make sense. Follow the model. (6 x 1 pt. each = 6 pts.)

modelo

El menú nos trae el entremes.

El camarero nos trae el entremes.

1. Comemos la ensalada con mantequilla.
____
2. El limón es una verdura.
____
3. Vamos a comer el plato principal y luego algunos entremeses.
____
4. Normalmente, las salchichas son de espárragos, de arvejas o de margarina.
____
5. Tengo sed; voy a beber un jugo de pimienta.
____
6. Si quieres merendar, puedes comer una langosta.
____

2 Categorías Write two items in each category. Do not repeat any words. (6 x 1 pt. each = 6 pts.)

Las verduras	El desayuno	Las bebidas
________	________	________
________	________	________

3 Escribir Write a dinner menu to mark an important occasion. The menu must describe two appetizers, two main dishes, and several beverages. (4 pts. for grammar + 4 pts. for style and creativity = 8 pts.)

____
____
____
____
____
____
____
____

Quizzes

Nombre ______________________ Fecha ______________________

ESTRUCTURA 8.1 — Lección 8

Quiz A

1 Verbos Complete the chart with the correct verb forms. (5 x 1 pt. each = 5 pts.)

infinitivo	seguir	(1)
yo	(2)	morí
tú	seguiste	(3)
nosotras	seguimos	(4)
ellos	(5)	murieron

2 Completar Fill in the blanks with the correct preterite forms of the verbs in parentheses. (5 x 1 pt. each = 5 pts.)

1. Diego y Javier ______________________ (conseguir) un mapa.
2. Esta mañana usted ______________________ (pedir) mucho café.
3. Tú ______________________ (sentirse) mal ayer.
4. La semana pasada yo no ______________________ (dormir) bien.
5. Amparo ______________________ (preferir) comer en casa.

3 Oraciones Write sentences using the information provided. Use the preterite and make any necessary changes. (4 x 1 pt. each = 4 pts.)

modelo

Edgar / preferir / pollo asado

Edgar prefirió el pollo asado.

1. Álvaro y yo / servir / los entremeses

____

2. ¿quién / repetir / las instrucciones?

____

3. ayer / yo / vestirse / con ropa elegante

____

4. ustedes / dormirse / a las diez

____

4 La cena Fill in the blanks with the preterite form of the appropriate verbs from the box. Four verbs will not be used. (8 x 0.75 pt. each = 6 pts.)

abrir	**mirar**	**repetir**
conseguir	**pedir**	**sentirse**
escoger	**preferir**	**servir**
leer	**probar**	**vestirse**

Anoche Jorge, Iván y yo salimos a cenar a Mi Tierra, un restaurante guatemalteco. Nosotros (1) _____________ este lugar porque Jorge (2) _____________ una reseña (*review*) en Internet que decía (*said*) que la comida es auténtica y muy sabrosa. No es un restaurante elegante; entonces nosotros (3) ______________ con bluejeans. De verdad, en Mi Tierra mis amigos y yo (4) ______________ como (*like*) en casa. El camarero que nos (5) ______________ fue muy amable. Para empezar, Jorge e Iván (6) ______________ tamales, pero yo (7) ______________ esperar el plato principal: carne de res con arroz y frijoles. Comimos tanto (*so much*) que no (8) ______________ nada de postre (*dessert*). ¡Fue una cena deliciosa!

Quizzes

Nombre ______________________ Fecha ______________________

Quizzes

ESTRUCTURA 8.1 Lección 8

Quiz B

1 Completar Fill in the blanks with the preterite form of the appropriate verbs. (4 x 1 pt. each = 4 pts.)

1. Ayer tú ______________________ mal. (preferir, sentirse)
2. Usted ______________________ un mapa de Cuba. (conseguir, vestirse)
3. Esta mañana Diego y Javier ______________________ mucho café. (pedir, seguir)
4. La semana pasada yo no ______________________ bien. (pedir, dormir)

2 Frases Complete the sentences using the preterite. (4 x 1 pt. each = 4 pts.)

modelo

Yo conseguí un libro de arte, pero mis padres **consiguieron libros de historia.**

1. Tú te dormiste a las diez, pero Gloria ______________________
2. Los camareros sirvieron carne, pero nosotros ______________________
3. Mis amigos prefirieron ir de compras, pero yo ______________________
4. Eva y yo pedimos café, pero ustedes ______________________

3 Oraciones Write sentences using one element from each column. Use the preterite and make any necessary changes. (4 x 1 pt. each = 4 pts.)

yo	**conseguir**	**temprano**
Ángela	**dormir(se)**	**pizza**
mis amigos	**pedir**	**mal**
nosotras	**seguir**	**la profesora Rosales**
¿?	**sentirse**	**¿?**

1. ______________________
2. ______________________
3. ______________________
4. ______________________

4 Escribir Use four verbs from the box to describe a meal you ate recently in a restaurant. (5 pts. for grammar + 3 pts. for style and creativity = 8 pts.)

conseguir pedir probar servir escoger preferir recomendar

____

____

____

Nombre ________________ Fecha ________________

ESTRUCTURA 8.2 Lección 8

Quiz A

1 Oraciones Rewrite the sentences using pronouns. Follow the model. (5 x 1 pt. each = 5 pts.)

modelo

Nos va a traer los platos.

Nos los va a traer. / Va a traérnoslos.

1. Nos van a servir el café.
   ____
2. Le estoy mostrando el menú.
   ____
3. ¿Te sirvieron las papas fritas?
   ____
4. Me va a traer el salmón.
   ____
5. Les pedí una sopa de mariscos.
   ____

2 Combinar Write sentences using one element from each column. Make any necessary changes. (4 x 1 pt. each = 4 pts.)

modelo

¿Nos lo van a recomendar?

¿Van a recomendárnoslo?

1. Se la estamos preparando.
   ____
2. Te lo voy a repetir.
   ____
3. ¿Me lo estás preparando?
   ____
4. Se los debemos pedir.
   ____
5. Tienes que mostrármelos.
   ____

3 Preguntas Answer these questions in the affirmative, using pronouns. (5 x 1 pt. each = 5 pts.)

1. ¿Me estás recomendando ese libro?
____
2. ¿Les sirve el té helado a ustedes?
____
3. ¿Van a traerte la mantequilla?
____
4. ¿Ellos nos tienen que mostrar las fotos?
____
5. ¿Estás comprándole los camarones?
____

4 Completar Complete the conversation using pronouns. (5 x 1 pt. each = 5 pts.)

ARTURO ¿Me compraste el vino tinto?
LUIS Sí, (1) _______________
ARTURO Y ¿escogiste la música que vamos a escuchar?
LUIS Sí, (2) _______________
ARTURO ¿Me lavaste los platos?
LUIS Sí, acabo de (3) _______________
ARTURO ¿Qué me dices, Luis? ¿Debo ponerme esta corbata?
LUIS Sí, (4) _______________
ARTURO ¡Ay! ¿Y la comida? ¿Nos preparaste las chuletas de cerdo?
LUIS ¡Tranquilo, Arturo! Yo ya (5) _______________

Nombre ______________________ Fecha ______________________

ESTRUCTURA 8.2 Lección 8

Quiz B

Quizzes

1 Completar Provide Luis's responses. Use pronouns. (5 x 1 pt. each = 5 pts.)

ARTURO ¿Me compraste el vino tinto?
LUIS Sí, (1) ______________________
ARTURO Y ¿escogiste la música que vamos a escuchar?
LUIS (2) ______________________
ARTURO ¿Me lavaste los platos?
LUIS (3) ______________________
ARTURO ¿Qué me dices, Luis? ¿Debo ponerme esta corbata?
LUIS (4) ______________________
ARTURO ¡Ay! ¿Y la comida? A Elena le gustan las chuletas de cerdo.
LUIS ¡Tranquilo, Arturo! Yo voy a (5) ______________________

2 Preguntas Answer these questions using complete sentences. Use pronouns. (4 x 1 pt. each = 4 pts.)

1. ¿Les prestas dinero a tus amigos/as?
____
2. ¿Quién te va a preparar la cena hoy?
____
3. ¿Le compras regalos a tu madre? ¿Cuándo?
____
4. ¿Quién te enseña el español?
____

3 Escribir Make a list of ten objects in your house, and write who bought them and for whom. Include other details if possible. (7 pts. for grammar + 4 pts. for style and creativity = 11 pts.)

modelo
espejo italiano: **Mi novio me lo compró en Roma.**

____
____
____
____
____

Nombre ______________________________ Fecha ____________________

ESTRUCTURA 8.3 Lección 8

Quiz A

1 Emparejar Match the sentence pairs. Three items from Column B will not be used. (5 x 1 pt. each = 5 pts.)

A

______ 1. Mi prima y yo tenemos doce años.

______ 2. Mi padre trabaja 45 horas cada semana y mi madre trabaja 60.

______ 3. A Tomás y a Natalia les encanta la fruta.

______ 4. Mateo y yo corremos cinco kilómetros todos los días.

______ 5. Luis tiene muchos libros, pero yo sólo tengo dos.

B

a. Ella es menor que yo.
b. Corro peor que él.
c. Él trabaja menos que ella.
d. Soy tan joven como ella.
e. Él es tan activo como yo.
f. Ella trabaja tantas horas como él.
g. Él lee más que yo.
h. Ella come tantas peras como él.

2 Completar Soraya and Adelia are very different. Complete the comparisons with the correct words from the box. Three words will not be used. (5 x 1 pt. each = 5 pts.)

de	**mejor**	**peor**
más	**menor**	**que**
mayor	**menos**	

1. A Soraya no le gusta trabajar. Ella trabaja ____________________ que Adelia.
2. Adelia es más tímida ______________________ Soraya.
3. Soraya tiene catorce años y Adelia tiene quince. Soraya es ______________________ que Adelia.
4. Adelia estudia más que Soraya; ella toma más ______________________ cinco clases avanzadas.

   Soraya es ______________________ estudiante que Adelia.

Nombre ______________________ Fecha ______________

Quizzes

3 Amigos idénticos Francisco and Omar are the same in every respect. Complete the comparisons. (5 x 1 pt. each = 5 pts.)

1. Omar es tan alto ______________ Francisco.
2. Francisco trabaja ______________ como Omar.
3. Hace tres años que ellos estudian ruso. Francisco habla ruso tan ______________ como Omar.
4. Omar tiene ______________ libros como Francisco.
5. Ellos tienen quince años; Francisco es ______________ como Omar.

4 Comparar Write comparisons using the information provided. Make any necessary changes. (5 x 1 pt. each = 5 pts.)

modelo

comida japonesa / comida francesa / delicioso (tan)

La comida japonesa es tan deliciosa como la comida francesa.

1. Argentina / Guatemala (grande).
____
2. Scarlett Johansson / Julia Roberts (joven)
____
3. entremeses / platos principales (sabroso)
____
4. Puerto Rico / República Dominicana / playas (tanto)
____
5. música rock / música clásica (bueno)
____

Quizzes

ESTRUCTURA 8.3 Lección 8

Quiz B

1 Comparar Write comparisons using the information provided. Make any necessary changes. (5 x 1 pt. each = 5 pts.)

modelo

comida japonesa / comida francesa / delicioso (tan)

La comida japonesa es tan deliciosa como la comida francesa.

1. Argentina / Guatemala / grande
2. entremeses / costar / más / quince dólares
3. Scarlett Johansson / Julia Roberts / joven
4. música rock / música clásica / bueno
5. Puerto Rico / República Dominicana / playas / tanto

2 Oraciones Write comparisons using one element from each column. Make any necessary changes. (6 x 1 pt. each = 6 pts.)

la música rap	**costar**	**el fútbol**
yo	**saber**	**el presidente de España**
las verduras	**ser**	**la fruta**
el presidente de los EE.UU.	**tener**	**los restaurantes japoneses**
el fútbol americano	**trabajar**	**el jazz**
los restaurantes mexicanos	**¿?**	**mis amigos/as**

1. ______________________________
2. ______________________________
3. ______________________________
4. ______________________________
5. ______________________________
6. ______________________________

3 Escribir Write a paragraph comparing members of your family. Use comparisons and the words from the box. (6 pts. for grammar + 3 pts. for style and creativity = 9 pts.)

alto/a cómico/a inteligente mayor menor trabajador(a)

____

____

____

____

Nombre ______________________ Fecha ______________

ESTRUCTURA 8.4 Lección 8

Quiz A

Quizzes

1 Transformar Write the superlative form of each adjective. (5 x 1 pt. each = 5 pts.)

1. alta ______________
2. buenos ______________
3. simpático ______________
4. viejas ______________
5. grande ______________

2 Absolutos Write the absolute superlative (**-ísimo/a**) form. (5 x 1 pt. each = 5 pts.)

1. difícil ______________
2. rica ______________
3. guapos ______________
4. pequeño ______________
5. trabajadora ______________

3 Emparejar Match the sentence pairs. Two items from Column B will not be used. (5 x 1 pt. each = 5 pts.)

A

_____ 1. Nadie quiere comer en ese restaurante.
_____ 2. No tengo mucho dinero; voy a comprar esa camisa en rebaja.
_____ 3. ¿Por qué no te gustan mis zapatos?
_____ 4. Carmen no tiene tiempo de leer el libro.
_____ 5. No queremos ver esas películas.

B

a. Es baratísima.
b. Son las más aburridas.
c. Es la mayor.
d. Son feísimos.
e. Es el peor de la ciudad.
f. Son los menos sabrosos.
g. Es larguísimo.

4 Superlativos Write comparisons using the superlative. Follow the model. (5 x 1 pt. each = 5 pts.)

modelo

Miami, Los Ángeles, Nueva York (interesante)
Nueva York es la ciudad más interesante de las tres.

1. el fútbol, el béisbol, la natación (divertido)
____
2. el presidente de los EE.UU., el presidente de España, el primer ministro de Canadá (famoso)
____
3. la comida japonesa, la comida cubana, la comida irlandesa (sabroso)r
____
4. el español, el francés, el ruso (fácil)
____
5. los huevos con salchichas, la leche con cereal, el pan tostado con café (barato)
____

Quizzes

Nombre ____________________ Fecha ____________________

ESTRUCTURA 8.4 Lección 8

Quiz B

1 Emparejar Match the sentence pairs. Three items from Column B will not be used. (5 x 1 pt. each = 5 pts.)

A	B
______ 1. ¿Por qué no te gustan mis zapatos?	a. Es baratísima.
______ 2. Nadie quiere comer en ese café.	b. Son las más aburridas.
______ 3. No queremos ver esas películas.	c. Son los mejores del café.
______ 4. Voy a comprar esa corbata en rebaja.	d. Es la mayor.
______ 5. María no tiene tiempo de leer el libro.	e. Son feísimos.
	f. Es el peor de la ciudad.
	g. Son los menos sabrosos.
	h. Es larguísimo.

2 Superlativos Write comparisons using the superlative. Follow the model. (4 x 1 pt. each = 4 pts.)

modelo

el francés, el alemán, el ruso

El francés es la lengua menos difícil de las tres.

1. Miami, Los Ángeles, Toronto
____
2. el presidente de los EE.UU., el presidente de México, el primer ministro de Canadá
____
3. la comida japonesa, la comida cubana, la comida irlandesa
____
4. el fútbol, la natación, el tenis
____

3 Escribir Using four superlatives and three absolute superlatives (**-ísimo/a**), write a radio ad for a new restaurant. (7 pts. for grammar + 4 pts. for style and creativity = 11 pts.)

____
____
____
____
____
____
____

Nombre ______________________ Fecha ______________________

Quizzes

CONTEXTOS

Lección 9

Quiz A

1 Seleccionar Select the item that does not belong. (5 x 1 pt. each = 5 pts.)

	a.	b.	c.	d.
1.	a. enamorarse	b. casarse	c. comprometerse	d. jubilarse
2.	a. helado	b. boda	c. dulce	d. galleta
3.	a. juventud	b. fiesta	c. cumpleaños	d. Navidad
4.	a. estado civil	b. soltero	c. invitados	d. divorciado
5.	a. recién casado	b. pareja	c. separados	d. vejez
6.	a. odiar	b. sonreír	c. reírse	d. divertirse

2 ¿Lógico o ilógico? Indicate whether each statement is **lógico** (L) or **ilógico** (I). (5 x 1 pt. each = 5 pts.)

______ 1. Luz odia a Samuel; ellos se llevan muy mal.

______ 2. Mi tío murió; por eso mi tía es separada.

______ 3. En la fiesta brindaron con flan.

______ 4. Mañana es el aniversario de mis padres y vamos a sorprenderlos con una fiesta.

______ 5. Muchas personas se gradúan de la universidad cuando están en la etapa de la niñez.

3 Analogías Complete the analogies. Follow the model. (5 x 1 pt. each = 5 pts.)

modelo

muerte : morir :: nacimiento : **nacer**

1. muerte nacimiento :: divorciarse de : ______________________
2. pareja : amor :: amigos : ______________________
3. tener una cita : salir con :: separase de : ______________________
4. juntos : separados :: divertirse : ______________________
5. estudiar : graduarse :: niñez : ______________________

4 Completar Complete the conversations. Two words will not be used. (4 x 1 pt. each = 4 pts.)

cambiar edad pastel regalar relajarse romper

1. —¿Piensas ______________________ de trabajo? —Si, estoy buscando algo más interesante.
2. — De postre vamos a servir ______________________ —¡Qué rico!
3. —¿Qué hacen ustedes en las fiestas? — Bailamos, comemos, hablamos y en general ______________________.
4. —¿Qué le vas a ______________________ a tu padre en Navidad? —Unos discos compactos. Le encanta la música andina.

Nombre ______________________ Fecha ______________________

CONTEXTOS Lección 9

Quiz B

1 Analogías Complete the analogies. Follow the model. (5 x 1 pt. each = 5 pts.)

modelo

tener una cita : salir con :: separarse de : **romper con**

1. estudiar : graduarse :: niñez : ______________________
2. muerte : nacimiento :: divorciarse de : ______________________
3. muerte : morir :: nacimiento : ______________________
4. pareja : amor :: amigos : ______________________
5. juntos : separados :: divertirse : ______________________

2 Oraciones ilógicas Edit the sentences so they make sense. (4 x 1 pt. each = 4 pts.)

1. La muerte es el principio de la vida.
____
2. Una chica que celebra sus quince años está en la etapa de la madurez.
____
3. Mi abuela murió y ahora mi abuelo es separado.
____
4. Ricardo se comprometió con Lola porque la odia.
____

3 Preguntas Answer the questions using complete sentences. (3 x 1 pt. each = 3 pts.)

1. ¿En qué año te gradúas de la escuela?______________________
2. ¿Con quién te llevas bien?______________________
3. ¿Qué hacen tú y tus amigos para relajarse?______________________

4 Escribir Imagine that you are 80 years old. Use the preterite and eight words from the box to describe the most important moments of your life. (4 pts. for grammar + 4 pts. for style and creativity = 8 pts.)

adolescencia	**boda**	**celebrar**	**enamorarse**	**jubilarse**	**niñez**
aniversario	**casarse**	**comprometerse**	**graduarse**	**nacer**	**salir**

____
____
____
____

Nombre ______________________ Fecha ______________________

ESTRUCTURA 9.1 Lección 9

Quiz A

Quizzes

1 Verbos Complete the chart with the correct verb forms. (12 x 0.5 pt. each = 6 pts.)

Infinitivo	conducir	(1)	(2)
yo	(3)	(4)	quise
usted	(5)	(6)	(7)
nosotras	(8)	(9)	(10)
ellos	(11)	pudieron	(12)

2 Completar Fill in the blanks with the preterite form of the appropriate verbs. (5 x 1 pt. each = 5 pts.)

1. Tú le ______________ (traer, estar) un regalo a Julián, ¿verdad?
2. Ayer ______________ (traducir, haber) una boda en el Club Campestre.
3. El sábado pasado yo ______________ (dar, saber) una fiesta en mi casa, pero no ______________ (poner, venir) nadie.
4. Alejandra y Cristian ______________ (decir, hacer) que quieren celebrar su aniversario en México.

Nombre ______________________ Fecha ______________________

Quizzes

3 Oraciones Write sentences using the information provided. Use the preterite and make any necessary changes. (5 x 1 pt. each = 5 pts.)

modelo

nosotros / decir / verdad

Nosotros dijimos la verdad.

1. ustedes / darle / beso / recién casado

____

2. ¿cuándo / saber / tú / fecha / de la graduación?

____

3. yo / poner / flan de caramelo / en / mesa

____

4. Antonio y yo / estar / Madrid / verano pasado

____

5. ¿qué / hacer / Nicolás y Fernanda / después de / divorcio?

____

4 El cumpleaños Fill in the blanks with the correct preterite form of the verbs from the box. Some verbs may be used more than once. Two verbs will not be used. (8 x 0.5 pt. each = 4 pts.)

dar	**poder**	**tener**	**haber**
estar	**poner**	**traducir**	**sonreír**
hacer	**saber**	**traer**	**jubilarse**

El mes pasado mi esposo y yo (1) ____________________ una gran fiesta para nuestra hija, quien cumplió tres años. Nosotros invitamos a treinta personas, pero en la fiesta sólo (2) ____________________ veintiocho invitados porque la señora Casas y su hija no (3) ____________________ venir. Mi madre (4) ____________________ unas lasañas deliciosas y mis hermanas (5) __________________ flores (*flowers*) y globos (*balloons*) para decorar la casa. Después de comer pastel, mi hermano (6) ____________________ música y todos bailamos. Los invitados se fueron a las cinco de la tarde. Luego mi esposo (7) __________________ que lavar los platos y yo (8) ________________ una lista de las tarjetas de agradecimiento (*thank-you cards*) que tenemos que escribir.

Nombre ____________________ Fecha ____________________

Quizzes

ESTRUCTURA 9.1 Lección 9

Quiz B

1 Completar Fill in the blanks with the preterite of the appropriate verb. (5 x 1 pt. each = 5 pts.)

1. Ayer ____________________ una boda en el Club Miramar. (traducir, haber)
2. El sábado pasado tú ____________________ una fiesta aquí en tu casa, pero no ____________________ nadie. (dar, saber); (poner, venir)
3. Ellos ____________________ que van a celebrar su aniversario. (decir, hacer)
4. Yo ____________________ un regalo para Julián. (traer, estar)

2 Oraciones Write sentences using one element from each column. Use the preterite and make any necessary changes. (4 x 1 pt. each = 4 pts.)

usted	**dar**	**una mentira**
Carme y yo	**decir**	**la boda de Rafael**
mis amigos	**estar**	**un poema de amor**
tú	**poner**	**una fiesta**
	traducir	**música bailable**

1. ____________________
2. ____________________
3. ____________________
4. ____________________

3 Preguntas Answer the questions using complete sentences. (3 x 1 pt. each = 3 pts.)

1. ¿Qué tuviste que hacer la semana pasada? ____________________
2. ¿Cuándo supiste la fecha de esta prueba? ____________________
3. ¿Quién no estuvo en clase ayer? ____________________

4 Escribir Using four verbs from the box, describe what you did on your last birthday. (5 pts. for grammar + 3 pts. for style and creativity = 8 pts.)

dar	estar	haber	hacer	tener	traer	venir

____

____

____

____

Quizzes

Nombre ______________________ Fecha ______________________

ESTRUCTURA 9.2 — Lección 9

Quiz A

1 **¿Lógico o ilógico?** Indicate whether each statement is **lógico** (**L**) or **ilógico** (**I**). (4 x 1 pt. each = 4 pts.)

____________ 1. Teresa supo que hice una fiesta y no la invité. Ahora está enojada conmigo.

____________ 2. Busqué por horas, pero no encontré la casa de David. No quise visitarlo.

____________ 3. Leila se rio mucho durante la película; no pudo divertirse.

____________ 4. Mis padres se conocieron en Japón; por eso celebran sus aniversarios en Tokio.

2 **Escoger** Select the correct option. (6 x 1 pt. each = 6 pts.)

1. Por fin (conocí, supe) por qué Marlene rompió con David. ¡Está enamorada de José Luis!
2. Ana Milena (quiso, no pudo) llamarte ayer, pero no contestaste el teléfono.
3. Santiago nunca me dijo cómo (conoció, supo) a su novia, pero sé que fue muy romántico.
4. Mañana me gradúo de la escuela. (Pude, No supe) aprobar (*pass*) todas mis clases.
5. Martín se jubiló el año pasado. (Quiso, No quiso) trabajar más.
6. Durante la boda, Daniela se durmió. (Quiso, No pudo) sacar fotos.

3 **Oraciones** Write sentences using the information provided. Use the preterite and make any necessary changes. (5 x 1 pt. each = 5 pts.)

modelo

yo / conocer / este / persona / hoy

Yo conocí a esta persona hoy.

1. el presidente / no querer / hablar con los reporteros
2. ¿cómo / saber / ustedes / lo que (*what*) / pasar / entre / Fabiana y Raúl?
3. tú / conocer / señor Castillo / anteayer
4. nosotros / no poder / comprar los regalos / porque / haber / mucho tráfico / en el centro
5. después de / los exámenes, / Natalia / poder / relajarse

4 **Completar** Fill in the blanks with the correct form of **conocer**, **poder**, **querer**, or **saber**. (5 x 1 pt. each = 5 pts.)

1. A Carlitos no le gustan nada las verduras y por eso no ________________________ comer el brocóli.
2. —¿Conoce usted a mi esposa? —Sí, la ________________________ el año pasado.
3. Después de muchas horas de estudio, Federico ________________________ aprobar el examen.
4. Yo ________________________ sorprender a Marisol el sábado, pero el viernes ella ________________________ todos mis planes.

Nombre ______________________ Fecha ______________________

ESTRUCTURA 9.2 Lección 9

Quiz B

1 Escoger Select the correct option. (6 x 1 pt. each = 6 pts.)

1. Santiago nunca me dijo cómo _______ a su novia, pero sé que fue en Italia.
   a. conoció b. supo
2. Daniela se durmió durante el matrimonio de Tomás y Eugenia. _______ sacar fotos de la pareja.
   a. No pudo b. Quiso
3. Ana Milena _______ llamarte ayer, pero no contestaste el teléfono.
   a. no pudo b. quiso
4. Mañana me gradúo de la escuela secundaria. _______ aprobar (*pass*) todas mis clases.
   a. Pude b. No supe
5. Por fin _______ por qué Marlene rompió con David. ¡Está saliendo con Pablo!
   a. conocí b. supe
6. El señor Iglesias se jubiló el año pasado. _______ trabajar más.
   a. Quiso b. No quiso

2 Completar Complete the sentences. (5 x 1 pt. each = 5 pts.)

1. El año pasado mis padres supieron...
   ____
2. Ayer mis amigos/as y yo quisimos...
   ____
3. Esta mañana no pude...
   ____
4. La semana pasada el/la profesor(a) de español no quiso...
   ____
5. Mi mejor amigo/a y yo nos conocimos...
   ____

3 Escribir Make a list of six things a public figure did (or did not do) over the past few months. Use **conocer**, **saber**, **poder**, **no poder**, **querer**, and **no querer**. (6 pts. for grammar + 3 pts. for style and creativity = 9 pts.)

____
____
____
____
____
____

Quizzes

Quizzes

Nombre ______________________ Fecha ______________

ESTRUCTURA 9.3 Lección 9

Quiz A

1 Escoger Fill in the blanks with **Qué**, **Cuál**, or **Cuáles**. (8 x 1 pt. each = 8 pts.)

1. ¿______________ estudias?
2. ¿______________ de los dos no te gusta?
3. ¿______________ película quieres ver?
4. ¿En ______________ etapa de la vida estás tú?
5. ¿______________ son los postres para la fiesta?
6. ¿______________ es tu opinión?
7. ¿______________ piensas de mis zapatos nuevos?
8. ¿______________ libros te gustan?

2 Emparejar Fill in the blanks in Column A with **cómo**, **cuál(es)**, **cuánto/a(s)**, **dónde**, **qué**, or **quién(es)**. Match the questions in Column A to the responses in Column B. (7 x 1 pt. each = 7 pts.)

A	B
______ 1. ¿_______ es la fecha de tu cumpleaños?	a. quince años
______ 2. ¿A _______ hora naciste?	b. el veinticinco de marzo
______ 3. ¿_______ celebras tu cumpleaños?	c. una chica que celebra sus quince años
______ 4. ¿Con _______ celebras tu cumpleaños?	d. en casa
______ 5. ¿_______ es una quinceañera?	e. a las tres y once de la mañana
______ 6. ¿_______ celebras tu cumpleaños?	f. con una gran fiesta
______ 7. ¿_______ años tienes?	g. con mis amigos

3 Preguntas Write a question for each situation using **qué**, **cuál**, or **cuáles**. (5 x 1 pt. each = 5 pts.)

modelo

Quieres saber la fecha de cumpleaños de tu novio.

¿Cuál es la fecha de tu cumpleaños?

1. Necesitas la definición de un "flan".

   ____

2. Tu madre te pide que abras (*you open*) la puerta, pero tienes muchas llaves.

   ____

3. Organizas una fiesta y quieres saber los postres que les gustan a tus amigos.

   ____

4. Necesitas saber el estado civil de tu vecina (*neighbor*).

   ____

5. Miras al cielo (*sky*) y ves algo muy raro (*strange*).

   ____

ESTRUCTURA 9.3 Lección 9

Quizzes

Quiz B

1 Escoger Fill in the blanks with **Qué**, **Cuál**, or **Cuáles**. (4 x 1 pt. each = 4 pts.)

1. ¿______________________ son los postres para la fiesta?
2. ¿______________________ película quieres ver?
3. ¿______________________ es tu número de teléfono?
4. ¿______________________ estudias?

2 Preguntas Fill in the blanks using interrogative words (**¿a qué hora?, ¿cómo?, ¿cuál(es)?, ¿cuándo?, ¿dónde?, ¿qué?**). Then answer the questions using complete sentences. (6 x 1 pt. each = 6 pts.)

1. ¿______________________ es tu fecha de cumpleaños?
   ____
2. ¿______________________ naciste?
   ____
3. ¿______________________ celebras tu cumpleaños?
   ____
4. ¿______________________ es tu estado civil?
   ____
5. ¿En ______________________ etapa de la vida están tus padres?
   ____
6. ¿______________________ es una quinceañera?
   ____

3 Escribir Write ten questions you would use to interview a famous person coming to visit your campus. Use **qué** and **cuál(es)**. (5 pts. for grammar + 5 pts. for style and creativity = 10 pts.)

____

____

____

____

____

____

____

Nombre ____ Fecha ____________________________

ESTRUCTURA 9.4 Lección 9

Quiz A

1 Escoger Select the correct option. (4 x 2 pts. each = 8 pts.)

1. —Bueno, ya conociste a mis padres. ¿Ellos te hablaron de _______?
   —Hablamos de muchas cosas, pero de _______ no me dijeron nada.
   a. yo; tú b. mí; ti c. mi; tú d. me; te
2. —Pienso ir al centro comercial. ¿Vienes tú?
   —No, no puedo ir _______. Tengo que estudiar.
   a. mi b. para ti c. mí d. contigo
3. —No puedo vivir sin _______.
   —¡Ay! Y yo quiero vivir mi vida dedicada a _______.
   a. ti, ti b. yo; mí c. te; mí d. tú; tú
4. —Entre _______ y _______, creo que mis padres se van a divorciar.
   —¿Verdad? Quizás el matrimonio no es para _______.
   a. te; me; ellos b. ti; mí; nosotros c. él; ella; ti d. tú; yo; ellos

2 Completar Complete the sentences with the appropriate preposition and pronoun. (8 x 1 pt. each = 8 pts.)

1. El regalo grande es _________________________. (*for him*)
2. Mañana salgo _________________________. (*without you*, pl. form.)
3. Hay un mensaje _________________________. (*for you*, sing. fam.)
4. _________________________, esos pantalones son muy feos. (*For me*)
5. Traigo este libro _________________________. (*for you*, sing. form.)
6. No me gusta estar _________________________. (*without them*, f.)
7. ¿Te interesa venir _________________________ a la playa? (*with me*)
8. Ellos no pueden celebrar _________________________. (*without us*, f.)

3 Oraciones Write sentences using the information provided. Use the preterite and pronouns and make any necessary changes. Follow the model. (4 x 1 pt. each = 4 pts.)

modelo

yo / no / querer / salir / con / (Guillermo)

No quise salir con él.

1. pastel / ser / para / (Lucía) ____
2. chicas / sentarse / al lado de / (Jaime y yo)____
3. para / (tú), / la fiesta / ser / aburrido ____
4. yo / estar / cine / (tú) ____

Nombre ______________________________ Fecha ____________________

ESTRUCTURA 9.4 Lección 9

Quiz B

Quizzes

1 Completar Complete the conversations with the appropriate pronouns. (8 x 1 pt. each = 8 pts.)

1. —No puedo vivir sin ____________________.
   —¡Ay! Yo también te quiero. Voy a vivir siempre junto a (*next to*) ____________________.
2. —Bueno, ya conociste a mis padres. ¿Ellos te hablaron de ____________________?
   —Hablamos de muchas cosas, pero de ____________________ no me dijeron nada.
3. —Pienso ir al centro comercial. ¿Vienes tú?
   —No, no puedo ir ____________________. Tengo que estudiar.
4. —Entre __________________ y __________________, creo que mis padres se van a divorciar.
   —¿Verdad? Quizás el matrimonio no es para ____________________.

2 Preguntas Answer the questions using complete sentences. Use pronouns. (3 x 1 pt. each = 3 pts.)

1. Cuando sales los fines de semana, ¿quiénes salen contigo? ____________________

   ____
2. Para ti, ¿cuál es el día de fiesta más divertido? ¿Por qué? ____________________

   ____
3. Piensa en alguien que conociste en tu niñez. ¿Sería (*Would it be*) diferente tu vida sin esa persona?

   ____

   ____

3 Escribir Write a conversation between two guests at a wedding. Use four different prepositions and six different pronouns. (5 pts. for grammar + 4 pts. for style and creativity = 9 pts.)

____

____

____

____

____

____

____

____

____

____

TEST A

Lección 1

1 Escuchar Read these statements. Then listen to the message that Jaime left on his colleague's voicemail and indicate whether each statement is **cierto** or **falso**. (5 x 2 pts. each = 10 pts.)

	Cierto	**Falso**
1. Jaime está regular.	______	______
2. Hay cuatro maletas en el autobús.	______	______
3. El libro es de los profesores.	______	______
4. Son las nueve de la noche.	______	______
5. El número de teléfono es el 24-30-12.	______	______

2 ¡Hola! Write a conversation based on what one of the groups in the picture might say. (6 pts. for vocabulary + 6 pts. for grammar + 3 pts. for style and creativity = 15 pts.)

____

____

____

____

____

____

____

____

____

____

____

Tests

Nombre ______________________________ Fecha ____________________

3 **¿Singular o plural?** Write the singular or plural form of the nouns. Follow the model.

modelo

—Hay una maleta.
—**No. Hay cuatro maletas.**

1. —Hay un lápiz. —No. Hay dos ________________.
2. —Hay dos mujeres. —No. Hay una ________________.
3. —Hay un pasajero. —No. Hay cuatro ________________.
4. —Hay una chica. —No. Hay dos ________________.
5. —Hay un estudiante. —No. Hay tres ________________.

4 **La hora** Reyes and Soledad meet at the school's cafeteria. Complete their conversation by writing out the times as words. (5 x 2 pts. each = 10 pts.)

1. —Hola, Reyes. ¿Qué hora es?
   —Hola, Soledad. (*It's 9:30 a.m.*) ________________________________.
2. —Gracias. ¿A qué hora es la clase de español?
   —La clase (*is at 10:15 a.m.*) ________________________________.
3. —¿Y la clase de matemáticas?
   —La clase (*is at 2:25 p.m.*) ________________________________.
4. —¿Y el partido (*game*) de tenis?
   —El partido (*is at 4:45 p.m.*) ________________________________.
5. —Gracias. ¿Y a qué hora es la fiesta (*party*)?
   —(*It's at 8:00 p.m.*) ________________________________.

5 **¿Qué tal?** Two students meet on the first day of class. Fill in the blanks with a Spanish word. (10 x 1 pt. each = 10 pts.)

DIANA Hola, (1) ________________ tardes. ¿Cómo (2) ________________ llamas?

TONI Hola, me (3) ________________ Toni, ¿y tú?

DIANA Diana. ¿De (4) ________________ eres?

TONI (5) ________________ de México. ¿Y tú?

DIANA De los Estados Unidos. Oye, ¿(6) ________________ hora es?

TONI Es (7) ________________ una de la tarde.

DIANA Gracias.

TONI De (8) ________________. (9) ________________ vemos en clase.

DIANA Sí. Hasta (10) ________________.

Tests

6 Preguntas Answer these questions with complete sentences. (5 x 3 pts. each = 15 pts.)

1. ¿Cómo estás? ________
2. ¿Cómo te llamas? ________
3. ¿Qué hora es? ________
4. ¿Cuántos estudiantes hay en la clase de español? ________
5. ¿Qué hay en tu mochila (*backpack*)? ________

7 Lectura Read these bulletin board notices and answer the questions with complete sentences. Write the numbers as words. (4 x 2 pts. each = 8 pts.)

Cuaderno

Hola, soy Mariana. Encontré[1] en la cafetería un cuaderno con números de teléfono.
Teléfono: 22-07-17

[1] *I found*

Tenis

Me llamo Julio y soy de España.
Busco[2] chico o chica para practicar tenis.
Teléfono: 25-14-23

[2] *I'm looking for*

1. ¿Cuál (*What*) es el nombre de la chica? ________
2. ¿Qué hay en el cuaderno? ________
3. ¿De qué país es el chico? ________
4. Escribe (*Write*) el número de teléfono del chico. ________

8 Saludos Write a conversation in which two students introduce themselves, ask each other how they are doing, ask each other where they are from, mention what time it is, and say goodbye. Use vocabulary and grammar from this lesson. (8 pts. for vocabulary + 8 pts. for grammar + 6 pts. for style = 22 pts.)

Tests

TEST B   Lección 1

1 Escuchar Read these statements. Then listen to the message that Don Fernando left on his colleague's voicemail and indicate whether each statement is **cierto** or **falso**. (5 x 2 pts. each = 10 pts.)

	Cierto	**Falso**
1. Don Fernando está regular.	______	______
2. Hay tres maletas y un libro en el autobús.	______	______
3. Las maletas son de los estudiantes.	______	______
4. Son las diez de la mañana.	______	______
5. El número de teléfono es el 25-13-07.	______	______

2 ¡Hola! Write a conversation based on what one of the groups in the picture might say. (6 pts. for vocabulary + 6 pts. for grammar + 3 pts. for style and creativity = 15 pts.)

____
____
____
____
____
____
____
____
____
____
____
____

Tests

3 ¿Singular o plural? Write the singular or plural form of the nouns. Follow the model. (5 x 2 pts. each = 10 pts.)

modelo

—Hay una maleta.
—**No. Hay cuatro maletas.**

1. —Hay quince fotos. —No. Hay una ____________.
2. —Hay tres profesores. —No. Hay un ____________.
3. —Hay un diccionario. —No. Hay cuatro ____________.
4. —Hay tres computadoras. —No. Hay una ____________.
5. —Hay un cuaderno. —No. Hay veintitrés ____________.

4 La hora María and Jorge meet at the school's cafeteria. Complete their conversation by writing out the times as words. (5 x 2 pts. each = 10 pts.)

1. —Hola, Jorge. ¿Qué hora es?
   —Hola. (*It's 9:20 p.m.*) ____________________.
2. —Gracias. ¿A qué hora es la clase de español?
   —La clase (*is at 11:00 a.m.*) ____________________.
3. —¿Y la clase de matemáticas?
   —La clase (*is at 2:45 p.m.*) ____________________.
4. —¿Y la clase de geografía?
   —La clase (*is at 4:30 p.m.*) ____________________.
5. —Gracias. ¿Y a qué hora es la fiesta (*party*)?
   —(*It's at 10:00 p.m.*) ____________________.

5 ¿Qué tal? Two students meet on the first day of class. Fill in the blanks with a Spanish word. (10 x 1 pt. each = 10 pts.)

SARA Hola, buenos (1) ____________. ¿Cómo te (2) ____________?

DIEGO Hola, (3) ____________ llamo Diego, ¿y (4) ____________?

SARA Sara. (5) ____________ gusto.

DIEGO El (6) ____________ es mío. ¿(7) ____________ estudiante?

SARA Sí, (8) ____________ estudiante.

DIEGO Yo también (*too*). ¿(9) ____________ qué hora es la clase de biología?

SARA La clase es a las cuatro.

DIEGO Gracias. Nos (10) ____________ en clase.

SARA Adiós.

Nombre ________________________ Fecha ____________

6 Preguntas Answer these questions with complete sentences. (5 x 3 pts. each = 15 pts.)

1. ¿Cómo te llamas? ____________
2. ¿De dónde eres? ____________
3. ¿A qué hora es la clase de español? ____________
4. ¿Cuántos profesores hay en la clase de español? ____________
5. ¿Hay cuadernos en la clase? ____________

7 Lectura Read these bulletin board notices and answer the questions with complete sentences. Write any numbers as words. (4 x 2 pts. each = 8 pts.)

Maleta

Hola, soy Javier y soy de Costa Rica. Soy estudiante. Encontré[1] una maleta con un diccionario, un mapa, una computadora y dos cuadernos.

[1] *I found*

Chica estudiante

Busca[2] chico de México para practicar español. Me llamo Sarah y soy estudiante. Teléfono: 34-29-06.

[2] *Is looking for*

1. ¿Cuál (*What*) es el nombre del chico? ____________
2. ¿De qué país es el chico? ____________
3. ¿Qué hay en la maleta? ____________
4. Escribe (*Write*) el número de teléfono de Sarah. ____________

____

8 Saludos Write a conversation in which a teacher and a student introduce themselves, ask each other how they are doing and where they are from, mention what time it is, and say goodbye. Use vocabulary and grammar from this lesson. (8 pts. for vocabulary + 8 pts. for grammar + 6 pts. for style = 22 pts.)

____

____

____

____

____

____

____

____

____

____

Tests

Nombre ______________________ Fecha ______________________

TEST C Lección 1

1 Escuchar You will hear five personal questions. Answer them with Spanish sentences. (5 x 2 pts. each = 10 pts.)

1. ______________________
2. ______________________
3. ______________________
4. ______________________
5. ______________________

2 El día de Lourdes Look at Lourdes' course load and answer the questions about her schedule with complete sentences. Write the numerals as words. (5 x 2 pts. each = 10 pts.)

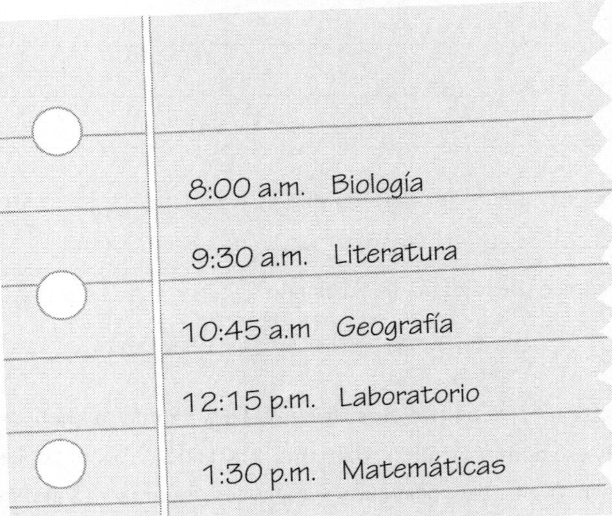

1. ¿A qué hora es la clase de biología? ______________________
2. ¿A qué hora es la clase de literatura? ______________________
3. ¿A qué hora es la clase de geografía? ______________________
4. ¿A qué hora es el laboratorio? ______________________
5. ¿A qué hora es la clase de matemáticas? ______________________

Tests

3 Lectura Read the message that a driver left for his colleague and answer the questions with complete sentences. Write any numbers as words. (5 x 3 pts. each = 15 pts.)

> Hola, Cristina. Soy Armando, un conductor de autobús de la agencia Ecoturista. ¿Cómo estás? Yo, bien. Oye, hay un problema. Hay cinco maletas y un libro en el autobús. Las maletas son de los estudiantes de los Estados Unidos. Pero ¿de quién es el libro? Por favor, necesito[1] la información hoy[2]. Es la una de la tarde. Mi número de teléfono es el 24-30-12. Perdón y hasta luego.

[1]*I need* [2]*today*

1. ¿Cuál (*What*) es el nombre del conductor? ____________
2. ¿Cuántas maletas hay en el autobús? ____________
3. ¿De quiénes son las maletas? ____________
4. ¿Qué hora es? ____________
5. Escribe (*Write*) el número de teléfono de Armando. ____________

4 ¡Hola! Write a conversation between two close friends. They should say hello, introduce a third person, ask each other how they are doing, mention what time it is, and say goodbye. Use the vocabulary and grammar from this lesson. (6 pts. for vocabulary + 6 pts. for grammar + 3 pts. for style = 15 pts.)

Nombre ______________________ Fecha ______________________

TEST D Lección 1

1 Escuchar You will hear five personal questions. Answer them with Spanish sentences. (5 x 2 pts. each = 10 pts.)

1. ______________________
2. ______________________
3. ______________________
4. ______________________
5. ______________________

2 El día de Iván Look at Iván's course load and answer the questions about his schedule with complete sentences. Write the numerals as words. (5 x 2 pts. each = 10 pts.)

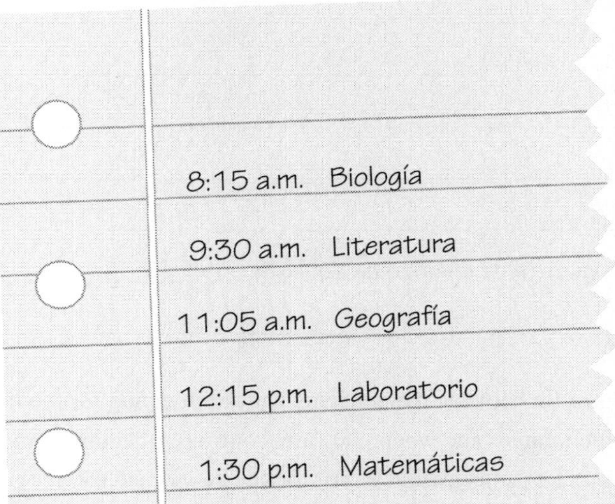

1. ¿A qué hora es la clase de biología? ______________________
2. ¿A qué hora es la clase de literatura? ______________________
3. ¿A qué hora es la clase de geografía? ______________________
4. ¿A qué hora es el laboratorio? ______________________
5. ¿A qué hora es la clase de matemáticas? ______________________

Tests

Nombre ______________________________ Fecha ____________________

3 Lectura Read the message that a travel agent left for one of the company's drivers, and answer the questions with complete sentences. Write any numbers as words. (5 x 3 pts. each = 15 pts.)

> Hola, Pedro. Soy Eduardo. ¿Qué tal? Yo, regular. Hay un problema y necesito[1] información. Hay dos maletas y cuatro libros en el autobús. Las maletas son de los turistas de México. Pero ¿de quién son los libros? Por favor, necesito la información hoy[2]. Son las seis de la tarde. Mi número de teléfono es el 23-06-15.
> Muchas gracias.

[1]*I need* [2]*today*

1. ¿Cuántas maletas hay en el autobús? ______________________________
2. ¿Cuántos libros hay en el autobús? ______________________________
3. ¿De quiénes son las maletas? ______________________________
4. ¿Qué hora es? ______________________________
5. Escribe (*Write*) el número de teléfono de Eduardo. ______________________________

4 ¡Hola! Write a conversation between two students who are meeting for the first time. They should say hello, ask each other their names and where they are from, ask what time it is, and say goodbye. Use the vocabulary and grammar from this lesson. (6 pts. for vocabulary + 6 pts. for grammar + 3 pts. for style = 15 pts.)

____

Tests

Nombre ______________________________ Fecha ______________________

TEST E Lección 1

1 Escuchar Some items were left behind in a classroom. Read the questions below, listen to the voicemail message from the custodian, and then answer the questions. (5 x 2 pts. each = 10 pts.)

1. ¿Para quién (*for whom*) es el mensaje?
   a. para los estudiantes b. para el profesor Valdivia c. para el profesor Martínez
2. ¿Cuántos videos hay en el laboratorio?
   a. cuatro videos b. veinte videos c. tres videos
3. ¿Cuántos diccionarios hay?
   a. dos diccionarios b. cuatro diccionarios c. un diccionario
4. ¿De quién son los cuadernos?
   a. de los estudiantes b. del profesor Martínez c. del profesor Valdivia
5. ¿Qué hora es?
   a. las 5:30 b. las 3:00 c. las 9:15

2 Emparejar Match the sentence fragments. (5 x 2 pts. each = 10 pts.)

______ 1. Hasta	a. está usted?
______ 2. Nos	b. Mari Carmen y a Claudia.
______ 3. Buenas	c. vemos, José Luis.
______ 4. Saludos a	d. noches, señora Sánchez.
______ 5. ¿Cómo	e. mañana.

3 En orden Order the lines of the dialogue from 1 to 5. (5 x 2 pts. each = 10 pts.)

______ a. ¿Qué hay de nuevo?

______ b. Chau.

______ c. Nada.

______ d. Hola, Sofía, regular.

______ e. Hola, Simón, ¿cómo estás?

Tests

4 Correcto o incorrecto Indicate whether each equation is **correcta** or **incorrecta**. (5 x 2 pts. each = 10 pts.)

	Correcta	**Incorrecta**
1. 7 x 4 = veintitrés	______	______
2. 6 + 6 = doce	______	______
3. 7 – 5 = diez	______	______
4. 5 x 3 = quince	______	______
5. 8 + 9 = diecisiete	______	______

5 ¿Ser o no ser? Fill in the blanks with the appropriate form of **ser**. (6 x 2 pts. each = 12 pts.)

1. Madrid ________________________ la capital de España.
2. Julieta y sus padres ________________________ de Puerto Rico.
3. Nosotros ________________________ estudiantes de la Escuela San José.
4. ________________________ un diccionario.
5. —¿Quién ________________________ (tú)?
6. —Yo ________________________ Héctor Camacho.

6 Identificar Match the words to the pictures. (6 x 2 pts. each = 12 pts.)

dos diccionarios	**un cuaderno**
dos fotos	**una escuela**
tres autobuses	**una maleta**

1. ________________________

2. ________________________

3. ________________________

4. ________________________

5. ________________________

6. ________________________

Tests

7 ¿Qué pasa? Fill in the blanks with words from the box. (9 x 2 pts. each = 18 pts.)

es	**mío**	**presento**
estás	**nada**	**se**
gusto	**nuevo**	**soy**

JOAQUÍN ¿Qué tal, Eva? ¿Qué hay de (1) ______________________?

EVA (2) ______________________, Joaquín. ¿Cómo (3) ______________________?

JOAQUÍN Bien, gracias.

EVA ¿Ella (4) __________________ tu hermana (*sister*)? ¿Cómo (5) ________________ llama?

JOAQUÍN Te (6) ______________________ a Isabel.

EVA Mucho (7) ______________________, Isabel. Yo (8) ______________________ Eva.

ISABEL El gusto es (9) ______________________.

8 Lectura Read Sofía's blog entry, then fill in the blanks. (6 x 3 pts. each = 18 pts.)

> Hola, me llamo Sofía. ¿Cómo están? Yo estoy muy bien. Gracias por entrar (*for entering*) a mi blog. Yo soy de Puerto Rico, pero vivo (*but I live*) en Los Ángeles. ¿De dónde son ustedes?
>
> Yo soy estudiante de la Escuela San Martin. ¿Ustedes son estudiantes? Mis clases son a las 8:15 de la mañana.
>
> ¿Tienen hermanos (*Do you have any siblings*)? Yo tengo (*I have*) dos hermanos: Pablo y Mario. Aquí hay tres fotografías de mi familia.

1. Sofía es de ______________________.
2. Ella vive (*lives*) en ______________________.
3. Ella es ______________________ de la Escuela San Martin.
4. Las clases de Sofía son a las ______________________ de la mañana.
5. Sofía tiene (*has*) ____________________ hermanos.
6. Sus hermanos se llaman Pablo y ____________________.

Tests

Nombre ______________________________ Fecha ____________________

TEST F

Lección 1

1 Escuchar Some items were left behind in a classroom. Read the questions below, listen to the voicemail message from the custodian, and then answer the questions. (5 x 2 pts. each = 10 pts.)

1. ¿Para quién (*for whom*) es el mensaje?
   a. para el profesor Pérez b. para el profesor de italiano c. para los estudiantes
2. ¿Cuántos mapas hay en el laboratorio?
   a. tres mapas b. cuatro mapas c. veinte mapas
3. ¿Cuántos diccionarios hay?
   a. dos diccionarios b. tres diccionarios c. cuatro diccionarios
4. ¿Qué hora es?
   a. las 5:30 b. las 10:00 c. las 9:00
5. ¿Hasta (*Until*) qué hora está Juan en la escuela?
   a. hasta las 5:30 b. hasta las 6:00 c. hasta las 6:30

2 Emparejar Match the sentence fragments. (5 x 2 pts. each = 10 pts.)

______ 1. Hasta	a. es usted?
______ 2. ¿Cómo	b. luego.
______ 3. Buenas	c. está?
______ 4. ¿Qué hay	d. tardes, don Daniel.
______ 5. ¿De dónde	e. de nuevo?

3 En orden Order the lines of the dialogue from 1 to 5. (5 x 2 pts. each = 10 pts.)

______ a. Hola, Luis, mucho gusto.

______ b. Buenos días, doña Rosita. ¿Cómo está?

______ c. El gusto es mío.

______ d. No muy bien, María, ¿y usted?

______ e. Bien, gracias. Éste es mi hermano Luis.

Tests

Nombre ________________________ Fecha ________________________

4 Correcto o incorrecto Indicate whether each equation is **correcta** or **incorrecta**. (5 x 2 pts. each = 10 pts.)

	Correcta	**Incorrecta**
1. 23 – 4 = diecinueve	______	______
2. 6 x 4 = treinta	______	______
3. 7 + 5 = doce	______	______
4. 3 x 3 = nueve	______	______
5. 8 + 8 = diecisiete	______	______

5 ¿Ser o no ser? Fill in the blanks with the appropriate form of **ser**. (6 x 2 pts. each = 12 pts.)

1. Washington D.C. ____________________ la capital de los Estados Unidos.
2. Juan Carlos ____________________ de Puerto Rico.
3. Yo ____________________ estudiante de español.
4. Tú ____________________ conductor.
5. —¿Quiénes ____________________ (ustedes)?
6. —Nosotros ____________________ Rosa y Diego Salcedo.

6 Identificar Match the words to the pictures. (6 x 2 pts. each = 12 pts.)

cuatro maletas	**tres hombres**
dos diccionarios	**una escuela**
dos fotos	**una maleta**

1. ____________________

2. ____________________

3. ____________________

4. ____________________

5. ____________________

6. ____________________

Tests

7 ¿Qué pasa? Fill in the blanks with words from the box. (9 x 2 pts. each = 18 pts.)

bien	estás	llama
el	gracias	nombre
es	hola	nuevo

PEDRO ¿Qué tal, Laura? ¿Cómo (1) ______________________?

LAURA Muy (2) ______________________, Pedro. ¿Qué hay de (3) ______________________?

PEDRO Nada nuevo. ¿Quién es la niña?

LAURA Ella (4) ______________________ mi sobrina (*niece*). Se (5) ______________________ Cristina.

PEDRO (6) ______________________ Cristina, mucho gusto.

CRISTINA Hola, Pedro, (7) ______________________ gusto es mío.

PEDRO Cristina es un (8) ______________________ muy bonito.

CRISTINA (9) ______________________, Pedro.

8 Lectura Read Clara's blog entry, then fill in the blanks. (6 x 3 pts. each = 18 pts.)

Hola, me llamo Clara. ¿Cómo están? Yo estoy bien. Gracias por entrar (*for entering*) a mi blog. Yo soy de Perú, pero estudio (*I study*) en Boston.

Yo soy estudiante de la Escuela San Gabriel. ¿Ustedes son estudiantes? Mis clases son a las 8:30 de la mañana.

¿Tienen hermanos (*Do you have any siblings*)? Yo tengo (*I have*) tres hermanos: Luis, Paco y José. Aquí hay unas fotografías de mi familia.

1. Clara es de ______________________.
2. Ella estudia (*studies*) en ______________________.
3. Ella es ______________________ de la Escuela San Gabriel.
4. Las clases de Clara son a las ______________________ de la mañana.
5. Clara tiene (*has*) ______________________ hermanos.
6. Sus hermanos se llaman Luis, Pablo y ______________________.

Tests

Nombre ______________________ Fecha ______________________

TEST A

Lección 2

1 Escuchar Read these statements. Then listen as Professor Sánchez addresses his students on the first day of classes and indicate whether each statement is **cierto** or **falso**. (5 x 2 pts. each = 10 pts.)

	Cierto	Falso
1. El profesor Sánchez enseña español.	______	______
2. La clase es los lunes, martes y viernes.	______	______
3. La clase es de diez a once de la mañana.	______	______
4. Necesitan practicar los lunes en el laboratorio.	______	______
5. El laboratorio está lejos de la biblioteca.	______	______

2 Este semestre Óscar and Deana are discussing the semester. Write a conversation with at least eight items from the box. (6 pts. for vocabulary + 6 pts. for grammar + 3 pts. for style and creativity = 15 pts.)

biblioteca	**hablar**	**prueba**
compañero/a	**lenguas**	**tarea**
desear	**mirar**	**trabajar**
gustar	**porque**	**viernes**

____

____

____

____

____

____

3 Una conversación Ana and David are talking about their classes. Fill in the questions. (5 x 2 pts. each = 10 pts.)

ANA David, ¿(1) ______________________________________?

DAVID El libro de literatura está encima de la mesa.

ANA Gracias. Necesito preparar la tarea para la clase.

DAVID ¿(2) ______________________________________?

ANA Sí, me gusta mucho estudiar literatura.

DAVID ¿(3) ______________________________________?

ANA Porque la materia es muy interesante.

DAVID ¿(4) ______________________________________?

ANA La profesora Diana Burgos enseña la clase de literatura.

DAVID ¿(5) ______________________________________?

ANA En la clase hay sesenta chicas.

DAVID ¡Qué bien! El próximo (*next*) semestre tomo la clase yo también.

Tests

Nombre ______________________ Fecha ______________________

4 Números Look at the report and answer the questions with complete sentences. Write the numerals as words. (5 x 2 pts. each = 10 pts.)

	Estudiantes	Lenguas extranjeras
1.	número total de estudiantes en la escuela: 1.500	número de estudiantes que[1] hablan español: 86
2.	número de chicos: 497	número de estudiantes que hablan otras[2] lenguas (no español): 72
3.	número de chicas: 903	número de estudiantes que estudian español: 750

[1]*that* [2]*other*

1. ¿Cuántos estudiantes hay en total? ______________________

____

2. ¿Cuántos chicos hay? ¿Y chicas? ______________________

____

3. ¿Cuántos estudiantes hablan español? ______________________

____

4. ¿Cuántos estudiantes hablan otras lenguas? ______________________

____

5. ¿Cuántos estudiantes estudian español? ______________________

____

5 En España Fill in the blanks with the present tense of the Spanish verb. (10 x 2 pts. each = 20 pts.)

Querida (*Dear*) Jessica:

¿Cómo estás? Yo (1) ______________________ (*to be*) muy bien. Me (2) ______________________ (*to like*) mucho estudiar español en el verano (*summer*) en Sevilla. Yo (3) ______________________ (*to study*) mucho todos los días. Las clases (4) ______________________ (*to finish*) a las 2 de la tarde. A las 2:30, yo (5) ______________________ (*to return*) al apartamento. El dueño (*owner*) del apartamento, Germán, (6) ______________________ (*to work*) en la universidad. Él (7) ______________________ (*to teach*) literatura en la Facultad de Filosofía y Letras. Por las tardes, la familia de Germán y yo (8) ______________________ (*to talk*) mucho porque yo necesito practicar español. Por las noches, nosotros (9) ______________________ (*to watch*) la televisión.

Bueno, ¿y tú? ¿Qué tal? ¿Qué día (10) ______________________ (*to arrive*) a España?

Adiós,

Jorge

Tests

Nombre ______________________ Fecha ______________

6 Preguntas Answer these questions with complete sentences. (5 x 2 pts. each = 10 pts.)

1. ¿Qué día es hoy? ______________________
2. ¿Caminas a la escuela? ______________________
3. ¿Escuchas música todos los días? ______________________
4. ¿Te gusta escuchar la radio? ______________________
5. ¿A qué hora termina la clase de español? ______________________

7 Lectura Read Mercedes' e-mail to her brother and answer the questions with complete sentences. (5 x 2 pts. each = 10 pts.)

Para Julio	**De** Mercedes	**Asunto** Saludo

Estoy en la cafetería, que está al lado de la biblioteca. Sólo[1] hay nueve estudiantes en la cafetería ahora. Estoy al lado de la ventana y, cuando deseo descansar, miro a los estudiantes que caminan al gimnasio. Estudio aquí para[2] el examen de biología porque Laura, mi hermana (*sister*), está en casa con unas chicas y yo necesito estudiar mucho. El examen es el jueves a las tres de la tarde. También necesito preparar la tarea de física. ¡Necesito estudiar mucho!

[1]*only* [2]*for*

1. ¿Dónde está la cafetería? ______________________
2. ¿Cuántos estudiantes hay en la cafetería? ______________________
3. ¿Cómo descansa Mercedes? ______________________
4. ¿Por qué estudia en la cafetería? ______________________

   ____
5. ¿Cuándo es el examen? ______________________

8 Tú Write a paragraph with at least five sentences in which you state your name and where you are from, where you go to school, the classes you are taking, whether you work (and, if so, where), and some of your likes and/or dislikes. Use vocabulary and grammar from this lesson. (6 pts. for vocabulary + 6 pts. for grammar + 3 pts. for style and creativity = 15 pts.)

____

____

____

____

____

____

Tests

Nombre ____________________ Fecha ____________________

TEST B

Lección 2

1 Escuchar Read these statements. Then listen as Professor Molina addresses her students on the first day of classes. Indicate whether each statement is **cierto** or **falso**. (5 x 2 pts. each = 10 pts.)

	Cierto	Falso
1. La profesora Molina enseña inglés.	______	______
2. La clase es los martes y los viernes.	______	______
3. La clase es de una a dos de la tarde.	______	______
4. Necesitan practicar los miércoles en el laboratorio.	______	______
5. El laboratorio está cerca de la librería.	______	______

2 Este semestre Dora and Julia are discussing the semester. Write a conversation with at least eight items from the box. (6 pts. for vocabulary + 6 pts. for grammar + 3 pts. for style and creativity = 15 pts.)

biblioteca	**comprar**	**horario**	**materia**
cafetería	**descansar**	**lejos de**	**necesitar**
clase	**enseñar**	**llevar**	**regresar**

____

____

____

____

____

____

____

3 Una conversación Javi and Raúl are talking about their classes. Write the questions. (5 x 2 pts. each = 10 pts.)

JAVI Raúl, ¿(1) ______________________________?
RAÚL El diccionario está encima de mi escritorio.
JAVI Gracias. Necesito estudiar para la prueba de español.
RAÚL ¿(2) ______________________________?
JAVI Sí, me gusta mucho estudiar español.
RAÚL ¿(3) ______________________________?
JAVI Porque deseo viajar a Latinoamérica.
RAÚL ¿(4) ______________________________?
JAVI El profesor Vicente Flores enseña la clase de español.
RAÚL ¿(5) ______________________________?
JAVI En la clase hay quince estudiantes.
RAÚL ¡Qué bien! El próximo (*next*) semestre tomo la clase yo también.

Tests

Nombre ______________________ Fecha ______________________

4 Números Look at the report and answer the questions with complete sentences. Write the numerals as words. (5 x 2 pts. each = 10 pts.)

	Estudiantes	Información académica
1.	número total de estudiantes: 2.650	especialidades: 35
2.	número de chicos: 1.134	actividades extraescolares: 42
3.	número de chicas: 1.516	profesores: 105

1. ¿Cuántos estudiantes en total hay en la escuela? ______________________

____

2. ¿Cuántos chicos hay en la escuela? ______________________

____

3. ¿Cuántas chicas hay en la escuela? ______________________

____

4. ¿Cuántas especialidades hay? ______________________

____

5. ¿Cuántos profesores enseñan en esta escuela? ______________________

____

Tests

5 Mi semestre Fill in the blanks with the present tense of the Spanish verb. (10 x 2 pts. each = 20 pts.)

Querido (*Dear*) Santiago:

¿Cómo estás? Yo (1) ______________ (*to be*) muy bien. Me (2) ______________ (*to like*) mucho estudiar español en el verano (*summer*) en Sevilla. Mi apartamento (3) ______________ (*to be*) muy cerca de la escuela. Yo (4) ______________ (*to study*) todos los días, pero los sábados (5) ______________ (*to rest*) y los domingos (6) ______________ (*to teach*) inglés al hijo (*son*) de la dueña (*owner*) de mi apartamento. Por las noches, mi compañera de cuarto, Claire, y yo 7) ______________ (*to prepare*) la tarea y (8) ______________ (*to listen*) música. Las dos (9) ______________ (*to need*) practicar español y hablamos mucho. Bueno, ¿y tú? ¿Qué tal? ¿Qué día (10) ______________ (*to arrive*) a España? Hasta pronto,

Irene

Nombre ______________________ Fecha ______________

6 Preguntas Answer these questions with complete sentences. (5 x 2 pts. each = 10 pts.)

1. ¿Qué día es mañana? ______________________
2. ¿Dónde preparas la tarea? ______________________
3. ¿Escuchas la radio por las noches? ______________________
4. ¿Te gusta viajar? ______________________
5. ¿A qué hora llegas a casa hoy? ______________________

____

7 Lectura Read Juan Antonio's e-mail to his sister and answer the questions with complete sentences. (5 x 2 pts. each = 10 pts.)

Para Tania	**De** Juan Antonio	**Asunto** Saludo

Estoy en la biblioteca, que está al lado del gimnasio. Me gusta la biblioteca porque sólo[1] hay once estudiantes ahora. Cuando deseo descansar, camino a la cafetería porque está muy cerca de la biblioteca y tomo un café[2]. Estudio aquí porque Dan, mi hermano (*brother*), está en casa con unos chicos y yo necesito preparar el examen de historia. El examen es el viernes a las 10 de la mañana. También necesito preparar la tarea de biología. Necesito estudiar mucho.

[1]*only* [2]*coffee*

1. ¿Dónde está la biblioteca? ______________________
2. ¿Cuántos estudiantes hay en la biblioteca? ______________________
3. ¿Cómo descansa Juan Antonio? ______________________
4. ¿Por qué estudia en la biblioteca? ______________________

____

5. ¿Cuándo es el examen? ______________________

8 Tú Write a paragraph with at least five sentences in which you mention the classes you are taking, when they are (day and time), whether you like the classes, whether you work, and the things you like to do when you are not studying. Use vocabulary and grammar from this lesson. (6 pts. for vocabulary + 6 pts. for grammar + 3 pts. for style and creativity= 15 pts.)

____

____

____

____

____

____

Tests

Nombre ______________________ Fecha ______________________

TEST C

Lección 2

1 Escuchar You will hear five personal questions. Answer them with Spanish sentences. (5 x 2 pts. each = 10 pts.)

1. ______________________
2. ______________________
3. ______________________
4. ______________________
5. ______________________

2 ¿Qué tal? Write a conversation between Jessica and Sebastián with at least eight items from the box. (4 pts. for vocabulary + 4 pts. for grammar + 2 pts. for style and creativity = 10 pts.)

bailar	**desear**	**hablar**	**tarea**
cafetería	**escuchar**	**materia**	**trabajar**
clase	**gustar**	**porque**	**viernes**

____

____

____

____

____

____

____

____

____

____

Tests

3 Lectura Read José's e-mail to his friend and answer the questions with complete sentences. (5 x 3 pts. each = 15 pts.)

Para Ana	**De** José	**Asunto** Saludo

Estoy en la biblioteca de la escuela. Me gusta la biblioteca: no hay muchos estudiantes. Ahora estoy al lado de la ventana y, cuando deseo descansar, miro a los estudiantes que caminan a clase. Hoy estudio aquí para[1] el examen de física porque Manuel, mi primo (*cousin*) está en casa con diez amigos y yo necesito estudiar mucho. El examen es el martes a las 10 de la mañana. Deseo regresar a casa a las 8 de la noche para tomar algo[2] y escuchar música.

[1]*for* [2]*something*

1. ¿Dónde estudia José? ____________________
2. ¿Por qué está en la biblioteca? ____________________
3. ¿Cómo descansa? ____________________
4. ¿Cuándo es el examen? ____________________
5. ¿Por qué desea llegar a casa a las ocho? ____________________

4 Tus clases Write a paragraph about yourself with at least five sentences in which you state your name and where you are from, the classes you are taking, and some of your likes or dislikes. Use vocabulary and grammar from this lesson.
(6 pts. for vocabulary + 6 pts. for grammar + 3 pts. for style and creativity = 15 pts.)

____

Nombre ________________ Fecha ________________

TEST D

Lección 2

1 Escuchar You will hear five personal questions. Answer them with Spanish sentences. (5 x 2 pts. each = 10 pts.)

1. ________________
2. ________________
3. ________________
4. ________________
5. ________________

2 ¿Qué tal? Write a conversation between Marina and José using at least eight items from the box. (4 pts. for vocabulary + 4 pts. for grammar + 2 pts. for style and creativity = 10 pts.)

biblioteca	**cantar**	**horario**	**porque**
buscar	**curso**	**laboratorio**	**tarea**
caminar	**esperar**	**mirar**	**terminar**

____

Tests

Nombre ______________________ Fecha ______________________

3 Lectura Read Mónica's e-mail to her friend and answer the questions with complete sentences. (5 x 3 pts. each = 15 pts.)

Para Pablo	**De** Mónica	**Asunto** Saludo

Estoy en casa. Hoy estudio aquí porque Sandra, mi hermana (*sister*), no está en casa. Ella trabaja hoy. Me gusta estudiar en mi cuarto y escuchar música. No me gusta estudiar en la biblioteca porque siempre[1] hay muchos estudiantes. Necesito estudiar para[2] el examen de historia; es mañana, lunes, a las cuatro de la tarde. Cuando deseo descansar, camino a la cafetería, que está muy cerca, y tomo un café[3]. Necesito estudiar mucho porque el examen es muy difícil (*difficult*).

[1]*always* [2]*for* [3]*coffee*

1. ¿Dónde estudia Mónica? ______________________

2. ¿Por qué estudia? ______________________

3. ¿Desea Mónica estudiar en la biblioteca? ¿Por qué? ______________________

4. ¿Cuándo es el examen? ______________________

5. ¿Cómo descansa? ______________________

4 Tus clases Write a paragraph about yourself with at least five sentences in which you state your name and where you are from, what you study, whether you work (if so, when and where), and some of your likes and/or dislikes. Use vocabulary and grammar from this lesson. (6 pts. for vocabulary + 6 pts. for grammar + 3 pts. for style and creativity = 15 pts.)

____

Tests

Nombre ____________________ Fecha ____________________

TEST E

Lección 2

1 Escuchar Read the statements. Then listen to Professor Sánchez on the first day of class and indicate whether each statement is **cierto** or **falso**. (5 x 2 pts. each = 10 pts.)

	Cierto	Falso
1. El profesor Sánchez enseña italiano (*Italian*).	______	______
2. El horario del curso está en la pizarra.	______	______
3. Los lunes y los miércoles, la clase es de ocho a nueve de la mañana.	______	______
4. Los viernes, la clase es de cinco a seis de la tarde.	______	______
5. Los estudiantes necesitan papel y calculadora.	______	______

2 Escribir Write the numbers as words. (5 x 2 pts. each = 10 pts.)

1. 546 ____________________
2. 205 ____________________
3. 38 ____________________
4. 1.116 ____________________
5. 809 ____________________

3 ¿Me ayudas? Fill in the blanks with words from the box. (5 x 2 pts. each = 10 pts.)

caminamos
horario
lado
química
trimestre

MARÍA Pablo, gracias por ayudarme (*helping me*) con el (1) ____________________.

PABLO De nada, María. Este (2) ____________________ hay mucho que estudiar.

MARÍA ¿Dónde está el laboratorio de (3) ____________________?

PABLO Está al (4) ____________________ de la biblioteca.

MARÍA ¿(5) ____________________ al laboratorio?

PABLO No, lo siento. Necesito descansar.

Tests

Nombre ______________________ Fecha ______________________

4 Emparejar Match the pictures and descriptions. (5 x 2 pts. each = 10 pts.)

1. ______________ 2. ______________ 3. ______________

4. ______________ 5. ______________

a. Juan y Patricia dibujan.
b. Hay muchos estudiantes en la biblioteca.
c. El reloj está cerca de la puerta.
d. El profesor explica la lección a Pedro y a Luz.
e. La pluma está sobre el escritorio.

5 Escoger Select the item that does not belong. (6 x 2 pts. each = 12 pts.)

1. a. la tiza b. la pluma c. la papelera
2. a. la geografía b. el libro c. la economía
3. a. la materia b. la especialización c. la librería
4. a. la residencia estudiantil b. la casa c. la tarea
5. a. la pizarra b. la especialización c. el mapa
6. a. el semestre b. la contabilidad c. el español

6 En la clase Fill in the blanks with the appropriate form of **estar**. (6 x 2 pts. each = 12 pts.)

¿Dónde (1) ______________ nosotros en la clase? Yo (2) ______________ enfrente de la pizarra. Al lado de mi escritorio (3) ______________ David. Él no habla con Diego y Luisa porque ellos (4) ______________ lejos de él. Tú (5) ______________ entre la ventana y Verónica. Ustedes (6) ______________ cerca de la puerta.

Tests

Nombre ______________________ Fecha ______________________

7 Completar Fill in the blanks with the present tense form of the verbs. (9 x 2 pts. each = 18 pts.)

1. Nosotros ______________________ (comprar) dos mochilas.
2. Marta y Raquel ______________________ (cenar) en casa de Ronaldo.
3. Yo ______________________ (desayunar) en el restaurante que está detrás de la librería.
4. Eduardo ______________________ (explicar) cómo llegar a la residencia estudiantil.
5. Los estudiantes ______________________ (dibujar) el mapa en la pizarra.
6. Yo ______________________ (preguntar): ¿qué hora es?
7. Maribel ______________________ (contestar) el teléfono.
8. Elena, Irene y José ______________________ (regresar) a clase el lunes.
9. Ustedes ______________ (necesitar) estudiar en la biblioteca.

8 Lectura Read the description of Daniela's semester, then answer the questions. (6 x 3 pts. each = 18 pts.)

> Daniela es mi amiga. Ella estudia en la universidad. Este semestre ella estudia cinco materias. Los lunes, miércoles y viernes toma clases de administración de empresas, contabilidad y economía. Los martes y jueves toma clases de geografía e historia. Daniela camina de la residencia estudiantil a la universidad y cena en la cafetería de la universidad porque termina sus clases a las nueve de la noche. Los fines de semana, ella trabaja en la biblioteca. Le gusta (*She likes*) bailar y escuchar la radio.

1. ¿Cuántas materias toma Daniela?
   a. 4 b. 5 c. 6
2. ¿Qué materia no toma este semestre?
   a. contabilidad b. economía c. computación
3. ¿Cómo llega Daniela a la universidad?
   a. Toma el autobús. b. Camina. c. Toma un taxi.
4. ¿A qué hora termina sus clases?
   a. a las 8 p.m. b. a las 9 p.m. c. a las 10 p.m.
5. ¿Qué pasa los fines de semana?
   a. Estudia en la biblioteca. b. Baila y canta. c. Trabaja en la biblioteca.
6. ¿Qué le gusta (*does she like*) a Daniela?
   a. bailar b. estudiar c. dibujar

Tests

Nombre ______________________________ Fecha ______________________________

TEST F

Lección 2

1 Escuchar Read the statements. Then listen to Professor Merino on the first day of class and indicate whether each statement is **cierto** or **falso**. (5 x 2 pts. each = 10 pts.)

	Cierto	**Falso**
1. El profesor Merino enseña química.	______	______
2. Los lunes, la clase es de ocho a nueve de la mañana.	______	______
3. Los viernes, la clase es a las nueve.	______	______
4. Hay clase de química los miércoles.	______	______
5. Los estudiantes necesitan una calculadora para la clase.	______	______

2 Escribir Write the numbers as words. (5 x 2 pts. each = 10 pts.)

1. 324 ______________________________
2. 111 ______________________________
3. 418 ______________________________
4. 1537 ______________________________
5. 819 ______________________________

3 ¿Me ayudas? Fill in the blanks with words from the box. (5 x 2 pts. each = 10 pts.)

caminamos
detrás
química
regresar
trimestre

ANA Pedro, gracias por (1) ______________________ al laboratorio conmigo.

PEDRO De nada, Ana.

ANA ¿Éste es el laboratorio de (2) ______________________?

PEDRO No, éste es el laboratorio de física. El laboratorio de química está (3) ______________________ de la biblioteca.

ANA ¡Ay, no! ¿(4) ______________________ a la biblioteca?

PEDRO Sí. Este (5) ______________________ necesitamos trabajar mucho.

ANA ¡Necesito unas vacaciones!

Tests

Nombre ______________________ Fecha ______________________

4 Emparejar Match the pictures and descriptions. (5 x 2 pts. each = 10 pts.)

1. ______________ 2. ______________ 3. ______________

4. ______________ 5. ______________

a. La pluma de Juan está sobre el escritorio.
b. El profesor explica el problema a María y a Carlos.
c. Los estudiantes estudian en la biblioteca.
d. Linda y José estudian arte.
e. La clase mira un mapa.

Tests

5 Escoger Select the item that does not belong. (6 x 2 pts. each = 12 pts.)

1. a. el estadio	b. la silla	c. el escritorio
2. a. el inglés	b. el español	c. la contabilidad
3. a. el examen	b. el papel	c. la prueba
4. a. la mochila	b. la puerta	c. la ventana
5. a. el lunes	b. el mes	c. el miércoles
6. a. la librería	b. la biblioteca	c. la economía

6 En la clase Fill in the blanks with the appropriate form of **estar**. (6 x 2 pts. each = 12 pts)

¿Dónde (1) ______________ mis compañeros de clase? Tania (2) ______________ a la derecha de mi escritorio. Yo (3) ______________ al lado de Carlos. Nosotros (4) ______________ enfrente de Lucas, que no mira a Diana porque (5) ______________ detrás de él. No hablas con ella porque tú (6) ______________ lejos de su escritorio.

7 Completar Fill in the blanks with the present tense form of the verbs. (9 x 2 pts. each = 18 pts.)

1. Yo ____________________ (cenar) con los padres de Camila.
2. Los hermanos Torres ____________________ (estudiar) física y matemáticas.
3. Mi tía (*aunt*) ____________________ (conversar) con el profesor de computación.
4. Pepe ____________________ (dibujar) en el cuaderno.
5. Los estudiantes ____________________ (preguntar) dónde está la residencia estudiantil.
6. Luisa ____________________ (trabajar) cerca de aquí.
7. Los profesores ____________________ (explicar) el horario de clases.
8. Mis vecinos (*My neighbors*) ____________________ (regresar) de sus vacaciones mañana.
9. Tú no ____________________ (desayunar) los fines de semana.

8 Lectura Read the description of Daniel's semester, then answer the questions. (6 x 3 pts. each = 18 pts.)

Daniel es mi amigo. Él estudia en la universidad. Este semestre él estudia cuatro materias. Los lunes y miércoles toma clases de historia y sociología. Los martes y jueves toma clases de computación y periodismo. Daniel toma el autobús para viajar a la universidad y desayuna en la cafetería de la universidad porque su primera (*first*) clase es a las siete de la mañana. Los fines de semana, él trabaja en un laboratorio. Le gustan (*He likes*) las lenguas extranjeras y viajar.

1. ¿Cuántas materias toma Daniel?
   a. 4 b. 5 c. 6
2. ¿Qué materia no toma este semestre?
   a. contabilidad b. periodismo c. sociología
3. ¿Cómo llega Daniel a la universidad?
   a. Toma un taxi. b. Camina. c. Toma el autobús.
4. ¿A qué hora es su primera clase?
   a. a las 6 a.m. b. a las 7 a.m. c. a las 8 a.m.
5. ¿Qué pasa los fines de semana?
   a. Prepara la cena. b. Estudia. c. Trabaja.
6. ¿Qué le gusta a Daniel?
   a. escuchar la radio b. viajar c. bailar

Nombre ______________________ Fecha ______________________

TEST A

Lección 3

1 Escuchar Read these statements. Then listen to a description of Esteban's life and indicate whether each statement is **cierto** or **falso**. (5 x 2 pts. each = 10 pts.)

	Cierto	Falso
1. Esteban es de Ecuador.	______	______
2. Esteban estudia biología.	______	______
3. Trabaja mucho.	______	______
4. Su novia tiene veintitrés años.	______	______
5. Su novia no trabaja mucho.	______	______

2 La familia de Graciela Look at the family tree and write how each person is related to Graciela. Follow the model. Then use your imagination to describe them, using at least six words from the box. (6 pts. for vocabulary + 6 pts. for grammar + 3 pts. for style and creativity = 15 pts.)

modelo

Beatriz es la abuela de Graciela.

antipático/a	**guapo/a**	**moreno/a**
bajo/a	**joven**	**rubio/a**
delgado/a	**malo/a**	**simpático/a**

____

____

____

____

____

____

____

____

____

____

Tests

3 Julia Julia is leaving a note for her sister, Inés. Fill in the blanks with one of the possessive adjectives in parentheses. Pay attention to the meaning of the whole sentence. (5 x 2 pts. each = 10 pts.)

(1) ______________________ (Mis, Sus, Su) amigos vienen mañana a casa para terminar (2) ______________________ (mis, sus, nuestro) proyecto (*project*) de ciencias. ¡Ah! Hoy debo terminar (3) ______________________ (mi, sus, mis) tarea de español. ¿Tienes que asistir a (4) ______________________ (mi, mis, tus) clases? Necesitas hablar con Alicia. Ella tiene (5) ______________________ (sus, mi, tus) libro de español.

Gracias.

4 La familia Pérez Fill in each blank with the correct present tense form of the verb in Spanish. (10 x 2 pts. each = 20 pts.)

La familia Pérez (1) ______________________ (*to live*) en Oaxaca. El padre se llama Joaquín y enseña español. La madre, Irene, trabaja en una biblioteca. Ella (2) ______________________ (*to open*) la biblioteca todos los días a las 7:30 de la mañana. Los dos (3) ______________________ (*to be*) muy simpáticos y trabajadores. Ellos (4) ______________________ (*to have*) dos hijas. La mayor, María, tiene veinte años y (5) ______________________ (*to attend*) a la UNAM, en la Ciudad de México. La menor, Marlene, tiene doce años. Las hermanas son muy buenas amigas y ellas (6) ______________________ (*to share*) todas las cosas. Cuando María no está en casa de sus padres, ella le (7) ______________________ (*to write*) mucho a su familia. Marlene (8) ______________________ (*to receive*) muchos mensajes electrónicos (*e-mails*) de ella. Marlene no estudia mucho. Sus padres no (9) ______________________ (*to understand*) a Marlene. Ellos creen que ella (10) ______________________ (*should*) preparar más sus clases.

5 Preguntas Answer these questions with complete sentences. (5 x 3 pts. each = 15 pts.)

1. ¿Cuántos años tienes? ______________________

2. ¿Cuál es tu color favorito? ______________________

3. ¿Tienes hermanos o hermanas? ¿Cuántos? ______________________

4. ¿Te gusta correr? ______________________

5. ¿A qué hora vienes a la clase de español? ______________________

Tests

Nombre ______________________ Fecha ______________________

6 Lectura Read the blog entry Javier wrote today about his older brother, Adrián. Then, answer the questions with complete sentences. (5 x 3 pts. each = 15 pts.)

http://www.javierorozco.net

Mi hermano Adrián tiene veintitrés años y estudia en la universidad. Trabaja por las tardes en la cafetería. Cuando trabaja en la cafetería, toma café y habla con sus amigos todo el tiempo. A las diez de la noche, regresa a casa y estudia. Él debe estudiar mucho. Necesita buenas notas[1] en química porque desea ser médico. Nuestros padres son médicos y a Adrián le gusta la profesión.
Este año comparte su apartamento con Vicente, un estudiante colombiano. Son buenos amigos. Ellos hablan en inglés y en español. El español no es difícil, pero necesita practicar más, porque desea estudiar un semestre en México. Yo admiro a[2] mi hermano.

[1] *grades* [2] *I admire*

1. ¿Cuántos años tiene Adrián? ______________________

2. ¿Qué hace (*does he do*) por las tardes? ______________________

3. ¿Qué materia necesita estudiar? ¿Por qué? ______________________

4. ¿Cuál es la profesión de su madre? ______________________

5. ¿Con quién vive Adrián? ______________________

7 Tu familia Write a paragraph with at least five sentences where you describe at least one member of your family. What is he or she like physically? What is his or her personality like? What does he or she do on a typical day? What does he or she do for fun? Use vocabulary you learned in this lesson.
(6 pts. for vocabulary + 6 pts. for grammar + 3 pts. for style and creativity = 15 pts.)

Tests

Nombre ____________________ Fecha ____________________

TEST B

Lección 3

1 Escuchar Read these statements. Then listen to a description of Manuela's life and indicate whether each statement is **cierto** or **falso**. (5 x 2 pts. each = 10 pts.)

	Cierto	Falso
1. Manuela es española.	______	______
2. Manuela trabaja por las mañanas.	______	______
3. Vive con su prima Tina.	______	______
4. Tina es estudiante de matemáticas.	______	______
5. Ellas corren los sábados.	______	______

2 La familia de Luis Miguel Look at the family tree and write how each person is related to Luis Miguel. Follow the model. Then use your imagination to describe some of them using at least six words from the box. (6 pts. for vocabulary + 6 pts. for grammar + 3 pts. for style and creativity = 15 pts.)

modelo

Ana María es la esposa de Luis Miguel.

antipático/a
bajo/a
delgado/a
guapo/a
interesante
joven
moreno/a
trabajador(a)
viejo/a

Tests

____

____

____

____

____

____

____

____

____

Nombre ______________________________ Fecha ____________________

3 Patricia Patricia is leaving a note for her sister, Tina. Fill in the blanks with one of the possessive adjectives in parentheses. Pay attention to the meaning of the whole sentence. (5 x 2 pts. each = 10 pts.)

> Necesito terminar esta tarde (1) ____________________ (mi, tu, su) tarea de cálculo para mañana y no tengo (2 ____________________ (mi, tu, tus) calculadora. Tú tienes una, ¿no? ¿Necesitas (3) ____________________ (mi, tu, su) calculadora hoy? Gracias. Otra cosa (*Another thing*): tienes un mensaje telefónico (*phone message*) de (4) ____________________ (nuestros, tu, sus) amiga Carla. Es (5) ____________________ (mi, tu, su) cumpleaños (*birthday*) este sábado y prepara una fiesta.

4 Mi familia Fill in each blank with the correct present tense form of the verb in Spanish. (10 x 2 pts. each = 20 pts.)

Mi papá y yo (1) ____________________ (*to live*) en Barcelona. Él es periodista y (2) ____________________ (*to write*) para (*for*) un periódico (*newspaper*) español. También (3) ____________________ (*to read*) mucho. Yo (4) ____________________ (*to attend*) a la escuela. Todas las mañanas a las 6:30, nosotros (5) ____________________ (*to run*) una hora. Después, nosotros (6) ____________________ (*to drink*) jugo (*juice*) y (7) ____________________ (*to eat*). Por las tardes, yo (8) ____________________ (*should*) estudiar mucho, pero a veces (*sometimes*) miro un poco la televisión. Mi papá siempre (9) ____________________ (*to come*) a casa tarde (*late*), pero yo (10) ____________________ (*to understand*) que los periodistas trabajan mucho.

5 Preguntas Answer these questions with complete sentences. (5 x 3 pts. each = 15 pts.)

1. ¿De qué tienes miedo? ______________________________
____
2. ¿Cuál es tu color favorito? ______________________________
____
3. ¿Cómo es tu familia? ______________________________
____
4. ¿Cuántos primos/as tienes? ______________________________
____
5. ¿Qué tienes que estudiar hoy? ______________________________
____

Tests

6 Lectura Read the blog entry María wrote today about her older sister, Anabel. Then, answer the questions with complete sentences. (5 x 3 pts. each = 15 pts.)

http://www.mariatotino.net

Mi hermana Anabel tiene veintidós años y estudia en la universidad de Chicago. Vive con su buena amiga Rosana; ella es de Argentina también. Las dos tienen muchas clases y mucha tarea este semestre. Por las mañanas, Anabel asiste a sus clases y por las tardes prepara su tarea en la biblioteca o en la cafetería. Los sábados trabaja de recepcionista en un hospital. Le gusta trabajar porque aprende mucho. Desea ser médica. Los domingos le gusta conversar con amigos, comer en restaurantes y bailar. Le gusta mucho vivir con su amiga Rosana porque es muy fácil compartir problemas con ella. Yo admiro a[1] mi hermana.

[1] *I admire*

1. ¿De dónde es Anabel? ______________________
2. ¿Con quién vive? ______________________
3. ¿Dónde prepara su tarea? ______________________
4. ¿Trabaja Anabel los domingos? ______________________
5. ¿Es difícil vivir con Rosana? ¿Por qué? ______________________

7 Tu amigo/a Write a paragraph with at least five sentences in which you describe one of your friends. What is he or she like physically? What is his or her personality like? What does he or she do on a typical day? What does he or she do for fun? Use vocabulary you learned in this lesson. (6 pts. for vocabulary + 6 pts. for grammar + 3 pts. for style and creativity = 15 pts.)

____

Tests

Nombre ______________________ Fecha ______________________

TEST C

Lección 3

1 Escuchar You will hear five personal questions. Answer them with Spanish sentences. (5 x 2 pts. each = 10 pts.)

1. ______________________
2. ______________________
3. ______________________
4. ______________________
5. ______________________

2 La familia de Manuela Look at the family tree and write how each person is related to Manuela. Follow the model. Use your imagination to describe these people, with at least six words from the box. (6 pts. for vocabulary + 6 pts. for grammar + 3 pts. for style and creativity = 15 pts.)

modelo

José Antonio es el hermano de Manuela.

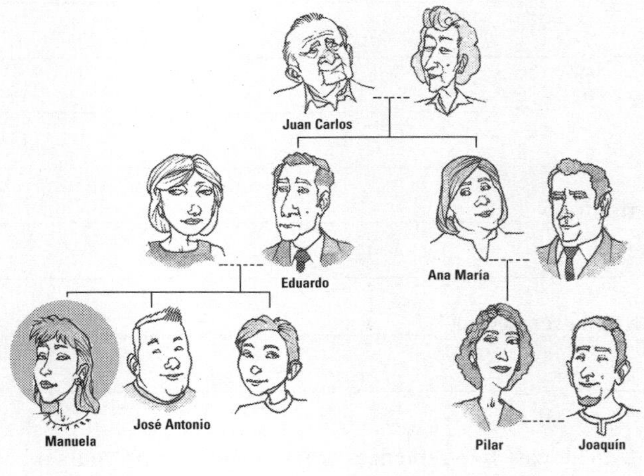

alto/a
feo/a
gordo/a
guapo/a
interesante
simpático/a
tonto/a
trabajador(a)

____

____

____

____

____

____

____

____

____

Tests

Nombre ______________________________ Fecha ____________________

3 Lectura Read the blog entry Cristina wrote today about her cousin, Rosa. Then, answer the questions with complete sentences. (5 x 2 pts. each = 10 pts.)

http://www.cristinarodriguez.net

Mi prima Rosa tiene veinte años y estudia en la universidad. Vive en la residencia estudiantil. Trabaja por las tardes en la biblioteca. Le gusta trabajar allí[1] porque cuando no hay estudiantes tiene tiempo para leer y estudiar. A las diez de la noche regresa a casa y estudia. Ella debe estudiar mucho. Debe tener buenas notas[2] en inglés porque desea ser periodista. Sus padres son periodistas. Tienen que viajar y trabajar en muchos países diferentes.

Su compañera de cuarto se llama Mónica y son buenas amigas. Ella es de Cuba, y Rosa y ella hablan en inglés y en español. El español no es difícil, pero necesita practicar más, porque desea estudiar un semestre en Perú. Yo admiro a[3] mi prima Rosa.

[1] *there* [2] *grades* [3] *I admire*

1. ¿Cuántos años tiene Rosa? ______________________________
2. ¿Por qué trabaja en la biblioteca? ______________________________
3. ¿Qué materia necesita estudiar? ¿Por qué? ______________________________
4. ¿Cuál es la profesión de su madre? ______________________________
5. ¿Con quién comparte el cuarto de la residencia? ______________________________

4 ¿Cómo eres? Write a paragraph with at least five sentences where you describe yourself. What are you like physically? What is your personality like? What is your favorite color? What do you do on a typical day? What do you do for fun? Use vocabulary from this lesson. (6 pts. for vocabulary + 6 pts. for grammar + 3 pts. for style and creativity = 15 pts.)

____

Tests

Nombre ______________________________ Fecha ______________________

TEST D

Lección 3

1 Escuchar You will hear five personal questions. Answer them with Spanish sentences. (5 x 2 pts. each = 10 pts.)

1. ______________________________
2. ______________________________
3. ______________________________
4. ______________________________
5. ______________________________

2 La familia de Eduardo Look at the family tree and write how each person is related to Eduardo. Follow the model. Use your imagination to describe them, using at least six words from the box. (6 pts. for vocabulary + 6 pts. for grammar + 3 pts. for style and creativity = 15 pts.)

modelo

Ana María es la hermana de Eduardo.

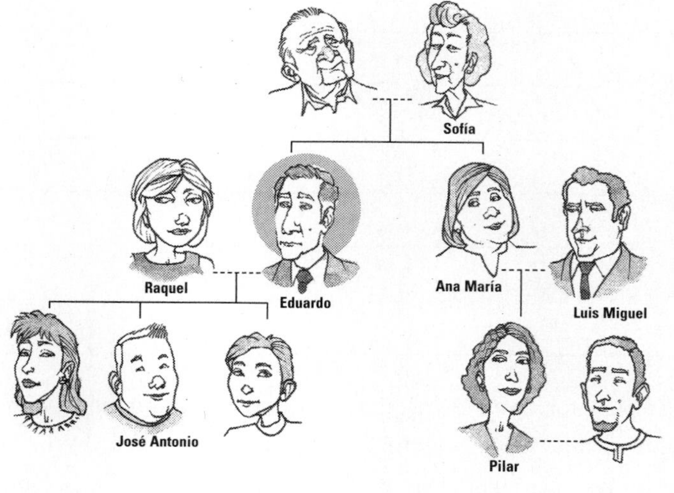

bajo/a
delgado/a
guapo/a
inteligente
malo/a
moreno/a
pelirrojo/a
viejo/a

____

____

____

____

____

____

____

____

____

Tests

Nombre ______________________ Fecha ______________________

3 Lectura Read the blog entry Carlos wrote today about his cousin, Raúl. Then, answer the questions with complete sentences. (5 x 2 pts. each = 10 pts.)

http://www.carlosmatute.net

Mi primo Raúl tiene diecinueve años, es mexicano y estudia en la Universidad de Vermont. Desea ser programador porque le gusta diseñar páginas web[1]. También le gusta hablar con sus amigos y conocer[2] gente. Este semestre debe estudiar mucho porque también trabaja por las tardes en el centro de computadoras. Este año está en el club de arte porque no desea estar todo el día con computadoras. Sus padres son artistas. Ahora vive en un apartamento con un viejo amigo. Se llama Peter y es de Maine. Ellos hablan inglés y español porque Peter desea estudiar un año en España y necesita practicar español. Yo admiro a[3] mi primo Raúl.

[1] *to design websites* [2] *to meet* [3] *I admire*

1. ¿De dónde es Raúl? ______________________

2. ¿Por qué debe estudiar mucho este semestre? ______________________

3. ¿Cuál es la profesión de su padre? ______________________

4. ¿Con quién vive Raúl? ______________________

5. ¿Por qué Raúl habla con Peter en español? ______________________

4 Una persona importante Write a paragraph with at least five sentences where you describe an important person in your life. Why is this person important in your life? What is this person like physically? What is his or her personality like? What is his or her favorite color? What does he or she do on a typical day? What does he or she do for fun? Use vocabulary from this lesson. (6 pts. for vocabulary + 6 pts. for grammar + 3 pts. for style and creativity = 15 pts.)

____

____

____

____

____

____

____

Tests

Nombre ______________________ Fecha ______________________

TEST E

Lección 3

1 Escuchar Read the statements. Then listen to Víctor Miguel's description of himself in his personal ad and indicate whether each statement is **cierto** or **falso**. (5 x 2 pts. each = 10 pts.)

	Cierto	Falso
1. Víctor Miguel es de Ecuador.	______	______
2. Víctor trabaja en una biblioteca.	______	______
3. El padre de Víctor es periodista.	______	______
4. Víctor es alto y moreno.	______	______
5. La novia ideal de Víctor debe tener 19 años.	______	______

2 Emparejar Match the pictures and descriptions. (5 x 2 pts. each = 10 pts.)

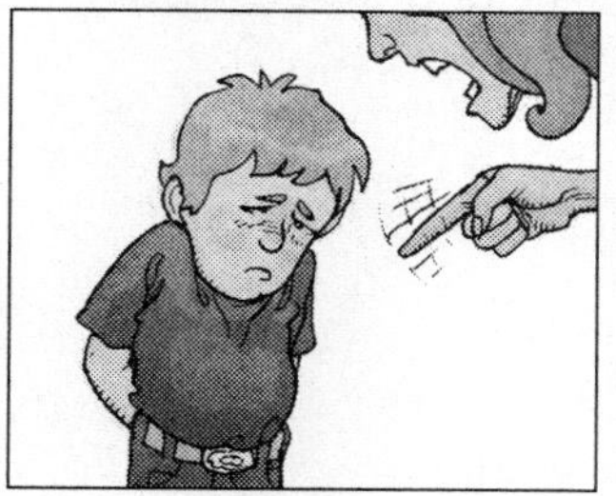

1. ______________________

2. ______________________

3. ______________________

4. ______________________

5. ______________________

a. Los señores López tienen un hijo y una hija.
b. Juan es bajo y José es muy alto, pero son hermanos.
c. Los papás y los abuelos de Diego están en la casa.
d. La madre reprende (*scolds*) a su hijo.
e. Juan y Marta son novios.

3 La familia Fill in the blanks with words from the box. (5 x 2 pts. each = 10 pts.)

1. La esposa de mi hermano es mi ______________________.
2. La hija de mis tíos es mi ______________________.
3. El esposo de mi hija es mi ______________________.
4. Mi ______________________ es la esposa de mi papá, pero no es mi mamá.
5. La madre de mi esposo es mi ______________________.

cuñada
madrastra
prima
suegra
yerno

Tests

Nombre ______________________ Fecha ______________________

4 Gloria Fill in the blanks with the appropriate form of the verbs. (5 x 2 pts. each = 10 pts.)

Hola, Diana:

Los tíos (1) ______________________ (venir) hoy a las cuatro de la tarde.

Tú (2) ______________________ (deber) abrir la puerta, por favor.

Yo (3) ______________________ (venir) a casa a las cinco. Hoy yo

(4) ______________________ (asistir) a la clase de economía de tres a cuatro y media. A las cinco menos quince, (5) ______________________ (correr) a tomar el autobús. Nos vemos.

Gracias,

Gloria

5 A trabajar Match the activities in Column A to the professions in Column B. (5 x 2 pts. each = 10 pts.)

A	B
_____ 1. dibujar	a. el/la artista
_____ 2. la biología	b. el/la profesor(a)
_____ 3. la computación	c. el/la periodista
_____ 4. preguntar y escribir	d. el/la doctor(a)
_____ 5. enseñar literatura	e. el/la programador(a)

6 Completar Fill in the blanks with words from the box. (7 x 2 pts. each = 14 pts.)

asistes	**comprendo**	**tienes**	**vienes**
comemos	**tengo**	**viene**	

SANDRA Hola, Anita. ¿Cuándo (1) ______________________ tu familia?

ANITA Viene el sábado. Con permiso, yo (2) ______________________ que estudiar para un examen.

SANDRA ¿Qué examen (3) ______________________?

ANITA Es un examen de química, y hay cosas que no (4) ______________________.

SANDRA Eso pasa (*That happens*) cuando no (5) ______________________ a clase.

ANITA ¿(6) ______________________ a mi casa a ayudarme (*to help me*)?

SANDRA Claro. Pero (7) ______________________ juntas (*together*).

Tests

7 Mi casa es su casa Fill in the blanks with the appropriate possessive adjectives. (9 x 2 pts. each = 18 pts.)

1. Él es ______________________ (*my*) primo.
2. ______________________ (*Your, form.*) amigos son franceses.
3. ______________________ (*Their*) cuadernos están en el autobús.
4. Victoria es la amiga de ______________________ (*our*) sobrina.
5. ______________________ (*My*) casa es blanca y verde.
6. El esposo de María es ______________________ (*your, fam.*) yerno.
7. ______________________ (*His*) cuadernos son azules.
8. Los hijos de tu hija son ______________________ (*your, fam.*) nietos.
9. ______________________ (*My*) abuelos están en Portugal.

8 Lectura Read about Pedro, then indicate whether each statement is **cierto** or **falso**. (6 x 3 pts. each = 18 pts.)

Pedro es de Chile, pero (*but*) sus padres son argentinos. Muchos de sus parientes viven en Chile. La familia de Pedro es muy grande. Su madre tiene cuatro hermanas y un hermano. Su padre tiene tres hermanos. Pedro estudia en la escuela y su materia favorita es la geografía. Él no tiene novia, pero tiene muchas amigas en la clase.

	Cierto	**Falso**
1. Los padres de Pedro son argentinos.	______	______
2. Pedro no tiene parientes en Chile.	______	______
3. La madre de Pedro tiene cinco hermanas.	______	______
4. Pedro es artista.	______	______
5. A Pedro le gusta la geografía.	______	______
6. Pedro tiene una novia en la escuela.	______	______

Nombre ______________________ Fecha ______________________

TEST F

Lección 3

1 Escuchar Read the statements. Then listen to Ana Isabel's description of herself in her personal ad and indicate whether each statement is **cierto** or **falso**. (5 x 2 pts. each = 10 pts.)

	Cierto	Falso
1. Ana Isabel es de los Estados Unidos.	______	______
2. Ana Isabel trabaja en una librería.	______	______
3. La madre de Ana Isabel es doctora.	______	______
4. El hermano de Ana Isabel no estudia.	______	______
5. El novio de Ana Isabel debe ser simpático.	______	______

2 Emparejar Match the pictures and descriptions. (5 x 2 pts. each = 10 pts.)

1. ______________________

2. ______________________

3. ______________________

4. ______________________

5. ______________________

a. Mi libro está en la ventana.
b. Pepe está con sus padres y sus abuelos.
c. La señora Díaz lee un libro.
d. Ana y Diego son novios.
e. La familia Pérez está en el parque.

3 La familia Complete the sentences with words from the box. (5 x 2 pts. each = 10 pts.)

1. Los padres de mis padres son mis ______________________.
2. Los hijos de mi hermana son mis ______________________.
3. La madre de mi esposo es mi ______________________.
4. El hijo de mis abuelos que (*that*) no es mi tío es mi ______________________.
5. Los padres de mis primos son mis ______________________.

abuelos
padre
sobrinos
suegra
tíos

Tests

4 Valeria Fill in the blanks with the appropriate form of the verbs. (5 x 2 pts. each = 10 pts.)

Hola, Mario:

Yo (1) ______________________ (estar) en la escuela. La clase de computación (2) ______________________ (ser) de una a dos. El tío Fernando y la tía Mercedes (3) ______________________ (venir) a comer hoy. A las dos (yo) (4) ______________________ (correr) al supermercado (*grocery store*). Tú (5) ______________________ (tener) que regresar a casa antes de las dos.

Hasta pronto.

Gracias,

Valeria

5 A trabajar Match the activities in Column A to the professions in Column B. (5 x 2 pts. each = 10 pts.)

A	B
_____ 1. escribir y preguntar	a. el/la programador(a)
_____ 2. trabajar con computadoras	b. el/la artista
_____ 3. las ciencias	c. el/la doctor(a)
_____ 4. bailar o dibujar	d. el/la profesor(a)
_____ 5. enseñar geografía	e. el/la periodista

6 Completar Fill in the blanks with appropriate words from the box. (7 x 2 pts. each = 14 pts.)

comemos	**creo**	**simpática**	**vives**
comprendo	**difícil**	**vienes**	

PEDRO Hola, Paula. ¿Cuándo es el examen de matemáticas?

PAULA Es el viernes, pero yo todavía (*still*) no (1) ______________________ muchas cosas.

PEDRO Yo (2) ______________________ que (*that*) la clase es muy fácil.

PAULA ¡No! La profesora es (3) ______________________, pero su clase es muy (4) ______________________.

PEDRO ¿Tú (5) ______________________ cerca de la escuela?

PAULA Sí. ¿(6) ______________________ a mi casa a ayudarme (*to help me*)?

PEDRO Claro. Pero (7) ______________________ juntos (*together*).

Tests

Nombre ______________________ Fecha ______________________

7 Los adjetivos posesivos Fill in the blanks with the appropriate possessive adjectives. (9 x 2 pts. each = 18 pts.)

1. Éste es ______________ (*my*) cuaderno.
2. ______________ (*our*) libros están encima del escritorio.
3. ______________ (*her*) padres están en España.
4. Mi hermana es la madre de ______________ (*my*) sobrinas.
5. ______________ (*their*) casa es amarilla.
6. Tu padre es el abuelo de ______________ (*your*) hijos.
7. ______________ (*your, form.*) primo es japonés.
8. Ése es ______________ (*his*) diccionario.
9. ______________ (*our*) abuela es alemana.

8 Lectura Read about Linda, then indicate whether each statement is **cierto** or **falso**. (6 x 3 pts. each = 18 pts.)

Linda es de Venezuela, pero sus padres son españoles. Linda y sus hermanos asisten a la escuela en Caracas. Linda es muy buena estudiante. Ella desea ser una doctora importante. Su hermano mayor, Carlos, también desea ser doctor. Fabián, su hermano menor, desea ser artista. Ellos viven lejos de la escuela. Por suerte (*luckily*), sus padres tienen un auto (*car*) grande..

	Cierto	Falso
1. Los padres de Linda son de España.	______	______
2. Linda asiste a la escuela en Maracaibo.	______	______
3. Linda tiene dos hermanos.	______	______
4. Linda y Carlos desean ser doctores.	______	______
5. Ellos viven muy cerca de la escuela.	______	______
6. Los padres de Linda tienen un auto grande.	______	______

Tests

Nombre ______________________ Fecha ______________________

TEST A Lección 4

1 Escuchar Read these statements and multiple-choice options. Then listen to the advertisement for **Club Cosmos** and select the correct option. (5 x 2 pts. each = 10 pts.)

1. El Club Cosmos está en...
   a. las montañas. b. el pueblo. c. la ciudad.
2. Las actividades son para...
   a. la familia. b. los aficionados al deporte. c. los niños.
3. En el Club Cosmos hay...
   a. dos gimnasios. b. dos cafeterías. c. dos piscinas.
4. Usted puede pasar en la cafetería...
   a. sus ratos libres. b. todos los días. c. sus vacaciones.
5. Cierran...
   a. a las doce de la noche. b. los ratos libres. c. los sábados.

2 En el campus Describe what people are doing in the picture. Write at least five sentences. (6 pts. for vocabulary + 6 pts. for grammar + 3 pts. for style and creativity = 15 pts.)

Tests

3 ¿Qué hacemos? Fill in the blanks with the present tense of the stem-changing verbs, irregular verbs, or verbs with an irregular **yo** form in parentheses. (10 x 2 pts. each = 20 pts.)

MARIANA ¿(1) (Nosotras) ______________ (*to see*) el partido en la televisión?

LUCÍA No, hoy yo (2) ______________ (*to prefer*) ir al cine. Yo (3) ______________ (*to want*) ver una película francesa.

MARIANA No me gustan las películas francesas. (4) ______________ (*to think*) que son aburridas (*boring*).

LUCÍA Tú no (5) ______________ (*to understand*) nada de películas extranjeras. Por favor, si hoy nosotras (6) ______________ (*to go*) al cine, mañana (7) ______________ (*can*) jugar al tenis.

MARIANA Bueno, vamos al cine. ¿A qué hora (8) ______________ (*to begin*) la película?

LUCÍA A las seis, (9) ______________ (*to suppose*). Voy a ver en el periódico. Sí, es a las seis.

MARIANA Vamos, pero ¿(10) ______________ (*to return*) pronto? Mañana tenemos que hacer muchas cosas.

4 Preguntas Answer the questions with complete sentences. (6 x 3 pts. each = 18 pts.)

1. ¿Qué te gusta hacer en tus ratos libres? ______________
2. ¿Qué vas a hacer este fin de semana? ______________
3. ¿Qué cosas traes a la clase de español? ______________
4. ¿Sales mucho? ¿Cuándo sales? ______________
5. ¿Eres aficionado/a a los deportes? ¿A cuáles? ______________
6. ¿Qué prefieres: ir a la playa o ver películas? ______________

Nombre ______________________ Fecha ______________

5 Lectura Sandra is writing a postcard to her friend Rubén. Read it and answer the questions. (6 x 2 pts. each = 12 pts.)

> Hola, Rubén:
> Por fin consigo un poco de tiempo para escribir una postal. Te escribo desde un parque de la ciudad. Hoy tengo ganas de descansar. Daniel y yo pensamos ir al museo y yo después quiero almorzar en un pequeño café que hay en la plaza Mayor. Laura y Sebastián van a pasear por el centro. Todos tenemos que volver a las siete al hotel porque mañana vamos de excursión. Vamos a escalar unas montañas. Daniel dice que son muy bonitas.
> Y tú, ¿cómo estás? Supongo que bien. Por ahora te digo adiós, pero hablamos pronto.
> Un beso,
> Sandra

1. ¿Por qué puede Sandra escribir la postal? ______________________
2. ¿Dónde está Sandra? ______________________
3. ¿Qué quiere hacer ella? ______________________
4. ¿Qué van a hacer Sandra y Daniel? ______________________
5. ¿Dónde va a comer Sandra? ______________________
6. ¿Qué piensa Daniel de las montañas? ______________________

6 Tus ratos libres Write a paragraph with at least five sentences where you talk about how you usually spend your free time, and how you will spend it tomorrow. Use vocabulary and grammar from this lesson. (10 pts. for vocabulary + 10 pts. for grammar + 5 pts. for style and creativity = 25 pts.)

Tests

Nombre ______________________ Fecha ______________________

TEST B

Lección 4

1 Escuchar Read these statements and multiple-choice options. Then listen to the advertisement for **Club Excursionista** and select the correct option. (5 x 2 pts. each = 10 pts.)

1. El Club Excursionista está en...
   a. la ciudad   b. el pueblo.   c. las montañas.
2. Pueden pasar...
   a. un fin de semana.   b. un rato.   c. su familia.
3. En el Club Excursionista hay...
   a. tres gimnasios.   b. dos cafeterías.   c. dos piscinas.
4. Cerca del club hay...
   a. una piscina.   b. un restaurante.   c. un parque.
5. Si desean más información, las personas pueden...
   a. leer el periódico.   b. escribir un mensaje electrónico.   c. escribir una carta.

2 En el parque Describe what people are doing in the picture. Write at least five sentences. (6 pts. for vocabulary + 6 pts. for grammar + 3 pts. for style and creativity = 15 pts.)

____

____

____

____

____

____

____

____

____

Tests

Nombre ______________________ Fecha ______________________

3 ¿Fútbol? Fill in the blanks with the present tense of the Spanish stem-changing verbs, irregular verbs, or verbs with an irregular **yo** form in parentheses. (10 x 2 pts. each = 20 pts.)

DAVID ¿(1) ______________________ (*to want*) ir al cine?

LUIS No, hoy (2)______________________ (*to prefer*) estar en el hotel. Nosotros (3) ______________________ (*can*) mirar la televisión. Esta tarde hay un partido de fútbol. Hoy (4) ______________________ (*to play*) mi equipo favorito.

DAVID Yo no (5) ______________________ (*to understand*) nada de fútbol. Yo (6) ______________________ (*to suppose*) que hoy vamos a ver el partido de fútbol, pero mañana nosotros (7) ______________________ (*to go*) al cine. ¿Qué (8) ______________________ (*to think*) tú?

LUIS Bueno, mañana vemos una película.

DAVID ¿A qué hora (9) ______________________ (*to begin*) el partido?

LUIS A ver... a las tres.

DAVID Pues, voy a ir a pasear un poco.

LUIS Bueno, pero (10) ______________________ (*to return*) pronto, ¿no? No quiero ver el partido solo (*alone*).

4 Preguntas Answer these questions with complete sentences. (6 x 3 pts. each = 18 pts.)

1. ¿Qué clases prefieres este (*this*) semestre? ______________________

____

2. ¿Eres aficionado/a al cine? ______________________

____

3. ¿Sales mucho los fines de semana? ¿Adónde vas? ______________________

____

4. ¿Juegas al fútbol? ¿Y al béisbol? ______________________

____

5. ¿Qué vas a hacer este fin de semana? ______________________

____

6. ¿Te gusta leer el periódico? ¿Qué periódico lees? ______________________

____

Tests

5 Lectura Sandra has received a postcard from her friend Rubén. Read it and answer the questions. (6 x 2 pts. each = 12 pts.)

> Hola, Sandra:
> Gracias por la postal. Te escribo desde la cafetería de la escuela. Luis, Marta y yo queremos salir esta tarde. Marta quiere ver una película mexicana, pero yo no soy aficionado a las películas y no tengo ganas de ir al cine. Hoy prefiero pasar tiempo en el gimnasio y después leer una revista. Este fin de semana, vamos a ir al museo y después a comer en un bonito restaurante del centro. Ahora tengo que ir a la biblioteca, porque tengo que estudiar para un examen de historia. ¡Necesito descansar! Espero recibir otra postal pronto.
> Un beso y saludos a tus amigos,
> Rubén

1. ¿Dónde está Rubén? ______________________
2. ¿Qué piensan hacer por la tarde él y sus amigos? ______________________
____
3. ¿Qué quiere hacer Rubén? ______________________
4. ¿Qué van a hacer este fin de semana? ______________________
____
5. ¿Adónde va a estudiar Rubén? ______________________
6. ¿Por qué tiene que estudiar Rubén? ______________________
____

6 Tus ratos libres Write a paragraph with at least five sentences where you talk about how you usually spend your free time and how you will spend it tomorrow. Use vocabulary and grammar from this lesson. (10 pts. for vocabulary + 10 pts. for grammar + 5 pts. for style and creativity = 25 pts.)

____
____
____
____
____
____
____
____
____
____

Tests

Nombre ______________________ Fecha ______________________

TEST C

Lección 4

1 Escuchar You will hear five personal questions. Answer them with Spanish sentences. (5 x 2 pts. each = 10 pts.)

1. ______________________
2. ______________________
3. ______________________
4. ______________________
5. ______________________

2 En la ciudad Look at the picture and imagine that some friends are going to spend the day in the city. Describe what they are going to do, using vocabulary from this lesson, based on what you see. Write at least five sentences. (6 pts. for vocabulary + 6 pts. for grammar + 3 pts. for style and creativity = 15 pts.)

____

____

____

____

____

____

____

____

____

____

____

Tests

3 Lectura Read this advertisement for the **Club Deportivo Mérida** and answer the questions with complete sentences. (5 x 2 pts. each = 10 pts.)

¿Es usted una persona activa? ¿Le gusta practicar deportes? Entonces visite el Club Deportivo Mérida, en el parque del centro de la ciudad. Tenemos actividades para los aficionados a todos los deportes. Puede practicar la natación y el ciclismo o jugar al tenis. También tenemos equipos de béisbol, vóleibol y baloncesto; hay partidos cada fin de semana. Nuestro club tiene una piscina, dos gimnasios y un café donde usted puede descansar y leer su correo electrónico. Si quiere más información, puede venir al club. Cerramos a las doce de la noche.

1. ¿Dónde está el Club Deportivo Mérida? ______________________
2. ¿Cuándo son los partidos de vóleibol en el Club Deportivo Mérida? ______________________
3. ¿Dónde puedes leer tu correo electrónico? ______________________
4. ¿Qué deportes puedes practicar en el Club Deportivo Mérida? ______________________
5. ¿Te gustan las actividades mencionadas aquí? ¿Cuáles? ______________________

Tests

4 El fin de semana Describe what you are doing this weekend. Use all the verbs in the box. (6 pts. for vocabulary + 6 pts. for grammar + 3 pts. for style and creativity = 15 pts.)

dormir	**pensar**	**querer**
ir	**poder**	**ver**

TEST D

Lección 4

1 Escuchar You will hear five personal questions. Answer them with Spanish sentences. (5 x 2 pts. each = 10 pts.)

1. ______________________
2. ______________________
3. ______________________
4. ______________________
5. ______________________

2 Un día en el parque Using the activities in the picture as a guide, write at least five sentences that say what some friends are going to do today. Use the vocabulary from the lesson. (6 pts. for vocabulary + 6 pts. for grammar + 3 pts. for style and creativity = 15 pts.)

____
____
____
____
____
____
____
____
____

Tests

Nombre ______________________ Fecha ______________________

3 Lectura Read this advertisement for the **Club Ciudad Azul** and answer the questions with complete sentences. When answering with numbers, write them as words. (5 x 2 pts. each = 10 pts.)

> El Club Ciudad Azul abre el próximo sábado en el centro de la ciudad, al lado del Museo de Arte. Es un lugar familiar donde va a encontrar actividades deportivas y sociales. Durante la primera semana, puede visitarnos y ver nuestras instalaciones[1]. El club tiene dos piscinas, dos gimnasios y un restaurante. También tiene una biblioteca donde puede pasar sus ratos libres o leer el periódico, y un café donde puede reunirse[2] con los amigos. Los fines de semana, tenemos actividades para todos: puede practicar la natación y el baloncesto o jugar al tenis. Si quiere más información, puede llamar al teléfono 24-98-50. Cerramos a las once de la noche.

[1]*facilities* [2]*meet*

1. ¿Dónde está el Club Ciudad Azul? ______________________
2. ¿Qué deportes puedes practicar en el Club Ciudad Azul? ______________________
3. ¿Dónde puedes leer el periódico? ______________________
4. ¿Cuál es el número de teléfono? ______________________
5. ¿Te gustan las actividades mencionadas aquí? ¿Cuáles? ______________________

4 Vacaciones Describe what you are going to do on your next vacation. Use all the verbs in the box. (6 pts. for vocabulary + 6 pts. for grammar + 3 pts. for style and creativity = 15 pts.)

jugar	**poder**	**preferir**	**querer**	**visitar**	**volver**

____

Nombre ______________________ Fecha ______________________

TEST E

Lección 4

1 Escuchar Read the statements. Then listen to the radio commercial and indicate whether each statement is **cierto** or **falso**. (5 x 2 pts. each = 10 pts.)

En el gimnasio Tarzán...	**Cierto**	**Falso**
1. tienen clases de baloncesto.	______	______
2. las clases empiezan a las nueve.	______	______
3. cierran a las diez de la noche.	______	______
4. hay clases todos los días.	______	______
5. te dan una pelota de fútbol si vas ahora.	______	______

2 Conjugar Complete the chart with the appropriate verb forms. (5 x 2 pts. each = 10 pts.)

Infinitive	yo	nosotros/as
conseguir	(1)	(2)
contar	(3)	
perder	(4)	
mostrar		(5)

3 Escribir Write sentences using **ir a** with the information provided. Follow the model. (5 x 2 pts. each = 10 pts.)

modelo

ustedes / dormir / en mi casa

Ustedes van a dormir en mi casa.

1. Patricia / leer el periódico / en los ratos libres

____

2. Jorge / visitar monumentos / en el centro

____

3. yo / jugar videojuegos / el fin de semana

____

4. nosotros / nadar / en el gimnasio

____

5. Lola y Daniel / ir / al parque

____

Tests

Nombre ______________________ Fecha ______________________

4 Escoger Select the item that does not belong. (5 x 2 pts. each = 10 pts.)

1. a. la patineta b. la bicicleta c. la natación
2. a. el equipo b. el golf c. el hockey
3. a. la iglesia b. el parque c. el museo
4. a. pasear en bicicleta b. patinar en línea c. jugar videojuegos
5. a. el periódico b. el videojuego c. la revista

5 Completar Fill in the blanks with the appropriate form of the verbs. (6 x 2 pts. each = 12 pts.)

1. Sofía ____________________ (empezar) a ver una película.
2. Los Pumas de la UNAM ____________________ (jugar) en el estadio.
3. El jugador ____________________ (pedir) una pelota de tenis.
4. Mariana ____________________ (oír) la radio por la tarde.
5. César y yo ____________________ (preferir) jugar al vóleibol
6. Tú ____________________ (seguir) el partido por la radio.

6 Escribir Fill in the blanks with the **yo** form of the appropriate verbs. (6 x 2 pts. each = 12 pts.)

decir	**salir**
hacer	**traer**
oír	**ver**

1. Por las mañanas, ____________________ de mi casa a las siete.
2. ____________________ la radio por las tardes.
3. Los fines de semana, ____________________ películas con mi novia.
4. ____________________ unos libros a la biblioteca.
5. Cuando mis amigos tienen hambre, ____________________ sándwiches.
6. Siempre (*Always*) ____________________ la verdad.

Tests

Nombre ______________________ Fecha ______________________

7 Mariela Fill in the blanks with the present tense form of the appropriate verbs. (9 x 2 pts. each = 18 pts.)

1. Los padres de Mariela __________________ (conseguir, jugar, oír) boletos para el partido de fútbol.
2. En la mañana, Mariela __________________ (poner, salir, jugar) al golf con sus primos.
3. Mariela __________________ (mostrar, oír, suponer) su colección de pelotas de fútbol.
4. Los hermanos de Mariela __________________ (poner, preferir, perder) jugar a videojuegos.
5. Mariela y yo __________________ (empezar, ver, salir) a hacer el desayuno.
6. La mamá de Mariela no __________________ (traer, recordar, volver) si hay fruta (*fruit*) para el desayuno.
7. El papá de Mariela __________________ (entender, dormir, traer) los boletos para el partido de fútbol.
8. Mariela y yo __________________ (contar, poder, repetir) ir al partido con nuestros amigos.
9. Y tú, ¿__________________ (contar, querer, repetir) ir con nosotros?

8 Lectura Read Fernanda's e-mail, then answer the questions. (6 x 3 pts. each = 18 pts.)

> Hola, Cristina:
> Mi familia y yo vamos a hacer muchas cosas este fin de semana. Hoy, a las 10:00 a.m., voy a pasear en bicicleta. Mi hermano, Marcos, va a ir de excursión al lago (*lake*) y piensa nadar toda la mañana. A las 2:00 p.m. voy a almorzar con mis papás. Mañana hay un partido de fútbol. Pienso que el equipo de Marcos va a ganar. Después (*After*) del partido vamos a la piscina para tomar el sol y nadar. ¿Puedes ir conmigo a la piscina el próximo (*next*) fin de semana? ¡La natación es fantástica!
> Hasta pronto,
> Fernanda

1. ¿Qué le cuenta Fernanda a Cristina en su mensaje?
   a. sus planes b. cómo llegar al lago c. cuántos hermanos tiene
2. ¿A qué hora va a pasear en bicicleta Fernanda?
   a. a las 2:00 p.m. b. a las 9:00 a.m. c. a las 10:00 a.m.
3. ¿Qué actividad piensa hacer Marcos en el lago?
   a. natación b. esquí acuático c. buceo
4. ¿Qué va a hacer Fernanda con sus papás?
   a. almorzar b. jugar al golf c. ir de excursión
5. ¿Adónde quiere ir Fernanda con Cristina?
   a. al lago b. al partido de fútbol c. a la piscina
6. ¿Quién piensa que la natación es fantástica?
   a. sus papas b. Fernanda c. Cristina

Tests

Nombre ______________________ Fecha ______________________

TEST F

Lección 4

1 Escuchar Read the statements. Then listen to the radio commercial and indicate whether each statement is **cierto** or **falso**. (5 x 2 pts. each = 10 pts.)

En el gimnasio Sansón...	**Cierto**	**Falso**
1. tienen clases de tenis.	______	______
2. las clases empiezan a las nueve.	______	______
3. cierran a las diez de la noche.	______	______
4. hay clases todos los días.	______	______
5. te dan una pelota de fútbol si vas ahora.	______	______

2 Conjugar Complete the chart with the appropriate verb forms. (5 x 2 pts. each = 10 pts.)

Infinitive	**yo**	**nosotros/as**
decir	(1)	(2)
dormir	(3)	
entender		(4)
volver		(5)

3 Tiempo libre Write sentences using **ir a** with the information provided. Follow the model. (5 x 2 pts. each = 10 pts.)

modelo

ustedes / dormir / en mi casa

Ustedes van a dormir en mi casa.

1. yo / escribir una carta / a las tres de la tarde

____

2. Camilo y Natalia / andar en patineta / en el parque

____

3. nosotros / jugar al tenis

____

4. Paula / pasear en bicicleta / en el centro

____

5. Daniel / ir / a la iglesia / el domingo

____

Tests

Nombre ______________________________ Fecha ____________________

4 Escoger Select the item that does not belong. (5 x 2 pts. each = 10 pts.)

1. a. tomar el sol b. ver películas c. la pelota
2. a. la iglesia b. el museo c. el partido
3. a. el correo b. el béisbol c. el ciclismo
4. a. escribir una carta b. ir de excursión c. leer un mensaje electrónico
5. a. el café b. el centro c. el restaurante

5 Completar Fill in the blanks with the appropriate form of the verbs. (6 x 2 pts. each = 12 pts.)

1. Francisco ____________________ (cerrar) su correo electrónico.
2. Tú ____________________ (repetir) la excursión porque te gusta mucho.
3. Juliana ____________________ (ver) un partido de vóleibol.
4. David y yo ____________________ (recordar) este día importante.
5. El equipo ____________________ (conseguir) ganar.
6. Clara y Andrea ____________________ (comenzar) a practicar hockey el sábado.

6 Escribir Fill in the blanks with the **yo** form of the appropriate verbs. (6 x 2 pts. each = 12 pts.)

decir	**poner**
hacer	**traer**
oír	**ver**

1. Todos los días, ____________________ música por la mañana.
2. Por las tardes, ____________________ muchos libros a casa.
3. Mi hermano lee y yo ____________________ la tarea.
4. Por la noche, ____________________ mis libros en el escritorio.
5. Los domingos, ____________________ la televisión por la tarde.
6. ¡Yo ____________________ que los partidos de fútbol son fantásticos!

Tests

Nombre ______________________ Fecha ______________________

7 Valentina Fill in the blanks with the present tense form of the appropriate verbs. (9 x 2 pts. each = 18 pts.)

1. El fin de semana Valentina ________________ (dormir, querer, cerrar) ir de excursión a las montañas.
2. Valentina y sus hermanos ____________________ (volver, contar, empezar) a casa a las tres.
3. Después (*After*) de la escuela, Valentina y tú __________________ (pensar, conseguir, salir) en lo que van a hacer por la tarde.
4. Su hermanito ____________________ (cerrar, seguir, salir) a Valentina por toda la casa.
5. Valentina ___________________ (oír, pedir, dormir) a su mamá una pelota de fútbol para su hermano.
6. Todos los días, Valentina ____________________ (almorzar, preferir, traer) con su familia.
7. Cuando Valentina y sus hermanos van al centro, tú ____________________ (pedir, visitar, entender) monumentos con ellos.
8. Valentina _________________ (poner, contar, recordar) que tiene que contestar su correo electrónico.
9. Hoy, Valentina y yo ____________________ (traer, perder, repetir) una mascota (*pet*) a la casa.

8 Lectura Read Victoria's e-mail, then answer the questions. (6 x 3 pts. each = 18 pts.)

> Hola, Marcela:
> ¿Recuerdas el complejo deportivo (*sports complex*) que está al lado del estadio? Voy todos los fines de semana porque puedo hacer muchas actividades. Este fin de semana hay partidos de tenis, fútbol y baloncesto para niños y adultos. También hay paseos en bicicleta por el parque todas las mañanas. Yo nado por las tardes en la piscina. Varias chicas de la escuela también vienen los fines de semana. Puedes practicar todos los deportes menos (*but*) golf. Si quieres, te consigo una invitación.
> Hasta pronto,
> Victoria

1. ¿Dónde practica deportes Victoria?
   a. en el estadio   b. en el complejo deportivo   c. en el parque
2. ¿Qué pasa este fin de semana?
   a. hay partidos de tenis y fútbol   b. hay exhibición de golf   c. hay excursiones
3. ¿Cuándo hay paseos en bicicleta?
   a. todas las noches   b. los fines de semana   c. todas las mañanas
4. ¿Qué hace Victoria por las tardes?
   a. pasea en bicicleta   b. juega al béisbol   c. nada en la piscina
5. ¿Qué deporte no puedes practicar en el complejo deportivo?
   a. el baloncesto   b. el golf   c. la natación
6. ¿Qué puede conseguir Victoria para Marcela?
   a. una invitación   b. una bicicleta   c. una piscina

Tests

Nombre ______________________ Fecha ______________________

TEST A

Lección 5

1 Escuchar Read these statements and multiple-choice options. Then listen to the advertisement for a travel agency and select the correct answer. (5 x 2 pts. each = 10 pts.)

1. La agencia de viajes se llama ____________________.
   a. Agencia Puerto Rico b. Agencia Sol y Mar c. Agencia Sol y Playa
2. La agencia ofrece (*offers*) ____________________ en San Juan.
   a. un fin de semana b. una semana c. una vuelta
3. Si tienes un mes de vacaciones puedes ____________________.
   a. tomar un barco b. tomar el sol c. montar a caballo
4. Boquerón es ____________________.
   a. una agencia b. una playa c. un hotel
5. En Boquerón puedes ____________________.
   a. acampar b. pescar c. ir de compras

2 Vacaciones Two friends are on vacation at the beach. Describe their vacation using at least eight words from the box. Use the present progressive at least twice.
(6 pts. for vocabulary + 6 pts. for grammar + 4 pts. for style and creativity = 16 pts.)

aburrido/a	**agosto**	**estación**	**hacer calor**	**llave**	**mar**
acampar	**caballo**	**estar**	**jugar a las cartas**	**maletas**	**pescar**

____

____

____

____

____

3 Hotel Colón Use this hotel directory to answer the questions. Answer with ordinal numbers (e.g., *first, second,* etc.) in complete Spanish sentences. (5 x 1 pt. each = 5 pts.)

Hotel Colón	**Piso 5**	Restaurante Vistas	Habitaciones 58–72
	Piso 4		Habitaciones 40–57
	Piso 3	Gimnasio	Habitaciones 31–39
	Piso 2	Cafetería Ecuador	Habitaciones 21–29
	Piso 1	Biblioteca	Habitaciones 1–20

1. ¿En qué piso está la biblioteca? ______________________________
2. ¿En qué piso está la habitación cuarenta y nueve? ______________________________
3. ¿En qué piso está el restaurante Vistas? ______________________________
4. ¿En qué piso está el gimnasio? ______________________________
5. ¿En qué piso está la cafetería? ______________________________

Tests

Nombre ______________________ Fecha ______________________

4 De viaje The Gómez family is taking a trip to San Juan, Puerto Rico. Rewrite the sentences, changing the underlined direct object nouns to direct object pronouns. (8 x 1 pt. each = 8 pts.)

1. Toda la familia hace las maletas. ______________________
2. Juan pone el equipaje y la cámara de fotos en el automóvil. ______________________
3. Mariselis lleva los pasaportes. ______________________
4. Su hijo, Emilio, pide las cartas. ______________________
5. La abuela, Rosa, busca el periódico. ______________________
6. Juan tiene los pasajes de avión. ______________________
7. Mariselis va a comprar mapas de Puerto Rico. ______________________
8. La abuela y Mariselis quieren visitar los monumentos de San Juan. ______________________

5 Amigos Fill in the blanks with the appropriate forms of **ser** or **estar**. (10 x 1.5 pts. each = 15 pts.)

DIANA ¡(1) ______________ lloviendo!

MIGUEL Claro, (2) ______________ otoño, ¿no?

DIANA Mmm... no me gusta la lluvia y tengo que ir al hospital y (3) ______________ lejos.

MIGUEL ¿Al hospital? ¿(4) ______________ preocupada por algo (*anything*)?

DIANA No, el padre de Noé (5) ______________ médico y (6) ______________ trabajando allí.

MIGUEL ¿Noé y tú (7) ______________ novios?

DIANA No, él (8) ______________ muy enamorado de otra chica. Nosotros (9) ______________ solamente (*just*) amigos.

MIGUEL Oye, yo (10) ______________ aburrido, ¿quieres ir a tomar un café?

DIANA No, lo siento, no puedo... tengo que ir al hospital. Quizás el fin de semana...

6 Preguntas Answer these questions with complete sentences. (6 x 3 pts. each = 18 pts.)

1. En verano, ¿prefieres ir de vacaciones al campo o a la playa? ______________________
2. En invierno, ¿adónde vas de vacaciones? ______________________
3. ¿Qué tiempo hace hoy en tu ciudad? ______________________
4. ¿En qué piso tomas la clase de español? ______________________
5. ¿Te gusta viajar en tren? ¿Por qué? ______________________
6. ¿Cuáles son tres cosas que haces cuando vas de vacaciones a la playa? ______________________

Tests

Nombre ______________________ Fecha ______________________

7 Lectura Read this advertisement and answer the questions with complete sentences. (5 x 2 pts. each = 10 pts.)

Agencia Turistar

PUERTO RICO TE ESTÁ ESPERANDO.
Ahora puedes pasar unos días fantásticos por muy pocos dólares. ¿Te gusta viajar en barco? ¿Te gusta el Caribe[1]? Puedes pasar unas magníficas vacaciones visitando las bonitas playas puertorriqueñas.

Pero si prefieres las ciudades, puedes visitar San Juan. ¿Dónde dormir? El hotel El Gran Sol está abierto todo el año. Tenemos habitaciones dobles al lado del mar. Puedes tomar el sol en la playa durante[2] el día y pasear por la interesante ciudad por la noche.

Actividades del hotel: pescar, excursiones, montar a caballo, nadar.
Puedes hacer una reservación en el teléfono 684-250-4399.

[1]*Caribbean* [2]*during*

1. ¿Cómo puedes pasar unas buenas vacaciones en Puerto Rico? ______________________
2. ¿Quiénes deben ir a San Juan? ______________________
3. ¿Cuándo cierra el hotel El Gran Sol? ______________________
4. ¿Qué pueden hacer los huéspedes del hotel por la noche? ______________________
5. ¿Qué actividades hay en el hotel? ______________________

6 ¿Cómo soy? ¿Cómo estoy? Write a paragraph with at least five sentences describing yourself. Say what you are like in general, how you are feeling today, and what you are doing right now. Use at least five different adjectives and the vocabulary and grammar from this lesson. (7 pts. for vocabulary + 7 pts. for grammar + 4 pts. for style and creativity = 18 pts.)

____

Tests

Nombre ______________________ Fecha ______________________

TEST B

Lección 5

1 Escuchar Read these statements and multiple-choice options. Then listen to the advertisement for a travel agency and select the correct answer. (5 x 2 pts. each = 10 pts.)

1. La agencia de viajes se llama ________________.
   a. Agencia Sol y Playa   b. Agencia El Gran Sol   c. Agencia Puerto Rico
2. La agencia ofrece (*offers*) ________________ en San Juan.
   a. un fin de semana   b. una semana   c. una vuelta
3. Si tienes dos semanas de vacaciones puedes ________________.
   a. acampar en la playa   b. montar a caballo   c. jugar a las cartas
4. Boquerón es ________________.
   a. una agencia   b. una playa   c. un hotel
5. En Boquerón puedes ________________.
   a. pescar   b. acampar   c. ir de compras

2 Vacaciones Two friends are on vacation in the mountains. Describe their vacation using at least eight words from the box. Use the present progressive at least twice.
(6 pts. for vocabulary + 6 pts. for grammar + 4 pts. for style and creativity = 16 pts.)

aeropuerto	**enojado/a**	**excursión**	**hacer frío**	**llover**	**pescar**
cama	**equipaje**	**habitación**	**limpio/a**	**nevar**	**seguro/a**

____

____

____

____

____

3 Hotel Sol Use this hotel directory to answer the questions. Answer with ordinal numbers (e.g., *first, second,* etc.) in complete Spanish sentences. (5 x 1 pt. each = 5 pts.)

Hotel Sol	**Piso 5**		Habitaciones 58–72
	Piso 4	Restaurante Vistas	Habitaciones 40–57
	Piso 3	Agencia de viajes Sol	Habitaciones 31–39
	Piso 2	Biblioteca	Cafetería Luz del Mar
	Piso 1	Gimnasio	Habitaciones 1–30

1. ¿En qué piso está la biblioteca? ________________
2. ¿En qué piso está la habitación sesenta y dos? ________________
3. ¿En qué piso está el restaurante Vistas? ________________
4. ¿En qué piso está el gimnasio? ________________
5. ¿En qué piso está la agencia de viajes Sol? ________________

Tests

4 De viaje The Fernández family is taking a trip to San Juan, Puerto Rico. Rewrite the sentences, changing the underlined direct object nouns to direct object pronouns. (8 x 1 pt. each = 8 pts.)

1. Vicente pone las maletas en el automóvil. ______________________
2. Isabel lleva los documentos. ______________________
3. Su hijo, José Manuel, tiene la cámara de fotos. ______________________
4. Su hija, Anabel, busca un mapa de la isla. ______________________
5. Vicente tiene los pasajes de avión. ______________________
6. La abuela e Isabel quieren visitar los museos de San Juan. ______________________
7. Vicente e Isabel quieren escribir cartas a sus amigos. ______________________
8. Todos quieren tomar café puertorriqueño. ______________________

5 Amigos Fill in the blanks with the appropriate forms of **ser** or **estar**. (10 x 1.5 pts. each = 15 pts.)

NANCY ¡(1) ______________ nevando!

ANDRÉS Claro, (2) ______________ febrero, ¿no?

NANCY Tengo que ir a visitar a un amigo y su casa (3) ______________ lejos.

ANDRÉS ¿(4) ______________ cansada? ¿Dónde (5) ______________ su casa?

NANCY En el centro. Él (6) ______________ triste y necesita hablar conmigo.

ANDRÉS ¿Ustedes (7) ______________ novios?

NANCY Nosotros sólo (8) ______________ amigos. Él (9) ______________ enamorado de otra chica.

ANDRÉS Bueno, últimamente (*lately*) yo (10) ______________ trabajando mucho y necesito hablar. ¿Vamos a tomar un café el sábado?

6 Preguntas Answer these questions with complete sentences. (6 x 3 pts. each = 18 pts.)

1. Cuando haces un viaje, ¿prefieres acampar o ir a un hotel? ______________________
2. ¿Cuáles son tres cosas que haces cuando vas de vacaciones al campo? ______________________
3. ¿Te gusta viajar en avión? ¿Por qué? ______________________
4. ¿Cuántos pisos tiene la biblioteca de tu escuela? ______________________
5. ¿Cuál es la fecha de hoy? ______________________
6. ¿Qué tiempo hace esta (*this*) semana en tu ciudad? ______________________

Tests

Nombre ______________________ Fecha ______________________

7 Lectura Read this advertisement and answer the questions with complete sentences. (5 x 2 pts. each = 10 pts.)

Agencia de viajes Sol

PUERTO RICO TE ESTÁ ESPERANDO.
¿Te gusta explorar paisajes exóticos? Puedes explorar las bonitas playas puertorriqueñas y pasar horas nadando y buceando. También puedes viajar en barco y montar a caballo. Pero si prefieres descansar, las playas de Puerto Rico son ideales para tomar el sol y pescar.

El hotel Mar Azul es el lugar perfecto para las personas que buscan aventura y para las personas que quieren descansar. Puedes hacer muchas actividades durante[1] el día y por la tarde puedes visitar la ciudad. Por la noche puedes cenar en fantásticos restaurantes y bailar en las discotecas.

Actividades del hotel: excursiones en barco, excursiones a caballo, clases de salsa. Puedes hacer una reservación en el teléfono 684-250-4399. El hotel Mar Azul está abierto todo el año.

[1] *during*

1. ¿Qué pueden hacer las personas activas en Puerto Rico? ______________________
2. ¿Qué puedes hacer en Puerto Rico si estás cansado/a? ______________________
3. ¿Qué puedes hacer por la tarde? ¿Y por la noche? ______________________
4. ¿En qué meses puedes visitar el hotel Mar Azul? ______________________
5. ¿Qué actividades hay en el hotel? ______________________

6 ¿Cómo es? ¿Cómo está? Write at least five sentences describing a friend of yours. Say what your friend is like in general, how he or she is feeling today, and what he or she is doing right now. Use at least five different adjectives and vocabulary and grammar from this lesson. (7 pts. for vocabulary + 7 pts. for grammar + 4 pts. for style and creativity = 18 pts.)

Tests

Nombre ____________________ Fecha ____________________

TEST C

Lección 5

1 Escuchar You will hear five personal questions. Answer them with Spanish sentences. (5 x 2 pts. each = 10 pts.)

1. ____________________
2. ____________________
3. ____________________
4. ____________________
5. ____________________

2 Vacaciones Two friends are on vacation at the beach. Describe their vacation (whether they enjoy the weather, what activities they do to have fun, whether they run into problems, etc.) using at least six words from the box. Use the present progressive and include two direct object pronouns. (4 pts. for vocabulary + 4 pts. for grammar + 2 pts. for style and creativity = 10 pts.)

alegre	**equipaje**	**jugar**	**nervioso/a**	**primer**	**triste**
amable	**hacer**	**llave**	**preocupado/a**	**quinto/a**	**verano**

____

____

____

____

____

____

____

3 Hotel Colón Use the hotel directory to answer the questions. Use ordinal numbers (e.g., *first, second,* etc.) in complete sentences. (5 x 1 pt. each = 5 pts.)

Hotel Colón	**Piso 5**	Biblioteca	Habitaciones 59–72
	Piso 4	Restaurante Latino	Habitaciones 40–58
	Piso 3	Gimnasio	Habitaciones 31–39
	Piso 2	Agencia de viajes Turistar	Habitaciones 21–30
	Piso 1	Cafetería Quito	Habitaciones 1–20

1. ¿En qué piso está el restaurante Latino? ____________________
2. ¿En qué piso está la habitación veintidós? ____________________
3. ¿En qué piso está la biblioteca? ____________________
4. ¿En qué piso está la cafetería? ____________________
5. ¿En qué piso está el gimnasio? ____________________

Tests

4 Lectura Read the advertisement and answer the questions with complete sentences. (5 x 2 pts. each = 10 pts.)

Agencia Marina

SAN JUAN, PUERTO RICO, TE ESTÁ ESPERANDO.
Ahora puedes pasar unos días fantásticos por muy poco dinero[1].

¿Dónde dormir? El hotel Casals está en el Viejo San Juan. Cerca del hotel hay cafés, monumentos y restaurantes. Si deseas ir a la playa, tenemos un autobús que lleva allí a nuestros huéspedes.

El hotel Morro está abierto todo el año. Tenemos habitaciones dobles al lado del mar. Puedes tomar el sol en la playa durante[2] el día y pasear en la bonita ciudad en la noche.

Actividades organizadas por el hotel: pescar, excursiones, montar a caballo, nadar.
Puedes hacer una reservación ahora mismo en el teléfono 346-825-9490.

[1] *money* [2] *during*

1. ¿Cómo pueden ir a la playa los huéspedes del hotel Casals? ____________________
2. ¿Qué hay en el Viejo San Juan? ____________________
3. ¿Qué mes cierra el hotel Morro? ____________________
4. ¿Qué pueden hacer los huéspedes del hotel Morro por la mañana? ____________________
5. ¿Qué actividades hay en el hotel Morro? ____________________

5 ¿Cómo es? ¿Cómo está? Write a paragraph with at least five sentences describing a friend or family member. Say what he or she is like in general, how he or she is feeling today, and what he or she is doing right now. Use at least five different adjectives and the vocabulary and grammar from this lesson. (6 pts. for vocabulary + 6 pts. for grammar + 3 pts. for style and creativity = 15 pts.)

____

Tests

Nombre ______________________ Fecha ______________________

TEST D

Lección 5

1 Escuchar You will hear five personal questions. Answer them with Spanish sentences. (5 x 2 pts. each = 10 pts.)

1. ______________________
2. ______________________
3. ______________________
4. ______________________
5. ______________________

2 Vacaciones Two friends are on vacation in the mountains. Describe their vacation (whether they enjoy the weather, what activities they do, whether they run into problems, etc.) using at least six words from the box. Use the present progressive and include two direct object pronouns. (4 pts. for vocabulary + 4 pts. for grammar + 2 pts. for style = 10 pts.)

amable	**cansado/a**	**empleado/a**	**habitación**	**invierno**	**llegada**
avergonzado/a	**cómodo/a**	**estación**	**hacer sol**	**listo/a**	**sacar**

____

____

____

____

____

____

____

3 Hotel Viejo San Juan Use the hotel directory to answer the questions. Use ordinal numbers (e.g., *first, second,* etc.) in complete sentences. (5 x 1 pt. each = 5 pts.)

Hotel Viejo San Juan	**Piso 6**	Restaurante Tostones	Habitaciones 73–90
	Piso 5	Gimnasio	Habitaciones 58–72
	Piso 4		Habitaciones 40–57
	Piso 3	Agencia de viajes Sol	Habitaciones 31–39
	Piso 2	Biblioteca	Habitaciones 21–30
	Piso 1	Cafetería Luz del Mar	Habitaciones 1–20

1. ¿En qué piso está el restaurante Tostones? ______________________
2. ¿En qué piso está la habitación cuarenta y tres? ______________________
3. ¿En qué piso está la biblioteca? ______________________
4. ¿En qué piso está la cafetería? ______________________
5. ¿En qué piso está la agencia de viajes Sol? ______________________

Tests

4 Lectura Read the advertisement and answer the questions with complete sentences. (5 x 2 pts. each = 10 pts.)

Agencia Marina

SAN JUAN, PUERTO RICO, TE ESTÁ ESPERANDO.
Ahora puedes pasar unos días fantásticos y económicos.
El hotel Conquistador está en el Viejo San Juan. Cerca del hotel hay museos, monumentos y muy buenos restaurantes. Todos los días, el hotel ofrece[1] viajes a la playa en autobús.
El hotel Coquí está abierto todo el año. Tenemos para usted espectaculares habitaciones al lado del mar. Puede tomar el sol, nadar y bucear en la playa y bailar salsa en las discotecas de la ciudad.
Actividades organizadas en el hotel: clases de salsa, excursiones en bicicleta, excursiones a caballo.
Puedes hacer una reservación en el teléfono 346-825-9490.

[1] *offers*

1. ¿Cómo pueden ir a la playa los huéspedes del hotel Conquistador? ________________
2. ¿Qué hay en el Viejo San Juan? ________________
3. ¿En qué meses puedes visitar el hotel Coquí? ________________
4. ¿Qué actividades acuáticas pueden hacer los huéspedes del hotel Coquí? ________________
5. ¿Qué actividades hay en el hotel Coquí? ________________

5 ¿Cómo eres? ¿Cómo estás? Write a paragraph with at least five sentences describing yourself. Say what you are like in general, how you are feeling today, and what you are doing right now. Use at least five different adjectives and the vocabulary and grammar from this lesson. (6 pts. for vocabulary + 6 pts. for grammar + 3 pts. for style and creativity = 15 pts.)

____

Nombre ______________________________ Fecha ____________________

TEST E Lección 5

1 Escuchar Read the statements. Then listen to the podcast about **Isla del Sol** and indicate whether each statement is **cierto** or **falso**. (5 x 2 pts. each = 10 pts.)

	Cierto	Falso
1. Las playas de Isla del Sol son muy limpias.	______	______
2. En invierno hace mucho frío.	______	______
3. En la Isla del Sol hay un hotel excelente.	______	______
4. En la planta baja de Solimar usted puede montar a caballo.	______	______
5. En el sitio web de Solimar usted puede comprar pasajes de avión.	______	______

2 ¿Hace calor o hace frío? Match the pictures and descriptions. (5 x 2 pts. each = 10 pts.)

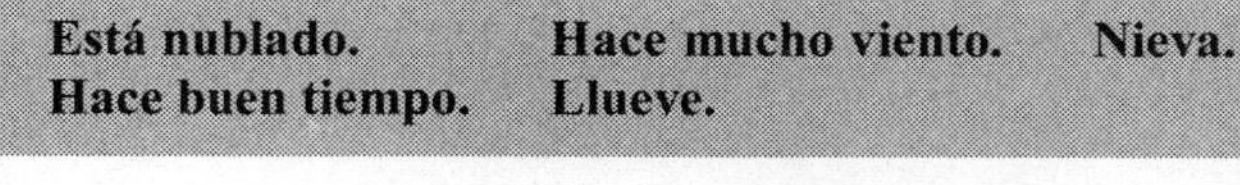

1. ____________________

2. ____________________

3. ____________________

4. ____________________

5. ____________________

3 Escoger Match the sentences that form logical pairs. Two items from Column B will not be used. (5 x 2 pts. each = 10 pts.)

A	B
_____ 1. Omar tiene un examen mañana.	a. Están listas.
_____ 2. Luis y Ana son novios.	b. Estoy equivocado.
_____ 3. Son las once de la noche.	c. Están de mal humor.
_____ 4. Mis primas no duermen bien.	d. Estoy feliz.
_____ 5. Voy de vacaciones a Puerto Rico.	e. Están enamorados.
	f. Está nervioso.
	g. El museo está cerrado.

Tests

Nombre ______________________________ Fecha ______________________

4 Oraciones Fill in the blanks with the present progressive form of the verbs. (5 x 2 pts. each = 10 pts.)

1. Sandra __________ __________ (leer) una revista en la playa.
2. Nosotros __________ __________ (jugar) al golf.
3. Tú __________ __________ (comer) en el restaurante Las Brisas.
4. El viajero __________ __________ (oír) música clásica.
5. Mis sobrinas __________ __________ (dormir) en la habitación.

5 *Ser* o *estar* Write complete sentences using **ser** or **estar** with the information provided. (6 x 2 pts. each = 12 pts.)

modelo

yo / bien

Yo estoy bien.

1. la puerta / abierta ______________________________
2. Víctor y Carlos / de Puerto Rico ______________________________
3. la clase / a las doce ______________________________
4. nosotros / lejos de la estación ______________________________
5. tú / muy inteligente ______________________________
6. yo / haciendo windsurf ______________________________

6 Pronombres Select the sentence that uses the appropriate direct object pronoun. (6 x 2 pts. each = 12 pts.)

1. El botones lleva unas maletas a la habitación.
   a. La lleva. b. Los lleva. c. Las lleva.
2. Están haciendo un viaje de dos semanas.
   a. Están haciéndolo. b. Están haciéndolas. c. Están haciéndolos.
3. Fabiola me invita a la fiesta y también invita a Sabrina.
   a. Las invita. b. Me invita. c. Nos invita.
4. Tú tienes que conseguir tres mapas de la ciudad.
   a. Tienes que conseguirlas. b. Tienes que conseguirlos. c. Tienes que conseguirnos.
5. Norma quiere comprar una motocicleta.
   a. Quiere comprarlo. b. Quiere comprarla. c. Quiere comprarlas.
6. El empleado no entiende a una huésped.
   a. No la entiende. b. No lo entiende. c. No me entiende.

Tests

7 Completar Select the appropriate verb forms or pronouns. (9 x 2 pts. each = 18 pts.)

Para: carla83@correo.es	**De:** sabrinagarcía@correo.es	**Asunto:** Saludos

Querida Carla:

Hoy mis padres y yo (1) (están/estamos/estar) en San Juan, Puerto Rico. Mañana vamos a viajar en tren. (2) (Nos/Me/Te) va a llevar a Bayamón, donde vive la familia de mi amiga Lisa. Lisa y su familia (3) (son/están/estamos) estadounidenses, pero ahora (*now*) están (4) (vivir/viven/viviendo) aquí. Hace buen tiempo en San Juan. Hoy está (5) (hacemos/haciendo/hacer) calor y mañana va a hacer frío. Mis padres practican el tenis, pero yo no (6) (los/lo/me) practico. Yo (7) (soy/estar/estoy) al lado de la piscina y estoy (8) (descansando/ descansamos/descansar).

¡Te extraño! (*I miss you!*) ¿(9) (Te/Los/Me) escribes pronto?

Tu prima,

Sabrina

8 Lectura Read about Mr. and Mrs. Ortega's bus trip from Arecibo to Mayagüez, Puerto Rico, then answer the questions. (6 x 3 pts. each = 18 pts.)

El señor y la señora Ortega están en la estación de autobuses, listos para ir a Mayagüez. El señor Ortega está nervioso porque no quiere tomar el autobús equivocado. Ellos siempre (*always*) viajan en avión o en automóvil. La señora Ortega está contenta porque puede tomar muchas fotos en el camino (*on the way*).

El conductor confirma que es el autobús que va a Mayagüez. Ahora el señor Ortega está de buen humor. Ya no está preocupado, y piensa en el mar, el paisaje y los amigos que va a visitar. Además (*Besides*), en Mayagüez hace sol.

1. ¿En qué van los señores Ortega a Mayagüez?
   a. en avión b. en autobús c. en automóvil
2. ¿Por qué está nervioso el señor Ortega?
   a. Pueden tomar el autobús equivocado. b. Van a viajar en avión. c. No pueden viajar.
3. ¿Por qué está contenta la señora Ortega?
   a. Va a tomar sol. b. Quiere viajar en autobús. c. Puede tomar fotos.
4. ¿Quién confirma que el autobús va a Mayagüez?
   a. el señor Ortega b. la señora Ortega c. el conductor
5. ¿En qué piensa el señor Ortega cuando está de buen humor?
   a. en el mar y los amigos b. en el viaje en autobús c. en el avión
6. ¿Qué tiempo hace en Mayagüez?
   a. Llueve. b. Hace sol. c. Hace frío.

Nombre ______________________ Fecha ______________________

TEST F — Lección 5

1 Escuchar Read the statements. Then listen to the podcast about Vieques, Puerto Rico, and indicate whether each statement is **cierto** or **falso**. (5 x 2 pts. each = 10 pts.)

	Cierto	Falso
1. Vieques tiene playas muy limpias.	______	______
2. Allí hay un hotel muy malo.	______	______
3. En Viequemar puedes montar a caballo.	______	______
4. No puedes hacer windsurf.	______	______
5. En el sitio web de Viequemar, puedes comprar los boletos.	______	______

2 ¿Cómo está el clima? Match the pictures and descriptions. (5 x 2 pts. each = 10 pts.)

Está lloviendo. **Está nublado.** **Hace mucho viento.**
Está nevando. **Hace buen tiempo.**

1. ______________________

2. ______________________

3. ______________________

4. ______________________

5. ______________________

3 Escoger Match the sentences that form logical pairs. Two items from Column B will not be used. (5 x 2 pts. each = 10 pts.)

A	B
______ 1. Juan tiene una fiesta (*party*) mañana.	a. Está feliz.
______ 2. Leticia y Julio son novios.	b. Están listas.
______ 3. Lorena y Salomón no duermen bien.	c. Estoy nervioso.
______ 4. Mi compañera explica la lección.	d. Están enamorados.
______ 5. Tengo un examen hoy.	e. Estoy enamorado.
	f. Están cansados.
	g. Está segura.

Tests

4 Oraciones Fill in the blanks with the present progressive form of the verbs. (5 x 2 pts. each = 10 pts.)

1. Rubén __________ __________ (jugar) *ping-pong* con su hermano.
2. María y Luis __________ __________ (leer) el mismo libro.
3. Tú __________ __________ (nadar) en la piscina del hotel.
4. El Sr. Velázquez __________ __________ (comer) la ensalada (*salad*).
5. Tus primas __________ __________ (estudiar) en la habitación.

5 *Ser* o *estar* Write complete sentences using **ser** or **estar** with the information provided. (6 x 2 pts. each = 12 pts.)

modelo

yo / bien

Yo estoy bien.

1. Carla y yo / en el museo ______________________________
2. la fiesta (*party*) / a las diez ______________________________
3. tú / costarricense ______________________________
4. el café / cerrado ______________________________
5. yo / montar a caballo ______________________________
6. José y Roberto / primos ______________________________

6 Pronombres Select the sentence that uses the appropriate direct object pronoun. (6 x 2 pts. each = 12 pts.)

1. Enrique quiere comprar una tabla de windsurf.
   a. Quiere comprarlo. b. Quiere comprarla. c. Quiere comprarlas.
2. Están haciendo un viaje de tres semanas.
   a. Están haciéndolas. b. Están haciéndolos. c. Están haciéndolo.
3. Tú tienes que conseguir los pasajes de avión.
   a. Tienes que conseguirlas. b. Tienes que conseguirlos. c. Tienes que conseguirnos.
4. El huésped no entiende a una empleada.
   a. No la entiende. b. No lo entiende. c. No me entiende.
5. Teresa me invita a la fiesta y también invita a Gustavo.
   a. Los invita. b. Me invita. c. Nos invita.
6. El agente confirma la reservación.
   a. La confirma. b. Los confirma. c. Las confirma.

Nombre ______________________ Fecha ______________________

7 Completar Select the appropriate verb forms or pronouns. (9 x 2 pts. each = 18 pts.)

Para: fabián82@correo.es	**De:** victoriagarzón@correo.es	**Asunto:** Saludos

Querido Fabián:

Esta semana, mis padres (1) (estamos/están/estar) en Bayamón, Puerto Rico. Mañana van a viajar en tren. (2) (Nos/Me/Los) va a llevar a San Juan, donde van a estar otra semana. Mi hermano y yo (3) (son/están/estamos) en casa de mis tíos Sandra y Ramón en el campo (*country*) y estamos un poco (4) (equivocados/aburridos/ordenados) aquí. Yo tomo fotos todos los días (*everyday*), pero mi hermano no (5) (los/las/la) mira. Él está (6) (enojado/ contento/ocupado) porque quiere regresar a la ciudad a ver a sus amigos. Hoy, está (7) (hacemos/haciendo/hacer) calor y mañana va a hacer frío. Yo (8) (soy/ estar/estoy) junto a la piscina descansando. ¡(9) (Es/Soy/Está) un día hermoso!

Tu amiga,

Victoria

8 Lectura Read about Ana and Jaime's trip from Mayagüez to Ponce, Puerto Rico, then answer the questions. (6 x 3 pts. each = 18 pts.)

Ana y Jaime están en la estación de autobuses. Ana lleva dos maletas y Jaime, una. Ellos van a Ponce a visitar a unos amigos. La puerta del autobús está cerrada y Ana está confundida. Piensa que es tarde (*late*). Jaime pide información a un señor. El señor es el conductor del autobús que va a Ponce y confirma que es temprano (*early*). Dice que el autobús va a estar listo en media hora. Ana está de mal humor porque tienen que esperar. Ella quiere salir ahora mismo (*right now*). Media hora después (*after*), Ana oye el motor del autobús y ahora está contenta.

1. ¿Dónde están Ana y Jaime?
   a. en la estación de autobuses b. en el aeropuerto c. en el autobús

2. ¿Cuántas maletas llevan Ana y Jaime?
   a. dos maletas b. tres maletas c. cuatro maletas

3. ¿Por qué está confundida Ana?
   a. Piensa que es tarde. b. Tiene hambre. c. La puerta está abierta.

4. ¿Quién confirma que es temprano?
   a. Ana b. Jaime c. el conductor del autobús

5. ¿Cuánto tiempo tienen que esperar Ana y Jamie?
   a. una hora b. media hora c. una hora y media

6. ¿Por qué Ana está contenta?
   a. Oye el ruido del tren. b. Oye a Jaime hablar. c. Oye el motor del autobús.

Tests

Nombre ______________________ Fecha ______________________

TEST A

Lección 6

1 Escuchar Read the sentence fragments and multiple-choice options. Then listen to the advertisement and select the correct option. (5 x 2 pts. each = 10 pts.)

1. El Caribe es...
   a. una tienda de computadoras. b. un mercado. c. un almacén.
2. Los clientes no tienen que gastar mucho dinero porque...
   a. no tienen mucho dinero. b. van a conseguir las mejores rebajas c. tienen tarjeta de crédito.
3. En la tienda para niños venden...
   a. pantalones de todos los colores. b. sombreros. c. faldas.
4. En la tienda para hombres tienen...
   a. camisetas y pantalones. b. chaquetas y pantalones. c. camisas y pantalones.
5. En la tienda las señoras pueden comprar...
   a. vestidos y guantes. b. blusas y zapatos. c. cinturones que hacen juego con la ropa.

2 De compras Write a dialogue between the customer and the sales clerk based on the picture. Use indirect object pronouns and at least six words from the box. (7 pts. for vocabulary + 7 pts. for grammar + 2 pts. for style and creativity = 16 pts.)

barato/a	**dar**	**pantalones**	**suéter**
caja	**efectivo**	**rebajas**	**talla**
corbata	**gris**	**regalo**	**tarjeta de crédito**

Tests

3 ¿Qué desea? Fill in the blanks of this conversation with demonstrative pronouns. (7 x 2 pts. each = 14 pts.)

VENDEDOR ¿Quiere ver aquellas faldas?

DORA Prefiero ver (1) ______________________ (*these ones here*). ¿Y esa camiseta?

VENDEDOR ¿(2) ______________________ (*That one*) o (3) ______________________ (*that one over there*)?

DORA (4) ______________________ (*That one over there*). Y, ¿puede mostrarme esos vestidos?

VENDEDOR ¿(5) ______________________ (*These*) o (6) ______________________ (*those*)?

DORA Éstos. Me gustaría (*I would like*) comprar guantes. ¿Cuánto cuestan (7) ______________________ (*those over there*)?

VENDEDOR Cuestan cincuenta y ocho dólares.

DORA Los compro.

4 En el centro comercial Read the paragraph and write the preterite forms in the blanks. (10 x 2 pts. each = 20 pts.)

El sábado pasado, Eugenia y yo fuimos (*went*) al centro comercial a comprar ropa. El centro (1) ______________________ (abrir) a las nueve y nosotras (2) ______________________ (llegar) a las nueve y treinta de la mañana. Primero, (3) ______________________ (tomar) café en la cafetería del centro comercial. Después, (4) ______________________ (visitar) las tiendas. Luego, a las dos de la tarde, (5) ______________________ (volver) a la cafetería para comer algo (*something*). Yo no (6) ______________________ (comprar) nada, pero Eugenia compró muchas cosas, porque (7) ______________________ (recibir) mucho dinero de sus padres la semana pasada. Yo (8) ______________________ (ver) una falda muy bonita, pero muy corta para mí. Eugenia (9) ______________________ (gastar) todo su dinero: compró dos vestidos, unos zapatos, una blusa y una falda. A las nueve de la noche, nosotras (10) ______________________ (salir) del centro.

5 Preguntas Answer these questions with Spanish sentences. (5 x 3 pts. each = 15 pts.)

1. ¿Qué ropa llevas cuando vas a clase? ______________________
2. ¿Te prestan dinero tus amigos? ______________________
3. ¿Sabes qué ropa está de moda? ______________________
4. ¿A qué hora volviste ayer a casa? ______________________
5. ¿Cuándo empezaste a estudiar español? ______________________

Tests

Nombre ______________________________ Fecha ______________________

6 Lectura Read this advertisement and answer the questions. (3 x 2 pts. each = 6 pts.)

COLECCIÓN PRIMAVERA-VERANO

Acaba de salir la moda de primavera-verano. Viene en muchos colores y es muy cómoda. Ya no tenemos que decidir entre estar cómodos y sentirnos elegantes.

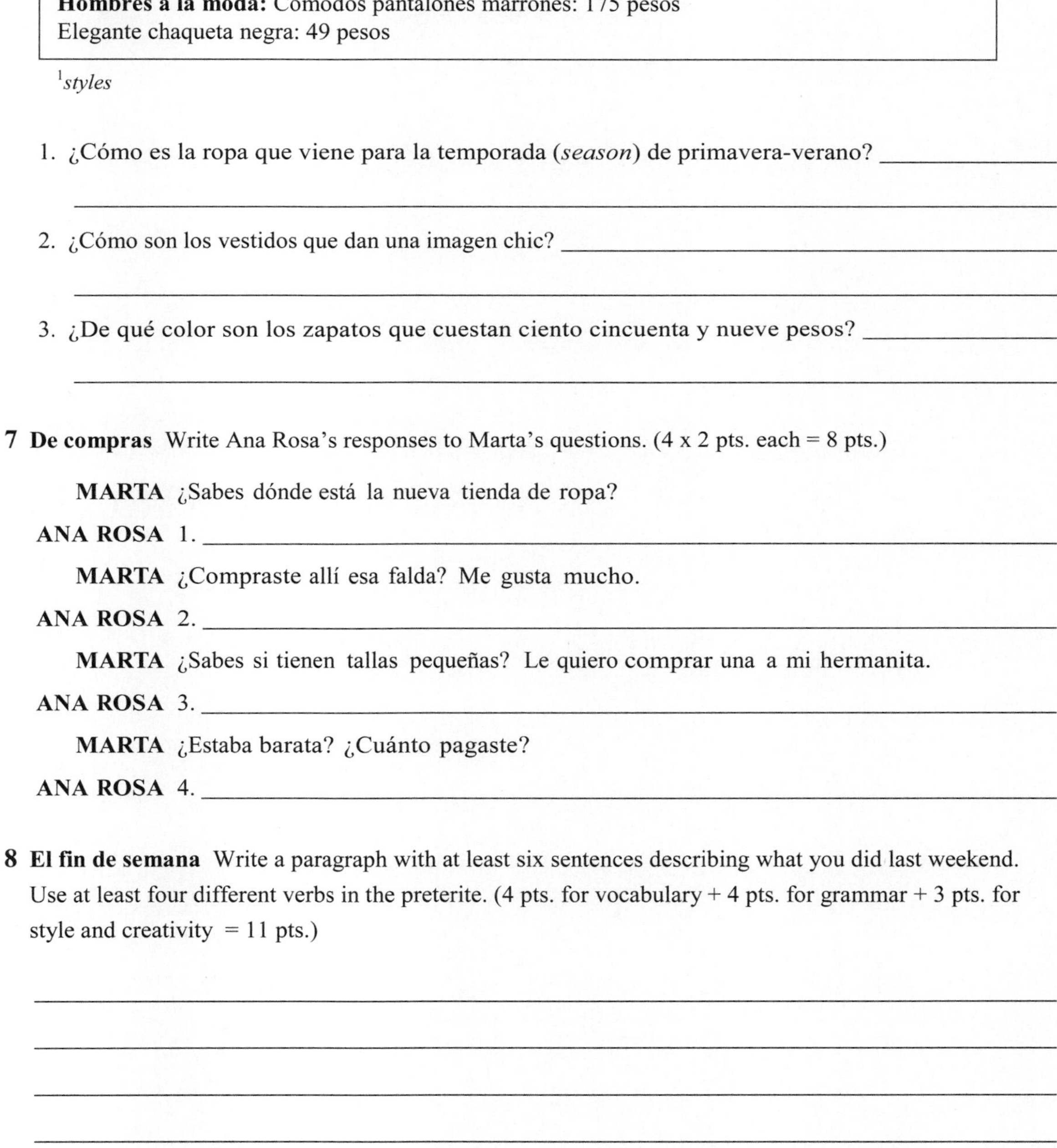

Mujeres a la moda: Esta primavera pueden comprar diferentes estilos[1] de botas, de minifaldas y de camisetas de colores. Este verano pueden llevar vestidos con variedad de estilos y colores para dar una imagen chic.

Vestidos anaranjado y rosado: 250 pesos Zapatos rojos: 150 pesos
Zapatos marrones: 159 pesos

Hombres a la moda: Cómodos pantalones marrones: 175 pesos
Elegante chaqueta negra: 49 pesos

[1] *styles*

1. ¿Cómo es la ropa que viene para la temporada (*season*) de primavera-verano? ______________

____

2. ¿Cómo son los vestidos que dan una imagen chic? ______________________

____

3. ¿De qué color son los zapatos que cuestan ciento cincuenta y nueve pesos? ______________

____

7 De compras Write Ana Rosa's responses to Marta's questions. (4 x 2 pts. each = 8 pts.)

MARTA ¿Sabes dónde está la nueva tienda de ropa?

ANA ROSA 1. ____

MARTA ¿Compraste allí esa falda? Me gusta mucho.

ANA ROSA 2. ____

MARTA ¿Sabes si tienen tallas pequeñas? Le quiero comprar una a mi hermanita.

ANA ROSA 3. ____

MARTA ¿Estaba barata? ¿Cuánto pagaste?

ANA ROSA 4. ____

8 El fin de semana Write a paragraph with at least six sentences describing what you did last weekend. Use at least four different verbs in the preterite. (4 pts. for vocabulary + 4 pts. for grammar + 3 pts. for style and creativity = 11 pts.)

____

____

____

____

Nombre ______________________ Fecha ______________________

TEST B Lección 6

1 Escuchar Read the statements and multiple-choice options. Then listen to the advertisement and select the correct option. (5 x 2 pts. each = 10 pts.)

1. El Prado es...
   a. un mercado al aire libre. b. un centro comercial. c. un supermercado.
2. El/La cliente/a puede llevar ropa de moda...
   a. a precios de ganga. b. pagando con tarjeta de crédito. c. y de muy buena calidad.
3. En la tienda para niños venden _______________ para los días de frío.
   a. abrigos b. impermeables c. camisetas
4. En la tienda de señoras pueden comprar _______________ que hacen juego con todo.
   a. cinturones y corbatas b. vestidos c. medias, sombreros y guantes
5. En la tienda para hombres hay una excelente rebaja en...
   a. chaquetas y pantalones. b. cinturones y corbatas. c. camisas y pantalones.

2 De compras Write a dialogue between the customer and the sales clerk based on the picture. Use indirect object pronouns and at least six words from the box. (7 pts. for vocabulary + 7 pts. for grammar + 2 pts. for style and creativity = 16 pts.)

anaranjado/a	**chaqueta**	**precio**	**regatear**
camisa	**corbata**	**rebajas**	**saber**
caro/a	**costar**	**regalo**	**tarjeta de crédito**

____

____

____

____

____

____

____

____

____

____

____

____

____

____

Tests

3 ¿Qué desea? Fill in the blanks of this conversation with demonstrative pronouns. (7 x 2 pts. each = 14 pts.)

VENDEDOR Tenemos muchos pantalones en rebaja. ¿Quiere ver (1) ______________ (*those over there*)?

PABLO No, gracias. Prefiero ver (2) ______________ (*these*). Y necesito una camisa. ¿Puedo ver (3) ______________ (*that one*)?

VENDEDOR ¿(4) ______________ (*That one*) o (5) ______________ (*that one over there*)?

PABLO (6) ______________ (*That one over there*). Me gustaría (*I would like*) comprar un cinturón también. ¿Cuánto cuesta (7) ______________ (*this one*)?

VENDEDOR Cuesta setenta y ocho dólares.

PABLO Lo compro.

4 En el centro comercial Read the paragraph and write the preterite forms in the blanks. (10 x 2 pts. each = 20 pts.)

El domingo pasado, mi novia, Marcela, y yo fuimos (*went*) al centro comercial a comprar ropa. Nosotros (1) ______________ (llegar) a las nueve y media de la mañana, pero ese día el centro no (2) ______________ (abrir) hasta las diez. Entonces, nosotros (3) ______________ (esperar) en una cafetería cerca del centro. A las diez en punto, nosotros (4) ______________ (empezar) a visitar las tiendas. Primero, Marcela (5) ______________ (comprar) un traje muy bonito. Después, un dependiente me (6) ______________ (mostrar) una chaqueta muy elegante, pero demasiado corta para mí. Al fin, yo (7) ______________ (encontrar) una tienda de ropa con tallas para personas altas. Yo (8) ______________ (ver) unos pantalones perfectos y otras cosas que necesitaba (*I needed*). Nosotros no (9) ______________ (salir) de la tienda hasta que los dependientes la (10) ______________ (cerrar).

5 Preguntas Answer the questions with Spanish sentences. (5 x 3 pts. each = 15 pts.)

1. ¿Qué ropa llevas a una fiesta (*party*)? ______________
2. ¿Conoces a muchas personas que siguen la moda? ______________
3. ¿Cuál es tu ropa favorita? ______________
4. ¿Gastaste mucho dinero la última vez (*the last time*) que visitaste otra ciudad? ______________
5. ¿A qué hora saliste de tu casa esta mañana? ______________

Tests

Nombre _______________ Fecha _______________

6 Lectura Read this advertisement and answer the questions. (3 x 2 pts. each = 6 pts.)

COLECCIÓN OTOÑO-INVIERNO

Acaba de salir la moda de otoño-invierno. Este año la moda viene en muchos colores para darles alegría a los días fríos.

Mujeres a la moda: Este otoño pueden comprar muchos estilos[1] de faldas y pantalones en rojo, marrón y anaranjado. Y lo más nuevo: impermeables de color verde y rosado con botas y bolsas que hacen juego.

Impermeable rosado: 165 pesos
Impermeable gris: 176 pesos
Chaqueta: 100 pesos
Abrigo largo: 315 pesos

Hombres a la moda: Cómodos pantalones y suéteres: 65 pesos
Elegante chaqueta negra: 250 pesos

[1] *styles*

1. ¿Cómo es la nueva moda para la temporada (*season*) de otoño-invierno? _______________

2. ¿De qué colores son las nuevas botas? _______________

3. ¿De qué color es el impermeable que cuesta ciento setenta y seis pesos? _______________

7 Conversación Write Ana's responses to Cristina's questions. (4 x 2 pts. each = 8 pts.)

CRISTINA ¿Conoces el nuevo centro comercial?
ANA 1. _______________
CRISTINA ¿Compraste allí esos zapatos?
ANA 2. _______________
CRISTINA ¿Cuánto te costaron?
ANA 3. _______________
CRISTINA Eso es mucho dinero. ¿Sabes cuándo van a tener rebajas?
ANA 4. _______________

8 El fin de semana Write a paragraph with at least six sentences describing what you did during the most recent long weekend. Use at least four different verbs in the preterite. (4 pts. for vocabulary + 4 pts. for grammar + 3 pts. for style and creativity = 11 pts.)

Tests

Nombre ______________________ Fecha ______________________

TEST C

Lección 6

1 Escuchar You will hear five personal questions. Answer them with Spanish sentences. (5 x 2 pts. each = 10 pts.)

1. ______________________
2. ______________________
3. ______________________
4. ______________________
5. ______________________

2 De compras Write a dialogue between the customer and the sales clerk based on the picture. Use indirect object pronouns and at least eight words from the box. (6 pts. for vocabulary + 6 pts. for grammar + 3 pts. for style and creativity = 15 pts.)

aquéllos/as	**conocer**	**estos**	**saber**
barato/a	**dar**	**precio**	**tarjeta de crédito**
caro/a	**esta**	**regalo**	**traje**

____

Tests

Nombre ______________________ Fecha ______________

3 Lectura Read this advertisement and answer the questions with sentences. Write numbers as words. (5 x 2 pts. each = 10 pts.)

COLECCIÓN OTOÑO-INVIERNO

Acaba de salir la moda de otoño-invierno. Viene en colores marrón y anaranjado y, como es muy cómoda, ya no tenemos que decidir entre estar cómodos y sentirnos elegantes.

Mujeres a la moda: Este otoño pueden comprar diferentes estilos[1] de botas, de faldas largas y de vestidos de hermosos colores. En invierno van a ver elegantes abrigos que hacen juego con trajes de pantalón y chaqueta.

Abrigo de color rojo: 430 pesos
Abrigo de color marrón: 375 pesos
Falda larga de muchos colores: 250 pesos
Botas de color gris: 135 pesos

Hombres a la moda: Suéter morado de lana: 200 pesos
Pantalones marrones para ir al trabajo: 120 pesos

[1] *styles*

1. ¿Cómo es la ropa que viene para la temporada (*season*) de otoño-invierno? ______________
2. ¿Qué ropa pueden llevar con los abrigos? ______________
3. ¿De qué material es el suéter negro? ______________
4. ¿De qué color es el abrigo que cuesta cuatrocientos treinta pesos? ______________
5. ¿En qué ocasiones pueden llevar los pantalones marrones? ______________

4 Sábado Write a paragraph with at least six sentences describing what you did last Saturday. Use at least four different verbs in the preterite. (6 pts. for vocabulary + 6 pts. for grammar + 3 pts. for style and creativity = 15 pts.)

Tests

Nombre ______________________ Fecha ______________________

TEST D

Lección 6

1 Escuchar You will hear five personal questions. Answer them with Spanish sentences. (5 x 2 pts. each = 10 pts.)

1. ____________________
2. ____________________
3. ____________________
4. ____________________
5. ____________________

2 De compras Write a dialogue between the customer and the sales clerk based on the picture. Use indirect object pronouns and at least six words from the box. (6 pts. for vocabulary + 6 pts. for grammar + 3 pts. for style and creativity = 15 pts.)

abrigo	**caro/a**	**esos**	**regatear**
aquel	**conocer**	**éstos**	**saber**
barato/a	**dar**	**regalo**	**talla**

____

Tests

Nombre ______________________ Fecha ______________________

3 Lectura Read this advertisement and answer the questions with sentences. Write numbers as words. (5 x 2 pts. each = 10 pts.)

COLECCIÓN PRIMAVERA-VERANO

Acaba de salir la moda de primavera-verano. Este año mucha ropa viene en colores morado y rosado, y en estilos[1] muy cómodos, pero elegantes.

Mujeres a la moda: Esta primavera pueden comprar diferentes estilos de faldas largas y trajes de pantalón y chaqueta para ir al trabajo, con los nuevos colores de este año. En verano van a ver en las tiendas elegantes vestidos que hacen juego con zapatos y bolsas de muchos estilos. Y para ir a la playa, pantalones cortos y sandalias de todos los colores.

Vestido morado: 250 pesos   Falda larga: 150 pesos   Sandalias de color gris: 135 pesos

Hombres a la moda: Trajes elegantes en colores claros[2]: 300 pesos
Cómodas camisetas para las vacaciones: 129 pesos

[1] *styles* [2] *light*

1. ¿Cómo es la moda de primavera-verano? ______________________
2. ¿Qué pueden llevar con los vestidos? ______________________
3. En esta primavera, ¿qué ropa para mujeres está de moda? ______________________
4. ¿Qué venden para ir a la playa? ______________________
5. ¿Qué ropa para hombres está a la moda? ______________________

4 Domingo Write a paragraph with at least six sentences describing what you did last Sunday. Use at least four different verbs in the preterite. (6 pts. for vocabulary + 6 pts. for grammar + 3 pts. for style and creativity = 15 pts.)

____

Nombre ______________________ Fecha ______________________

TEST E

Lección 6

1 Escuchar Read the statements. Then listen to the store advertisement and indicate whether each statement is **cierto** or **falso**. (5 x 2 pts. each = 10 pts.)

	Cierto	Falso
1. El almacén empezó a vender la semana pasada.	______	______
2. El almacén vende ropa para hombre y para mujer.	______	______
3. Tienen bluejeans, camisas y chaquetas.	______	______
4. Tienen pocas tallas.	______	______
5. No puedes pagar con tarjeta de crédito.	______	______

2 Julio y Lupita Match the sentences that form logical pairs. (5 x 2 pts. each = 10 pts.)

A	B
_____ 1. Julio y Lupita van a la piscina.	a. Llevan pantalones cortos y zapatos de tenis y tienen una pelota.
_____ 2. Julio y Lupita van a jugar al baloncesto.	b. Llevan impermeables y botas.
_____ 3. Julio y Lupita van a esquiar a las montañas.	c. Él lleva una corbata y ella lleva un vestido.
_____ 4. Julio y Lupita van a salir, pero está lloviendo.	d. Llevan gafas de sol y trajes de baño.
_____ 5. Julio y Lupita van a un restaurante muy elegante.	e. Llevan suéteres, chaquetas y guantes.

Tests

3 Completar Fill in the blanks with the present tense form of **saber** or **conocer.** (5 x 2 pts. each = 10 pts.)

1. Yo no ________________________ a qué hora abre el almacén.
2. Tú ________________________ un mercado muy barato.
3. Luisa ________________________ nadar muy bien.
4. Nosotros ________________________ a la vendedora de zapatos de tenis.
5. Juan y José ________________________ conducir.

Nombre ______________________ Fecha ______________________

4 Ya pasó Fill in the blanks with the preterite form of the verbs. (5 x 2 pts. each = 10 pts.)

1. Ellos ______________________ (buscar) el mercado.
2. El dependiente ______________________ (vender) una camisa.
3. Nosotros ______________________ (escribir) cartas a nuestros amigos.
4. ¿Tú ______________________ (pagar) en efectivo por la ropa interior?
5. Juan ______________________ (llegar) ayer de su viaje a la playa.

5 Escoger Match the pictures and descriptions. (6 x 2 pts. each = 12 pts.)

1. ______________

2. ______________

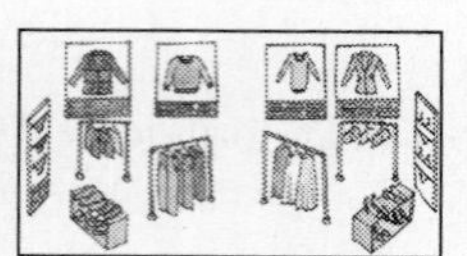

3. ______________

4. ______________

5. ______________

6. ______________

a. Hay un sombrero y un traje de baño.
b. El dependiente ayuda a dos personas.
c. Julia paga por el vestido.
d. María paga en efectivo en la caja.
e. En la tienda hay ropa de hombre y de mujer.
f. Voy a esquiar este fin de semana.

6 Escribir Rewrite the sentences to include indirect object pronouns. Follow the model. (6 x 2 pts. each = 12 pts.)

modelo

Ana presta la falda. (*to her*)
Ana <u>le</u> presta la falda.

1. Mario presta dinero. (*to you,* pl.)

____

2. Ellos escriben mensajes electrónicos. (*to me*)

____

3. Juana vende una cartera. (*to him*)

____

4. La vendedora dice dónde comprar trajes de baño. (*to us*)

____

5. Lola da los calcetines. (*to you,* fam. sing.)

____

6. El vendedor ofrece un descuento. (*to them*)

____

7 Juanita va al almacén Fill in the blanks with words from the box. (9 x 2 pts. each = 18 pts.)

bolsa	**efectivo**	**número**	**rebaja**	**traje**
caras	**esta**	**ofrecer**	**tenis**	

VENDEDOR Buenas tardes.

JUANITA Hola, ¿me puede ayudar?

VENDEDOR Sí. ¿Qué le puedo (1) ____________________?

JUANITA Voy de vacaciones a la playa y necesito un par de sandalias. No pueden ser muy (2) ____________________ porque no tengo mucho dinero.

VENDEDOR Muy bien. Yo creo que usted necesita también unos zapatos de (3) ____________________. Son más cómodos y si paga en (4) ____________________ le hacemos una (5) ____________________.

JUANITA ¡Qué bien!

VENDEDOR ¿Qué (6) ____________________ calza?

JUANITA Calzo 7. También quiero comprar un (7) ____________________ de baño, unas gafas de sol y una (8) ____________________ anaranjada.

VENDEDOR Mire. Tenemos (9) ____________________ bolsa anaranjada y es muy elegante.

JUANITA Gracias por su ayuda, y por la rebaja.

8 Lectura Read the description of the store, then answer the questions. (6 x 3 pts. each = 18 pts.)

> El almacén Azul vende ropa casual de hombre y de mujer. Tiene una gran variedad (*variety*) de colores y tallas. Los bluejeans cuestan de $30 a $50. Las vendedoras están listas si los clientes necesitan ayuda (*help*). Estas muchachas estudian diseño (*design*) de modas. A mí me gusta mucho este almacén. Tiene muy buenos precios y una gran selección.

1. ¿Qué tipo de ropa vende el almacén Azul?
   a. ropa elegante b. ropa casual c. ropa deportiva
2. ¿De qué tiene una gran variedad el almacén?
   a. de colores y tallas b. de precios c. de bluejeans
3. ¿Cuánto cuestan los bluejeans en el almacén?
   a. de $30 a $40 b. de $20 a $50 c. de $30 a $50
4. Si los clientes necesitan ayuda, ¿cómo están las vendedoras?
   a. listas b. aburridas c. enamoradas
5. ¿Qué estudian las muchachas que trabajan en el almacén?
   a. contabilidad b. diseño de modas c. matemáticas
6. ¿Por qué le gusta este almacén a María?
   a. Los precios son fijos. b. Puede regatear. c. Tiene una gran selección.

Nombre ______________________ Fecha ______________________

TEST F

Lección 6

1 Escuchar Read the statements. Then listen to the store advertisement and indicate whether each statement is **cierto** or **falso**. (5 x 2 pts. each = 10 pts.)

	Cierto	**Falso**
1. El almacén está en el centro comercial San Juan.	______	______
2. La entrada está en la calle Constitución.	______	______
3. El almacén vende sólo ropa de hombre.	______	______
4. Tienen bluejeans.	______	______
5. Los precios del almacén son caros.	______	______

2 Juan y Lucy Match the sentences that form logical pairs. (5 x 2 pts. each = 10 pts.)

A	B
_____ 1. Juan y Lucy van a jugar fútbol.	a. Llevan pantalones cortos y zapatos de tenis.
_____ 2. Juan y Lucy van a nadar.	b. Llueve mucho.
_____ 3. Juan y Lucy compran pantalones cortos en la tienda.	c. Pagan con tarjeta de crédito.
_____ 4. Juan y Lucy van a esquiar.	d. Llevan trajes de baño.
_____ 5. Juan y Lucy compran unos impermeables.	e. Llevan suéteres y guantes.

3 Completar Fill in the blanks with the present tense form of **saber** or **conocer**.

1. Ana ________________________ hablar español y francés.
2. Ustedes no ________________________ a mi amigo Daniel.
3. Tú ________________________ jugar al tenis como un profesional.
4. Nosotros ________________________ el castillo del rey (*King*) Juan.
5. Los estudiantes ________________________ dónde está la biblioteca.

Tests

Nombre ______________________________ Fecha ____________________

4 ¿Qué pasó ayer? Fill in the blanks with the preterite form of the verbs. (5 x 2 pts. each = 10 pts.)

1. María ______________________ (comprar) tres trajes de baño ayer.
2. Ustedes ______________________ (ofrecer) un descuento a los clientes la semana pasada.
3. Yo ______________________ (buscar) zapatos de tenis ayer.
4. Nosotros ______________________ (pagar) con tarjeta de crédito en el almacén.
5. Tú ______________________ (empezar) a leer esta novela.

5 Escoger Match the pictures and descriptions. (6 x 2 pts. each = 12 pts.)

1. ______________

2. ______________

3. ______________

4. ______________

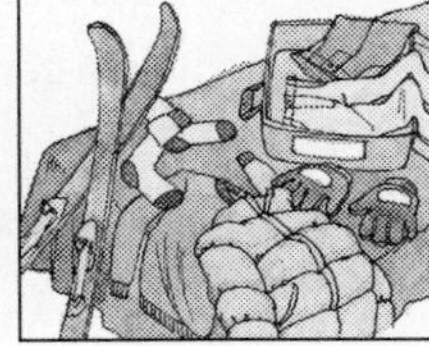

5. ______________

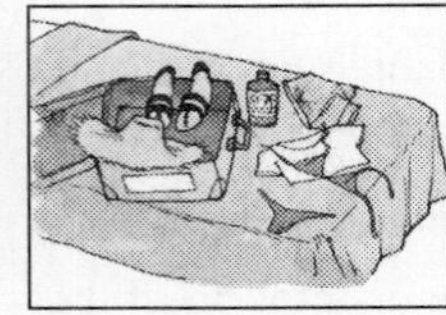

6. ______________

a. Voy a esquiar este fin de semana.
b. Hay un sombrero y un traje de baño.
c. Julia paga por el vestido.
d. María paga en efectivo en la caja.
e. En la tienda hay ropa de hombre y de mujer.
f. El dependiente ayuda a dos personas.

6 Escribir Rewrite the sentences to include indirect object pronouns. Follow the model. (6 x 2 pts. each = 12 pts.)

modelo

Ana presta la falda. (*to her*)
Ana le presta la falda.

1. Luis paga con tarjeta de crédito. (*to them*)

   ____

2. Mariana trae la ropa. (*to you,* pl.)

   ____

3. Félix escribe un mensaje electrónico. (*to me*)

   ____

4. La vendedora muestra los trajes de baño. (*to you,* fam. sing.)

   ____

5. Elisabeth compra calcetines. (*to him*)

   ____

6. Los padres dan dinero. (*to us*)

   ____

Tests

Nombre ______________________________ Fecha ______________________

7 Juanita va de compras Fill in the blanks with words from the box. (9 x 2 pts. each = 18 pts.)

baratas	**estos**	**servirle**
calza	**gafas**	**vestido**
efectivo	**rebaja**	**zapatos**

VENDEDOR Buenas tardes

JUANITA Hola, ¿me puede ayudar?

VENDEDOR Sí. ¿En qué puedo (1) ______________________?

JUANITA Voy de vacaciones a la playa y necesito un par de sandalias (2) ______________________ porque no tengo mucho dinero.

VENDEDOR Muy bien. Yo creo que usted necesita también unos (3) ______________________ de tenis. Son más cómodos y si paga en (4) ______________________ le hacemos una (5) ______________________.

JUANITA ¡Qué bien!

VENDEDOR ¿Qué número (6) ______________________?

JUANITA Calzo 7. También quiero comprar unas (7) ______________________ de sol, una falda y un (8) ______________________ morado.

VENDEDOR Mire. Tenemos (9) ______________________ vestidos y son muy elegantes.

JUANITA Gracias por su ayuda, y por la rebaja.

8 Lectura Read the description of a store at a mall, then answer the questions. (6 x 3 pts. each = 18 pts.)

> La semana pasada abrió las puertas la tienda de ropa deportiva El campeón. Esta tienda está en el tercer piso del centro comercial. La tienda tiene una gran variedad de zapatos de tenis, pantalones cortos, camisetas y trajes de baño de todos los colores. Muchas personas buscaron los zapatos de tenis Mercurio en todas las tiendas deportivas de la ciudad y sólo los encontraron en ésta. Esos zapatos son especiales para correr largas distancias. A los primeros cien clientes les dieron una gran rebaja.

1. ¿Cuándo abrió la tienda de ropa deportiva El campeón?
   a. ayer b. la semana pasada c. el mes pasado
2. ¿Dónde está la tienda?
   a. en el primer piso b. en el segundo piso c. en el tercer piso
3. ¿Qué puedes encontrar en El Campeón?
   a. trajes de baño b. suéters c. sombreros
4. ¿Qué buscaron muchas personas?
   a. zapatos de tenis b. pantalones cortos c. calcetines deportivos
5. ¿Para qué son especiales esos zapatos?
   a. para caminar en la playa b. para correr largas distancias c. para ir de excursión
6. ¿Qué les dieron a los primeros clientes?
   a. una camiseta b. una gran rebaja c. tres pares de zapatos

Nombre ______________________ Fecha ______________________

TEST A

Lección 7

1 Escuchar Read these statements and listen as Vicente talks about his plans for tomorrow. Then mark each statement as **cierto** or **falso**. (5 x 2 pts. each = 10 pts.)

	Cierto	Falso
1. Va a estar siete días en Perú.	______	______
2. Le molesta viajar.	______	______
3. Se preocupa por llevar las cosas que necesita.	______	______
4. Se despierta a las ocho.	______	______
5. Nunca come antes de un viaje.	______	______

2 Buenos días Describe what Ángel is doing, using at least five reflexive verbs. (5 x 3 pts. each = 15 pts.)

____

____

____

____

____

____

____

3 ¿Qué le gusta? Write a paragraph about someone you know well. Describe that person's habits, likes, and dislikes, using at least four words or expressions from each box. (6 pts. for vocabulary + 6 pts. for grammar + 3 pts. for style and creativity = 15 pts.)

aburrir	**importar**	**molestar**	**preocuparse**
fascinar	**interesar**	**ponerse**	**sentirse**

algunos días	**en casa**	**nervioso/a**	**por la noche**
contento/a	**mucho**	**nunca**	**siempre**

____

____

____

____

____

____

Tests

Nombre ______________________ Fecha ______________________

4 Te espero Read the conversation and fill in the blanks with one of the words in parentheses. (5 x 2 pts. each = 10 pts.)

INÉS Tengo hambre.

ANDY Lo siento. No hay (1) ________________ (nada, ningún) para comer. Luego podemos comer (2) ________________ (nunca, algo) en el restaurante al lado del Museo de Arte Contemporáneo.

INÉS Está bien. Oye, tengo que llamar a mi compañero de clase para preguntarle cuándo es el próximo examen. ¿Puedo usar el teléfono?

ANDY Lo siento. Mi hermano (3) ________________ (siempre, nunca) está hablando por teléfono con su novia. Acaba de llamarla y todavía están hablando. Puedes usarlo más tarde. ¿Puedes esperar aquí? Voy a quitarme esta camisa. Voy a ver si me puedo poner (4) ________________ (alguna, ninguna) que sea (*that is*) más elegante.

INÉS Bueno, puedo esperar. ¿Tienes algún libro divertido?

ANDY No, lo siento, no tengo (5) ________________ (nadie, ninguno). Pero estoy listo en cinco minutos.

INÉS Bueno, aquí te espero.

5 Preguntas Answer these questions with complete sentences, using the preterite of **ser** and **ir**. (5 x 3 pts. each = 15 pts.)

1. ¿Fuiste al cine el mes pasado? ¿Con quién fuiste? ________________
2. ¿Cuál fue tu clase favorita el semestre pasado? ________________
3. ¿Cómo fueron tus vacaciones de invierno? ________________
4. ¿Adónde fuiste ayer después de las clases? ________________
5. ¿Fuiste de compras la semana pasada? ¿Qué compraste? ________________

Nombre ____________________ Fecha ____________________

6 Lectura Read this excerpt of an interview with actor Fernando León and answer the questions with complete sentences. (5 x 3 pts. each = 15 pts.)

PERIODISTA Bienvenido.

FERNANDO LEÓN Muchas gracias por invitarme. Me encanta su columna de los domingos.

PERIODISTA Gracias. A todos nos interesa aprender un poco más de usted. ¿Le gusta su estilo de vida[1]?

FERNANDO LEÓN No siempre. Muchas veces me molesta tener que viajar. Bueno, y también tengo que levantarme muchas veces a las cuatro o cinco de la mañana para llegar al plató[2]. Ahora estoy trabajando en una nueva película: ***Las bodas[3] de Drácula***. Me visto en unos diez minutos, y luego tienen que maquillarme y peinarme. Trabajamos dieciocho horas seis días por semana. Cuando llego a casa, no tengo ganas de nada. Sólo quiero quitarme la ropa, ponerme el pijama[4] y acostarme.

PERIODISTA Y su novia, ¿qué piensa de su rutina?

FERNANDO LEÓN A mi novia tampoco le gusta mucho. Mi rutina no le gusta a nadie. Ni a mi familia, ni a mis amigos, ni a mi novia. Ella trabaja en la universidad y tiene un horario muy bueno. Pienso que en el futuro voy a tener que trabajar en otra profesión.

[1]*lifestyle* [2]*set* [3]*weddings* [4]*pajamas*

1. ¿Le interesa el trabajo del periodista a Fernando León? ____________________

____

2. ¿Le gusta levantarse temprano? ____________________

____

3. ¿Cuánto tiempo necesita para ponerse la ropa? ____________________

____

4. ¿Qué hace después de llegar a casa? ____________________

____

5. ¿A quién le gusta la rutina de Fernando León? ____________________

____

7 Tu rutina Write a paragraph about your daily routine. Use sequencing expressions. (8 pts. for vocabulary + 8 pts. for grammar + 4 pts. for style and creativity = 20 pts.)

____

____

____

____

____

____

Tests

Nombre ______________________ Fecha ______________________

TEST B Lección 7

1 Escuchar Read these statements and listen as Iván talks about his plans for tomorrow. Then mark each statement as **cierto** or **falso**. (5 x 2 pts. each = 10 pts.)

	Cierto	Falso
1. Iván va a estar tres semanas en Panamá.	______	______
2. A Iván le encantan los viajes largos.	______	______
3. Jamás se duerme en el avión.	______	______
4. Todavía necesita comprar regalos para sus amigos.	______	______
5. Le preocupa no tener tiempo para preparar todo.	______	______

2 ¡Buenos días! ¡Buenas noches! Look at the pictures and use your imagination to write what Alicia and Jennifer do every morning and every night. Use at least five reflexive verbs. (5 x 3 pts. each = 15 pts.)

____

____

____

____

____

____

3 ¿Qué le gusta? Write a paragraph about your best friend. Describe that person's habits, likes, and dislikes, using at least four words or expressions from each box. (6 pts. for vocabulary + 6 pts. for grammar + 3 pts. for style and creativity = 15 pts.)

bañarse	**encantar**	**faltar**	**lavarse**
despertarse	**enojar**	**fascinar**	**quedar**

algunas mañanas	**en clase**	**por la noche**	**siempre**
dormido/a	**jamás**	**preocupado/a**	**tampoco**

____

____

____

____

____

Tests

Nombre ______________________ Fecha ______________________

4 Carla y Ángel Read the conversation and fill in the blanks with one of the words in parentheses. (5 x 2 pts. each = 10 pts.)

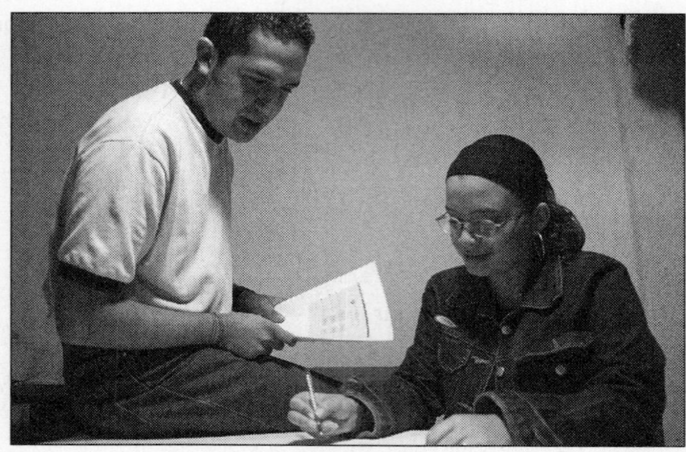

CARLA Tengo sed.

ÁNGEL Lo siento. No hay (1) ______________________ (nada, ningún) para beber. Necesito ir al supermercado. Luego podemos comprar (2) ______________________ (nunca, algo) en la tienda.

CARLA Está bien. ¿Puedo usar el baño?

ÁNGEL Creo que mi hermano está bañándose. (3) ______________________ (siempre, nunca) se baña por las tardes y (4) ______________________ (algunos, ningunos) días está una hora en el cuarto de baño.

CARLA Bueno, puedo esperar.

ÁNGEL Mi hermano no tiene (5) ______________________ (algún, ningún) respeto. Me molesta mucho.

CARLA No te preocupes. No hay ningún problema. Seguimos estudiando. ¡Tenemos mucho que hacer!

5 Preguntas Answer these questions with complete sentences, using the preterite of **ser** and **ir**. (5 x 3 pts. each = 15 pts.)

1. ¿Cuál fue tu película favorita del año pasado? ______________________
2. ¿Cómo fueron tus clases el semestre pasado? ______________________
3. ¿Fuiste a algún museo el mes pasado? ¿A qué museo y con quién? ______________________
4. ¿Adónde fuiste el fin de semana pasado? ______________________
5. ¿Cómo fueron tus últimas (*last*) vacaciones de verano? ______________________

Tests

Nombre ____________________ Fecha ____________________

6 Lectura Read this excerpt of an interview with Arturo Brito Ríos, a famous journalist, and then answer the questions with complete sentences. (5 x 3 pts. each = 15 pts.)

PRESENTADORA Bienvenido.

ARTURO Muchas gracias por invitarme a esta entrevista[1].

PRESENTADORA De nada. A todos nos interesa aprender un poco más sobre usted. ¿Le gusta su estilo de vida[2]?

ARTURO No siempre me gusta. Muchas veces me molesta tener que viajar. Bueno, y también tengo que levantarme muchas veces a las tres o cuatro de la mañana para llegar al aeropuerto. Algunos días me ducho en dos minutos, me visto, y muchas veces no tengo tiempo de afeitarme. Muchos días trabajo dieciocho horas y cuando llego a casa, no tengo ganas de nada. Sólo quiero quitarme la ropa, ponerme el pijama[3] y acostarme.

PRESENTADORA Y su esposa, ¿qué piensa de su rutina?

ARTURO A mi esposa tampoco le gusta mucho. La verdad es que mi rutina no le gusta a nadie. Ni a mis amigos, ni a mis hijos, ni a mi esposa. Ella es profesora y tiene un horario muy bueno. Ahora estoy trabajando también en mi primera novela, pero me falta tiempo para escribir. Pienso que en el futuro voy a tener que trabajar en otra área. Me fascina escribir novelas y puedo trabajar en casa y estar cerca de mi familia.

[1]*interview* [2]*lifestyle* [3]*pajamas*

1. ¿Qué piensa Arturo Brito Ríos de su estilo de vida? ____________________

2. ¿Qué hace al llegar a casa después de un día largo? ____________________

3. ¿Les gusta a los hijos de Arturo Brito Ríos la rutina de su padre? ____________________

4. ¿Qué le gusta a Arturo Brito Ríos? ____________________

5. ¿Por qué quiere cambiar de (*to change*) trabajo? ____________________

7 La rutina de tu amigo/a Write a paragraph about your best friend's daily routine. Use sequencing expressions. (8 pts. for vocabulary + 8 pts. for grammar + 4 pts. for style and creativity = 20 pts.)

____

Tests

TEST C Lección 7

1 Escuchar You will hear five personal questions. Answer them with Spanish sentences. (5 x 1 pt. each = 5 pts.)

1. ______
2. ______
3. ______
4. ______
5. ______

2 Buenos días Describe what Lupe is doing, using at least five reflexive verbs. (5 x 2 pts. each = 10 pts.)

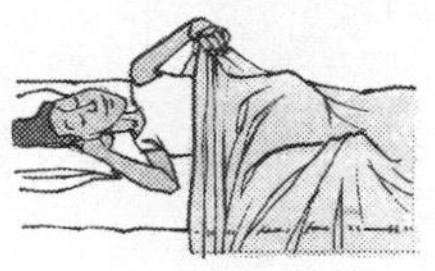    

3 ¿Qué te gusta? Describe your habits, likes, and dislikes, using at least four words or expressions from each box. (4 pts. for vocabulary + 4 pts. for grammar + 2 pts. for style and creativity = 10 pts.)

acordarse	**encantar**	**interesar**	**ponerse**
acostarse	**enojarse**	**llamarse**	**sentirse**

contento/a	**jamás**	**nervioso/a**	**siempre**
en clase	**mucho**	**por la mañana**	**también**

Tests

4 Lectura Read this excerpt of a conversation between two friends. Then, answer the questions with complete sentences. (5 x 2 pts. each = 10 pts.)

ANA Pame, ¡hola! Hace mucho[1] que no te veo.

PAMELA ¡Hola! Sí, es que mi hermana y yo hicimos un viaje maravilloso de dos meses por Latinoamérica.

ANA ¡Qué interesante! Y ¿a qué países fueron?

PAMELA Pues mira, empezamos en Ecuador; allí visitamos Quito, Ibarra y, por supuesto[2], fuimos a las islas Galápagos y a varias ciudades cerca de los Andes. Después fuimos a México. Allí, primero paseamos juntas[3] por la Ciudad de México, luego yo fui a Acapulco, Mérida y Cancún y mi hermana fue a Monterrey, Guadalajara y Puebla.

ANA ¿Fueron a otros lugares?

PAMELA Sí, por último fuimos a Puerto Rico, con sus playas espectaculares y tantos sitios[4] históricos increíbles.

ANA ¿Qué lugar les gustó más?

PAMELA Mmm, bueno, a mí me encantó San Juan, Puerto Rico. Y a mi hermana... le fascinaron las islas Galápagos en Ecuador.

[1] *It's been a while* [2] *of course* [3] *together* [4] *so many sites*

1. ¿Adónde fueron Pamela y su hermana de vacaciones? ________________
2. ¿Adónde fueron primero? ________________
3. En México, ¿a qué ciudades fue sola (*by herself*) Pamela? ¿Y su hermana? ________________
4. ¿A qué lugares fueron antes de terminar su viaje? ________________
5. ¿Cuál fue el lugar favorito de Pamela? ¿Y el de su hermana? ________________

5 Su rutina Write a paragraph about the daily routine of someone you know. Use sequencing expressions. (6 pts. for vocabulary + 6 pts. for grammar + 3 pts. for style and creativity = 15 pts.)

____

Nombre ______________________ Fecha ______________________

TEST D

Lección 7

1 Escuchar You will hear five personal questions. Answer them with Spanish sentences. (5 x 1 pt. each = 5 pts.)

1. ______________________
2. ______________________
3. ______________________
4. ______________________
5. ______________________

2 ¡Buenos días! ¡Buenas noches! Look at the pictures and use your imagination to describe what Tomás and Enrique do every morning and every night. Use at least five reflexive verbs. (5 x 2 pts. each = 10 pts.)

____

3 ¿Cómo es? Describe your best friend's habits, likes, and dislikes, using at least four words or expressions from each box. (4 pts. for vocabulary + 4 pts. for grammar + 2 pts. for style and creativity = 10 pts.)

aburrir	**encantar**	**levantarse**
acostarse	**faltar**	**preocuparse**
despedirse	**fascinar**	

antes	**los fines de semana**	**por la noche**
dormido/a		**siempre**
en casa	**ni... ni**	**tranquilo/a**

____

Tests

Nombre ______________________ Fecha ______________________

4 Lectura Read this excerpt of a conversation between two friends. Then, answer the questions with complete sentences. (5 x 2 pts. each = 10 pts.)

JOSELO Enrique, ¡hola! Hace mucho[1] que no te veo.

ENRIQUE ¡Hola! Sí, es que mi hermano y yo hicimos un viaje maravilloso de dos meses por España y Latinoamérica.

JOSELO ¡Qué interesante! Y ¿a qué países fueron?

ENRIQUE Pues mira, primero fuimos a España. Allí, primero paseamos juntos[2] por Madrid, luego yo fui a Salamanca, Zaragoza y Barcelona y mi hermano fue a Ibiza, Mallorca y Menorca. Después fuimos a Puerto Rico, donde visitamos San Juan, Ponce, Arecibo y la isla de Vieques.

JOSELO ¿Fueron a otros países?

ENRIQUE Sí, por último fuimos a Perú, con sus ciudades incas espectaculares en los Andes y tantas[3] historias increíbles.

JOSELO ¿Y qué lugar les gustó más?

ENRIQUE Mmm, bueno, a mí me encantó Machu Picchu en los Andes peruanos. Y a mi hermano... le fascinó la isla de Vieques, en Puerto Rico.

[1] *It's been a while* [2] *together* [3] *so many*

1. ¿Adónde fueron Enrique y su hermano de vacaciones? ______________________

2. En España, ¿a qué lugares fue solo (*by himself*) Enrique? ¿Y su hermano? ______________________

3. ¿Adónde fueron en Puerto Rico? ______________________

4. ¿A qué país fueron antes de terminar su viaje? ______________________

5. ¿Cuál fue el lugar favorito de Enrique? ¿Y el de su hermano? ______________________

5 Su rutina Write a paragraph where you imagine the daily routine of your favorite actor or actress. Use sequencing expressions. (6 pts. for vocabulary + 6 pts. for grammar + 3 pts. for style and creativity = 15 pts.)

Nombre ______________________ Fecha ______________________

TEST E Lección 7

1 Escuchar Read the questions. Then listen to Ana's description of the Hernández dormitory and select the appropriate answers. (5 x 2 pts. each = 10 pts.)

1. ¿Qué oyen los estudiantes de la residencia todas las mañanas?
   a. el despertador b. a los compañeros c. los platos de la cafetería
2. ¿Cuánto tiempo tienen los estudiantes para desayunar?
   a. una hora y media b. una hora c. media hora
3. ¿Qué les molesta a algunos de los estudiantes?
   a. comer tarde b. descansar c. despertarse temprano
4. ¿Qué les gusta a algunos de los estudiantes?
   a. volver a la cama b. llegar temprano a las clases c. peinarse y maquillarse
5. ¿Qué prefiere hacer Ana?
   a. levantarse temprano b. dormir c. lavarse la cara

2 Emparejar Match the pictures and descriptions. (5 x 2 pts. each = 10 pts.)

1. __________

2. __________

3. __________

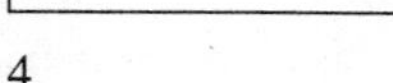

4. __________

5. __________

a. Sofía se cepilla los dientes después de la comida.
b. Francisco canta en la ducha.
c. Mi hermano se afeita todos los días.
d. Sofía se maquilla por la mañana.
e. El chico se cepilla el pelo dos veces al día.

3 Verbos Complete the chart with the appropriate reflexive verb forms. (5 x 2 pts. each = 10 pts.)

infinitivo	tú	ella	nosotros
probarse			(1)
irse		(2)	
secarse		(3)	
sentirse	(4)		(5)

4 Escoger Select the appropriate indefinite or negative words. (5 x 2 pts. each = 10 pts.)

1. En la playa, siempre hay ______________________ que hacer.
   a. algún b. nada c. algo
2. Hoy ______________________ va a ir a la escuela porque hay mucha nieve.
   a. nadie b. jamás c. siempre
3. Alicia va a escoger (*choose*) ______________________ de estos colores.
   a. nunca b. alguno c. ninguno
4. El martes no va a llover y el miércoles ______________________.
   a. jamás b. nunca c. tampoco
5. ¿______________________ puede ayudarte?
   a. Alguien b. Ningún c. Algún

5 *¿Ir* o *ser*? Fill in the blanks with the preterite form of **ser** or **ir**. Then indicate whether the infinitive is **ser** or **ir**. (6 x 2 pts. each = 12 pts.)

	ser	**ir**
1. Ricardo y yo ______________________ al museo por la mañana.	______	______
2. Los papás de María ______________________ muy generosos.	______	______
3. La profesora de historia ______________________ a una reunión.	______	______
4. Esta tarde tú ______________________ a probarte las camisas.	______	______
5. Ayer por la mañana yo ______________________ a desayunar con mis primos.	______	______
6. Ustedes no ______________________ al cine el lunes por la noche.	______	______

6 La rutina de Perla Fill in the blanks with words from the box. (9 x 2 pts. each = 18 pts.)

se cambia	**despertador**	**se maquilla**	**nada**	**se sienta**
se cepilla	**entonces**	**le molesta**	**pantuflas**	

El (1) ______________________ de Perla suena (*rings*) a las cinco de la mañana. Perla se pone las (2) ______________________ y entra al baño a ducharse. Luego se seca, (3) ______________________ los dientes y (4) ______________________ en la cama para cepillarse el pelo. A Perla (5) ______________________ no saber qué ponerse. (6) ____________________ de ropa cada dos minutos, pero (7) ____________________ le gusta. (8) ______________________ mira el reloj y decide ponerse o el vestido azul o el traje gris. Cuando está vestida (9) ____________________ la cara y sale para la escuela.

Nombre ______________________ Fecha ______________________

7 Completar Fill in the blanks with the present tense form of the verbs. (6 x 2 pts. each = 12 pts.)

modelo

A mí **me gusta** (gustar) bañarme.

1. A Marisa ______________________ (aburrir) las matemáticas.
2. A Juan y a Bella ______________________ (encantar) ir al cine.
3. A mí no ______________________ (importar) si llueve esta noche.
4. ¿A ti ______________________ (gustar) los museos?
5. A ellos ______________________ (faltar) diez dólares para comprar los boletos.
6. A Nora y a mí ______________________ (molestar) la música muy alta (*loud*).

8 Lectura Read the note from a travel agent to her clients, then answer the questions. (6 x 3 pts. each = 18 pts.)

> Sres. Valdivia:
>
> Por la mañana van a llegar al hotel La Palmera. Este elegante hotel les va a fascinar. Yo me quedé allí cuando fui a Arequipa el año pasado. Todas las habitaciones tienen ventanas con vista (*view*) al volcán (*volcano*) El Misti. Los cuartos de baño son muy grandes, con ducha, dos lavabos y una mesa con espejo. Por la tarde, pueden comer o en el restaurante Los Sabores o en el café Vistahermosa. También, si les interesa la historia, pueden visitar la Casa del Moral. A las ocho de la noche, Francisco Ramírez va a encontrarse (*meet*) con ustedes para llevarlos a cenar a un restaurante en la Plaza de Armas. Más tarde les voy a dar el itinerario (*itinerary*) para los otros días de su viaje.
>
> Hasta pronto,
>
> Sofía Enríquez
>
> Agente de viajes

1. ¿Adónde van los señores Valdivia?
   a. a Iquitos b. a Arequipa c. a Lima
2. ¿Por qué Sofía conoce Arequipa?
   a. Porque ella fue allí. b. Porque ella vive allí. c. Porque sus padres viven allí.
3. ¿Qué tienen todas las habitaciones?
   a. ventanas con vistas al volcán b. espejos grandes c. sillas cómodas
4. ¿Dónde pueden comer?
   a. en la Casa del Moral b. en El Misti c. en Los Sabores
5. ¿Adónde pueden ir si les interesa la historia?
   a. a La Palmera b. a la Casa del Moral c. a Vistahermosa
6. ¿Qué va a hacer Francisco Ramírez?
   a. mostrarles el volcán b. llevarlos a cenar c. darles el itinerario

Tests

Nombre ______________________ Fecha ______________________

TEST F Lección 7

1 Escuchar Read the questions. Then listen to Javier's description of the González dormitory and select the appropriate answers. (5 x 2 pts. each = 10 pts.)

1. ¿Qué oyen los estudiantes de la residencia todas las mañanas?
   a. el despertador   b. los platos de la cafetería   c. a la gente de la calle
2. ¿Cuánto tiempo tienen los estudiantes para desayunar?
   a. una hora y media   b. una hora   c. media hora
3. ¿Qué les gusta a algunos de los estudiantes?
   a. volver a la cama   b. llegar temprano a las clases   c. peinarse y maquillarse
4. ¿Qué les molesta a algunos de los estudiantes?
   a. comer tarde   b. descansar   c. despertarse temprano
5. ¿Qué prefiere hacer Javier?
   a. dormir   b. afeitarse   c. levantarse temprano

2 Emparejar Match the pictures and descriptions. (5 x 2 pts. each = 10 pts.)

1. ______________________

2. ______________________

3. ______________________

4. ______________________

5. ______________________

a. Leticia se cepilla los dientes.
b. Luis se afeita todas las mañanas.
c. Mario se lava la cara.
d. Ella se maquilla.
e. Olivia se ducha.

3 Verbos Complete the chart with the appropriate reflexive verb forms. (5 x 2 pts. each = 10 pts.)

infinitivo	tú	él	nosotros
irse	(1)		(2)
cepillarse		(3)	
lavarse		(4)	
quedarse			(5)

Nombre ______________________ Fecha ______________________

4 Escoger Select the appropriate indefinite or negative words. (5 x 2 pts. each = 10 pts.)

1. María Elena ______________________ estudia mucho para los exámenes.
   a. nada b. siempre c. ningún
2. José y Leticia ______________________ compran este champú.
   a. nunca b. nadie c. alguna
3. Yo ______________________ tengo un pantalón azul.
   a. nada b. alguno c. también
4. No sé si ______________________ vio ese avión.
   a. alguien b. tampoco c. nunca
5. ______________________ Juana ______________________ Julia van a ir a la fiesta (*party*).
   a. O, y b. Ni, y c. Ni, ni

5 *¿Ir* o *ser*? Fill in the blanks with the preterite form of **ser** or **ir**. Then indicate whether the infinitive is **ser** or **ir**. (6 x 2 pts. each = 12 pts.)

	ser	ir
1. Alexa y tú ______________________ de vacaciones a la playa.	______	______
2. Nosotros ______________________ muy buenos estudiantes.	______	______
3. Tú ______________________ a Perú el verano pasado.	______	______
4. Los estudiantes ______________________ a la biblioteca por la tarde.	______	______
5. Gerardo ______________________ muy simpático el sábado por la noche.	______	______
6. Yo ______________________ muy feliz ese año.	______	______

6 La rutina de Josefina Fill in the blanks with words from the box. (9 x 2 pts. each = 18 pts.)

baño	**durante**	**se maquilla**	**nunca**	**toalla**
champú	**le encanta**	**le molesta**	**o**	

Josefina no tiene clases (1) ______________________ la mañana.
(2) ______________________ se levanta temprano. Va al cuarto de
(3) ______________________ y lleva el (4) ______________________, el jabón y la
(5) ______________________. No los deja (*leave*) allí porque a su hermano menor
(6) ______________________ el champú que ella usa. Josefina almuerza a mediodía y por
la tarde se viste, se peina y (7) ______________________. Para ir a la escuela, o va en autobús
(8) ______________________ su hermano la lleva. A él sólo
(9) ______________________ llevarla cuando llueve.

Tests

7 Completar Fill in the blanks with the present tense form of the verbs. (6 x 2 pts. each = 12 pts.)

modelo

A mí **me gusta** (gustar) bañarme.

1. A mis amigos y a mí ____________________ (encantar) los animales.
2. A mis papás ____________________ (molestar) el ruido (*noise*) de la fiesta (*party*).
3. Ese pantalón no ____________________ (quedar) bien a Luisa.
4. A mí sólo ____________________ (faltar) tres páginas para terminar el libro.
5. Tú ____________________ (aburrir) cuando estás solo.
6. A ustedes ____________________ (interesar) la clase de ciencias.

8 Lectura Read the note from a travel agent to his clients, then answer the questions. (6 x 3 pts. each = 18 pts.)

> Sres. Forero:
>
> Al mediodía van a llegar al hotel Dorado. Este hotel les va a encantar. Yo me quedé allí cuando fui a Iquitos el mes pasado. Su habitación tiene ventanas con vista (*view*) al río Amazonas (*Amazon River*). Los cuartos de baño no son muy grandes, pero son cómodos. Tienen ducha, un lavabo y un espejo grande. Por la tarde, pueden comer o en el restaurante El Dorado o en el café Recuerdos, que está cerca del hotel. También, si les interesa la historia, pueden visitar el Museo Amazónico. A las ocho de la noche, Diego Gutiérrez va a encontrarse (*meet*) con ustedes para llevarlos a cenar a un restaurante en la Plaza de Armas. Luego les voy a dar el itinerario (*itinerary*) para los otros días de su viaje.
>
> Hasta pronto,
> Manuel Peña
> Agente de viajes

1. ¿Adónde van los señores Forero?
   a. a Iquitos   b. a Arequipa   c. a Lima
2. ¿Por qué Manuel conoce Iquitos?
   a. Porque él vive allí.   b. Porque sus padres viven allí.   c. Porque él fue allí.
3. ¿Qué tiene la habitación de los señores Forero?
   a. espejos grandes   b. vistas al río   c. sillas cómodas
4. ¿Dónde pueden comer?
   a. en el hotel   b. en el café Recuerdos   c. en el Museo Amazónico
5. ¿Qué va a hacer Diego Gutiérrez?
   a. llevarlos a cenar   b. mostrarles el río   c. darles el itinerario
6. ¿Dónde van a cenar?
   a. en el restaurante El Dorado   b. en el café Recuerdos   c. en la Plaza de Armas

Nombre ______________________ Fecha ______________________

TEST A

Lección 8

1 Escuchar Read these questions and listen to what the waiter is saying about the menu. Then, choose the correct option. (5 x 2 pts. each = 10 pts.)

1. ¿Qué sopas sirve el restaurante?
   a. salmón, espárragos y champiñones b. salmón, espárragos y camarones c. pollo, espárragos y champiñones
2. ¿Cón qué se sirve el bistec?
   a. con verduras b. con arroz c. con queso
3. ¿Qué recomienda el camarero?
   a. carne de res b. chuleta de cerdo c. arroz con pollo
4. ¿Cuál es el plato del día?
   a. pollo asado b. pavo asado c. marisco asado
5. ¿Qué bebida es la especialidad del restaurante?
   a. té helado b. jugos naturales c. vinos

2 Mi comida favorita Using words from the box, write a paragraph about the foods you like and don't like, when and where you eat them, whether you frequently order those foods, etc. (6 pts. for vocabulary + 6 pts. for grammar + 3 pts. for style and creativity = 15 pts.)

buenísimo	más	el mejor	menos	que	riquísima	tan	tanto

____

____

____

____

____

____

3 El mejor Write sentences about the following items, using superlatives. (5 x 2 pts. each = 10 pts.)

1. El plato del día
   ____
2. Esta sopa
   ____
3. El jugo de naranja
   ____
4. El pollo asado
   ____
5. El café de Colombia
   ____

Tests

Nombre ______________________ Fecha ______________________

4 ¿Qué desea? Fill in the blanks in the conversation with double object pronouns. (5 x 2 pts. each = 10 pts.)

CAMARERO Buenos días.

CLIENTE Buenos días. ¿Puede decirme el menú del día?

CAMARERO (1) ________________ digo ahora mismo. Para empezar, tenemos unos entremeses deliciosos.

CLIENTE ¿(2) ________________ recomienda?

CAMARERO (3) ________________ recomiendo especialmente. También le recomiendo las chuletas de cerdo. Son buenísimas. Si quiere, (4) ________________ sirvo después de los entremeses.

CLIENTE Sí, gracias. Ah, y, por favor, ¿me puede traer pan?

CAMARERO (5) ________________ traigo ahora mismo.

5 Una cita (*date*) Fill in the blanks in this paragraph with the preterite form of the stem-changing verbs in parentheses. (8 x 1 pt. each = 8 pts.)

Paula (1) ________________ (vestirse) con prisa. Nerviosa por su cita con Federico, salió de su casa puntualmente. Ellos fueron a un restaurante muy romántico. Federico (2) ________________ (pedir) sopa y bistec, pero Paula (3) ________________ (preferir) comer una ensalada y atún. La camarera les (4) ________________ (servir) la comida muy tarde. Pero ellos no se enojaron, porque estuvieron hablando todo el tiempo. Después, fueron a pasear y (5 ________________ (seguir) hablando de muchas cosas. Los dos (6) ________________ (sentirse) muy bien. Ellos (7) ________________ (despedirse) a las doce de la noche, pero (8) ________________ (volver) a verse pronto.

6 Preguntas Answer these questions with complete sentences. (5 x 3 pts. each = 15 pts.)

1. ¿Qué comiste ayer en el desayuno? ________________
2. Cuando lo necesitas, ¿a quién le pides dinero? ________________
3. ¿Qué cenaste ayer? ________________
4. ¿A qué hora te dormiste ayer? ________________
5. ¿Quién duerme más horas que tú? ________________

Tests

7 Lectura Read this article and answer the questions. (5 x 2 pts. each = 10 pts.)

A muchos jóvenes les interesa estar bien, practicar deportes y estar delgados. Sin embargo[1], ellos normalmente no se preocupan mucho por la comida que ofrecen las cafeterías de sus universidades. Para saber más sobre los hábitos alimenticios de los estudiantes universitarios, veinte universidades del país hicieron una encuesta[2].

Los resultados muestran que de almuerzo muchos estudiantes comen un sándwich y toman un refresco. También comen mucho entre comidas. Consumen pocas verduras, mucha carne y muchos refrescos. Ellos saben que comer verduras y pescados es bueno, pero no lo hacen.

La encuesta también dice que el 60 por ciento de los estudiantes piensan que la comida en los campus universitarios es muy buena, y un 77 por ciento dice que en las cafeterías encuentran todos los tipos de comida que les gustan. Este estudio, sin embargo, muestra que las universidades tienen que enseñar a sus estudiantes a darle más importancia a una buena nutrición en el almuerzo.

[1]*However* [2]*did a survey*

1. ¿Para qué se hizo este estudio? ______________________________
____
2. ¿Qué les interesa a los estudiantes? ______________________________
____
3. ¿Les gusta a los estudiantes el tipo de comida que les dan en las universidades? ______________
____
4. ¿Qué comen y qué toman los estudiantes al mediodía? ______________________________
____
5. ¿Son buenos los hábitos de los estudiantes? ______________________________
____

8 La cena Describe what happened at this dinner. Use the preterite and include direct and indirect object pronouns. (9 pts. for vocabulary + 9 pts. for grammar + 4 pts. for style and creativity = 22 pts.)

____
____
____
____
____
____
____

Tests

Nombre ______________________ Fecha ______________

TEST B

Lección 8

1 Escuchar Read these questions and listen to what the waiter is saying about the menu. Then choose the correct option. (5 x 2 pts. each = 10 pts.)

1. ¿Cuáles son los entremeses favoritos del camarero?
   a. espárragos y champiñones b. jamón y camarones c. jamón y champiñones
2. ¿Qué tipo de sopa sirven?
   a. sopa de marisco b. sopa de verduras c. sopa de pescado
3. ¿Qué carne recomienda el dueño del restaurante?
   a. carne de res b. chuleta de cerdo c. pollo
4. ¿Cuál es el plato del día?
   a. pollo asado b. pavo asado c. salmón con patatas fritas
5. ¿Qué bebida es la especialidad del restaurante?
   a. té helado b. jugos de frutas c. vinos

2 Nuestra comida favorita Using words from the box, write a paragraph about the foods you and your friends like and don't like, when and where you eat them, whether you frequently order those foods, etc. (6 pts. for vocabulary + 6 pts. for grammar + 3 pts. for style and creativity = 15 pts.)

como	**más de**	**menos... que**	**sabrosa**
delicioso	**la mejor**	**peor**	**tantos... como**

____

____

____

____

____

____

3 El mejor Write sentences about the following items, using superlatives. (5 x 2 pts. each = 10 pts.)

1. Este camarero
   ____
2. El pollo asado
   ____
3. Este restaurante
   ____
4. El café de Costa Rica
   ____
5. El desayuno
   ____

Tests

Nombre ______________________________ Fecha ______________________

4 ¿Qué desea? Fill in the blanks in the conversation with double object pronouns. (5 x 2 pts. each = 10 pts.)

CLIENTE Hola. ¿Puede decirme qué platos principales sirven hoy?

CAMARERO Hoy tenemos una carne excelente. Pero puede ver el menú. Ahora mismo (1) ______________________ traigo.

CLIENTE ¿Qué me recomienda usted?

CAMARERO El plato del día es muy bueno. Yo (2) ______________________ recomiendo. De primer plato hay sopa de mariscos; las sopas son la especialidad de la casa.

CLIENTE Gracias. Voy a empezar con la sopa. ¿(3) ______________________ puede traer ahora? Tengo muchísima hambre.

CAMARERO Ahora mismo (4) ______________________ traigo.

CLIENTE Me gusta mucho la carne de res, ¿(5) ______________________ puede servir con papas fritas?

CAMARERO Claro que sí.

5 Una ocasión especial Fill in the blanks in this paragraph with the preterite form of the stem-changing verbs in parentheses. (8 x 1 pt. each = 8 pts.)

Ayer mi familia y yo (1) ______________________ (vestirse) muy elegantes para una ocasión muy especial: el cumpleaños (*birthday*) de mi abuela. Ella (2) ______________________ (preferir) ir a un restaurante y después ir a ver una película. Mi hermano (3) ______________________ (conseguir) boletos (*tickets*) para las ocho de la noche. En el restaurante todos (nosotros) (4) ______________________ (pedir) el plato del día. La comida estuvo (*was*) riquísima, pero el camarero nos la (5) ______________________ (servir) muy tarde y nosotros no (6) ______________________ (empezar) a comer hasta las siete y media. Pero no nos enojamos, porque estuvimos (*we were*) hablando todo el tiempo. Nosotros (7) ______________________ (sentirse) muy bien hablando con mi abuela. Nosotros (8) ______________________ (volver) a casa a las doce de la noche.

6 Preguntas Answer the questions with complete sentences. (5 x 3 pts. each = 15 pts.)

1. ¿Qué almorzaste ayer? ____
2. ¿Quién te ayuda con la tarea? ____
3. ¿Cuál fue la clase más interesante que tomaste el año pasado? ______________________
4. ¿Cuántas horas dormiste ayer? ____
5. ¿Conoces a alguna persona famosa? ____

Tests

Nombre ______________________ Fecha ______________________

7 Lectura Read the letter from Clara to Eduardo and answer the questions. (5 x 2 pts. each = 10 pts.)

> Hola, Eduardo:
>
> ¡Qué bien me lo pasé el verano con mis papás en España! Visitamos, vimos, conocimos, conversamos, paseamos, tomamos cientos de fotos, pero sobre todo[1], ¡comimos! ¡Qué comida tan buena! Y lo más interesante es que, en un país tan pequeño, varía mucho de región a región. Por eso lo probamos todo.
>
> Comimos ensaladas, sopas, la famosa paella, todo tipo de pescados y mariscos..., y todo preparado de una manera muy simple, con ajo, perejil[2] y aceite de oliva[3]. Por eso todo tenía un sabor muy natural y auténtico. El aceite de oliva fue lo más nuevo e interesante. Los españoles lo usan para todo.
>
> ¿Y de postre? Los dulces son muy variados, muy ricos y no tan "dulces"; por eso, no tienes que preocuparte... comí mucho, sí, pero llevo la misma ropa de siempre, la que a ti te gusta.
>
> ¿Y las tapas? ¡Qué buena idea! Son pequeñísimos platos preparados con una gran variedad de ingredientes. Comer tapas es una excelente oportunidad para conocer gente y conversar. Este verano vamos tú y yo. A ti también te va a encantar.
>
> Clara

[1]*above all* [2]*parsley* [3]*olive oil*

1. ¿Por qué le escribe Clara esta carta a Eduardo? ______________________
2. ¿Qué es lo que más le gustó a Clara de su viaje a España? ______________________
3. Según Clara, ¿por qué la comida española es muy natural y auténtica? ______________________
4. ¿Qué piensa Clara de las tapas? ______________________
5. ¿Qué relación piensas que existe entre Clara y Eduardo y por qué lo piensas (*believe that*)? ______________________

8 En el restaurante Describe what happened at this dinner. Use the preterite and include direct and indirect object pronouns. (9 pts. for vocabulary + 9 pts. for grammar + 4 pts. for style and creativity = 22 pts.)

Tests

Nombre ______________________ Fecha ______________________

TEST C

Lección 8

1 Escuchar You will hear five personal questions. Answer them with Spanish sentences. (5 x 2 pts. each = 10 pts.)

1. ______________________
2. ______________________
3. ______________________
4. ______________________
5. ______________________

2 Buen provecho (*Bon appétit*) Write a paragraph about the foods you like and don't like, when and where you eat them, which restaurants you prefer, etc. Include at least six words from the box. (6 pts. for vocabulary + 6 pts. for grammar + 3 pts. for style and creativity = 15 pts.)

buenísimo	**más**	**menos**	**recomendar**	**tan**
escoger	**el mejor**	**el peor**	**riquísima**	**tanto**

____

____

____

____

____

____

____

____

____

____

Tests

4 Lectura Read this article and answer the questions. (5 x 2 pts. each = 10 pts.)

¿Qué comen los estudiantes?

Varias universidades hicieron una encuesta[1] para saber qué almuerzan los estudiantes universitarios. Los resultados muestran que existe una gran diferencia entre lo que comen los días que tienen que ir a clase y los fines de semana.

La encuesta muestra que, durante los días de clases, muchos estudiantes almuerzan caminando de un lugar a otro, en sólo quince minutos. No tienen suficiente tiempo para comer y con demasiada frecuencia comen lo mismo. En el almuerzo muchos estudiantes comen sándwiches y toman refrescos. Los días de clases también consumen muchos refrigerios[2] entre comidas.

Otro aspecto interesante es que muchos piensan que la comida de las cafeterías es buena para lo que necesitan. Pero en realidad las comidas de las cafeterías no son muy buenas. Por otra parte[3], los fines de semana, a los estudiantes les gusta probar comidas nuevas, muchas veces de otros países. También pasan más tiempo comiendo y socializando al mismo tiempo.

[1]*did a survey* [2]*snacks* [3]*On the other hand*

1. ¿Por qué hicieron (*did they do*) esta encuesta? ______
2. ¿Cómo almuerzan los estudiantes los días de clases? ______
3. ¿Qué almuerzan durante la semana? ______
4. ¿Qué piensan de la comida de las cafeterías? ______
5. ¿Qué cambia (*changes*) los fines de semana? ______

5 La cena Using your imagination to describe what happened at this dinner. Use direct and indirect object pronouns, and the preterite of at least four verbs from the box. (6 pts. for vocabulary + 6 pts. for grammar + 3 pts. for style and creativity = 15 pts.)

pedir	repetir	seguir	sentirse	servir	vestirse

______

Tests

Nombre ______________________ Fecha ______________________

TEST D

Lección 8

1 Escuchar You will hear five personal questions. Answer them with Spanish sentences. (5 x 2 pts. each = 10 pts.)

1. ______________________
2. ______________________
3. ______________________
4. ______________________
5. ______________________

2 Sabor latino Write a paragraph about the foods you like and do not like, when and where you eat them, if you frequently cook those foods, etc. Include at least six words from the box. (6 pts. for vocabulary + 6 pts. for grammar + 3 pts. for style and creativity = 15 pts.)

buenísimo	**malísimo**	**el más... de**	**menos**	**recomendar**
escoger	**el más sabroso**	**el mayor**	**peor**	**tan... como**

____

____

____

____

____

____

____

____

____

____

Tests

4 Lectura Read the comments about eating habits around the world and answer the questions with complete sentences. (5 x 2 pts. each = 10 pts.)

Elisa Eiroa, España: Los estadounidenses almuerzan en poco tiempo y comen poco. En mi país, el almuerzo es la comida principal del día. Los españoles, por lo general, dedicamos dos o tres horas para comer y descansar.
Daniel Castillo, México: El horario de las comidas es muy diferente. Los estadounidenses cenan muy temprano, a las 5 o las 6 de la tarde, y después no comen nada más antes de acostarse. La cena es su comida principal. En México, almorzamos a las 2 o a las 3 y cenamos a las 8 o a las 9 de la noche. La cena, por lo general, es más pequeña.
Rebeca Guardia, Panamá: En los restaurantes de los países hispanos, la idea de pedir comida para llevar[1] no es común[2]. En mi país, nos gusta sentarnos y almorzar sin prisa. Nadie lleva comida a la oficina. También nos gusta descansar un poco antes de regresar al trabajo. Generalmente, tampoco llevamos a casa la comida que no podemos terminar en el restaurante; siempre se queda en el plato.

[1] *ordering take-out* [2] *common*

1. ¿Cuál es una de las diferencias entre el almuerzo español y el estadounidense? ______
2. ¿Qué hacen los españoles a la hora del almuerzo? ______
3. ¿Cuál es la comida principal para los mexicanos? ______
4. ¿Por qué dice Rebeca que no es popular pedir comida para llevar en Panamá? ______
5. ¿Qué hacen en Panamá con lo que no se come en un restaurante? ______

5 Un almuerzo Samuel and his friends went out for lunch. Describe what happened, using direct and indirect object pronouns and the preterite forms of at least four verbs from the box. (6 pts. for vocabulary + 6 pts. for grammar + 3 pts. for style and creativity = 15 pts.)

conseguir despedirse pedir preferir seguir servir

______

Nombre ______________________ Fecha ______________________

TEST E

Lección 8

1 Escuchar Read the questions. Then listen to the conversation between Carlos and the waiter and select the appropriate answers. (5 x 2 pts. each = 10 pts.)

1. ¿Cómo se llama el restaurante donde están Carlos y su hijo?
   a. El Cocinero Veloz b. Neptuno c. Plutón
2. ¿Quién pide el jugo de naranja?
   a. Carlos b. el hijo de Carlos c. el camarero
3. ¿Qué recomienda el camarero para Carlos?
   a. ensalada b. hamburguesa c. salmón
4. ¿Qué va a comer el hijo de Carlos?
   a. hamburguesa b. paella c. un huevo
5. ¿Qué pide Carlos al final?
   a. un poco de sal b. un poco de pan c. un poco de limón

2 Identificar Select the item that does not belong. (5 x 2 pts. each = 10 pts.)

1. a. limón b. naranja c. champiñón
2. a. mantequilla b. ajo c. cebolla
3. a. yogur b. sal c. pimienta
4. a. vinagre b. sopa c. aceite
5. a. comida b. bebida c. dueño

3 Comparar Fill in the blanks with the appropriate comparative words. (5 x 2 pts. each = 10 pts.)

1. El restaurante Del Mar es ______________________ (*more*) caro que el restaurante Los Amigos.
2. Lalo y Susi piden ______________________ (*as many*) platos como sus amigos.
3. En el café hay ______________________ (*fewer*) personas que en la heladería (*ice cream shop*).
4. El pollo con papas es el ______________________ (*best*) plato del menú.
5. Inés es la ______________________ (*youngest*) de todas las estudiantes.

4 Ayer Fill in the blanks with the preterite form of the verb. (5 x 2 pts. each = 10 pts.)

1. Tú ______________________ ______________________ (servirle) la merienda a tu familia.
2. Yo me ______________________ (dormir) en el sofá.
3. Mis hermanos ______________________ (pedir) langosta con mantequilla.
4. Ustedes ______________________ (preferir) tomar chocolate.
5. Nati ______________________ ______________________ (vestirse) de rojo para la fiesta (*party*).

Tests

Nombre ______________________ Fecha ______________________

5 Emparejar Match the pictures and descriptions. (6 x 2 pts. each = 12 pts.)

1. _____

2. _____

3. _____

4. _____

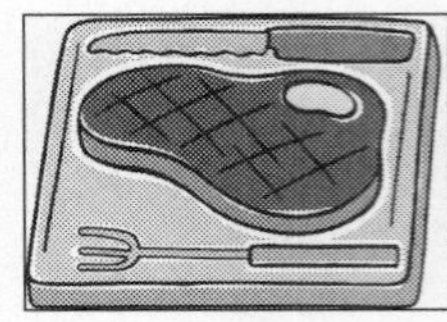
5. _____

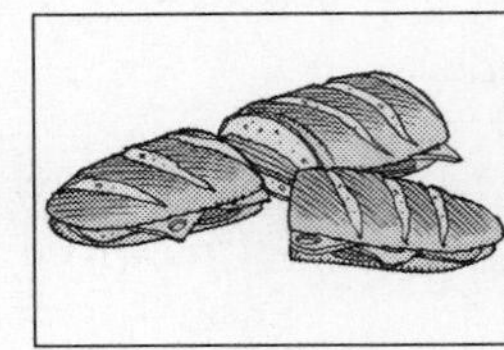
6. _____

a. A mi hermano y a su novia les gusta mucho la pizza.
b. Mis papás van a comer pescado, camarones y langosta.
c. A mi prima Mariela le encantan las hamburguesas con papas fritas.
d. Vamos a pedir sándwiches de jamón con queso.
e. Esta noche vamos a cenar carne asada.
f. Ayer desayuné cereal con leche.

Tests

6 Escoger Select the option that uses the appropriate pronouns. (6 x 2 pts. each = 12 pts.)

1. Laura nos sirvió el refresco y el café.
   a. Nos lo sirvió. b. Nos los sirvió.
2. Carmen y yo le trajimos una ensalada a Ileana.
   a. Nos la trajimos. b. Se la trajimos.
3. Le compro cuatro manzanas a Eduardo.
   a. Se las compro. b. Se lo compro.
4. Ellos te recomiendan este restaurante.
   a. Te los recomiendan. b. Te lo recomiendan.
5. Le pidieron una taza de té y una copa de vino.
   a. Se las pidieron. b. Se la pidieron.
6. Minerva me consigue unos quesos italianos.
   a. Me los consigue. b. Me la consigue.

Nombre ______________________ Fecha ______________________

7 ¿Qué van a comer? The waiter is reading back an order to make sure he has understood it correctly. Fill in the blanks with words from the box. (9 x 2 pts. each = 18 pts.)

hamburguesas	**pidieron**	**se las**
leche	**prefirió**	**se los**
más	**refrescos**	**tinto**

El señor y la señora (1) ______________ agua mineral ahora, y vino con la comida: vino (2) ______________ para ella y vino blanco para él. Los jóvenes van a tomar (3) ______________ y el niño quiere (4) ______________. Los platos principales (5) ______________ voy a traer en diez minutos. La señora y los jóvenes van a comer (6) ______________ con queso. El señor (7) ______________ la langosta con mantequilla. Y el niño pidió el plato (8) ______________ sencillo (*simple*): la ensalada de frutas. ¿Sí? ¿Las bebidas? (9) ______________ voy a servir ahora mismo.

8 Lectura Read the description of Ana and José's dinner, then answer the questions. (6 x 3 pts. each = 18 pts.)

Ana y José cenaron en un restaurante nuevo que está cerca de la casa de Ana. José le pidió el menú al camarero. El camarero les dijo las especialidades del día: sopa de cebolla, ensalada de lechuga y tomate, y jamón con puré de papas. Ana pidió la sopa y el jamón. A José no le gusta la carne de cerdo. Prefiere la carne de res. No le gusta la cebolla, pero le encantan los champiñones. El camarero le recomendó los champiñones con aceite y ajo, y la hamburguesa con queso. La cena estuvo excelente.

1. ¿Dónde está el restaurante nuevo?
   a. cerca de la casa de José   b. cerca de la casa de Ana   c. en el centro
2. ¿Quién pidió el menú?
   a. José   b. Ana   c. el camarero
3. ¿De qué es la sopa del día?
   a. de pollo   b. de cebolla   c. de espárragos
4. ¿Qué tipo (*kind*) de carne pidió Ana?
   a. una hamburguesa   b. pollo   c. jamón
5. ¿Qué no le gusta a José?
   a. la carne de cerdo   b. la carne de res   c. los champiñones
6. ¿Qué le recomendó el camarero a José?
   a. la hamburguesa con queso   b. el jamón con papas   c. la sopa de cebolla

Nombre ______________________ Fecha ______________________

TEST F

Lección 8

1 Escuchar Read the questions. Then listen to the conversation between Marta and the waiter and select the appropriate answers. (5 x 2 pts. each = 10 pts.)

1. ¿Cómo se llama el restaurante donde están Marta y su hija?
   a. Restaurante Paco   b. La Langosta Feliz   c. Restaurante Lola
2. ¿Quién pide el jugo de naranja?
   a. el camarero   b. Marta   c. la hija de Marta
3. ¿Qué recomienda el camarero para Marta?
   a. langosta   b. pizza   c. una hamburguesa
4. ¿Qué va a comer la hija de Marta?
   a. pollo   b. pescado   c. ensalada
5. ¿Qué pide Marta al final?
   a. un poco de limón   b. un poco de sal   c. un poco de pan

2 Identificar Select the item that does not belong. (5 x 2 pts. each = 10 pts.)

1. a. el desayuno   b. el ajo   c. el almuerzo
2. a. el pescado   b. la carne   c. el maíz
3. a. la sal   b. el jamón   c. el queso
4. a. el café   b. el refresco   c. el atún
5. a. la naranja   b. la cerveza   c. la manzana

3 Comparar Fill in the blanks with the appropriate comparative words. (5 x 2 pts. each = 10 pts.)

1. El restaurante argentino es ______________________ (*as*) caro como el restaurante italiano.
2. El menú del almuerzo tiene ______________________ (*fewer*) platos que el menú de la cena.
3. Las papas al horno (*baked potatoes*) son ______________________ (*better*) que las papas fritas.
4. La carne de res con verduras es el plato ______________________ (*most*) caro del menú.
5. Rocío es la ______________________ (*oldest*) de sus hermanos.

4 Ayer Fill in the blanks with the preterite form of the verbs. (5 x 2 pts. each = 10 pts.)

1. Usted ______________________ (vestirse) para la fiesta (*party*).
2. Yo ______________________ (pedir) ensalada con pollo.
3. Mis hermanos no ______________________ (dormir) anoche.
4. Los estudiantes ______________________ (repetir) el examen.
5. El camarero ______________________ ______________________ (servirle) las bebidas a los señores.

Tests

5 Emparejar Match the pictures and descriptions. (6 x 2 pts. each = 12 pts.)

1. _____ 2. _____ 3. _____

4. _____ 5. _____ 6. _____

a. En el hotel sirven huevos, pan tostado, café y jugo en el desayuno.
b. La leche es muy buena para la salud.
c. El pollo asado del restaurante peruano es delicioso.
d. No me siento muy bien; voy a tomar un té.
e. Para la cena hay carne asada, ensalada y sopa.
f. Voy a comer hamburguesa con papas fritas y té helado.

6 Escoger Select the option that uses the appropriate pronouns. (6 x 2 pts. each = 12 pts.)

1. Tus amigos te recomiendan el pollo asado.
   a. Te los recomiendan. b. Te lo recomiendan.

2. Sandra me consigue unos panes franceses.
   a. Me los consigue. b. Me la consigue.

3. Teresa y yo le trajimos una hamburguesa a Úrsula.
   a. Nos la trajimos. b. Se la trajimos.

4. Le pidieron una cerveza y una taza de té.
   a. Se las pidieron. b. Se la pidieron.

5. Laura nos sirvió el jugo y el refresco.
   a. Nos lo sirvió. b. Nos los sirvió.

6. Le compro cinco peras a Fausto.
   a. Se las compro. b. Se lo compro.

Tests

Nombre ______________________ Fecha ______________________

7 ¿Qué van a comer? The waiter is reading back an order to make sure he has understood it correctly. Fill in the blanks with words from the box. (9 x 2 pts. each = 18 pts.)

camarones	**más**	**se las**
entremeses	**pidió**	**se los**
jugo	**prefirieron**	**vino**

El señor (1) ____________________ el coctel (*cocktail*) de (2) ____________________. La señora y los niños (3) ______________________ la ensalada César. De tomar, los señores quieren (4) ______________________ blanco y los niños van a tomar (5) ____________________ de manzana. De plato principal todos van a probar el plato (6) ______________________ rico del menú: la paella con pollo y mariscos. (7) ______________________ voy a traer cuando terminen (*they finish*) de comer los (8) ____________________. ¿Sí? ¿Los entremeses? (9) ____________________ voy a servir ahora mismo.

8 Lectura Clara and her friends had lunch at a restaurant. Read the description and answer the questions. (6 x 3 pts. each = 18 pts.)

Clara invitó a sus amigas a comer en un restaurante que está cerca de la escuela. Decidieron compartir varios platos. Pidieron camarones fritos, queso y verduras con salsa de yogur como entremeses. También pidieron una ensalada con aceite y vinagre. Bebieron agua mineral. Después el camarero les sirvió chuletas de cerdo con papas al horno (*baked potatoes*) y pimientos rellenos de langosta (*lobster stuffed peppers*). Como la comida y el servicio (*service*) fueron excelentes, Clara y sus amigas le dejaron una muy buena propina (*tip*) al camarero.

1. ¿Dónde está el restaurante?
   a. cerca de la escuela　b. cerca de la casa de Clara　c. cerca de la casa de su amiga
2. Las amigas decidieron...
   a. pedir arvejas y arroz.　b. comer en el restaurante más caro.　c. compartir varios platos.
3. ¿Qué tipo de ensalada pidieron?
   a. ensalada de queso　b. ensalada con aceite y vinagre　c. ensalada de camarones
4. ¿Qué bebieron?
   a. leche　b. jugo de naranja　c. agua mineral
5. ¿Con qué les sirvieron las chuletas de cerdo?
   a. con papas al horno　b. con ensalada　c. con salsa de yogur
6. Como la comida y el servicio fueron excelentes,...
   a. dejaron una buena propina.　b. pidieron más comida.　salieron corriendo.

Tests

Nombre ______________________________ Fecha ______________

TEST A Lección 9

1 Escuchar Read these sentence fragments and multiple-choice options. Then, listen to the message that Yolanda leaves on Ana's voicemail and select the correct option. (5 x 2 pts. each = 10 pts.)

1. Yolanda llama a Ana para...
   a. darle las gracias. b. preparar la fiesta. c. felicitarla por su cumpleaños.
2. Yolanda está comenzando su...
   a. vejez. b. juventud. c. madurez.
3. Yolanda cree que el restaurante colombiano...
   a. es excelente. b. está lejos. c. es el peor.
4. De postre, sirvieron...
   a. helado. b. pan. c. flan.
5. Ricardo y Ana...
   a. pasearon por la ciudad. b. no se conocieron. c. bailaron mucho.

2 ¡Fiesta! Look at the picture and describe the celebration using your imagination and the questions as a guide. Write at least five sentences with vocabulary from this lesson. (6 pts. for vocabulary + 6 pts. for grammar + 3 pts. for style and creativity = 15 pts.)

- ¿Qué tipo de fiesta es? ¿Para quién es?
- ¿Qué platos van a comer? ¿Qué beben?
- ¿Qué están haciendo los invitados?

Tests

Nombre ______________________ Fecha ______________

3 La fiesta sorpresa Fill in the blanks in the conversation with words from the box. Use the verbs in the present or in the preterite. You may use some options more than once. (10 x 2 pts. each = 20 pts.)

conocer	**cuál**	**poder**	**qué**	**querer**	**saber**

RICARDO ¿(1) ______________ quieres tomar?

ANA Nada, gracias. Estoy muy contenta con la fiesta sorpresa para Yolanda. ¿(2) ______________ día es su cumpleaños?

RICARDO Es el martes. El año pasado, ella (3) ______________ celebrarlo, pero se enfermó y no (4) ______________ hacerlo.

ANA Yo, este año, (5) ______________ regalarle un disco. ¿(6) ______________ cuál es su grupo favorito?

RICARDO Pues no. Ayer le pregunté por su música favorita y no la (7) ______________ oír bien. Cuando ella me iba a (*was going to*) contestar, la llamó por teléfono Susana.

ANA No (8) ______________ a Susana. ¿Quién es?

RICARDO Es una amiga de Yolanda muy divertida. La (9) ______________ el semestre pasado, en la fiesta de Yolanda a la que tú no (10) ______________ ir, porque tenías (*you had*) un examen.

Tests

4 La boda Complete this paragraph with the preterite form of the verbs in parentheses. (10 x 2 pts. each = 20 pts.)

Ana y mi primo Ricardo (1) ______________ (*to get married*) el sábado pasado. Ellos (2) ______________ (*to get engaged*) hace un mes y este fin de semana (3) ______________ (*to celebrate*) su boda en el restaurante más bonito de Valparaíso. Susana y yo estuvimos en la celebración. Mis padres no (4) ______________ (*to be able to*) venir, pero me (5) ______________ (*to give*) un regalo para ellos. Yo (6) ______________ (*to drive*) el carro de los novios hasta el restaurante. Ana (7) ______________ (*to become*) muy nerviosa, pero al fin (8) ______________ (*to say*) "SÍ". Durante la fiesta, empezó a llover, y los novios (9) ______________ (*to have*) que cancelar el baile (*dance*) al aire libre. Después, el padre del novio (10) ______________ (*to bring*) un champán muy bueno para brindar por la pareja. Todos lo pasamos muy bien. ¡Vivan los novios!

5 Lectura Match the pictures and descriptions. (6 x 2 pts. each = 12 pts.)

Boda de Alejandro y Lucía

El día sábado 30 de octubre, a las seis de la tarde, Alejandro Gómez y Lucía Tudela se casaron en la Iglesia de San Juan. La ceremonia fue oficiada[1] por el pastor Roberto Marín. Después de la ceremonia, los padres de los recién casados invitaron a todos los amigos de la familia a una fiesta en el restaurante Monti.

Fiesta de Antonia Llanos

El 17 de marzo, Antonia Llanos, hija de Enrique Llanos y María Martín de Llanos, celebró su fiesta de quince años. Todos los amigos de la familia asistieron a una cena en el restaurante El Pardo, donde comieron, bailaron y se divirtieron. El hermano de Antonia, Miguel Ángel Llanos, que vive en Roma, también asistió a la fiesta con su esposa Carmen.

[1] *was officiated*

1. ¿Qué hicieron Alejandro y Lucía el 30 de octubre? ______________________
2. ¿Qué hicieron después de salir de la iglesia? ______________________
3. ¿Quiénes fueron a la fiesta? ______________________
4. ¿Cómo celebraron la fiesta de quince años de Antonia Llanos? ______________________
5. ¿Qué relación tienen Miguel Ángel y Carmen? ______________________

6 Una fiesta Write a paragraph about a party you recently attended. Use the preterite of at least four verbs from the box and include at least two pronouns after prepositions. (8 pts. for vocabulary + 8 pts. for grammar + 4 pts. for style and creativity = 20 pts.)

conducir	**enamorarse**	**llevarse bien/mal**	**pasarlo bien/mal**	**poner**	**saber**

Tests

Nombre ______________________ Fecha ______________________

TEST B

Lección 9

1 Escuchar Read these sentence fragments and multiple-choice options. Then, listen to the message that Rúper leaves on Paco's voicemail and select the correct option. (5 x 2 pts. each = 10 pts.)

1. Rúper llama a Paco para...
   a. darle las gracias. b. preparar la fiesta. c. invitarlo a su fiesta.
2. Rúper...
   a. cumplió 21 años. b. se casó. c. se graduó.
3. Rúper habla de un restaurante argentino porque...
   a. es de Paco. b. no es muy bueno. c. Paco lo recomendó.
4. El regalo sorpresa es...
   a. una computadora. b. una moto. c. un carro.
5. Paco y Noemí...
   a. hablaron mucho. b. no se conocieron. c. pasearon por la ciudad.

2 ¡Fiesta! Look at the picture and describe what is happening, using your imagination and the questions as a guide. Write at least five sentences with vocabulary from this lesson. (6 pts. for vocabulary + 6 pts. for grammar + 3 pts. for style and creativity = 15 pts.)

- ¿Qué tipo de fiesta es? ¿Qué celebran?
- ¿Qué están comiendo? ¿Qué beben?
- ¿Qué están haciendo los invitados?

____

____

____

____

____

____

____

Tests

3 La fiesta sorpresa Fill in the blanks in this dialogue with words from the box. Use the verbs in the present or in the preterite. You may use some options more than once. (10 x 2 pts. each = 20 pts.)

conocer	**poder**	**querer**
cuál	**qué**	**saber**

ALFONSO Hola, hermanita. ¿(1) ______________ quieres tomar?

PILAR Un té, por favor. ¿Sabes? Estoy muy contenta con la fiesta sorpresa de aniversario para papá y mamá. Sabes cuándo es, ¿verdad? A ver, ¿(2) ______________ día es?

ALFONSO Pues, sí. Es el viernes.

PILAR ¡Muy bien, Alfonso! ¿Te acuerdas que el año pasado nosotros planeamos (*planned*) una fiesta, pero no la (3) ______________ celebrar? Cuando papá (4) ______________ que la abuela estaba (*was*) en el hospital, no (5) ______________ celebrar una fiesta.

ALFONSO Sí, pero este año la abuela está muy bien y va a bailar toda la noche. ¿Y (6) ______________ es el menú para la fiesta?

PILAR Los platos favoritos de los dos. Y Antonio Suárez les va a hacer su pastel favorito.

ALFONSO ¿Y (7) ______________ es su pastel favorito?

PILAR El pastel de chocolate.

ALFONSO ¿Y quién es Antonio Suárez? No lo (8) ______________.

PILAR Es el dueño del restaurante favorito de mamá. Yo lo (9) ______________ el mes pasado y es un hombre muy simpático. Alfonso, parece que no (10) ______________ muchas cosas sobre papá y mamá. ¿Cuándo fue la última vez que hablaste con ellos?

4 La graduación Fill in the blanks in this paragraph using the preterite form of the verbs in parentheses. (10 x 2 pts. each = 20 pts.)

El sábado pasado yo (1) ______________ (*to be*) en la fiesta de graduación de Isabel, mi mejor amiga. Ella (2) ______________ (*to want*) celebrarlo al aire libre con su familia y todos sus amigos. (3) ______________ (*There was*) mucha comida muy buena. Isabel (4) ______________ (*to become*) muy contenta cuando sus padres le (5) ______________ (*to give*) una sorpresa: un viaje a San Francisco. Yo también le (6) ______________ (*to bring*) un regalo y le gustó mucho. En la fiesta, el padre de Isabel (7) ______________ (*to say*) unas palabras y todos (8) ______________ (*to laugh*) porque él es muy simpático. Todos (9) ______________ (*to have fun*). Pero, qué lástima (*a shame*) que empezó a llover y todos nosotros (10) ______________ (*to have*) que entrar (*go in*) a la casa. Por suerte (*luckily*), tienen una casa muy grande.

Nombre ______________________ Fecha ______________________

5 Lectura Read these society notes from a newspaper and answer the questions with complete sentences. (5 x 3 pts. each = 15 pts.)

Aniversario de César Antón y Estela Parada de Antón

César Antón y Estela Parada celebraron su 25º aniversario de bodas el día sábado 6 de marzo, a las siete de la tarde, con una cena en el elegante restaurante San Marcos. Sus hijos, María Luisa, Francisco y Sofía, invitaron a toda la familia y amigos de la pareja y los sorprendieron con una fiesta con cincuenta invitados. Después, todos los invitados fueron a la Sala Conde Luna, donde bailaron felices hasta muy tarde.

Bautizo[1] de María Esmeralda Cárdenas Obregón

Ayer, Justo Cárdenas y Liliana Obregón de Cárdenas celebraron el bautizo de su hija, María Esmeralda. La ceremonia fue en la catedral[2] de Santa María. Entre los invitados estuvieron los padres de Liliana, Raimundo y Esmeralda Obregón. Después de la ceremonia, los familiares y amigos fueron al restaurante La Codorniz de Oro. La dueña del restaurante, Elena Cárdenas, preparó una comida maravillosa para celebrar el bautizo de su primera sobrina.

[1]*Baptism* [2]*cathedral*

1. ¿Qué hicieron los hijos de César y Estela el 6 de marzo? ______________________
2. ¿Qué hicieron todos después de la cena? ______________________
3. ¿Dónde fue el bautizo de María Esmeralda? ______________________
4. ¿Quién es doña Esmeralda? ______________________
5. ¿Qué relación tiene Elena Cárdenas con María Esmeralda? ______________________

6 Los cumpleaños Write a paragraph about a birthday celebration that you recently attended. Use the preterite of at least four verbs from the box and include at least two pronouns after prepositions. (8 pts. for vocabulary + 8 pts. for grammar + 4 pts. for style and creativity = 20 pts.)

cambiar	**divertirse**	**llevarse bien/mal**	**salir con**	**sonreír**	**tener una cita**

____

____

____

____

____

____

____

Tests

Nombre ______________________ Fecha ______________________

TEST C

Lección 9

1 Escuchar You will hear five personal questions. Answer them with Spanish sentences. (5 x 2 pts. each = 10 pts.)

1. ______________________
2. ______________________
3. ______________________
4. ______________________
5. ______________________

2 ¡A divertirse! Look at the picture and, using the questions as a guide, describe the celebration. Write at least five sentences, using vocabulary from this lesson. (6 pts. for vocabulary + 6 pts. for grammar + 3 pts. for style and creativity = 15 pts.)

- ¿Qué tipo de fiesta es? ¿Para quién es?
- ¿Qué platos van a comer? ¿Y qué beben?
- ¿Qué van a hacer los invitados?

Tests

Nombre ______________________ Fecha ______________________

3 Lectura Read these society notes from a newspaper and answer the questions with complete sentences. (5 x 2 pts. each = 10 pts.)

Nacimiento de Alberto Araneda Ochoa

El día domingo 8 de julio nació Alberto Araneda en el hospital de San Telmo. Es hijo de José Luis Araneda y de Luisa Ochoa. Los padres del niño quieren compartir la alegría de su nacimiento y van a celebrarlo el día domingo 31 de julio en el restaurante Soler. En la fiesta se va a brindar por la felicidad de la familia Araneda Ochoa.

Cena benéfica[1]

El viernes pasado, se celebró en la Sala Milenio una cena benéfica[1] para la educación pública. Fueron muchos los periodistas y profesores que asistieron al evento. Todos se divirtieron gracias a la excelente Ángeles Rueda, que organizó todo a la perfección. Entre los famosos que fueron a la cena, pudimos ver a Amalia Rodríguez, que, para sorpresa de todos, fue con su ex esposo, Manuel Flores.

[1] *charity*

1. ¿En qué etapa de la vida está Alberto Araneda? ______________________
2. ¿Por qué celebran la fiesta los padres de Alberto? ______________________
3. ¿Quiénes fueron invitados a la cena en la Sala Milenio? ______________________
4. ¿Cómo lo pasaron los invitados a la Sala Milenio? ______________________
5. ¿Cuál es el estado civil de Amalia Rodríguez? ______________________

4 Una fiesta Write a paragraph about a party that you recently attended. Use the preterite of at least four verbs from the box and include at least two pronouns after prepositions. (6 pts. for vocabulary + 6 pts. for grammar + 3 pts. for style and creativity = 15 pts.)

conducir	poder	querer	saber	tener	venir

Tests

Nombre ______________________ Fecha ______________________

TEST D

Lección 9

1 Escuchar You will hear five personal questions. Answer them with Spanish sentences. (5 x 2 pts. each = 10 pts.)

1. ______________________
2. ______________________
3. ______________________
4. ______________________
5. ______________________

2 ¡A divertirse! Look at the picture and describe what's happening, using the questions as a guide. Write at least five sentences with vocabulary from this lesson. (6 pts. for vocabulary + 6 pts. for grammar + 3 pts. for style and creativity = 15 pts.)

- ¿Qué celebran los invitados? ¿Dónde están?
- ¿Qué platos van a comer? ¿Qué beben?
- ¿Qué hacen los invitados?

Tests

3 Lectura Read these society notes from a newspaper and answer the questions with complete sentences. (5 x 2 pts. each = 10 pts.)

Matrimonio de Javier y Noemí

El pasado sábado 10 de octubre Javier González y Noemí del Pozo celebraron su boda en la Iglesia de San Andrés. A la ceremonia asistieron la familia y los amigos de la pareja, incluidos[1] Iván y Susana, los dos hijos que Javier tuvo en su primer matrimonio. Marta, la primera esposa de Javier, también asistió. La celebración siguió en el restaurante Palacio con una comida para los cien invitados.

Doña Matilde Sánchez de Higuera cumplió 91 años

La familia de doña Matilde Sánchez de Higuera organizó una fiesta sorpresa para celebrar su cumpleaños. Asistieron a la fiesta los hijos y nietos de doña Matilde, entre otros familiares y amigos. La fiesta fue el pasado domingo. Nieves Higuera, la hija menor de doña Matilde, habló sobre la interesante y larga vida de su madre y recordó la vida de su padre, quien murió cuando Matilde tenía ochenta y tres años.

[1] *including*

1. ¿Es la primera vez que se casa Javier? ______________________
2. ¿Quiénes son Iván, Susana y Marta? ______________________
3. ¿En qué etapa de la vida está doña Matilde Sánchez? ______________________
4. ¿Qué hizo la familia Higuera Sánchez? ______________________
5. ¿Qué hizo Nieves? ______________________

4 Los cumpleaños Write a paragraph about a birthday party that you recently attended. Use the preterite of at least five verbs from the box and include at least two pronouns after prepositions. (6 pts. for vocabulary + 6 pts. for grammar + 3 pts. for style and creativity = 15 pts.)

estar	poder	querer	saber	tener	traer

____

Nombre ______________________________ Fecha ______________________

TEST E

Lección 9

1 Escuchar Read the statements. Then listen to a short biography of María Muñoz, and indicate whether each statement is **cierto** or **falso**. (5 x 2 pts. each = 10 pts.)

	Cierto	**Falso**
1. María Muñoz nació en Madrid.	______	______
2. Su madre le regaló un cuaderno.	______	______
3. María estudió computación.	______	______
4. María se casó después de graduarse.	______	______
5. María vive en California.	______	______

2 Emparejar Match the pictures and descriptions. (5 x 2 pts. each = 10 pts.)

1. _____

2. _____

3. _____

4. _____

5. _____

a. Ana cumple veintiún años.
b. Saúl abrió una botella de vino tinto.
c. Celebramos el Año Nuevo con champán.
d. La fiesta de cumpleaños de Marisa fue muy divertida.
e. Alberto y sus amigos celebran la Navidad.

3 ***¿Qué* o *cuál*?** Fill in the blanks using **qué**, **cuál**, or **cuáles**. (5 x 2 pts. each = 10 pts.)

1. ¿______________________ es tu número de teléfono?
2. ¿______________________ pastel quieres comprar para la fiesta?
3. ¿______________________ son los colores de la bandera (*flag*) de México?
4. ¿______________________ vamos a hacer para el cumpleaños de la abuela?
5. ¿______________________ es el vino que prefieres?

4 **Verbos** Fill in the blanks with the preterite form of the verbs. (11 x 2 pts. each = 22 pts.)

1. Yo ______________________ (tener) que comprar los boletos de autobús.
2. Sus amigas le ______________________ (decir) que hace las mejores galletas de la ciudad.
3. Carla y tú ______________________ (traer) un regalo para María a la estación de autobuses.
4. Nosotros no ______________________ (saber) qué hacer cuando vimos a Virginia.
5. Tú ______________________ (estar) estudiando en España durante cuatro años.
6. Los hermanos Salas ______________________ (querer) comprar un carro nuevo.
7. Tú ______________________ (poder) terminar la tarea a tiempo.
8. Lisa no ______________________ (saber) lo que pasó en la fiesta.
9. Marcia y tú ______________________ (conocer) a Carolina en ese restaurante.
10. Ella no ______________________ (querer) preparar la ensalada para la cena.
11. Yo le ______________________ (dar) diez dólares a mi sobrinito.

5 **Preposiciones** Fill in the blanks with the appropriate pronouns and prepositions. (6 x 2 pts. each = 12 pts.)

1. Lorena no quiere ir a la fiesta ______________________ (*with me*).
2. Ellos tienen que traer el flan ______________________ (*for him*).
3. Leonardo se va a sentar ______________________ (*with you,* form.).
4. Sandra se lleva muy bien ______________________ (*with you,* fam.).
5. Celebré el Año Nuevo ______________________ (*with her*).
6. Vamos a comprar unos postres ______________________ (*for you,* fam.).

Nombre ______________________ Fecha ______________________

6 ¡Viva la fiesta! Fill in the blanks with words from the box. (9 x 2 pts. each = 18 pts.)

aniversario	**condujo**	**pudieron**
brindaron	**hizo**	**quiso**
con	**para**	**trajo**

Liliana y Patricia prepararon una fiesta de (1) ____________ para sus amigos Victoria y David. Invitaron a todos los amigos de la pareja y, (2) ____________ ellas, lo mejor es que todos (3) ____________ asistir. Liliana (4) ____________ la reservación en un restaurante muy elegante del centro. Patricia (5) ____________ de la casa de Victoria y David al restaurante y llegó (6) ____________ ellos a la mesa donde estaban (*were*) todos esperando. Victoria (7) ____________ agradecer a sus amigos, pero no pudo porque empezó a llorar (*to cry*) de alegría. Todos (8) ____________ por la pareja y compartieron los postres y los dulces que el camarero (9) ____________ a la mesa.

7 Lectura Read the description, then answer the questions. (6 x 3 pts. each = 18 pts.)

El viernes Mirta hizo una fiesta para celebrar su cumpleaños. Ella cumplió 15 años. Luisa hizo un pastel y un flan. Sandra y Tomás trajeron el jugo y los refrescos. Sebastián quiso venir, pero no pudo porque vive en otra ciudad. Así que, Sebastián le pidió a Luisa comprar unos dulces para Mirta y dárselos en la fiesta. Ella se puso muy contenta cuando supo que los dulces venían (*came*) de Sebastián. Fue una noche muy divertida. Estuvieron bailando y cantando hasta las diez de la noche.

1. ¿Cuántos años cumplió Mirta?
   a. quince b. veintidós c. diecisiete
2. ¿Qué hizo Luisa?
   a. una ensalada b. unos dulces c. un pastel y un flan
3. ¿Quiénes trajeron el jugo y los refrescos?
   a. Sandra y Tomás b. Mirta y Sebastián c. Sandra y Luisa
4. ¿Fue Sebastián a la fiesta?
   a. sí b. no sé c. no
5. ¿Cómo se puso Mirta cuando vio los dulces?
   a. alegre b. confundida c. preocupada
6. Mirta y sus amigos bailaron hasta las...
   a. diez. b. once. c. doce.

Tests

Nombre ______________________ Fecha ______________________

TEST F — Lección 9

1 Escuchar Read the statements. Then listen to a short biography of Carlos Cruz, and indicate whether each statement is **cierto** or **falso**. (5 x 2 pts. each = 10 pts.)

	Cierto	Falso
1. Carlos Cruz nació en Buenos Aires.	______	______
2. Su madre le regaló un cuaderno.	______	______
3. Carlos estudió arte y matemáticas.	______	______
4. Carlos se casó antes de graduarse.	______	______
5. Carlos vive en Valparaíso.	______	______

2 Emparejar Match the pictures and descriptions. (5 x 2 pts. each = 10 pts.)

1. _____

2. _____

3. _____

4. _____

5. _____

a. Los amigos de Miguel le prepararon una fiesta sorpresa.
b. A Patricia le encantan los dulces.
c. Mi postre favorito es el flan de caramelo.
d. Samuel quiere el helado de vainilla y Marco quiere el pastel de chocolate.
e. ¿Qué prefieren: pastel, flan o galletas?

Tests

Nombre ______________________ Fecha ______________________

3 ***¿Qué* o *cuál*?** Fill in the blanks using **qué**, **cuál**, or **cuáles**. (5 x 2 pts. each = 10 pts.)

1. ¿______________________ es el dulce de leche?
2. ¿______________________ es el mejor postre que tienen?
3. ¿______________________ estudia Leticia?
4. ¿______________________ son los hijos de Sonia?
5. ¿______________________ pastel vas a comprar para la fiesta?

4 Lo que pasó, pasó Fill in the blanks with the preterite form of the verbs. (11 x 2 pts. each = 22 pts.)

1. Anoche, yo ______________________ (hacer) una fiesta.
2. Mónica ______________________ (traducir) las instrucciones para sus amigos que no hablan español.
3. Marcelo y Nati ______________________ (poner) el pastel y los dulces sobre la mesa.
4. Tú ______________________ (conducir) tres horas para llegar a la fiesta.
5. Paola y yo no ______________________ (querer) tomar vino.
6. Ayer, yo ______________________ (conocer) a los padres de mi novia.
7. Ustedes no ______________________ (saber) los resultados (*results*) de las pruebas.
8. Nosotros ______________________ (poder) hacer las compras antes de la lluvia (*rain*).
9. Mariela ______________________ (querer) estudiar el fin de semana, pero fue imposible.
10. Mi hermana y yo ______________________ (saber) la noticia (*news*) el martes por la noche.
11. Tú me ______________________ (dar) veinte dólares el sábado pasado.

5 Preposiciones Fill in the blanks with the appropriate pronouns and prepositions. (6 x 2 pts. each = 12 pts.)

1. El pastel es ______________________ (*for you,* fam. sing.).
2. Josefina no quiere ir a la fiesta ______________________ (*with him*).
3. ¿Vienes a la fiesta ______________________ (*with me*)?
4. Ellos compraron un flan ______________________ (*for me*).
5. Yo tengo un mensaje ______________________ (*for her*).
6. Andrés llegó a la clase ______________________ (*with you,* fam. sing.).

Tests

Nombre ______________________ Fecha ______________________

6 ¡Viva la fiesta! Fill in the blanks with words from the box. (9 x 2 pts. each = 18 pts.)

alegría	**con**	**hicieron**
botellas	**condujeron**	**postres**
celebrar	**estuvo**	**quiso**

Los señores Ortiz y sus dos hijas (1) ______________________ una fiesta para (2) ____________________ el Año Nuevo con todos sus amigos. La señora Ortiz preparó unos (3) ______________________ muy ricos. El señor Ortiz compró unas (4) ______________________ de champán. Alejandra, la hija menor, (5) ____________________ leer un poema para sus papás, pero no pudo porque empezó a llorar (*to cry*) de (6) ______________________. Su hermana Esther vino a ayudarle y (7) ______________________ poniendo música. Los amigos de la familia (8) ______________________ desde muchas partes de la ciudad. Todos se divirtieron mucho (9) ______________________ la familia Ortiz.

7 Lectura Read the description, then answer the questions. (6 x 3 pts. each = 18 pts.)

El sábado Rosa hizo una fiesta para celebrar su cumpleaños. Ella cumplió 14 años. Isela preparó un flan y unos dulces. Julio y Amalia trajeron el jugo y los refrescos. Antonio quiso venir, pero no pudo porque vive en otra ciudad. Por eso, Antonio le pidió a Isela comprar un pastel para Rosa y dárselo en la fiesta. Ella se puso muy contenta cuando supo que el pastel venía (*came*) de Antonio. Fue una noche muy divertida. Estuvieron bailando y cantando hasta las diez de la noche.

1. ¿Cuántos años cumplió Rosa?
   a. dieciséis　　b. veintidós　　c. catorce
2. ¿Qué preparó Isela?
   a. unos sándwiches　　b. un flan y unos dulces　　c. un pastel
3. ¿Quiénes trajeron el jugo y los refrescos?
   a. Rosa y Antonio　　b. Isela y Amalia　　c. Julio y Amalia
4. ¿Fue Antonio a la fiesta?
   a. no　　b. no sé　　c. sí
5. ¿Cómo se puso Rosa cuando vio el pastel?
   a. confundida　　b. alegre　　c. preocupada
6. Rosa y sus amigos bailaron hasta las...
   a. diez.　　b. once.　　c. doce.

Tests

Nombre ______________________________ Fecha ______________________

EXAM A — Lecciones 1–4

1 Escuchar Read these statements. Then listen to the recommendations that a guide is giving to a group of tourists and select the option that best completes each statement. (5 x 2 pts. each = 10 pts.)

1. Al llegar a la Ciudad de México, los turistas _________.
   a. pueden descansar b. tienen que ir a pasear c. tienen que salir a comer
2. Esta noche van a _________.
   a. ir a un restaurante b. salir a bailar c. pasear por la ciudad
3. Por las noches, _________.
   a. tienen cuidado b. salen mucho c. hace más fresco
4. El número de teléfono del hotel es el _________.
   a. 57-38-67 b. 23-17-89 c. 22-37-89
5. Los turistas van a visitar _________.
   a. un estadio b. dos museos c. la biblioteca

2 ¿Qué hacemos hoy? Hernán, Laura, and Silvia are deciding what they are going to do on their first day of vacation in Spain. Write what they plan to do, using at least six verbs from the list and the vocabulary from Lessons 1 to 4. (3 pts. for vocabulary + 3 pts. for grammar + 1 pt. for style and creativity = 7 pts.)

asistir a	**comprar**	**decidir**	**llegar**	**preferir**	**salir**
comer	**deber**	**desear**	**jugar**	**regresar**	**tener suerte**

Exams

Nombre ______________________ Fecha ______________________

3 La clase Look at the picture and answer the questions with complete sentences. (5 x 2 pts. each = 10 pts.)

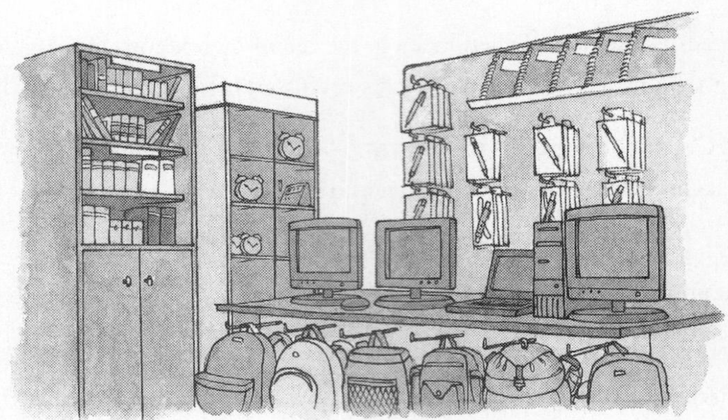

1. ¿Cuántas mochilas hay?
____
2. ¿Cuántos relojes hay?
____
3. ¿Qué hora es?
____
4. ¿Dónde están las computadoras?
____
5. ¿Cuántos cuadernos hay?
____

4 De paseo While Hernán shops, Laura and Silvia are walking around the city. Fill in the blanks in their conversation with the verb **tener** and the words from the box. (5 x 1 pt. each = 5 pts.)

años	frío	hambre	razón	sueño
calor	ganas	miedo	sed	suerte

SILVIA ¿(1) ______________________? Yo ya quiero comer.

LAURA No, ahora no. Podemos comer un poco más tarde. Pero (2) ______________________ de tomar un café. Estoy muy cansada y (3) ______________________.

SILVIA Bueno, vamos a buscar un café. Espera un momento, voy a quitarme el suéter (*sweater*) porque (4) ______________________.

LAURA Sí, es verdad. ¡Qué calor hace! ¿Por qué no vamos con Hernán a la biblioteca? Hace demasiado calor para estar en la calle (*street*).

SILVIA (5) ______________________, vamos a la biblioteca.

Exams

Nombre ______________________________ Fecha ______________________

5 Mensaje electrónico Complete the e-mail Cristina writes to Francisco with the correct form of the verbs in the box. Do not repeat verbs. (5 x 1 pt. each = 5 pts.)

empezar	**mostrar**	**pensar**	**querer**	**volver**

Hola, Francisco:

¿Qué tal? ¿Cuándo (1) ______________ las clases en tu ciudad? Yo (2) ______________que aquí empezamos el cinco de septiembre. Yo no (3) ____________comenzar la escuela todavía (*yet*). ¡Me encanta el verano (*summer*)! Ahora tengo mucho tiempo libre para andar en patineta, ver películas y pasear en bicicleta, mis actividades favoritas. Si tú (4) ____________ de visita al verano que viene, yo te (5) _____________ mi bicicleta nueva. Bueno, hablamos pronto.

Un saludo,

Cristina

6 Oraciones Write complete sentences with the information provided. Write numbers as words. (5 x 2 pt. each = 10 pts.)

1. yo / salir / de casa / 7:15 a.m. / todos los días
____
2. el gimnasio / cerrar / 10:45 p.m.
____
3. Mario / ir a / visitar / museo / fin de semana
____
4. yo / jugar / fútbol / 365 días al año
____
5. tú / dormir / 7 horas / todos los días
____

7 Preguntas Answer these questions with complete sentences. (5 x 2 pts. each = 10 pts.)

1. ¿Cuántos años tienes?
____
2. ¿Qué día es hoy?
____
3. ¿Qué programas de televisión te gustan?
____
4. ¿Cuántas personas hay en tu familia?
____
5. ¿Adónde te gusta ir con tus amigos?
____

Nombre ______________________ Fecha ______________________

8 Los pasatiempos Write sentences using **ir a** to explain what these people are going to do. (5 x 2 pts. each = 10 pts.)

1. Rafael 2. Paola 3. Sr. Barrera 4. Elena y José Fernando 5. Francisco y José

1. ______________________
2. ______________________
3. ______________________
4. ______________________
5. ______________________

9 Tu familia Pick a family member and write about him or her. Be sure to cover the topics below. (3 pts. for vocabulary + 3 pts. for grammar + 1 pt. for style and creativity = 7 pts.)

- What is his or her name?
- What is your relationship with him or her?
- Where does he or she live?
- What is he or she like?
- What does he or she like to do in his or her free time?

____

10 Lectura Read this pamphlet and answer the questions with complete sentences. When answering with numbers, write the numbers as words. (5 x 2 pts. each = 10 pts.)

CLUB VERANO

El Club Verano abre el próximo domingo. Aquí va a encontrar actividades deportivas y sociales para toda la familia. ¡El club va a ser el lugar favorito de sus hijos!

¿Dónde está?

El Club Verano está cerca del centro de la ciudad, a la derecha de la biblioteca pública.

¿Qué hay?

El club tiene tres piscinas, dos gimnasios (uno para niños y otro para adultos) y un restaurante.

¿Qué actividades se pueden hacer?

Usted puede practicar la natación y jugar al tenis. También tenemos equipos de vóleibol, tenis y baloncesto.

¿Dónde se puede comer?

Si[1] tienes hambre y sed, puedes ir a nuestro fabuloso restaurante.

¿Qué horario tiene?

El Club Verano abre a las 7:30 a.m y cierra a las 10:45 p.m todos los días de la semana.

¡Esperamos tu llamada[2]!

[1]*if* [2]*call*

1. ¿Cómo se llama el club? _______________
2. ¿Dónde está la biblioteca pública? _______________
3. ¿Cuántos gimnasios hay para niños? _______________
4. ¿A qué hora abre y cierra el club? _______________
5. ¿Cuáles son tus actividades favoritas del club? ¿Por qué? _______________

Exams

Nombre ______________________ Fecha ______________________

11 El verano Write a paragraph with at least six sentences that describes what you usually do in the summer. Use the grammar and vocabulary from Lessons 1 to 4. (6 pts. for vocabulary + 6 pts. for grammar + 4 pts. for style and creativity = 16 pts.)

Exams

Nombre ______________________ Fecha ______________________

EXAM B

Lecciones 1–4

1 Escuchar Read these statements. Then listen to the recommendations that a guide is giving to a group of tourists and select the option that best completes each statement. (5 x 2 pts. each = 10 pts.)

1. Los turistas tienen unas horas para _________.
   a. visitar la ciudad b. descansar en sus cuartos c. leer una revista
2. Por la tarde van a _________.
   a. visitar monumentos b. salir sin el grupo c. pasear por la ciudad
3. Por la noche el grupo va a _________.
   a. comer en un restaurante b. tener cuidado con el frío c. ir a la biblioteca
4. El número de teléfono del hotel es el _________.
   a. 57-38-67 b. 23-17-89 c. 53-32-13
5. Por la mañana tienen que salir del hotel _________.
   a. a las 8:30 b. a las 9 c. a las 9:15

2 ¿Qué hacemos hoy? Lola, Estefanía, and Álvaro are deciding what they are going to do on their first day of vacation in Spain. Write what they plan to do, using at least six verbs from the list and the vocabulary from Lessons 1 to 4. (3 pts. for vocabulary + 3 pts. for grammar + 1 pt. for style and creativity = 7 pts.)

almorzar	**comprar**	**empezar**	**llevar**	**preferir**	**regresar**
buscar	**descansar**	**leer**	**nadar**	**querer**	**viajar**

____

____

____

____

____

____

____

____

Exams

Nombre ______________________ Fecha ______________________

3 La clase Look at the picture and answer the questions with complete sentences. (5 x 2 pts. each = 10 pts.)

1. ¿Cuántas computadoras hay?
____
2. ¿Dónde están las mochilas?
____
3. ¿Qué hora es?
____
4. ¿Cuántos cuadernos hay?
____
5. ¿Cuántos relojes hay?
____

4 En el parque While Lola is shopping, Estefanía and Álvaro are sitting on a park bench at sunset. Fill in the blanks in their conversation with verb **tener** and a word from the box, without repeating any words. (5 x 1 pt. each = 5 pts.)

años	**frío**	**hambre**	**razón**	**sueño**
calor	**ganas**	**miedo**	**sed**	**suerte**

ESTEFANÍA Álvaro, ¿puedes venir conmigo al hotel? (1) ______________ y necesito una chaqueta (*jacket*).

ÁLVARO ¿Puedes ir tú sola (*alone*)? Estoy cansado y no (2) ______________ de caminar.

ESTEFANÍA No, no quiero ir sola. No hay mucha gente por la calle (*street*) y (3) ______________.

ÁLVARO Está bien. (4) ______________, no debes caminar sola por la noche. Podemos ir al hotel y comer algo allí. ¿No (5) ______________? Yo sí.

ESTEFANÍA Sí, yo también. Buena idea.

Exams

5 Mensaje electrónico Complete the e-mail Marta writes to Esteban with the correct form of the verbs in the box. Do not repeat verbs. (5 x 1 pt. each = 5 pts.)

almorzar	encontrar	pensar	querer	suponer

Hola, Esteban:
¿Qué tal? Tengo una pregunta para ti. ¿En qué restaurante de tu pueblo (1) __________ tú?
Mi amigo Pablo (2) ___________ ir allí y (3) ___________ recomendaciones.
Yo (4) __________ que voy a ir con él. Bueno, si (*if*) quieres venir con nosotros, el sábado nos podemos (5) ___________ a las once y media en la biblioteca de tu pueblo.
Un saludo,
Marta

6 Oraciones Write complete sentences with the information provided. Write numbers as words. (5 x 2 pt. each = 10 pts.)

1. yo / ver / partido de baloncesto / televisión / 7:45 p.m.
____
2. nosotros / jugar / vóleibol / martes / y / jueves
____
3. María y su hermana / ir a / cenar / restaurante / centro
____
4. la biblioteca / cerrar / 7:30 p.m.
____
5. ellos / dormir / 8 horas / todos los días
____

7 Preguntas Answer these questions with complete sentences. (5 x 2 pts. each = 10 pts.)

1. ¿De dónde eres?
____
2. ¿Qué tiempo hace hoy?
____
3. ¿Cuál es tu película favorita?
____
4. ¿Cómo se llaman tus padres?
____
5. ¿Cuáles son los pasatiempos favoritos de tu mejor amigo/a?
____

Nombre ________________________ Fecha ________________________

8 Los pasatiempos Write sentences using **ir a** to explain what these people are going to do. (5 x 2 pts. each = 10 pts.)

1. ______________________________
2. ______________________________
3. ______________________________
4. ______________________________
5. ______________________________

9 Tu familia Pick a family member and write about him or her. Be sure to cover the topics below. (3 pts. for vocabulary + 3 pts. for grammar + 1 pt. for style and creativity = 7 pts.)

- What is his or her name?
- What is your relationship with him or her?
- What does he or she do?
- What is he or she like?
- What does he or she like to do in his or her free time?

____

____

____

____

____

____

____

____

____

____

Exams

Nombre ______________________ Fecha ______________________

10 Lectura Read this pamphlet and answer the questions with complete sentences. When answering with numbers, write the numbers as words. (5 x 2 pts. each = 10 pts.)

CLUB DIVERSIÓN

El Club Diversión abre el próximo sábado. Aquí va a encontrar actividades deportivas y sociales para toda la familia. ¡El club va a ser el lugar favorito de sus hijos!

¿Dónde está?

El Club Diversión está cerca del centro de la ciudad, a la izquierda de la escuela pública.

¿Qué hay?

El club tiene tres gimnasios, dos piscinas y un café.

¿Qué actividades se pueden hacer?

Usted puede jugar al vóleibol y al tenis. También tenemos equipos de béisbol, natación y baloncesto. Y para descansar, puede ir a la biblioteca y leer un libro o mirar su correo electrónico.

¿Dónde comer?

Si[1] tienes hambre y sed, puedes ir a nuestro fabuloso café.

¿Qué horario tiene?

El Club Diversión abre a las 7:45 a.m y cierra a las 9:30 p.m de lunes a sábado.

¡Esperamos tu llamada[2]!

[1]*if* [2]*call*

1. ¿Cómo se llama el club? ______________________

____

2. ¿Dónde está la escuela pública? ______________________

____

3. ¿Cuántas piscinas hay? ______________________

____

4. ¿A qué hora abre y cierra el club? ______________________

____

5. ¿Cuáles son tus actividades favoritas del club? ¿Por qué? ______________________

____

Exams

Nombre ______________________ Fecha ______________________

11 Mi fin de semana Write a paragraph with at least six sentences that describes one of your typical weekends. Use the grammar and vocabulary from Lessons 1 to 4. (6 pts. for vocabulary + 6 pts. for grammar + 4 pts. for style and creativity = 16 pts.)

Exams

Nombre ______________________ Fecha ______________________

EXAM A Lecciones 1–9

1 Escuchar Francisco and Irene are thinking of going to Puerto Rico on vacation. Julio, their friend, is telling them what he did when he was there. Listen to his description, and mark these statements as **cierto** or **falso.** (5 x 2 pts. each = 10 pts.)

	Cierto	**Falso**
1. Julio es soltero.	______	______
2. Se divirtió en Puerto Rico.	______	______
3. Fue a Puerto Rico para ir de compras.	______	______
4. Le fascinaron todos los postres.	______	______
5. Prefiere la playa Ocean Park.	______	______

2 Los planes Irene and Francisco have decided to go visit relatives in Ponce. They have gotten together to discuss what they are going to do. Describe their plans, using at least six words from the box. (4 pts. for vocabulary + 4 pts. for grammar + 2 pts. for style and creativity = 10 pts.)

caro/a	**divertirse**	**pasaje**	**regalo**	**ropa**
dinero	**maleta**	**rebaja**	**relajarse**	**salir**

____
____
____
____
____
____
____
____

Exams

Nombre ______________________ Fecha ______________________

3 Rutina Describe what Carolina is doing before going to work. Use the present progressive. (4 x 2 pts. each = 8 pts.)

____
____
____
____
____
____
____
____

4 Hola Fill in the blanks in this conversation with **ser** or **estar**. (10 x 1 pt. each = 10 pts.)

MAURICIO Hola, Carolina. ¿Cómo (1) ______________? ¡Te veo muy bien!

CAROLINA Hola, hombre. Pues yo (2) ______________ muy bien. ¿Y tú? Parece que (3) ______________ un poco más delgado.

MAURICIO Sí, hace unos meses que empecé a ir al gimnasio. Bueno, pero hablemos de otras cosas. Me dijeron que tienes novio. ¿Quién (4) ______________? ¿Lo conozco?

CAROLINA No, no lo conoces. Se llama Raúl. Él (5) ______________ de México y ahora (6) ______________ aquí estudiando en mi escuela. Y tú, ¿qué haces ahora?

MAURICIO Ya ves, últimamente (7) ______________ muy buen estudiante. Pronto acabo la escuela secundaria. Oye, y ¿sabes algo de Irene y Francisco? (8) ______________ muy simpáticos, pero hace mucho (*it's been a while*) que no los veo.

CAROLINA Ellos (9) ______________ ahora en Puerto Rico con la escuela. Yo los veo a menudo. La casa de Francisco (10) ______________ al lado de la mía (*mine*).

MAURICIO Quiero verlos. A ver si salimos con ellos pronto.

Exams

Nombre ______________________________ Fecha ____________________

5 De compras Francisco and Irene are shopping in Puerto Rico. Change the underlined words to direct object pronouns and change the indirect objects to indirect object pronouns. (5 x 1 pt. each = 5 pts.)

modelo

Puedes darle la maleta al botones.
Se la puedes dar.

FRANCISCO Puedes comprarle un reloj a tu hermana.
IRENE No, no (1) __________ __________ puedo comprar. No tengo dinero.
FRANCISCO Le puedes pedir dinero a tu primo.
IRENE No, no (2) __________ __________ quiero pedir.
FRANCISCO Mira, camisetas. Tú y yo debemos regalarle una camiseta a Sonia.
IRENE Sí, (3) __________ __________ debemos regalar. Fue muy simpática con nosotros.
FRANCISCO Yo también le quiero dar las gracias a tus tíos.
IRENE Sí, fueron muy amables. (4) __________ __________ tenemos que dar.
FRANCISCO Oye, quiero comprar estos discos para mí.
IRENE Qué coincidencia, yo también (5) __________ __________ quiero comprar.

6 La cena Fill in the blanks with the preterite of the verbs. (7 x 1 pt. each = 7 pts.)

Irene y Francisco salieron ayer por la noche. Ellos dos (1) __________________ (vestirse) muy elegantemente (*elegantly*) y fueron a un restaurante muy bueno. Francisco (2) ______________ (pedir) mucha comida, pero Irene (3) ______________ (preferir) comer poco. El camarero les (4) ______________ (servir) la comida rápidamente. Ellos dos hablaron mucho durante la cena. Después, (5) __________________ (despedirse) del dueño del restaurante. Francisco, nervioso, no (6) ____________ (dormir) nada porque se dio cuenta de (*realized*) que (7) ____________ (perder) la cartera en el restaurante.

7 Tu opinión Pick one of your favorite cities and describe why you like it so much and what you like to do there. Make sure to answer these questions. (4 pts. for vocabulary + 4 pts. for grammar + 2 pts. for style and creativity = 10 pts.)

- ¿Qué es lo que más te gusta de la ciudad? ¿Qué es lo que menos te gusta?
- ¿Vive algún familiar tuyo (*relative of yours*) allí?
- ¿Qué hiciste la última vez que estuviste allí?
- ¿Cuál es tu restaurante favorito de la ciudad? ¿Cuál es el plato que más te gusta del restaurante?

____

____

____

____

____

____

____

Exams

8 Qué precios Answer the questions. Write the numbers as words. (4 x 2 pts. each = 8 pts.)

1. ¿Cuánto cuestan los zapatos de tenis? ______________________________

____

2. ¿Cuánto cuestan las blusas de seda? ______________________________

____

3. ¿A qué hora cierra la tienda? ______________________________

____

4. ¿De qué números tiene botas la tienda? ______________________________

____

Exams

Nombre ______________________ Fecha ______________________

9 Preguntas Answer these questions with complete sentences. (5 x 2 pts. each = 10 pts.)

1. ¿Qué vas a hacer estas vacaciones? ______________________

2. ¿Qué hiciste anoche? ______________________

3. ¿A qué hora te fuiste ayer a tu casa? ______________________

4. ¿Conducen tus padres para llevarte a la escuela? ______________________

5. ¿Qué materias te interesan más? ______________________

10 Lectura Read this gossip column from a Spanish magazine. Then answer the questions with complete sentences. (5 x 2 pts. each = 10 pts.)

Rumores

Francisco Ruiz y Verónica Cortés celebraron ayer su fiesta de aniversario de bodas. Esta famosa pareja se conoció en la fiesta de Fin de Año del año 2009 en Cancún. Francisco y Verónica se comprometieron cuatro meses más tarde, en abril de 2010. Poco tiempo después se casaron. La fiesta de ayer, sólo para la familia, fue en el restaurante Olivas. La comida, como siempre en ese restaurante, estuvo sabrosísima. De postre sirvieron pastel de frutas y champán. Después de la cena todos los invitados brindaron por la felicidad de la joven pareja. Fueron a la fiesta casi todos los miembros de las dos familias, menos Carmen, la hermana del feliz esposo, que no pudo asistir. Ayer, durante la fiesta, supimos que Carmen está disfrutando de[1] unas largas vacaciones por el Caribe. ¿Quién sabe? Quizás Carmen quiere olvidar a Pablo, su ex novio. Alguien me dijo que se está divirtiendo con un nuevo amigo.

[1] *enjoying*

1. ¿Cuál es el estado civil de Verónica Cortés? ______________________

2. ¿Cuándo decidieron casarse Francisco y Verónica? ______________________

3. ¿Quiénes fueron invitados a la fiesta? ______________________

4. ¿Le gustó la comida al/a la periodista? ______________________

5. ¿Por qué no fue Carmen a la fiesta? ______________________

Exams

Nombre ________________________ Fecha ________________

11 Escribir Write a paragraph with at least five sentences about what you did last weekend. Use the preterite and vocabulary words. (5 pts. for vocabulary + 5 pts. for grammar + 2 pts. for style and creativity = 12 pts.)

Exams

Nombre ______________________ Fecha ______________________

EXAM B

Lecciones 1–9

1 Escuchar Pedro and Concepción are thinking of going to Puerto Rico on vacation. Magdalena, their friend, is telling them what she did when she was there. Listen to her description, and then mark these statements as **cierto** or **falso.** (5 x 2 pts. each = 10 pts.)

	Cierto	Falso
1. Magdalena fue a Puerto Rico tres veces.	______	______
2. Ella nunca visitó ningún museo.	______	______
3. Se divirtió más en el primer viaje.	______	______
4. A Magdalena le fascina ir de compras.	______	______
5. Les recomienda un restaurante en el Viejo San Juan.	______	______

2 Los planes Pedro and Concepción have decided to visit relatives in San Juan. Describe their plans, using at least six words from the list. (4 pts. for vocabulary + 4 pts. for grammar + 2 pts. for style and creativity = 10 pts.)

barato/a	**descansar**	**gastar**	**llegar**	**probar**
cambiar	**equipaje**	**juntos**	**pasaporte**	**riquísimo/a**

____

____

____

____

____

____

____

____

____

____

Exams

Nombre ______________________ Fecha ______________________

3 Rutina Describe what Magdalena is doing in each photo. Use the present progressive. (4 x 2 pts. each = 8 pts.)

____

____

____

____

____

____

____

4 Hola Fill in the blanks in this conversation with **ser** or **estar**. (10 x 1 pt. each = 10 pts.)

ALFREDO Hola, Concepción. ¿Cómo (1) ______________? ¡Te veo muy bien!

CONCEPCIÓN Hola, hombre. Pues yo (2) ______________ muy bien. ¿Y tú? Pareces cansado.¿(3) ______________ estudiando mucho?

ALFREDO Sí, (4) ______________ muy buen estudiante. Pronto acabo la escuela secundaria. Mi clase de física (5) ______________ muy interesante, pero siempre hay mucho que hacer. Bueno, y ¿a ti cómo te va? Me dijeron que tienes novio. ¿Quién (6) ______________? ¿Lo conozco?

CONCEPCIÓN No, no lo conoces. Se llama Pedro. Él (7) ______________ de Los Ángeles y (8) ______________ muy inteligente y generoso. Y tú, ¿tienes novia?

ALFREDO Pues, sí. ¿Te acuerdas de Marta, la amiga de mi hermana? Ella y yo (9) ______________ saliendo.

CONCEPCIÓN Me alegro mucho por ti. Es muy buena chica.

ALFREDO Muchas gracias. Bueno, me voy, (10) ______________ un poco tarde. Otro día hablamos más.

CONCEPCIÓN Está bien, ¡hasta pronto!

Exams

5 De compras Pedro and Concepción are shopping in Puerto Rico. Change the underlined words to direct object pronouns and change the indirect objects to indirect object pronouns. (5 x 1 pt. each = 5 pts.)

modelo

Puedes darle la maleta al botones.
Se la puedes dar.

PEDRO Puedes comprarles un libro a tus padres.
CONCEPCIÓN Sí, (1) __________ __________ voy a comprar. Y a tu hermana, ¿le llevamos este sombrero?
PEDRO Sí, (2) __________ __________ vamos a llevar. Me gusta.
CONCEPCIÓN También quiero comprar esta blusa para mí. ¿No es bonita?
PEDRO Sí, pero yo (3) __________ __________ compro, mi amor. Es mi regalo de cumpleaños.
CONCEPCIÓN Gracias, querido. Yo quiero darte las gracias por este viaje tan maravilloso.
PEDRO Muy bien. (4) __________ __________ puedes dar esta noche invitándome a cenar.
CONCEPCIÓN Bien. Tú me das el dinero y yo te invito.
PEDRO ¡Qué lista eres! Pues, claro, yo (5) __________ __________ doy.

6 La cena Fill in the blanks with the preterite of the verbs. (7 x 1 pt. each = 7 pts.)

Concepción y Pedro salieron a cenar ayer por la noche. Concepción (1) ______________ (vestirse) elegantemente (*elegantly*), pero Pedro siempre lleva traje para trabajar y anoche (2) __________ (preferir) vestirse con ropa informal. A su novia no le importó. (Ellos) (3) ____________________ (pedir) champán y unos platos deliciosos. El camarero les (4) ______________________ (traer) la comida rápidamente y todo (5) ______________________ (estar) riquísimo. Cuando (ellos) (6) ____________________ (salir) del restaurante, (7) ______________________ (dar) un paseo (*took a walk*) muy largo.

7 Tu opinión Pick one of your favorite seasons and describe why you like it so much and what you like to do during that season. Make sure to answer these questions. (4 pts. for vocabulary + 4 pts. for grammar + 2 pts. for style and creativity = 10 pts.)

- ¿Qué te gusta más de esta estación?
- ¿Qué te gusta menos?
- ¿Qué hiciste en esta estación el año pasado?
- ¿Qué cosas haces durante esta estación que no haces el resto del año (por ejemplo, con respecto a la comida, los viajes, los pasatiempos, la ropa)?

____

____

____

____

____

____

____

____

Exams

Nombre ______________________ Fecha ______________________

8 Qué precios Answer the questions. Write the numbers as words. (4 x 2 pts. each = 8 pts.)

1. ¿Cuánto cuestan los zapatos de tenis? ______________________

2. ¿Cuánto cuestan las blusas de seda? ______________________

3. ¿A qué hora cierra la tienda? ______________________

4. ¿De qué números tiene botas la tienda? ______________________

Exams

Nombre ______________________ Fecha ______________

9 Preguntas Answer these questions with complete sentences. (5 x 2 pts. each = 10 pts.)

1. ¿Qué vas a hacer esta noche? ______________________
2. ¿Qué tiempo hace hoy? ______________________
3. ¿A qué hora llegaste a la escuela esta mañana? ______________________
4. ¿Cuál es tu comida favorita? ______________________
5. ¿Qué materias no te interesan mucho? ______________________

10 Lectura Read this gossip column from a Spanish magazine. Then answer the questions with complete sentences. (5 x 2 pts. each = 10 pts.)

Rumores

El doctor Ignacio Cuevas, padre del conocido[1] artista español Pepe Cuevas, y su joven esposa Corina Bran celebraron el pasado sábado 22 de mayo el nacimiento de su primer hijo. Es el primer hijo para ella, pero el tercero para él. La interesante pareja —él tiene 87 años y ella tiene 47 años menos que su esposo— se casó el primero de marzo de 2010 en Florida. La fiesta del sábado pasado, para unas cien personas, fue en el hotel Hilton de Miami. En la cena sirvieron varios platos de mariscos —la comida favorita del feliz papá y de este periodista— y de postre hubo pastel de frutas y chocolate. Después de la espectacular[2] cena, los invitados pudieron bailar durante horas en el bello salón Diamante. Todos estuvieron muy contentos de ver bailar a los nuevos papás. Pero nadie pudo ver al niño después de la cena; la sobrina del doctor Cuevas, Juana, lo llevó a su habitación para dormir. Los nietos del doctor Cuevas, los conocidos jóvenes artistas Emilio y Pepe Junior, no pudieron asistir, pero Pepe Cuevas sí estuvo allí al lado de su padre y de su nuevo hermanito. Los invitados pidieron oír cantar a Pepe, pero él no cantó.

[1] *well-known, famous* [2] *spectacular*

1. ¿Cuál es el estado civil de Corina Bran? ______________________
2. ¿Cuántos años tiene ella? ______________________
3. ¿Quién es Pepe Cuevas? ¿Por qué estuvo en la fiesta? ______________________
4. ¿Por qué no bailó Juana en la fiesta? ______________________
5. ¿Qué piensa el periodista de la pareja? ¿Por qué? ______________________

Exams

Nombre ______________________ Fecha ______________________

11 Escribir Write a paragraph with at least five sentences about what you did this past week. Use the preterite and vocabulary words. (5 pts. for vocabulary + 5 pts. for grammar + 2 pts. for style and creativity = 12 pts.)

Exams

PERFORMANCE TASK Lección 1

All responses and communication must be in Spanish.

Context

You are meeting many students in Spanish class for the first time. You will prepare a brief presentation to introduce yourself to the class.

Interpretive task

Watch the **Fotonovela** episode in Lesson 1 and make a list of expressions people use to greet new acquaintances and to introduce themselves. Also, identify a few questions people use when they meet someone.

Interpersonal task

Work with a partner. You are meeting each other for the first time. Use the expressions and questions you identified in the **Fotonovela** to have a short conversation.

Presentational task

With your partner, prepare a brief presentation to introduce yourselves to the class. First greet the class, say your name, where you are from, and say you are a student. Don't forget to mention that you are pleased to meet the class! Then say that you want to introduce your partner to the class.

ASSESSMENT Lección 1

Integrated Performance Assessment Rubric and Suggestions

Because students have limited linguistic ability at this stage, keep your expectations simple and concrete. These criteria will become more complex as students' abilities develop.

	5 points	3 points	1 point
Interpretive	The student can identify several expressions people use to greet new acquaintances and to introduce themselves. The student can also identify a few questions people use when they meet someone.	The student can identify only a few expressions people use to greet new acquaintances and to introduce themselves. They can identify a few questions people use when they meet someone.	The student has difficulty identifying expressions and questions people use when meeting new acquaintances and introducing themselves.
Interpersonal	The student can have a short conversation demonstrating mutual understanding.	The student can have a short conversation with only some difficulty in mutual understanding.	The student can have a short conversation but does not reach mutual understanding.
Presentational	The student can introduce himself/herself to the class using the appropriate expressions.	The student can introduce himself/herself to the class using a few appropriate expressions, but details are missing.	The student has difficulty introducing himself/herself to the class, and the most relevant details are missing.

Nombre ____________________ Fecha ____________________

PERFORMANCE TASK Lección 2

All responses and communication must be in Spanish.

Context

You and your classmates want to know about each other's class schedules and your opinions about the classes you take. First, you will interview one of your classmates to find out about his/her classes. Then you will present your own schedule to the class.

Interpretive task

Watch the **Fotonovela** episode for Lesson 2 and make a list of expressions people use to talk about their classes, their schedules, and to ask about their favorite classes. Then look at the schedule on page 68 in your textbook to see how it is organized.

Interpersonal task

Make your own class schedule in Spanish and share it with a classmate. Ask your classmate what classes he/she takes, what time each class starts, and how he/she likes them.

Presentational task

Present your schedule to the class, including the times and days of the week of each class. Don't forget to mention which classes you like and which ones you don't!

ASSESSMENT Lección 2

Integrated Performance Assessment Rubric

	5 points	3 points	1 point
Interpretive	The student can easily identify several expressions people use to talk about their classes and schedules.	The student can identify only a few expressions people use to talk about their classes and schedules.	The student has difficulty identifying expressions people use to talk about their classes and schedules.
Interpersonal	The student can complete a basic conversation demonstrating mutual understanding. The result of the conversation is a clear comparison with his/her classmate's classes and schedule.	The student can complete a basic conversation with only some difficulty in mutual understanding. The result of the conversation is a clear comparison with his/her classmate's classes and schedule.	The student can complete a basic conversation but does not reach mutual understanding. The student is not able to make comparisons with his/her classmate's classes and schedule.
Presentational	The student can provide relevant information about his/her classes and schedule, and about the classes he/she likes or dislikes.	The student can provide relevant information about his/her classes and schedule, but there are some spelling or grammar errors.	The student fails to provide relevant information about his/her classes and schedule, and about the classes he/she likes or dislikes.

Nombre ______________________ Fecha ______________________

PERFORMANCE TASK Lección 3

All responses and communication must be in Spanish.

Context

You and a classmate are spending Spring vacation in a Spanish-speaking country, and the coordinator of the trip needs to place you with host families. You are going to read about six different people. Decide which person is the best host for your classmate. Then, present your recommendation to the class, describing your classmate and explaining your choice of host.

Interpretive task

Read the article **Gente… Las familias** on pages 106–107 of the textbook. Then, with a partner, choose two of the people profiled as your partner's possible host. List two reasons for each host as to why the person you chose is a good match for your partner.

Interpersonal task

Prepare a list of five questions to ask your partner that will help you decide which of the two candidates would be the best host for him/her. Then, interview your partner to determine who will best suit him/her. Take turns asking and answering each other's questions.

Presentational task

Present your recommendation to the class. Give at least three reasons why you chose the host you did for your partner.

ASSESSMENT Lección 3

Integrated Performance Assessment Rubric

	5 points	3 points	1 point
Interpretive	The student can identify reasons for choosing each potential host.	The student can identify reasons for choosing each potential host, with some difficulty.	The student cannot identify reasons for choosing each potential host.
Interpersonal	The student can complete an interview demonstrating mutual understanding. The result of the interview is a clear decision on the recommendation to the class.	The student can complete an interview with only some difficulty in mutual understanding. The result of the interview is a clear decision on the recommendation to the class.	The student can complete an interview but does not reach mutual understanding. The student is not able to make a clear recommendation to the class.
Presentational	The student can provide relevant information about his or her recommendation and the reasons for his or her choice.	The student can provide relevant information but some details are missing from his or her recommendation.	The presentation lacks detail and the student does not provide clear reasons for the decision.

Nombre ______________________ Fecha ______________________

PERFORMANCE TASK Lección 4

All responses and communication must be in Spanish.

Context

Your school is having an election for student council, and you need to decide what attributes are important in the person you elect. You are going to listen to two people describe themselves. Then, you and a partner will talk about the characteristics that would make each of them a better candidate. Finally, you will describe the characteristics of your ideal candidate to the class.

Interpretive task

Listen to the audio for the **Escuchar** activity on page 145 of your textbook. As you listen to the two people describe themselves, make a list of three characteristics that would make each of them good members of your school's student council. Then, make a list of three additional characteristics you would like to see in your student council members.

Interpersonal task

Compare your lists with your partner's lists. Take turns asking each other what characteristics you wrote down, and why you feel those characteristics are important. Work together to write a description of your ideal candidate, including at least five characteristics you think are important.

Presentational task

Prepare a presentation describing your ideal candidate to the class. Mention at least five characteristics of your ideal student council member, and describe why those characteristics are important for you and your school.

ASSESSMENT Lección 4

Integrated Performance Assessment Rubric

	5 points	3 points	1 point
Interpretive	The student can identify characteristics of each speaker.	The student can identify characteristics of each speaker with some difficulty.	The student can barely identify characteristics of each speaker.
Interpersonal	The student can complete an interview demonstrating mutual understanding. The result of the interview is a clear description for the class.	The student can complete an interview with only some difficulty in mutual understanding. The result of the interview is a clear description for the class.	The student can complete an interview but does not reach mutual understanding. The student is not able to prepare a clear description for the class.
Presentational	The student can provide relevant information about his or her recommendation and the reasoning for his or her choice.	Details are missing about the student's recommendation.	The presentation lacks detail, and the reasoning for the decision is unclear.

Nombre ______________________ Fecha ______________

PERFORMANCE TASK Lección 5

All responses and communication must be in Spanish.

Context

Six students from your Spanish class will be chosen to spend a week in Puerto Rico, at the **Hotel Vistahermosa** in Lajas. Students will be chosen in pairs based on their presentation to the selection committee.

Interpretive task

Read the brochure for the **Hotel Vistahermosa** on pages 180–181 of your textbook and make a list of the top three activities you would like to do or places you'd like to visitwhile you are there and why.

Interpersonal task

Share your list with a partner, telling him or her why you chose the activities or locations you did. Ask your partner what he or she chose, and ask questions about them. Collaborate to choose the best three to present.

Presentational task

Prepare slideshow for the selection committee with an audio narration. Your presentation should highlight the three activities or locations you chose, including your reasons for choosing each for when you stay at the **Hotel Vistahermosa**.

ASSESSMENT Lección 5

Integrated Performance Assessment Rubric

	5 points	3 points	1 point
Interpretive	The student can identify activities he or she would like to do.	The student can identify activities he or she would like to do, with some difficulty.	The student can only identify 1 activity he or she would like to do.
Interpersonal	The student can complete an interview demonstrating mutual understanding. The result of the interview is a recommendation for the selection committee.	The student can complete an interview with only some difficulty in mutual understanding. The result of the interview is a clear recommendation for the selection committee.	The student can complete an interview but does not reach mutual understanding. The student is not able to make a clear recommendation for the selection committee.
Presentational	The student can provide relevant information about his or her recommendation and the reasoning for his or her choice.	Details are missing about the student's recommendation.	The presentation lacks detail, and the reasoning for the decision is unclear.

Nombre ______________________ Fecha ______________________

PERFORMANCE TASK Lección 6

Integrated Performance Assessment

All responses and communication must be in Spanish.

Context

You are traveling to Colombia. Two of your friends have given you money to bring back clothing for them because they are interested in getting something unique from the Spanish-speaking world. Each of your friends, one male and one female, has given you $25, so you'll need to check the current exchange rate to find out how many **pesos** you have to spend.

Interpretive task

Read the brochure for **Almacén Corona** on pages 216–217 of your textbook. Make a list of the items you plan to buy, and their respective prices, for each of your friends.

Interpersonal task

When you arrive at the store, you ask a salesperson to help you find the items you'd like to buy. Work with a partner to play the roles of the customer and the salesperson. Describe at least four items you are looking for and how much you intend to pay for each of them. The salesperson can tell you what colors, sizes, and patterns are available.

Presentational task

Write an email to each of your friends from home. Describe at least two items you bought for each of them. Include as much detail as you can.

ASSESSMENT Lección 6

Integrated Performance Assessment Rubric

	5 points	3 points	1 point
Interpretive	The student can identify several items he or she would like to buy.	The student can identify a few items he or she would like to buy.	The student has difficulty identifying items he or she would like to buy.
Interpersonal	The student can complete an interview demonstrating mutual understanding. The result of the interview is a clear list of what the student will purchase.	The student can complete an interview with only some difficulty in mutual understanding. The result of the interview is a clear list of what the student will purchase.	The student can complete an interview but does not reach mutual understanding. The student is not able to make a clear list of what he or she will purchase.
Presentational	The student can provide relevant information about what he or she purchased for each friend, with sufficient details.	Details are missing about what the student purchased.	The email lacks detail and it is not clear what the student purchased.

Nombre ______________________ Fecha ______________________

PERFORMANCE TASK Lección 7

All responses and communication must be in Spanish.

Context

You are writing a short blog post about a celebrity you just heard interviewed, Julián Larrea. Your goal is to describe how his life is the same and different from your own.

Interpretive task

Listen to the interview from page 255 of your textbook. Write down three things he does as part of his daily routine, and two additional things he likes to do.

Interpersonal task

Compare your list with a partner's. Ask your partner how his or her routine and interests are similar or different from Julián's and your own, referring to at least three different activities.

Presentational task

Write a short blog post describing at least two things Julián does as part of his daily routine, and comparing your routine to his. Also include a comparison of your interests. Include as much detail as possible.

ASSESSMENT Lección 7

Integrated Performance Assessment Rubric

	5 points	3 points	1 point
Interpretive	The student can identify several things Julián does as part of his daily routine.	The student can identify only a few things Julián does as part of his daily routine.	The student can hardly identify things Julián does as part of his daily routine.
Interpersonal	The student can complete an interview demonstrating mutual understanding. The result of the interview is a clear list showing similarities and differences with Julián's daily routine.	The student can complete an interview with only some difficulty in mutual understanding. The result of the interview is a clear list showing similarities and differences with Julián's daily routine.	The student can complete an interview but does not reach mutual understanding. The student is not able to list similarities and differences with Julián's daily routine.
Presentational	The student can write a short blog entry describing Julián's daily routine and interests, and comparing them with his or her own.	The student has some difficulty writing a short blog entry describing Julián's daily routine and interests, and comparing them with his or her own.	The student writes a short blog entry but does not clearly describe Julián's daily routine and interests, and cannot compare them with his ot her own.

Integrated Performance Assessment

PERFORMANCE TASK Lección 8

All responses and communication must be in Spanish.

Context

You and a friend are in Antigua, Guatemala, and you are deciding on a restaurant to have dinner. Then you tell a group of friends (your classmates) about your decision.

Interpretive task

Read the menu and the review of **La feria del maíz** on pages 290–291 of your textbook. Make a list of the things that appeal to you about the restaurant and those that don't appeal to you. Mention at least four characteristics, citing specific examples from the text.

Interpersonal task

Talk with a partner about why you would or would not want to eat at **La feria del maíz.** Ask your partner about at least four characteristics of the restaurant, including those that were most appealing and those that were least appealing.

Presentational task

Together with your partner, prepare a presentation for the class about why you would or would not want to eat at **La feria del maíz.** Describe at least four characteristics of the restaurant.

ASSESSMENT Lección 8

Integrated Performance Assessment Rubric

	5 points	3 points	1 point
Interpretive	The student can identify 4 or more characteristics of the restaurant.	The student can identify 3 or more characteristics of the restaurant.	The student can identify 2 or more characteristics of the restaurant.
Interpersonal	The student can complete an interview demonstrating mutual understanding. The result of the interview is a clear opinion about the restaurant.	The student can complete an interview with only some difficulty in mutual understanding. The result of the interview is a clear opinion about the restaurant.	The student can complete an interview but does not reach mutual understanding. The student is not able to clearly articulate an opinion about the restaurant.
Presentational	The student can provide relevant information about the restaurant and why he or she would or would not want to eat there, with sufficient details.	Details are missing about the restaurant and why the student would or would not want to eat there.	The presentation lacks detail about the restaurant and it is not clear why the student would or would not want to eat there.

Nombre ______________________ Fecha ______________________

PERFORMANCE TASK

Lección 9

All responses and communication must be in Spanish.

Context

You recently met a new student from Puerto Rico who just moved to your town. Your new friend wants to know about the most important or fun celebration in your area.

Interpretive task

Watch the **Flash cultura** episode in Lesson 9 about **fiestas de la calle San Sebastián**. Write down at least three features of this celebration.

Interpersonal task

Compare your list with a partner's and discuss the similarities and differences you find between **San Sebastián** and a popular celebration in your area.

Presentational task

With your partner, record a short video in which you describe a popular celebration in your area to your new Puerto Rican acquaintance. In your video, compare this celebration to **las fiestas de la calle San Sebastián** described in the **Flash cultura** episode.

ASSESSMENT Lección 9

Integrated Performance Assessment Rubric

	5 points	3 points	1 point
Interpretive	The student can identify 3 or more characteristics of the celebration.	The student can identify 2 or more characteristics of the celebration.	The student can identify fewer than 2 characteristics of the celebration.
Interpersonal	The student can complete an interview demonstrating mutual understanding. The result of the interview is a clear comparison of two celebrations.	The student can complete an interview with only some difficulty in mutual understanding. The result of the interview is a clear comparison of two celebrations.	The student can complete an interview but does not reach mutual understanding. The student is not able to clearly compare the two celebrations.
Presentational	The student can provide a clear description with sufficient details.	Details are missing from the student's description.	The description lacks detail and it is not clear what the student is describing.

TEST AUDIO SCRIPTS

Lección 1

TEST A

Hola Marisa. Soy Jaime, el conductor del autobús. ¿Cómo estás? Yo estoy regular. Oye, hay un problema. Hay tres maletas y un libro en el autobús. Las maletas son de los pasajeros de Costa Rica. Pero ¿de quién es el libro? Son las diez de la mañana y mi número de teléfono es el 24-30-12. Muchas gracias.

TEST B

Hola, Carmen. Soy don Fernando, el conductor del autobús. ¿Cómo estás? Yo estoy bien. Oye, hay un problema. Hay dos maletas y tres libros en el autobús. Las maletas son de los turistas de Argentina. Pero ¿de quién son los libros? Son las doce del mediodía y el número de teléfono es el 25-13-07. Perdón y gracias.

TEST C

1. ¿Cómo te llamas?
2. ¿Cómo estás?
3. ¿De dónde eres?
4. ¿A qué hora es la clase de español?
5. ¿Cuántos profesores hay en la clase?

TEST D

1. ¿Qué tal?
2. ¿Qué hora es?
3. ¿Cómo se llama tu profesor(a) de español?
4. ¿Cuántas chicas hay en la clase?
5. ¿Hay chicos en la clase?

TEST E

Buenos días, profesor Martínez. ¿Cómo está? Soy Mauricio Valdivia. Hay cuatro videos, unos cuadernos y un diccionario en el laboratorio. Los cuadernos son de los estudiantes, pero ¿de quién son los videos y el diccionario? Son las nueve y cuarto de la mañana. Estoy en la escuela hasta las cinco y media, y mañana de diez de la mañana a tres de la tarde. Gracias.

TEST F

Buenos días, profesor Pérez. ¿Cómo está? Soy Juan López. Hay tres mapas, unos cuadernos y dos diccionarios en el laboratorio. Los cuadernos son de los estudiantes, pero ¿de quién son los mapas y los diccionarios? Son las diez de la mañana. Estoy en la escuela hasta las seis y media, y mañana de diez de la mañana a dos y media de la tarde. Gracias.

Lección 2

TEST A

Buenos días. Me llamo Enrique Sánchez y soy el profesor de química. Ahora deseo hablar sobre el curso. A ver, la clase es los lunes, miércoles y viernes de diez a once de la mañana. Necesitan preparar la tarea todos los días y estudiar mucho para la clase. También necesitan practicar todos los lunes en el laboratorio. El laboratorio está cerca de la biblioteca. Bueno, ¿desean preguntar algo?

TEST B

Buenas tardes, soy la profesora Molina. Enseño biología y soy la profesora este semestre. Ahora deseo hablar sobre el curso. A ver, la clase es los martes y los jueves de doce a una de la tarde. Necesitan preparar la tarea todos los días y estudiar mucho para esta clase. También necesitan practicar todos los miércoles en el laboratorio. El laboratorio está cerca de la librería. Bueno, ¿desean preguntar algo?

TEST C

1. ¿Qué día es hoy?
2. ¿Trabajas los sábados?
3. ¿Practicas mucho el español?
4. ¿Te gusta la clase de español?
5. ¿A qué hora termina la clase de español?

TEST D

1. ¿Qué clases tomas este semestre?
2. ¿Qué días es tu clase de español?
3. ¿Estudias en la biblioteca?
4. ¿A qué hora llegas a casa o a la residencia los lunes?
5. ¿Qué días descansas?

TEST E

Buenos días, me llamo Ernesto Sánchez. Soy el profesor de arqueología. El horario del curso está en la pizarra. Hay clase tres días a la semana. Los lunes y los miércoles, la clase es de ocho a nueve de la mañana. Los viernes, la clase es de cinco a seis de la tarde. Para esta clase necesitan el libro del curso, papel y pluma.

TEST F

Buenos días. Me llamo Enrique Merino. Soy el profesor de química. El horario del curso está en la pizarra. Hay clase cuatro días a la semana. Los lunes y los jueves, la clase es de ocho a nueve de la mañana. Los martes y los viernes, la clase es de nueve a diez de la mañana. Para esta clase necesitan una calculadora, papel y pluma.

Lección 3

TEST A

Esteban es de México y vive en Ecuador. Tiene treinta años y es muy inteligente. Estudia química en la universidad y por las tardes trabaja como programador. Tiene que trabajar mucho todos los días. Cuando termina de trabajar, asiste a sus clases. Su novia se llama Matilde y tiene veinticuatro años. Ella comprende que Esteban tiene que estudiar mucho porque ella también es muy trabajadora. Esteban y Matilde descansan los sábados y los domingos.

TEST B

Manuela es estudiante de matemáticas en la universidad. Es de España y tiene veinticinco años. Manuela trabaja en la biblioteca por las tardes y por eso no tiene mucho tiempo para salir con sus amigos. Su compañera de apartamento se llama Tina y es una chica muy simpática. Por las mañanas, Tina asiste a clases de japonés y por las tardes trabaja en un café. Manuela y Tina son muy buenas amigas. Comen en la cafetería todos los días y asisten a clase de yoga los sábados.

TEST C

1. ¿Dónde vives?
2. ¿Cuántos años tienes?
3. ¿Te gusta leer el periódico?
4. ¿Qué lenguas extranjeras comprendes?
5. ¿Tienes ganas de aprender español este semestre?

TEST D

1. ¿Cómo eres?
2. ¿Cuántos hermanos o hermanas tienes?
3. ¿Qué debes preparar esta tarde?
4. ¿Qué aprendes en la clase de español?
5. ¿Qué profesión te gusta?

TEST E

Hola, amigas:

Me llamo Víctor Miguel. Tengo veintidós años y soy ecuatoriano. Por las mañanas estudio medicina en la universidad y por las tardes trabajo en una librería. Mi padre es médico y mi madre es artista. Tengo un hermano menor. Él también es estudiante. Soy alto, moreno y muy, muy guapo. Mi novia ideal debe ser una muchacha bonita, simpática e inteligente, y debe tener entre veinte y veinticuatro años.

Saludos, muchachas.

TEST F

Hola, amigos:

Me llamo Ana Isabel. Tengo veintitrés años y soy estadounidense. Por las mañanas estudio periodismo en la universidad y por las tardes trabajo en una biblioteca. Mi padre es programador y mi madre es doctora. Tengo un hermano mayor. Él también es estudiante. Soy alta, pelirroja y muy simpática. Mi novio ideal debe ser un muchacho guapo, inteligente y bueno, y debe tener entre veintidós y veinticinco años.

Saludos, muchachos.

Lección 4

TEST A

¿Le gusta practicar deportes? El lugar que necesita es el Club Cosmos, en el centro de la ciudad. Tenemos actividades para los aficionados a todos los deportes: puede jugar al golf, practicar la natación y jugar al tenis. También hay una piscina, dos gimnasios y una cafetería donde usted puede pasar sus ratos libres. Si quiere más información, puede venir al club. Cerramos a las doce de la noche.

TEST B

¿Desea pasar más tiempo con su familia? ¿Les gusta practicar deportes o pasear en bicicleta? El lugar que usted y su familia necesitan es el Club Excursionista. Pueden pasar un fin de semana en las montañas. Tenemos diversiones para toda la familia. En el Club Excursionista hay dos piscinas, dos gimnasios y un restaurante. Cerca del club hay un parque donde pueden pasear en bicicleta y caminar. Si quiere más información, puede escribir un mensaje electrónico.

TEST C

1. ¿Qué vas a hacer mañana?
2. ¿Dónde piensas comer hoy?
3. ¿Qué vas a hacer este fin de semana?
4. ¿Cuál es tu película favorita?
5. ¿Te gusta practicar deportes?

TEST D

1. ¿Qué vas a hacer esta noche?
2. ¿Qué piensas comer hoy?
3. ¿Sales los fines de semana?
4. ¿A qué hora empieza la clase de español?
5. ¿Qué te gusta hacer los fines de semana?

TEST E

¿Te gustan los deportes? Entonces tienes que venir al gimnasio Tarzán. Tenemos todo lo que necesitas para practicar tu deporte favorito. En el gimnasio Tarzán tenemos clases de baloncesto, natación y muchos deportes más. El gimnasio abre cada día a las seis de la mañana y cierra a las diez de la noche. Las clases empiezan a las diez de la mañana. Los domingos no hay clases. ¡Y si vienes hoy, te damos una pelota de fútbol!

TEST F

¿Te gustan los deportes? Entonces tienes que venir al gimnasio Sansón. Tenemos todo lo que necesitas para practicar tu deporte favorito. En el gimnasio Sansón tenemos clases de fútbol americano, tenis y muchos deportes más. El gimnasio abre cada día a las siete de la mañana y cierra a las nueve de la noche. Las clases empiezan a las nueve de la mañana. Los domingos no hay clases. ¡Y si vienes hoy, te damos una pelota de baloncesto!

Lección 5

TEST A

Si deseas ir de vacaciones a Puerto Rico este verano, tu agencia de viajes es la Agencia Sol y Playa. En nuestra agencia puedes conseguir las vacaciones que necesitas. ¿Tienes pocos días de vacaciones? Puedes pasar un fin de semana en San Juan de Puerto Rico. En nuestra agencia tenemos pasajes de ida y vuelta. ¿Quieres un mes de vacaciones? Puedes conseguir unas magníficas vacaciones en barco, visitando las magníficas playas del mar Caribe. Si te gusta la naturaleza, puedes acampar dos semanas en la playa Boquerón. La Agencia Sol y Playa es para ti; ¡Puerto Rico te espera!

TEST B

Si deseas ir de vacaciones a Puerto Rico, tu agencia de viajes es la Agencia El Gran Sol. En nuestra agencia puedes conseguir las vacaciones que necesitas. ¿Tienes pocos días de vacaciones? Puedes pasar un fin de semana paseando por San Juan de Puerto Rico. En nuestra agencia vendemos un pasaje de ida y vuelta con habitación de hotel y excursiones a museos y lugares históricos. ¿Quieres dos semanas de vacaciones? Puedes conseguir unas fabulosas vacaciones acampando en la playa Boquerón y viendo los bonitos paisajes de la isla. La Agencia El Gran Sol es para ti; ¡Puerto Rico te espera!

TEST C

1. ¿Cuál es la fecha de hoy?
2. ¿Qué tiempo hace hoy?
3. ¿Qué quieres hacer en las vacaciones?
4. ¿Qué prefieres: viajar en avión o viajar en tren?
5. ¿Cómo estás hoy?

TEST D

1. ¿En qué estación del año estamos?
2. ¿Qué te gusta hacer cuando llueve?
3. ¿Cómo son tus vacaciones ideales?
4. Para tus vacaciones, ¿prefieres dormir en un hotel o acampar? ¿Por qué?
5. ¿Qué estás haciendo ahora mismo?

TEST E

Isla del Sol es un lugar excelente para ir de vacaciones. Sus playas son muy limpias. En verano hace calor y en invierno ¡también! En Isla del Sol hay un hotel excelente. Se llama Solimar. En la planta baja de Solimar puedes jugar cartas y videojuegos. Algunas actividades que ofrece el hotel son montar a caballo por la playa y hacer windsurf. En su sitio web, puedes hacer reservaciones y comprar los boletos de autobús del aeropuerto al hotel. ¡Es un lugar fantástico!

TEST F

Vieques es un lugar excelente para ir de vacaciones este verano. Sus playas son hermosas y limpias. En invierno hace fresco y en verano hace mucho calor. En Vieques hay un hotel excelente. Se llama Viequemar. En Viequemar puedes montar a caballo por la playa, bucear y hacer windsurf. En su sitio web, puedes hacer reservaciones y comprar los boletos de barco o avión. ¡Es un lugar fantástico!

Lección 6

TEST A

Bienvenidos al almacén El Caribe. En nuestras exclusivas tiendas de moda van a encontrar toda la ropa que ustedes necesitan para esta primavera. No tienen que gastar mucho dinero porque nuestros clientes siempre consiguen las mejores rebajas. En la tienda para niños, venden pantalones de todos los colores y camisetas a precios baratos. También tienen vestidos para niñas con bonitos diseños en color rosado. En la tienda para hombres, tienen chaquetas y pantalones que se pueden usar todo el año. También hay corbatas, zapatos y cinturones que hacen juego con toda su ropa. En la tienda de señoras, pueden comprar los vestidos más elegantes con guantes del mismo color.

TEST B

Bienvenidos al centro comercial El Prado. En nuestras exclusivas tiendas van a encontrar toda la ropa que necesitan para este invierno y pueden ir a la moda a precios de ganga. En la tienda para niños Globos, vendemos pantalones y camisetas a precios baratos y vestidos de bonitos diseños para niñas. También tenemos abrigos de todos los colores para los días de frío. En la tienda de señoras Detalles, pueden comprar los vestidos más elegantes y las más hermosas sandalias. También hay medias, sombreros y guantes que hacen juego con todo. En la tienda para hombres Modas Martino, tenemos chaquetas, pantalones y suéteres con los colores de moda. También hay una excelente rebaja en cinturones y corbatas.

TEST C

1. ¿A qué hora llegaste ayer a tu casa?
2. ¿Te prestan dinero tus amigos?
3. ¿En qué año empezaste a estudiar en la universidad?
4. ¿Qué ropa llevas ahora?
5. ¿Dónde comiste ayer?

TEST D

1. ¿Sabes hablar francés?
2. ¿Te compra ropa tu familia?
3. ¿Cuándo empezaste a estudiar en la universidad?
4. ¿Qué ropa te gusta llevar en verano?
5. ¿Dónde gastaste diez dólares la semana pasada?

TEST E

El almacén Toda Ropa abre sus puertas este fin de semana. Toda Ropa ofrece ropa para hombre y para mujer. Tenemos bluejeans, camisas, chaquetas, camisetas y muchas cosas más. Toda Ropa tiene muchos colores y tallas. Los precios son muy bajos y la ropa es hermosa y elegante. Usted puede pagar con tarjeta de crédito o en efectivo, pero no puede regatear, por favor. Nuestros vendedores están aquí para vender ropa buena, bonita y barata.

TEST F

El almacén Buena Pinta abre sus puertas este lunes. Estamos en el centro comercial San Juan. La entrada está frente al parque. En el almacén tenemos ropa para hombre y para mujer. Tenemos bluejeans y una gran colección de zapatos, carteras, corbatas y mucho más. Nuestros precios son baratos y nuestra ropa es buena y elegante. Usted puede pagar con tarjeta de crédito o en efectivo. Los vendedores le pueden dar más información.

Lección 7

TEST A

Mañana martes me voy a Perú por una semana. Me fascina viajar, pero siempre me pongo muy nervioso cuando tengo que irme. Me preocupa no tener tiempo para preparar todo lo que necesito, porque algunas veces no me acuerdo de llevar cosas importantes. Todavía me falta comprar el champú, la crema de afeitar y una toalla pequeña para el viaje. A ver, mañana me levanto a las siete, después me ducho, me visto y salgo a comprar las cosas que faltan. Luego vuelvo, como algo y llamo un taxi. Ah, también tengo que llevar un despertador.

TEST B

Mañana jueves me voy a Panamá por dos semanas. Me encanta viajar y me pongo especialmente contento cuando visito a mis amigos. Pero me molestan los viajes muy largos, por eso siempre me duermo en el avión y, cuando me despierto, estoy en mi destino. Todavía me falta comprar regalos para mis amigos. Me preocupa no tener tiempo para preparar todo lo que necesito.

TEST C

1. ¿A qué hora te levantaste hoy?
2. ¿Adónde fuiste en tus vacaciones?
3. ¿Te preocupas por tus amigos?
4. ¿Te molesta la música para estudiar?
5. ¿Te enojas mucho?

TEST D

1. ¿A qué hora te acostaste ayer?
2. ¿Prefieres ducharte o bañarte?
3. ¿Te preocupas por tus clases?
4. ¿Cuál fue tu película favorita el año pasado?
5. ¿Adónde fuiste ayer después de la clase de español?

TEST E

La rutina de mis compañeros de la residencia estudiantil Hernández es bastante normal. Todas las mañanas oyen el despertador a las cinco. Tienen una hora para bañarse, vestirse y arreglarse. Después, desayunan de seis a siete en la cafetería. A algunos estudiantes les molesta despertarse y levantarse temprano, pero a muchos les gusta. Dicen que es bueno siempre llegar temprano a las clases y que les aburre quedarse en la cama todo el día. ¡Yo prefiero dormir!

TEST F

La rutina de mis compañeros de la residencia estudiantil González es bastante normal. Todas las mañanas oyen el despertador a las cinco y media. Tienen una hora para bañarse, vestirse y arreglarse. Después, desayunan de seis y media a siete y media en la cafetería. A muchos estudiantes les gusta despertarse y levantarse temprano porque llegan temprano a sus clases, y les aburre quedarse en la cama todo el día. A otros, les molesta despertarse y levantarse temprano. Yo prefiero levantarme temprano y tomarme mi tiempo.

Lección 8

TEST A

Buenas tardes. Les voy a explicar los platos que ofrecemos hoy para el almuerzo. Para empezar tenemos cuatro deliciosas sopas: sopa de salmón, sopa de espárragos, sopa de verduras y también una rica sopa de champiñones. También tenemos bistec con verduras, un excelente jamón con patatas y, bueno, yo personalmente les recomiendo la carne de res con pimienta y limón. El plato del día es marisco asado. Para beber, los jugos naturales son nuestra especialidad o, si lo desean, les puedo traer el menú de vinos.

TEST B

Buenas noches. Les voy a explicar los platos que ofrecemos hoy para la cena. Para empezar tenemos sabrosos entremeses. Yo personalmente les recomiendo el jamón y los camarones. También ofrecemos cuatro deliciosos primeros platos: arroz con mariscos, pasta con espárragos, arvejas con jamón y también una sabrosa sopa de verduras. El dueño siempre recomienda la carne de res con pimientos. El plato del día es el pollo asado. Para beber, los jugos de frutas son nuestra especialidad o, si lo desean, les puedo traer agua mineral, refrescos o el menú de vinos.

TEST C

1. ¿Qué almorzaste ayer?
2. ¿Quién come más que tú?
3. ¿Comes muchas verduras?
4. ¿Les prestas tus libros a tus amigos?
5. ¿Crees que el pescado es mejor que la carne?

TEST D

1. ¿Les ofreces meriendas a tus amigos cuando van a tu casa?
2. ¿Qué te gusta beber cuando cenas en un restaurante?
3. ¿Dónde cenas los fines de semana?
4. ¿Qué desayunaste esta mañana?
5. ¿Cuándo cocinas?

TEST E

CAMARERO Buenas noches. Bienvenidos al restaurante Neptuno.

CARLOS Muchas gracias.

CAMARERO ¿Qué les puedo servir para beber?

CARLOS Un jugo de naranja para mí y agua mineral para mi hijo.

CAMARERO ¿Y para comer?

CARLOS ¿Qué nos recomienda?

CAMARERO A usted le recomiendo el salmón con espárragos y tomates. Al niño, le recomiendo la hamburguesa con papas fritas. En Neptuno tenemos las mejores hamburguesas de la ciudad.

CARLOS Voy a probar el salmón, pero lo quiero con un poco de limón, por favor. Para el niño prefiero un huevo con papas fritas y una ensalada de frutas.

CAMARERO Muy bien, enseguida se lo traigo todo.

CARLOS Muchas gracias. Tráiganos un poco de pan también, por favor.

TEST F

CAMARERO Buenos días. Bienvenidos al Restaurante Lola.
MARTA Gracias.
CAMARERO ¿Qué les puedo servir para beber?
MARTA Jugo de naranja para mí y agua mineral para la niña.
CAMARERO ¿Y para comer?
MARTA ¿Qué nos recomienda?
CAMARERO A usted le recomiendo la langosta con verduras. A la niña, le recomiendo la hamburguesa con papas fritas. En el Restaurante Lola tenemos las mejores hamburguesas de la ciudad.
MARTA La langosta no me gusta mucho. Voy a probar el salmón. Lo quiero con champiñones, por favor. Para la niña, prefiero la hamburguesa sin papas fritas, y una ensalada de lechuga.
CAMARERO Muy bien, enseguida se lo traigo todo.
MARTA Muchas gracias. Tráiganos un poco de pan también, por favor.

Lección 9

TEST A

Hola, Ana: soy Yolanda. Llamo para darte las gracias por venir a mi fiesta de cumpleaños ayer. Ya tengo dieciocho años y soy mayor de edad. ¡Qué bien! La verdad, me divertí mucho en la fiesta y todo salió muy bien. Ese restaurante colombiano es uno de los mejores y la comida fue muy buena. Me gustaron mucho los postres: el flan y el pastel de chocolate. Pero lo que me encantó fue el regalo sorpresa de mis padres: ¡un carro nuevo! Pero bueno, ya vi que bailaste mucho con mi primo Ricardo. Él me llamó hoy y creo que le interesa conocerte más. Así que llámame pronto y nos vamos los tres a pasear en el nuevo Toyota.

TEST B

Hola, Paco: soy Rúper. Llamo para darte las gracias por venir a mi fiesta ayer. Ya me gradué. ¡Qué bien! No lo puedo creer. ¿Te divertiste? Yo sí. Me divertí mucho con todos. Gracias también por recomendarme ese restaurante argentino. Me encantó la comida y los postres estuvieron riquísimos. Y... ¿qué te pareció el regalo sorpresa de mis padres? ¡Una moto! Tenemos que probarla. Tú puedes pasear a mi hermana Noemí en mi moto nueva. Ya vi que hablaste mucho con ella en la fiesta. Creo que a ella también le interesa conocerte más. Te llamo otra vez mañana y nos vamos los tres a tomar algo.

TEST C

1. ¿Qué hiciste ayer?
2. ¿Estudió alguien contigo para esta prueba?
3. ¿Pudiste dormir bien ayer?
4. ¿Te dieron algún regalo el día de tu cumpleaños?
5. ¿Cuándo supiste que ibas a venir a esta escuela?

TEST D

1. ¿Con quién te llevas muy bien en tu familia?
2. ¿Cuándo es tu cumpleaños?
3. ¿Con quién saliste el fin de semana pasado?
4. ¿Tuviste una cita el mes pasado?
5. ¿Cómo te gusta celebrar tu cumpleaños?

TEST E

María Muñoz nació en Barcelona en 1980. Cuando cumplió nueve años, su padre le regaló un cuaderno y María empezó a escribir muchísimo. Fue a la Universidad de Barcelona, donde estudió lengua y literatura. Cuando se graduó de la universidad, se casó con José Martínez. A los dos años se fueron a vivir a California. Los dos son muy felices y escriben cada día en el jardín de su preciosa casa.

TEST F

Carlos Cruz nació en Buenos Aires en 1979. Cuando cumplió diez años, su madre le regaló un cuaderno y lápices de colores, y Carlos empezó a dibujar muchísimo. Fue a la Universidad de Buenos Aires, donde estudió dibujo y teatro. Cuando se graduó de la universidad, se casó con Marta Jiménez. Al año siguiente se fueron a vivir a Madrid. Los dos son muy felices y trabajan cada día en el jardín de su preciosa casa.

EXAM AUDIO SCRIPTS

Lecciones 1–4

EXAM A

Bueno, amigos, ya estamos en la Ciudad de México. Ahora pueden descansar unas horas en sus cuartos. Esta noche vamos a ir a pasear por la ciudad. Por las noches normalmente hace más fresco. Si quieren salir sin el grupo, deben tener cuidado. Tienen que tener siempre un mapa y el número de teléfono del hotel. El número de teléfono es el 22-37-89. Mañana por la mañana tenemos que salir temprano para ir de excursión. Vamos a hacer muchas actividades: vamos a visitar dos museos y los monumentos del centro de la ciudad. Supongo que también vamos a pasear en biciclecta. Bueno, esto es todo. Nos vemos más tarde.

EXAM B

Bueno, amigos, ya estamos en la Ciudad de México. Ahora tienen unas horas para descansar en sus cuartos. Esta tarde vamos a ir a visitar los monumentos más importantes. Por la noche, todos vamos a ir al centro a un restaurante muy bueno. En la Ciudad de México siempre hace fresco por las noches. Si quieren salir sin el grupo, deben tener cuidado. Deben llevar siempre un mapa y el número de teléfono del hotel. El número de teléfono es el 53-32-13. Por la mañana tenemos que salir del hotel a las nueve. Vamos a ir al Museo de Arte Diego Rivera. Y, bueno, eso es todo. Nos vemos más tarde.

Lecciones 1–9

EXAM A

Puerto Rico es maravilloso. Les va a gustar mucho, estoy seguro. Cuando yo estuve allí, me lo pasé muy bien. El Viejo San Juan es muy bonito. Yo fui con mi esposa para celebrar nuestro aniversario de bodas y fue un viaje muy divertido. A mí no me interesa mucho, pero, si les gusta ir de compras, hay tiendas para todos. Para comer, les recomiendo un restaurante en el centro que se llama Don José. Allí tienen que probar el arroz con pollo y los pasteles de carne. De postre, tienen que pedir el flan; los otros postres no me gustaron. Mi playa favorita cerca de San Juan es Ocean Park. Es una de las playas más hermosas y tiene muchas actividades durante los fines de semana.

EXAM B

Puerto Rico es una isla bellíííísima. Yo volví de allí el mes pasado y éste fue mi tercer viaje. En mi primer viaje visité las playas más conocidas. En mi segundo viaje conocí un poco más el interior, visité muchos museos interesantísimos y compré libros de historia y cultura puertorriqueñas. Pero en este último viaje me divertí muchísimo más, porque ahora ya sé dónde ir de compras y a mí... ¡¡me encanta ir de compras!! También me encanta el paisaje y la comida me fascina. Estoy segura de que a ustedes también les va a encantar esta hermosa e interesante isla. Para comprar regalos, les recomiendo una tienda en el Viejo San Juan que se llama Perlas. Allí pueden encontrar regalos para todos a muy buenos precios.

OPTIONAL TEST SECTIONS

Fotonovela Video Test Items — **Lección 1**

1 ¿De dónde son? Write where the characters are from using complete sentences.

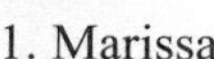

1. Marissa 2. Sra. Díaz 3. Sr. Díaz 4. Jimena y Felipe

1. ______________________________
2. ______________________________
3. ______________________________
4. ______________________________

Fotonovela Video Test Items — **Lección 2**

1 Las materias Write at least two sentences about each of the characters using words from the box.

1. Marissa 2. Felipe 3. Juan Carlos

administración	**ciencias ambientales**	**español**	**historia del arte**
arqueología	**computación**	**geografía**	**literatura**
biología	**economía**	**historia**	**química**

1. Marissa: ______________________________
____
2. Felipe: ______________________________
____
3. Juan Carlos: ______________________________
____

Optional Test Sections

Fotonovela Video Test Items — **Lección 3**

1 La familia Describe at least two members of the Díaz family using what you remember from the **Fotonovela**.

alto/a	**bonito/a**	**gordo/a**	**guapo/a**	**simpático/a**	**viejo/a**
antipático/a	**delgado/a**	**grande**	**pequeño/a**	**trabajador(a)**	

____

____

____

____

____

____

Fotonovela Video Test Items — **Lección 4**

1 ¿Qué pasó? Write the conversation that is taking place in the picture using what you remember from the **Fotonovela** and at least seven words from the box.

cine	**fin de semana**	**hacer**	**museo**	**salir**
esquí acuático	**golf**	**ir**	**pasatiempos**	**tenis**
excursión	**gustar**	**montañas**	**ratos libres**	

____

____

____

____

____

____

____

____

____

Fotonovela Video Test Items — **Lección 5**

1 ¿Qué pasó? Select one of the pictures and use what you remember from the **Fotonovela** to write the conversation that is taking place. Use the present progressive at least twice.

____

____

____

____

____

____

Fotonovela Video Test Items — **Lección 6**

1 ¿Qué pasó? Write sentences in the preterite to describe what happened in each scene. What did the girls buy? What did the boys buy? Were they happy with their purchases? Were the items inexpensive or expensive?

____

____

____

____

____

____

____

____

____

____

____

____

Optional Test Sections

Fotonovela Video Test Items **Lección 7**

1 Yo llegué primero Look at the pictures and write what the characters were doing or needed to do using what you remember from the **Fotonovela**. Mention at least two things for each character.

Optional Test Sections

Fotonovela Video Test Items **Lección 8**

1 Platos Recreate the dialogue that took place during this "romantic dinner" using what you remember from the **Fotonovela**. Mention some of the dishes the waiter offered them.

Fotonovela Video Test Items **Lección 9**

1 ¿Qué pasó? Describe what is talking place in the picture using what you remember from the **Fotonovela** and at least four words from the box.

calaveras de azúcar	**comida**	**flores**
cementerio	**disfraces**	**música**

Optional Test Sections

Fotonovela Video Test Items — **Lecciones 1–4**

1 Protagonistas Write a description of one of the **Fotonovela** characters. Mention his/her personality and what he/she likes to do.

____

____

____

____

____

____

____

____

Fotonovela Video Test Items — **Lecciones 1–9**

1 Protagonistas Describe an event that the characters shared using the preterite and what you remember from the **Fotonovela**.

____

____

____

____

____

____

____

____

Panorama Textbook Section Test Items — **Lección 1**

1 ¿Cierto o falso? Indicate whether these statements about the United States and Canada are **cierto** or **falso**. Correct the false statements.

	Cierto	**Falso**
1. La comida mexicana es muy popular en los Estados Unidos. ____	_____	_____
2. La Pequeña Habana es un barrio (*neighborhood*) de Cuba. ____	_____	_____
3. El desfile puertorriqueño (*Puerto Rican Parade*) se celebra en Miami. ____	_____	_____
4. Toronto, Vancouver y Montreal son las ciudades con más población hispana de Canadá. ____	_____	_____
5. Las enchiladas y las quesadillas son platos de Puerto Rico. ____	_____	_____
6. El cali-mex es una variación de la comida mexicana en los Estados Unidos. ____	_____	_____

Panorama Textbook Section Test Items — **Lección 2**

1 España Fill in the blanks with the appropriate words.

1. ________________________ es un plato típico de España.
   a. La paella b. El tomate c. La fajita
2. España tiene varias ________________________ oficiales.
   a. universidades b. lenguas c. ciudades
3. España es resultado de la combinación de diversas ________________________.
   a. lecciones b. tizas c. culturas
4. El chef José Andrés vive en ________________________.
   a. Nueva York b. Washington, DC c. Los Ángeles
5. José Andrés es dueño de varios ________________________ en los EE.UU.
   a. restaurantes b. laboratorios c. estadios
6. El Prado es ________________________ famoso.
   a. un pueblo (*town*) b. un artista c. un museo

Panorama Textbook Section Test Items — **Lección 3**

1 ¿Cierto o falso? Indicate whether these statements about Ecuador are **cierto** or **falso**. Correct the false statements.

	Cierto	**Falso**
1. El Cotopaxi es un volcán. ______	____	____
2. Muchas personas van a las islas Galápagos por sus playas. ______	____	____
3. Charles Darwin estudió (*studied*) las especies del volcán Cotopaxi. ______	____	____
4. Las islas Galápagos son famosas por sus tortugas (*tortoises*). ______	____	____
5. Oswaldo Guayasamín es un político ecuatoriano famoso. ______	____	____
6. Los Andes dividen Ecuador en varias regiones. ______	____	____
7. Los turistas no practican deportes (*sports*) en la Sierra. ______	____	____
8. La Mitad del Mundo es un monumento ecuatoriano. ______	____	____

Panorama Textbook Section Test Items — **Lección 4**

1 ¿Cierto o falso? Indicate whether these statements about Mexico are **cierto** or **falso**. Correct the false statements.

	Cierto	**Falso**
1. Los incas dominaron (*dominated*) en México del siglo (*century*) XIV al XVI. ______	____	____
2. Frida Kahlo era (*was*) la esposa de Octavio Paz. ______	____	____
3. Puedes ver obras (*works*) de Diego Rivera en el Museo de Arte Moderno de la Ciudad de México. ______	____	____
4. El D.F. es otro (*another*) nombre para la Ciudad de México. ______	____	____
5. México es el mayor productor de esmeraldas (*emeralds*) en el mundo. ______	____	____
6. Hay muchas ruinas en la Ciudad de México. ______	____	____
7. La ciudad de Monterrey es el centro económico y cultural de México. ______	____	____
8. La Ciudad de México está situada en Tenochtitlán, la capital de la cultura azteca. ______	____	____

Panorama Textbook Section Test Items — **Lección 5**

1 Conectar Match the descriptions in Column A to the words in Column B.

A	B
______ 1. Su uso es obligatorio en los documentos oficiales.	a. Puerto Rico
______ 2. Actor puertorriqueño.	b. el Gran Combo de Puerto Rico
______ 3. Protegía la bahía (*protected the bay*) de San Juan.	c. Camuy
______ 4. Es un río subterráneo.	d. El Morro
______ 5. Se hizo (*became*) estado libre asociado en 1952.	e. el inglés
______ 6. Gracias a él, los científicos (*scientists*) pueden estudiar la atmósfera.	f. la salsa
______ 7. Tiene origen puertorriqueño y cubano.	g. el Observatorio de Arecibo
______ 8. Orquesta de salsa famosa.	h. Raúl Juliá

Panorama Textbook Section Test Items — **Lección 6**

1 Completar Fill in the blanks with items from the box.

Alicia Alonso	**Fidel Castro**	**el tabaco**	***Buena Vista Social Club***
colibrí abeja	**José Martí**	**europeos**	**inmigración**

1. ____________________ fue (*was*) un poeta y político famoso.
2. El ____________________ es el ave más pequeña del mundo.
3. En Cuba viven muchos descendientes de africanos, ______________ chinos y antillanos.
4. ____________________ bailó en el Ballet de Nueva York.
5. ____________________ es un producto importante para la economía cubana.
6. La mayoría de los músicos del ____________________ son mayores.

Optional Test Sections

Panorama Textbook Section Test Items — Lección 7

1 Conectar Match the descriptions in Column A to the words in Column B. Two items in Column B will not be used.

A	B
______ 1. Es una música con influencias africanas y españolas.	a. barroca colonial
______ 2. Es un animal importante para la economía peruana.	b. Lima
______ 3. Es una ciudad antigua del Imperio inca.	c. Barranco
______ 4. Son un gran misterio.	d. Machu Picchu
______ 5. Es la capital de Perú.	e. andina
______ 6. La iglesia de San Francisco tiene esta arquitectura.	f. Iquitos
	g. alpaca
	h. las Líneas de Nazca

Panorama Textbook Section Test Items — Lección 8

1 ¿Cierto o falso? Indicate whether these statements about Guatemala are **cierto** or **falso**. Correct the false statements.

	Cierto	**Falso**
1. El español es la única lengua de Guatemala. ________________	______	______
2. Los artesanos guatemaltecos utilizan mosquitos para poner color en las telas (*fabrics*). ________________	______	______
3. El quetzal es un tipo de pájaro (*bird*). ________________	______	______
4. El gobierno mantiene una reserva ecológica para los quetzales. ________________	______	______
5. La capital de Guatemala es Antigua Guatemala. ________________	______	______
6. Antigua Guatemala es internacionalmente famosa por su celebración de Semana Santa (*Holy Week*). ________________	______	______
7. Los mayas usaron el cero antes que los europeos. ________________	______	______
8. El *huipil* indica el pueblo de origen de la persona que lo lleva. ________________	______	______

Optional Test Sections

Panorama Textbook Section Test Items — Lección 9

1 Conectar Match the sentence parts.

1. Pablo Neruda ________________
2. La isla de Pascua ________________
3. El Parque Nacional Villarrica ________________
4. En los Andes ________________
5. El vino chileno ________________

a. constituye una parte importante de la actividad económica del país.
b. es un sitio popular para practicar el esquí.
c. es famosa por sus estatuas enormes.
d. fue un gran poeta.
e. hay observatorios para observar las estrellas.

Optional Test Sections

Panorama Textbook Section Test Items **Lecciones 1–4**

1 Conectar Match the descriptions in Column A to the countries in Column B.

A	B
______ 1. Los aztecas dominaron (*dominated*) este país.	a. Ecuador
______ 2. Una de sus lenguas oficiales es el catalán.	b. España
______ 3. Aquí celebran el día del orgullo puertorriqueño.	c. Estados Unidos
______ 4. El volcán Cotopaxi está en este país.	d. México
______ 5. El inglés y el francés son las lenguas oficiales de este país.	e. Canadá

Panorama Textbook Section Test Items **Lecciones 1–9**

1 Conectar Match the descriptions in Column A to the countries in Column B.

A	B
______ 1. El quetzal es un símbolo muy importante en este país.	a. Chile
______ 2. La isla de Pascua es famosa por sus estatuas enormes.	b. Cuba
______ 3. Machu Picchu es una ciudad antigua del Imperio inca.	c. Ecuador
______ 4. Los músicos de *Buena Vista Social Club* son de esta isla.	d. España
______ 5. La Pequeña Habana es un barrio (*neighborhood*) de este país.	e. Estados Unidos
	f. Guatemala
______ 6. Aquí está el Museo del Prado.	g. México
______ 7. Se hizo estado libre asociado en 1952.	h. Perú
______ 8. Las islas Galápagos, famosas por sus tortugas (*tortoises*), son de este país.	i. Puerto Rico
	j. Canadá
______ 9. El francés es una lengua oficial en este país.	
______ 10. Frida Kahlo nació en este país.	

Panorama cultural Video Test Items **Lección 1**

1 Los hispanos en Nueva York y Montreal Write English sentences describing what you remember about the video segments.

1. 

____
____
____

2. 

____
____
____

3. 

____
____
____

Panorama cultural Video Test Items **Lección 2**

1 El Festival de San Fermín Fill in the blanks with words from the box.

celebran	**detrás de**	**mañana**	**turistas**
delante de	**llevan**	**noche**	**viajan**

1. En España ______________________ muchas fiestas tradicionales.
2. Muchísimas personas ______________________ a Pamplona para ver los encierros (*the running of the bulls*).
3. En los encierros, muchas personas corren (*run*) ______________________ diecisiete toros (*bulls*).
4. Los encierros empiezan (*begin*) a las ocho de la ______________________.
5. Los participantes de los encierros ______________________ periódicos (*newspaper*) para defenderse de los toros.
6. Los hombres de la comunidad y muchos ______________________ participan en los encierros.

Optional Test Sections

Panorama cultural Video Test Items **Lección 3**

1 Las islas Galápagos Fill in the blanks with words from the box.

cerca	tiene	turistas	viven
observan	tienen	vive	

1. En las islas Galápagos ________________________ muchos animales.
2. El archipiélago ________________________ fascinantes especies de animales.
3. Algunas tortugas (*some tortoises*) ________________________ más de (*more than*) cien años.
4. Las islas Galápagos están ________________________ de la costa (*coast*) de Ecuador.
5. Las islas Galápagos reciben a muchos ________________________.

Panorama cultural Video Test Items **Lección 4**

1 Teotihuacán Look at the picture and select the appropriate words to complete the sentences.

1. Las personas están en ________________________.
   a. Chichén Itzá b. Teotihuacán c. la capital mexicana
2. Ellos ________________________ en las pirámides.
   a. toman el sol b. estudian arqueología c. nadan
3. Se está celebrando ________________________.
   a. la cultura indígena b. el equinoccio (*equinox*) c. la independencia
4. A las cinco de la mañana la gente comienza a ________________________.
   a. bailar b. cantar c. escalar
5. Todos quieren sentir la energía ________________________ en sus manos.
   a. de las pirámides b. del sol c. de Tenochtitlán

Optional Test Sections

Panorama cultural Video Test Items — **Lección 5**

1 El Viejo San Juan Describe each picture with at least three Spanish sentences using what you remember from the video segment.

____
____
____
____
____

____
____
____
____
____

Panorama cultural Video Test Items — **Lección 6**

1 La santería Select the appropriate words to complete the sentences.

1. La santería es una práctica religiosa muy ________________ en países latinoamericanos.
   a. nueva b. aburrida c. común
2. Los ________________ son las personas que practican la santería.
   a. Eggún b. cubanos c. santeros
3. Las personas visitan a los santeros para ________________ con ellos.
   a. recordar b. conversar c. comer
4. Los Eggún son hombres y mujeres ________________ en la santería.
   a. viejos b. importantes c. inteligentes
5. En las reuniones, los Eggún y las familias ________________.
   a. bailan b. escriben c. aprenden
6. La santería es una de las tradiciones cubanas más ________________.
   a. antiguas b. modernas c. simpáticas

Optional Test Sections

Panorama cultural Video Test Items — **Lección 7**

1 Los deportes de aventura Fill in the blanks with words from the box.

caminar con llamas	**el fútbol**	**ir de excursión**	**pasear en bicicleta**
el Camino Inca	**ir de compras**	**la pesca**	***sandboard***

En Perú, practican muchos deportes de aventura. Muchas personas van a Pachacamac a (1) ____________________ de montaña. Muchos aficionados al (2) ____________________van a la región de Ocucaje y es muy común (3) ____________________ a la cordillera Blanca. Un deporte tradicional es (4) ____________________: las personas van por varios días hasta Machu Picchu. Esta ruta se llama (5) ____________________ y tiene cuarenta y tres kilómetros. Otro deporte tradicional es (6) ____________________ en pequeñas canoas. ¡Este deporte es muy antiguo!

Panorama cultural Video Test Items — **Lección 8**

1 ¿Cierto o falso? Indicate whether each statement is **cierto** or **falso** using the pictures as a guide. Correct the false statements.

1. Esta ciudad es la capital de Guatemala.

   ____

2. En las calles de esta ciudad hay ruinas donde los turistas pueden sentir la atmósfera del pasado.

   ____

3. Para las celebraciones de Semana Santa (*Holy Week*), las mujeres hacen hermosas alfombras (*carpets*).

   ____

4. Chichicastenango es una ciudad más grande que Antigua.

   ____

5. Todos los días hay un mercado al aire libre en las calles y plazas de la ciudad.

   ____

6. Todos los productos tienen precios fijos y los clientes no tienen que regatear al hacer sus compras.

   ____

Panorama cultural Video Test Items **Lección 9**

1 **La isla de Pascua** Describe your recent visit to **La isla de Pascua** in an e-mail using at least six Spanish sentences.

Para:	De:	Asunto (*Subject*):

Optional Test Sections

Panorama cultural Video Test Items — **Lecciones 1–4**

1 Preguntas Answer the questions using Spanish sentences.

1. ¿Qué celebran en agosto los dominicanos en Nueva York? ______________________
2. ¿Qué tienen en común el canal de televisión Telelatino, la revista *Picante* y el periódico *El correo canadiense*? ______________________
3. ¿Cuál es la actividad central del Festival de San Fermín? ______________________
4. ¿Dónde están las islas Galápagos? ______________________
5. ¿Qué es Teotihuacán? ______________________

Panorama cultural Video Test Items — **Lecciones 1–9**

1 ¿Cierto o falso? Indicate whether these statements are **cierto** or **falso**. Correct the false statements.

1. En el estado de Nueva York hay mucha población hispana de origen puertorriqueño. ______________________
2. Ana María Seifert vive en Montreal. ______________________
3. En la actividad central del Festival de San Fermín muchas personas corren delante de diecisiete toros. ______________________
4. En las islas Galápagos no viven personas. ______________________
5. El Castillo de San Felipe del Morro es un sitio histórico nacional de México. ______________________
6. Regla es un barrio de La Habana donde se practica la santería. ______________________
7. En la isla de Pascua siempre hace mucho frío y también mucho viento. ______________________

Flash cultura Video Test Items — Lección 1

1 En la plaza Answer these questions using English sentences.

1. What is the importance of plazas in the cities and towns of the Hispanic world?

____
____
____
____

2. Describe the greetings in the Spanish-speaking countries.

____
____
____
____
____
____

Flash cultura Video Test Items — Lección 2

1 La UNAM Indicate whether these statements are **cierto** (true) or **falso** (false).

	Cierto	Falso
1. La Ciudad de México no es importante.	_____	_____
2. La UNAM está en México, D.F.	_____	_____
3. En la UNAM hay dos mil estudiantes.	_____	_____
4. En la UNAM hay estudiantes de diferentes nacionalidades.	_____	_____
5. No hay residencias estudiantiles en la UNAM.	_____	_____
6. Varias personas famosas son ex alumnos o ex profesores de la UNAM.	_____	_____

Flash cultura Video Test Items — **Lección 3**

1 Dos familias Describe each family using what you remember from the episode and words from the box.

feliz	**guapo**	**pequeño**	**tradicional**
grande	**numeroso**	**simpático**	**viejo**

La familia Valdivieso... ____________________

La familia Bolaños... ____________________

Flash cultura Video Test Items — **Lección 4**

1 ¡Fútbol en España! Write a summary of the episode using at least four Spanish sentences and words from the box.

aficionados	**equipo**	**ganar**	**importante**	**pasión**
celebrar	**favorito/a**	**jugar**	**ir**	**perder**

Flash cultura Video Test Items **Lección 5**

1 ¡Vacaciones en Perú! Write a summary of the episode using the present progressive. Include at least two direct object pronouns.

Flash cultura Video Test Items **Lección 6**

1 Comprar en los mercados Describe what happened in each picture using the preterite. What did Randy buy? Where did he go? What did he do there?

Optional Test Sections

Flash cultura Video Test Items **Lección 7**

1 Tapas y más tapas Write a summary of the episode. Include the answers to these questions: Where was Mari Carmen and what places did she go to? What did she do there? Did she interview anyone? What conclusions can you draw?

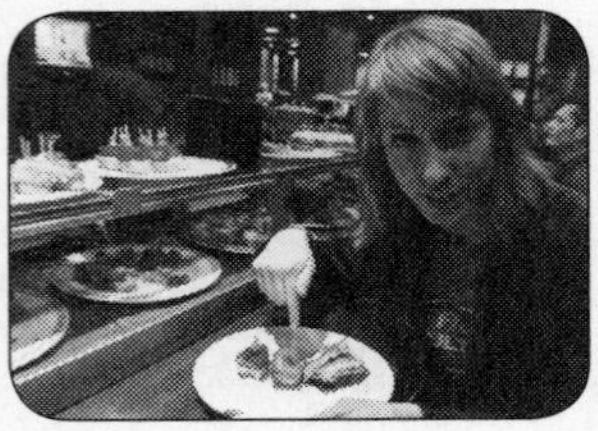

Flash cultura Video Test Items **Lección 8**

1 La comida latina Write a summary of what Leticia did in the episode. Include words from the box, comparisons, and double object pronouns.

arroz	**carne (picada/molida)**	**pedir**	**salsas**
bebida	**chile**	**probar**	**servir**
café	**comprar**	**recomendar**	**tortilla**

Flash cultura Video Test Items **Lección 9**

1 En la calle San Sebastián Describe what happened in the episode. Include words from the box and mention what makes the Christmas celebration in Puerto Rico so special.

artesanías	**Día de Reyes**	**Navidades**
cabezudos	**frituras**	**santos de palo**
canciones de Navidad	**música**	**tradición**

____
____
____
____
____
____
____
____
____

Optional Test Sections

Optional Test Sections

Flash cultura Video Test Items — Lecciones 1–4

1 Un episodio Select one of the pictures and write a summary of the corresponding **Flash cultura** episode.

Flash cultura Video Test Items — Lecciones 1–9

1 Un episodio Select one of the **Flash cultura** episodes you have seen and write a summary.

Alternate Listening Sections for **Tests A** and **B**

If you prefer that students complete a personalized task for the listening section, use these substitute scripts, and adapt **Tests A** and **B**.

Lección 1

1 Escuchar You will hear five personal questions. Answer them with Spanish sentences.

1. ¿Cómo se llama usted?
2. ¿Cómo está usted?
3. ¿De dónde es usted?
4. ¿A qué hora es la clase de español?
5. ¿Cuántos estudiantes hay en la clase?

Lección 2

1 Escuchar You will hear five personal questions. Answer them with Spanish sentences.

1. ¿Qué música escuchas?
2. ¿Qué materias tomas?
3. ¿Te gusta bailar?
4. ¿Qué llevas en la mochila?
5. ¿Trabajas los domingos?

Lección 3

1 Escuchar You will hear five personal questions. Answer them with Spanish sentences.

1. ¿Tienes hambre ahora?
2. ¿Tienes sobrinos o sobrinas?
3. ¿Crees que eres trabajador(a)?
4. ¿Crees que tienes suerte?
5. ¿Te gusta comer en la cafetería de la escuela?

Lección 4

1 Escuchar You will hear five personal questions. Answer them with Spanish sentences.

1. ¿Qué vas a comer hoy?
2. ¿Qué vas a hacer el sábado?
3. ¿Qué piensas hacer esta noche?
4. ¿Dónde te gusta pasar tus ratos libres?
5. ¿Te gusta ir al cine?

Lección 5

1 Escuchar You will hear five personal questions. Answer them with Spanish sentences.

1. ¿Qué tiempo crees que va a hacer el fin de semana?
2. ¿Cómo estás hoy?
3. ¿Qué quieres hacer en las vacaciones?
4. ¿Qué prefieres: las vacaciones en la playa o en la montaña?
5. ¿Cuál es la fecha de hoy?

Lección 6

1 Escuchar You will hear five personal questions. Answer them with Spanish sentences.

1. ¿Cuántas horas estudiaste para la prueba de español?
2. ¿Qué libro que leíste el año pasado te gustó más?
3. ¿Te compraron un regalo el mes pasado?
4. ¿A qué hora volviste a casa el fin de semana pasado?
5. ¿Viste ayer la televisión?

Lección 7

1 Escuchar You will hear five personal questions. Answer them with Spanish sentences.

1. ¿Te gusta quedarte en casa los domingos?
2. ¿Te enojas con tus amigos?
3. ¿Te molesta oír música cuando estudias?
4. ¿A qué hora te fuiste ayer a tu casa?
5. ¿Tienes algún amigo en Perú?

Lección 8

1 Escuchar You will hear five personal questions. Answer them with Spanish sentences.

1. ¿Merendaste algo ayer?
2. ¿Estudian tus amigos más que tú?
3. ¿Por qué escogiste estudiar español?
4. ¿Les recomiendas algún restaurante a tus compañeros?
5. Según tú, ¿cuál es el mejor restaurante de tu ciudad?

Lección 9

1 Escuchar You will hear five personal questions. Answer them with Spanish sentences.

1. ¿Cuándo supiste que ibas a venir a esta escuela?
2. ¿Condujiste ayer para volver a tu casa?
3. ¿Pudiste estudiar para esta prueba?
4. ¿Le diste un regalo a tu mejor amigo/a para su cumpleaños?
5. ¿Qué hiciste el fin de semana pasado?

Alternate Listening Section for **Exams A** and **B**

Lecciones 1–4

1 Escuchar You will hear five personal questions. Answer them with Spanish sentences.

1. ¿Cómo eres?
2. ¿Qué te gusta hacer?
3. ¿Cómo es tu familia?
4. ¿Qué haces los fines de semana?
5. ¿Qué vas a hacer este fin de semana?

Lecciones 1–9

1 Escuchar You will hear five personal questions. Answer them with Spanish sentences.

1. ¿Qué vas a hacer después del examen?
2. ¿Te dieron algún regalo el día de tu cumpleaños?
3. ¿A qué hora volviste ayer a tu casa?
4. ¿Qué hiciste las vacaciones pasadas?
5. ¿Qué materias te gustan más?

ANSWERS TO QUIZZES

Lección 1

Contextos

Quiz A

1 1. b 2. c 3. c 4. a 5. d

2 1. e 2. b 3. a 4. c 5. f

3 1. Buenos; está; usted 2. dónde; Soy

4 Some answers will vary. 1. Buenas tardes./Hola. 2. Me llamo Felipe./Soy Felipe. 3. Mucho gusto. 4. ¿De dónde eres? 5. ¿Y tú?

Quiz B

1 a. 6 b. 2 c. 4 d. 1 e. 3 f. 5

2 Answers will vary.

3 Answers will vary.

Estructura

1.1 Nouns and articles

Quiz A

1 1. el, la 2. las 3. el 4. los

2 1. un 2. una 3. unos, unas 4. unos

3 **People:** los hombres, el/la joven **Objects:** el diario, los mapas **Places:** las escuelas, el país

4 1. unos cuadernos 2. las lecciones 3. unas mujeres 4. los programas 5. las conductoras 6. los lápices

Quiz B

1 Answers will vary.

2 Some answers will vary. Sample answers: 1. la nacionalidad 2. el video 3. los/las turistas 4. los/las profesores/profesoras 5. el país 6. el diccionario 7. el día 8. el cuaderno 9. la maleta 10. los/las estudiantes

3 Answers will vary.

1.2 Numbers 0–30

Quiz A

1 a. once b. treinta c. veintidós d. nueve e. dieciséis

2 1. Cierto. 2. Falso. 3. Cierto. 4. Falso. 5. Cierto. 6. Falso.

3 1. veintitrés 2. veintinueve 3. trece 4. cero 5. catorce

4 1. Cuántas, Hay 2. un, seis

Quiz B

1 Answers will vary.

2 Answers will vary.

3 Answers will vary.

1.3 Present tense of *ser*

Quiz A

1 1. d 2. a 3. c 4. b 5. f

2 1. ser 2. soy 3. es 4. somos

3 1. Quién 2. Eres, soy 3. dónde, Somos

4 1. Carmen es profesora de arte. 2. ¿Tú eres de Canadá? 3. Ustedes son de España. 4. Las maletas son del pasajero. 5. ¿De quién son los lápices? 6. Yo soy estudiante.

Quiz B

1 Answers will vary.

2 Answers will vary.

3 Answers will vary.

1.4 Telling time

Quiz A

1 1. c 2. a 3. b 4. b

2 a. Son las once y cuarto/quince de la mañana. b. Son las diez menos cuarto/quince de la noche. c. Es la una menos veinticinco de la tarde. d. Es (la) medianoche./Son las doce de la noche. e. Son las seis y media/treinta de la mañana. f. Son las siete y veintitrés de la noche. g. Son las diez y diez de la mañana.

3 1. La clase de historia es a las dos y veinte. 2. Es la una. 3. El programa es a las nueve menos diez. 4. La prueba es a la una y cuarto/quince. 5. Son las cinco y media/treinta. 6. La clase de español es a las doce menos cuarto/quince.

Quiz B

1 Answers will vary.

2 Answers will vary.

3 Answers will vary.

Lección 2

Contextos

Quiz A

1 1. e 2. c 3. f 4. a 5. b

2 lunes, miércoles, viernes, sábado

3 1. L 2. I 3. L 4. L 5. I 6. I 7. I

4 1. prueba 2. física 3. examen 4. semana

Quiz B

1 Answers will vary.
2 Answers will vary.
3 Answers will vary.

Estructura

2.1 Present tense of *-ar* verbs

Quiz A

1 1. c 2. b 3. a 4. b

2 1. c 2. d 3. a 4. e

3 1. Ellas enseñan administración de empresas. 2. Yo necesito preparar la tarea. 3. Héctor y yo compramos libros en la librería. 4. A mí me gusta bailar los sábados. 5. Enrique desea escuchar música. 6. ¿Te gusta la psicología?

4 1. estudiamos 2. necesitan 3. toma 4. canta 5. desayuno 6. miro 7. gustan 8. mirar

Quiz B

1 Answers will vary.
2 Answers will vary.
3 Answers will vary.
4 Answers will vary.

2.2 Forming questions in Spanish

Quiz A

1 1. e 2. f 3. b 4. h 5. a 6. d

2 1. de dónde 2. Qué 3. verdad 4. Por qué

3 1. Sí, (yo) tomo seis clases este semestre. 2. Sí, (nosotros) necesitamos estudiar el sábado. 3. No, (el señor Ortiz) no enseña a las diez./No, (el señor Ortiz) enseña a [*time*]. 4. No, (Samuel y Lourdes) no miran la televisión.

4 1. ¿Qué buscas? 2. ¿Cómo se llama (el libro) 3. ¿Por qué buscas el libro?/¿Por qué buscas *Cien años de soledad*? 4. ¿El examen es mañana?/¿Es mañana el examen?/El examen es mañana, ¿verdad?/¿no? 5. ¿A qué hora es (el examen)? 6. ¿Enseña la clase el profesor Méndez?/El profesor Méndez enseña la clase, ¿verdad?/¿no?

Quiz B

1 Answers will vary.
2 Answers will vary.
3 Answers will vary.

2.3 Present tense of *estar*

Quiz A

1 1. están 2. estoy 3. estás 4. está 5. estamos

2 1. I 2. L 3. L 4. I 5. I

3 1. Las mochilas están detrás de las sillas. 2. La papelera está a la derecha del profesor. 3. ¿(Tú) Estás entre las ventanas y la puerta? 4. Nosotros estamos con Ramiro.

4 1. soy 2. Son 3. estamos 4. es 5. está 6. estoy

Quiz B

1 Answers will vary.
2 Answers will vary.
3 Answers will vary.

2.4 Numbers 31 and higher

Quiz A

1 a. treinta y ocho b. ciento dieciséis c. quinientos setenta y tres d. mil ochocientos veintiuno e. setecientos cincuenta y cuatro mil trescientos veintidós f. seis millones seiscientos quince mil diez

2 1. b 2. f 3. e 4. a

3 1. cien 2. novecientos mil 3. mil 4. sesenta y cinco 5. un millón

4 1. doscientos setenta mil 2. un millón ciento veinte mil cuatrocientos sesenta y un 3. cien, cien 4. doscientas cuarenta y una

Quiz B

1 Answers will vary.
2 Answers will vary.
3 Answers will vary.

Answers to Quizzes

Lección 3

Contextos

Quiz A

1 1. a 2. c 3. d 4. b

2 1. g 2. e 3. f 4. b 5. c

3 1. programador 2. familia 3. artista 4. gente 5. periodista 6. gemelos

4 1. abuelo 2. bisabuela 3. padre 4. nietos 5. tía

Quiz B

1 Suggested answers: 1. Es programador. 2. Es mi cuñado. 3. Es artista. 4. Es médica. 5. Es mi nuera. 6. Son mis hermanastras.

2 Answers will vary.

3 Answers will vary.

4 Answers will vary.

Estructura

3.1 Descriptive adjectives

Quiz A

1 1. bajo 2. fácil 3. inteligente 4. pequeño 5. joven

2 1. Es argentina. 2. Es alemán. 3. Somos canadienses. 4. Es costarricense. 5. Son españoles. 6. Son inglesas.

3 1. La mujer pelirroja enseña periodismo. 2. Nosotros somos simpáticos y trabajadores. 3. ¿Los turistas japoneses esperan el autobús? 4. Ustedes toman muchas pruebas en la clase de español.

4 1. trabajadora 2. buena 3. difíciles 4. chino 5. gran

Quiz B

1 Answers will vary.

2 Answers will vary.

3 Answers will vary.

4 Answers will vary.

3.2 Possessive adjectives

Quiz A

1 1. Tus 2. su 3. Nuestros 4. mi 5. Sus

2 1. Mi 2. nuestra 3. mis 4. Sus 5. tus

3 1. Yo llevo mis papeles a la clase. 2. Gustavo y yo terminamos nuestras tareas. 3. Tú compras tu calculadora en la librería. 4. ¿Ustedes hablan con su abuela? 5. Ana estudia para sus exámenes.

4 1. Es su tiza. 2. Son tus mochilas. 3. Es su mapa. 4. Son sus cuadernos. 5. Es nuestra papelera.

Quiz B

1 Answers will vary.

2 Answers will vary.

3 Answers will vary.

3.3 Present tense of *-er* and *-ir* verbs

Quiz A

1 1. comprendo 2. comprendemos 3. comprenden 4. vivir 5. vives 6. viven

2 1. b 2. c 3. a 4. b 5. a 6. d

3 1. Ángel abre la puerta del laboratorio. 2. Mi cuñada y yo decidimos leer unos libros interesantes. 3. Ustedes aprenden a hablar español. 4. Yo corro en el estadio los domingos. 5. Tú asistes a la clase de historia.

4 1. asistimos 2. debe 3. beben 4. comemos 5. escribo 6. crees

Quiz B

1 Answers will vary.

2 Answers will vary.

3 Answers will vary.

4 Answers will vary.

3.4 Present tense of *tener* and *venir*

Quiz A

1 1. tener 2. tienen 3. vengo 4. venimos

2 1. b 2. f 3. h 4. i 5. d 6. e

3 1. tengo 2. vienen 3. venimos 4. tienen 5. tienes 6. viene

4 1. Yo vengo de Italia. 2. Nuestros primos vienen a las diez de la noche. 3. Tú tienes miedo de la película de horror. 4. Nosotras tenemos ganas de mirar la televisión. 5. Usted tiene mucha sed. 6. Ernesto decide venir a la casa.

Quiz B

1 Answers will vary.

2 Answers will vary.

3 Answers will vary.

Lección 4

Contextos

Quiz A

1 **Lugares:** gimnasio, restaurante **Pasatiempos:** escribir, jugar videojuegos **Deportes:** esquí, vóleibol

2 1. el tenis 2. el béisbol 3. la natación 4. el ciclismo

3 1. e 2. c 3. d 4. b 5. a

4 1. pasatiempo 2. equipo 3. partidos 4. videojuegos 5. parque

Quiz B

1 Suggested answers: 1. Es el centro. 2. Es un gimnasio. 3. Es un restaurante. 4. Es un café. 5. Es un museo.

2 Answers will vary.

3 Answers will vary.

4 Answers will vary.

Estructura

4.1 Present tense of *ir*

Quiz A

1 1. van 2. va 3. van 4. vas 5. vamos 6. voy

2 1. Yo voy a la biblioteca. 2. Nosotros vamos a la piscina. 3. Mis primas van al gimnasio. 4. Tú vas de excursión. 5. Ustedes van al parque municipal. 6. Alejandro va al museo de ciencias.

3 1. Va a patinar en línea mañana también. 2. Vamos a ver una película mañana también. 3. Vas a andar en patineta mañana también. 4. Voy a leer un mensaje electrónico mañana también. 5. Van a escribir una carta mañana también.

4 1. Yo voy a nadar en la piscina. 2. Carmela y yo vamos a caminar por la plaza. 3. Fernando va al parque a las cuatro de la tarde. 4. Doña Inés y don Mario van a comer en el café Alameda.

Quiz B

1 Answers will vary.

2 Answers will vary.

3 Answers will vary.

4.2 Stem-changing verbs: *e:ie, o:ue*

Quiz A

1 1. cuentas 2. cuentan 3. jugar 4. jugamos 5. muestras 6. muestran 7. empezar 8. empezamos

2 1. entiende 2. quieres 3. jugar 4. pierden 5. recordamos

3 1. Omar y Antonio almuerzan en un restaurante japonés. 2. Usted no puede ver la película porque no encuentra el cine. 3. ¿Cierran ellas las ventanas? 4. Yo vuelvo a casa a las seis de la tarde. 5. Nosotras dormimos ocho horas.

4 1. empieza 2. pueden/podemos 3. piensan/pensamos 4. queremos 5. prefiero 6. juega

Quiz B

1 Answers will vary.

2 Answers will vary.

3 Answers will vary.

4.3 Stem-changing verbs: *e:i*

Quiz A

1 1. d 2. b 3. a 4. b

2 1. d 2. e 3. a 4. f 5. b

3 1. Sí, (Verónica y Carlos) piden ayuda. 2. Sí, digo que quiero ver una película. 3. Sí, (nosotros) conseguimos videojuegos en el centro. 4. Sí, (Mateo) sigue una dieta. 5. Sí, (ustedes) repiten las actividades./Sí, (nosotros) repetimos las actividades. 6. Sí, pedimos muchos favores.

4 1. dice 2. pide 3. repito 4. sigue 5. conseguir

Quiz B

1 Answers will vary.

2 Answers will vary.

3 Answers will vary.

4.4 Verbs with irregular *yo* forms

Quiz A

1 1. Pongo 2. Traigo 3. Oigo 4. Hago 5. Supongo

2 1. buceamos 2. para 3. poner 4. con

3 1. oímos 2. salimos 3. trae 4. traigo 5. pongo 6. salgo 7. veo/vemos

4 1. Yo no oigo bien. 2. Usted ve el partido de tenis en la televisión. 3. Mis amigos oyen las instrucciones de la profesora. 4. Yo no digo mentiras.

Quiz B

1 Answers will vary.

2 Answers will vary.

3 Answers will vary.

Lección 5

Contextos

Quiz A

1 1. b 2. a 3. b 4. c 5. c 6. a

2 1. L 2. I 3. L 4. L 5. I

3 1. llegada 2. tercera 3. mar 4. sacar fotos 5. está nevando

4 1. pasaporte 2. primer 3. barco 4. ida y vuelta

Quiz B

1 Answers will vary.

2 Answers will vary.

3 Answers will vary.

Estructura

5.1 *Estar* with conditions and emotions

Quiz A

1 1. abierto 2. triste 3. desordenado 4. limpio

2 1. b 2. i 3. a 4. d 5. f 6. c

3 1. estamos; aburridas 2. está; enamorada 3. estás; listo 4. estoy; confundido/a / equivocado/a 5. están; abiertas 6. estar; cansado/a

4 1. Los viajeros están de buen humor. 2. Tomás y yo estamos preocupados por la situación en el aeropuerto. 3. Mi sobrina está avergonzada. 4. ¿(Tú) Estás seguro/a de que quieres ser médico/a?

Quiz B

1 Answers will vary.

2 Answers will vary.

3 Answers will vary.

5.2 The present progressive

Quiz A

1 1. están jugando 2. estás viviendo 3. estoy pudiendo 4. estamos aprendiendo 5. está yendo

2 1. f 2. b 3. d 4. a

3 1. estamos pasando 2. estoy escribiendo 3. está buceando 4. está pescando 5. están leyendo 6. estás haciendo

4 1. Estoy buscando 2. están tomando 3. estás durmiendo 4. Estamos pidiendo 5. está abriendo

Quiz B

1 Answers will vary.

2 Answers will vary.

3 Answers will vary.

5.3 *Ser* and *estar*

Quiz A

1 1. b 2. e 3. a 4. g 5. d

2 1. es 2. eres 3. estoy; es 4. es 5. están

3 1. somos 2. somos 3. estamos 4. somos 5. es 6. son 7. son/están 8. están 9. está 10. es 11. están 12. está

Quiz B

1 Answers will vary.

2 Answers will vary.

3 Answers will vary.

5.4 Direct object nouns and pronouns

Quiz A

1 1. a 2. b 3. c 4. c 5. b

2 1. Ustedes lo buscan. 2. Anabela lo está mirando./Anabela está mirándolo. 3. No la veo. 4. Debemos llamarlos./Los debemos llamar. 5. Las vamos a comprar./Vamos a comprarlas.

3 1. Las tengo que hacer mañana. 2. Puedo llevarte al aeropuerto. 3. Estoy aprendiéndolo. 4. Nos van a visitar hoy.

4 1. No, no te estoy llamando./No, no estoy llamándote. 2. No, (la agente de viajes) no la confirma. 3. No, (el botones) no nos/los espera. 4. No, no los vamos/van a traer./No, no vamos/van a traerlos. 5. No, (mis abuelos) no me vienen a visitar./No, (mis abuelos) no vienen a visitarme. 6. No, (Lola y Ricardo) no quieren hacerlo./No, (Lola y Ricardo) no lo quieren hacer.

Quiz B

1 Answers will vary.

2 Answers will vary.

3 Answers will vary.

Lección 6

Contextos

Quiz A

1 A. impermeable, sombrero B. sandalias, traje de baño C. abrigo, guantes

2 1. c 2. a 3. d 4. d 5. b 6. a 7. c

3 1. gris/rosado 2. anaranjada 3. marrón/café/ blanco 4. morada 5. negro/azul oscuro

4 1. pantalones cortos 2. par 3. ricas 4. barata 5. precio fijo

Quiz B

1 Answers will vary. Suggested answers: A. un traje de baño, unas gafas de sol B. un abrigo, unas botas C. un vestido, un traje D. unos (blue)jeans, una blusa

2 Answers will vary.

3 Answers will vary.

Estructura

6.1 Saber and conocer

Quiz A

1 1. a 2. b 3. b 4. a

2 1. conocen 2. conozco 3. Sabes 4. sabemos 5. Conoces 6. saben

3 1. sé 2. saber 3. conoce 4. sabe 5. conoces 6. conozco

4 1. parecen; (mis amigos) parecen estar contentos 2. conoces; (yo) no conozco personalmente a una persona famosa 3. conducen; (mis padres) no conducen un automóvil feo/(mis padres) conducen un automóvil bonito 4. Traducen; (nosotros) traducimos del inglés al español

Quiz B

1 Some answers will vary. Suggested answers: 1. Saben; Sí, (mis amigos y yo) sabemos bailar. 2. conocen; No, (nosotros) no conocemos un buen lugar para bailar en nuestra ciudad. 3. sabe; Mi padre no sabe cantar bien. 4. saben; No, (mis hermanos) no saben cómo se llaman mis profesores. 5. Conoces; No, (yo) no conozco a una persona famosa./Sí, (yo) conozco a Leonardo DiCaprio.

2 Answers will vary.

3 Answers will vary.

4 Answers will vary.

6.2 Indirect object pronouns

Quiz A

1 1. me 2. les 3. le 4. te 5. les 6. Nos

2 1. Sí, me ofrecen el trabajo. 2. Sí, (Carlos) nos describe la tarea (a Ana y a mí). 3. Sí, les puedo vender la computadora./Sí, puedo venderles la computadora. 4. Sí, me están explicando la verdad (a mí)./Sí, (a mí) me están explicando la verdad.

3 Some answers may vary slightly. 1. Yo te pido dinero (a ti). 2. La vendedora nos muestra muchas chaquetas (a Laura y a mí). 3. ¿Quién le paga los estudios a Manuel? 4. Nosotros les pensamos comprar regalos a nuestras madres./Nosotros pensamos comprarles regalos a nuestras madres.

4 1. Te 2. le 3. a mí 4. nos/me 5. Les 6. me 7. les 8. Le

Quiz B

1 1. Answers will vary. Suggested answers: 1. Sí, Carlos me explica tu problema. 2. No, no quiero venderte la computadora. 3. La vendedora les va a mostrar unas corbatas. 4. Sí, nos está mirando. 5. No le ofrezco el trabajo a Carolina porque no es trabajadora.

2 Answers will vary.

3 Answers will vary.

6.3 Preterite tense of regular verbs

Quiz A

1 1. leímos 2. leyeron 3. comencé 4. aprendí 5. aprendimos 6. abrió 7. abrieron 8. busqué

2 1. oyeron 2. Asististe 3. vio 4. pagué 5. almorzamos

3 1. escribir 2. empezó 3. vivieron 4. vender 5. juega

4 1. volviste 2. acabo 3. pasó 4. salimos 5. llevó 6. esperamos 7. compraste 8. decidí

Quiz B

1 Answers will vary. Suggested answers: 1. Sí, ya la abrieron. Encontré unas plumas. 2. Sí, lo compré. Me costó dos dólares. Pagué en efectivo. 3. Sí, le llevé tu tarea. No, no escribió tu nota en el papel. 4. Sí, los vi. Hablamos de la tarea.

2 Answers will vary.

3 Answers will vary.

6.4 Demonstrative adjectives and pronouns

Quiz A

1 1. Esta falda elegante está de moda.
2. ¿Compraste aquellos trajes marrones?
3. Este sombrero cuesta cuarenta dólares.
4. Pienso comprar aquella camisa verde.
5. Esas vendedoras están organizando los zapatos.

2 1. ésta 2. aquéllas 3. éste 4. ése 5. aquél

3 1. Esos 2. ésta 3. aquella 4. Eso

4 1. Yo llevé este reloj la semana pasada. 2. ¿Cuándo encontraste esa corbata? 3. Ayer nosotros oímos esta música en la fiesta. 4. Juanjo le vendió aquellos libros a Raquel.

Quiz B

1 Some answers may vary. 1. aquella 2. Ése 3. esta 4. Esas

2 Answers will vary.

3 Answers will vary.

Lección 7

Contextos

Quiz A

1 1. a 2. d 3. d 4. c 5. a

2 a. 1 b. 4 c. 2 d. 3 e. 5

3 1. I 2. I 3. L 4. I 5. L

4 1. dormirse 2. jabón 3. levantarse 4. vestirse 5. antes de

Quiz B

1 Some answers will vary. Suggested answers: 1. el jabón 2. despertarse 3. lavarse las manos 4. el pelo 5. vestirse 6. maquillarse 7. los dientes

2 Answers will vary.

3 Answers will vary.

Estructura

7.1 Reflexive verbs

Quiz A

1 1. a 2. b 3. b 4. b

2 1. se quita 2. se preocupan 3. te acuerdas 4. me seco 5. nos maquillamos

3 1. Miguel se enoja con su novia. 2. María Elena y yo nos dormimos a las once. 3. Antes de dormirse, ustedes se cepillan los dientes. 4. ¿(Te) Duchas o te bañas? 5. Yo me pongo triste cuando tengo que irme de la casa de mi abuela.

4 1. se despiertan 2. se ducha 3. se queda 4. mira 5. se lava 6. se afeita 7. nos sentamos 8. cepillarme

Quiz B

1 a. 1 b. 4 c. 2 d. 3 e. 5; Verbs: se despierta; se afeita; se cepilla; se pone

2 Answers will vary.

3 Answers will vary.

7.2 Indefinite and negative words

Quiz A

1 1. b 2. b 3. a 4. a

2 1. ningún 2. Tampoco 3. nada 4. algunas 5. pero 6. algo

3 1. ninguno 2. sino 3. ni, ni 4. algún, ningún

4 1. Yo tampoco me siento bien./Yo no me siento bien tampoco. 2. Nunca me llama nadie./No me llama nadie nunca./Jamás me llama nadie./No me llama nadie jamás. 3. No hay ninguna película interesante en el cine. 4. Hay algo bonito en los almacenes. 5. Tengo ganas de ir de compras o/y de ir al cine./Tengo ganas de ir de compras y de ir al cine. 6. Siempre veo a alguien.

Quiz B

1 Some answers may vary. Suggested answers: 1. No veo a nadie tampoco. 2. Nunca hay nada bonito en los almacenes. 3. No tengo ganas ni de ir de compras ni de ir al cine. 4. Hay algunas películas interesantes en el cine. 5. Yo también quiero hacer algo. 6. Siempre me llama alguien.

2 Answers will vary.

3 Answers will vary.

7.3 Preterite of *ser* and *ir*

Quiz A

1 1. fui 2. fue 3. fuimos 4. fueron

2 1. e; ir 2. h; ir 3. i; ir 4. f; ser 5. g; ir 6. b; ser

3 1. Anteayer Danilo fue a la playa. 2. ¿Cómo fueron tus vacaciones en Perú? 3. Yo fui presidente del club de ciencias. 4. Ustedes no fueron a clase el viernes pasado.

4 1. Usted fue muy inteligente. 2. Mario y yo fuimos al cine. 3. ¿Fuiste a trabajar? 4. Fuimos estudiantes de la escuela secundaria. 5. ¿Cómo fueron las películas de terror? 6. Fui al parque para jugar al tenis.

Quiz B

1 Answers will vary. Suggested answers: 1. Fui a un restaurante.; ir 2. Paulina, Carolina y David fueron. Sí, Enrique fue también.; ir 3. Fue muy cara.; ser 4. Fuimos a una discoteca.; ir 5. Sí, fue divertido. Enrique bailó con Paulina.; ser 6. Sí, fueron novios.; ser

2 Answers will vary.

3 Answers will vary.

7.4 Verbs like *gustar*

Quiz A

1 1. b 2. a 3. b 4. a 5. c

2 1. les fascina 2. le interesan 3. les aburre 4. me importa 5. nos molesta

3 1. (A ti) Te molesta despertarte temprano. 2. (A José) Le quedaron bien los zapatos anaranjados. 3. ¿(A ustedes) Les encantaron sus vacaciones en la playa? 4. (A Carlos y a mí) Nos aburren las clases de sociología.

4 1. encantó/fascinó 2. Esteban 3. aburrió 4. a 5. al 6. ti

Quiz B

1 Suggested answers: 1. A ellas les aburre el arte. 2. Al señor García le encanta enseñar filosofía. 3. A Daniela y a mí nos fascina esquiar. 4. A usted le falta dinero.

2 Answers will vary.

3 Answers will vary.

4 Answers will vary.

Lección 8

Contextos

Quiz A

1 **La cena:** espárragos, arroz con pollo; **El almuerzo:** refresco, sándwich de jamón, uvas; **El desayuno:** cereales, café con leche, huevos

2 1. d 2. a 3. b 4. b 5. c 6. a

3 1. I 2. L 3. I 4. L 5. I 6. L

4 1. langosta 2. probar; sabroso 3. Sabe

Quiz B

1 Some answers will vary. Suggested answers: 1. Comemos la ensalada con aceite y vinagre. 2. El limón es una fruta. 3. Vamos a comer algunos entremeses y luego el plato principal. 4. Normalmente, las salchichas son de carne, de pollo o de cerdo. 5. Tengo sed; voy a beber un jugo de naranja. 6. Si quieres merendar, puedes comer una banana.

2 Answers will vary.

3 Answers will vary.

Estructura

8.1 Preterite of stem-changing verbs

Quiz A

1 1. morir 2. seguí 3. moriste 4. morimos 5. siguieron

2 1. consiguieron 2. pidió 3. te sentiste 4. dormí 5. prefirió

3 1. Álvaro y yo servimos los entremeses. 2. ¿Quién repitió las instrucciones? 3. Ayer yo me vestí con ropa elegante. 4. Ustedes se durmieron a las diez.

4 1. escogimos/preferimos 2. consiguió/leyó 3. nos vestimos 4. nos sentimos 5. sirvió 6. escogieron/pidieron/probaron 7. preferí 8. escogimos/pedimos/probamos

Quiz B

1 1. te sentiste 2. consiguió 3. pidieron 4. dormí

2 Answers will vary.

3 Answers will vary.

4 Answers will vary.

8.2 Double object pronouns

Quiz A

1 1. Nos lo van a servir./Van a servírnoslo. 2. Se lo estoy mostrando./Estoy mostrándoselo. 3. ¿Te las sirvieron? 4. Me lo va a traer./Va a traérmelo. 5. Se la pedí.

2 1. Estamos preparándosela. 2. Voy a repetírtelo. 3. ¿Estás preparándomelo? 4. Debemos pedírselos. 5. Me los tienes que mostrar.

3 1. Sí, te lo estoy recomendando./Sí, estoy recomendándotelo. 2. Sí, nos lo sirve. 3. Sí, me la van a traer./Sí, van a traérmela. 4. Sí, nos las tienen que mostrar./Sí, tienen que mostrárnoslas./Sí, se las tienen que mostrar./Sí, tienen que mostrárselas. 5. Sí, estoy comprándoselos./Sí, se los estoy comprando.

4 1. te lo compré 2. la escogí 3. lavártelos 4. te la debes poner/debes ponértela 5. se las preparé

Quiz B

1 Some answers will vary. Suggested answers: 1. te lo compré 2. Sí, la escogí. 3. Sí, te los lavé. 4. Sí, debes ponértela. 5. preparárselas ahora mismo

2 Answers will vary.

3 Answers will vary.

8.3 Comparisons

Quiz A

1 1. d 2. c 3. h 4. e 5. g

2 1. menos 2. que 3. menor 4. de; peor

3 1. como 2. tanto 3. bien 4. tantos 5. tan joven

4 1. Argentina es más grande que Guatemala. 2. Scarlett Johansson es menor/más joven que Julia Roberts. 3. Los entremeses son más/ menos sabrosos que los platos principales./Los entremeses son tan sabrosos como los platos principales. 4. Puerto Rico tiene tantas playas como la República Dominicana. 5. La música rock es mejor que la música clásica./La música rock es tan buena como la música clásica.

Quiz B

1 Some answers may vary. Suggested answers: 1. Argentina es más grande que Guatemala. 2. Los entremeses cuestan más de quince dólares. 3. Scarlett Johansson es menor que Julia Roberts. 4. La música rock es mejor que la música clásica. 5. Puerto Rico tiene tantas playas como la República Dominicana.

2 Answers will vary.

3 Answers will vary.

8.4 Superlatives

Quiz A

1 1. la más alta 2. los mejores 3. el más simpático 4. las mayores 5. el/la mayor/más grande

2 1. dificilísimo 2. riquísima 3. guapísimos 4. pequeñísimo 5. trabajadorcísima

3 1. e 2. a 3. d 4. g 5. b

4 Answers will vary. Sample answers: 1. El béisbol es el deporte más divertido de los tres. 2. El presidente de España es el menos famoso de los tres. 3. La comida cubana es la más sabrosa de las tres. 4. El francés es la lengua menos fácil de las tres. 5. La leche con cereal es el desayuno más barato de los tres.

Quiz B

1 1. e 2. f 3. b 4. a 5. h

2 Answers will vary.

3 Answers will vary.

Lección 9

Contextos

Quiz A

1 1. d 2. b 3. a 4. c 5. d 6. a

2 1. L 2. I 3. I 4. L 5. I

3 1. casarse con 2. amistad 3. romper con/divorciarse de 4. pasarlo mal 5. adolescencia

4 1. cambiar 2. pastel 3. nos relajamos 4. regalar

Quiz B

1 1. adolescencia 2. casarse con 3. nacer 4. amistad 5. pasarlo mal

2 Some answers will vary. Suggested answers: 1. El nacimiento es el principio de la vida. 2. Una chica que celebra sus quince años está en la etapa de la adolescencia. 3. Mi abuela murió y ahora mi abuelo es viudo. 4. Ricardo rompió con Lola porque la odia.

3 Answers will vary.

4 Answers will vary.

Estructura

9.1 Irregular preterites

Quiz A

1 1. poder 2. querer 3. conduje 4. pude 5. condujo 6. pudo 7. quiso 8. condujimos 9. pudimos 10. quisimos 11. condujeron 12. quisieron

2 1. trajiste 2. hubo 3. di; vino 4. dijeron

3 1. Ustedes le dieron un beso al recién casado/a la recién casada. 2. ¿Cuándo supiste tú la fecha de la graduación? 3. Yo puse el flan de caramelo en la mesa. 4. Antonio y yo estuvimos en Madrid el verano pasado. 5. ¿Qué hicieron Nicolás y Fernanda después del divorcio?

4 1. dimos/hicimos 2. estuvieron/hubo 3. pudieron 4. hizo 5. trajeron 6. puso 7. tuvo 8. hice

Quiz B

1 1. hubo 2. diste; vino 3. dijeron 4. traje

2 Answers will vary.

3 Answers will vary.

4 Answers will vary.

9.2 Verbs that change meaning in the preterite

Quiz A

1 1. L 2. I 3. I 4. L

2 1. supe 2. quiso 3. conoció 4. Pude 5. No quiso 6. No pudo

3 1. El presidente no quiso hablar con los reporteros. 2. ¿Cómo supieron ustedes lo que pasó entre Fabiana y Raúl? 3. Tú conociste al señor Castillo anteayer. 4. Nosotros no pudimos comprar los regalos porque hubo mucho tráfico en el centro. 5. Después de los exámenes, Natalia pudo relajarse.

4 1. quiso 2. conocí 3. pudo 4. quise; supo

Quiz B

1 1. a 2. a 3. b 4. a 5. b 6. b

2 Answers will vary.

3 Answers will vary.

9.3 *¿Qué?* and *¿cuál?*

Quiz A

1 1. Qué 2. Cuál 3. Qué 4. qué 5. Cuáles 6. Cuál 7. Qué 8. Qué

2 1. Cuál; b 2. qué; e 3. Dónde; d/Cómo; f 4. quién/quiénes; g 5. Qué; c 6. Cómo; f/Dónde; d 7. Cuántos; a

3 1. ¿Qué es un flan? 2. ¿Cuál es (la llave)? 3. ¿Qué postres les gustan (a ustedes)? 4. ¿Cuál es tu/su estado civil? 5. ¿Qué es eso?

Quiz B

1 1. Cuáles 2. Qué 3. Cuál 4. Qué

2 Sentences will vary. 1. Cuál 2. A qué hora/Cuándo/Dónde 3. Cómo/Cuándo/Dónde 4. Cuál 5. qué 6. Qué

3 Answers will vary.

9.4 Pronouns after prepositions

Quiz A

1 1. b 2. d 3. a 4. d

2 1. para él 2. sin ustedes 3. para ti 4. Para mí 5. para usted 6. sin ellas 7. conmigo 8. sin nosotras

3 1. El pastel fue para ella. 2. Las chicas se sentaron al lado de nosotros. 3. Para ti, la fiesta fue aburrida. 4. Yo estuve en el cine contigo.

Quiz B

1 Some answers will vary. 1. ti; ti 2. mí; ti 3. contigo 4. tú; yo; ellos

2 Answers will vary.

3 Answers will vary.

ANSWERS TO TESTS

Lección 1

Test A

1 1. Cierto. 2. Falso. 3. Falso. 4. Falso. 5. Cierto.

2 Answers will vary.

3 1. lápices 2. mujer 3. pasajeros 4. chicas 5. estudiantes

4 1. Son las nueve y media/treinta de la mañana 2. es a las diez y cuarto/quince de la mañana 3. es a las dos y veinticinco de la tarde 4. es a las cinco menos cuarto/quince de la tarde 5. Es a las ocho de la noche

5 1. buenas 2. te 3. llamo 4. dónde 5. Soy 6. qué 7. la 8. nada 9. Nos 10. luego/pronto

6 Answers will vary.

7 1. El nombre de la chica es Mariana. 2. En el cuaderno hay números de teléfono. 3. El chico es de España. 4. El número de teléfono del chico es el veinticinco, catorce, veintitrés.

8 Answers will vary.

Test B

1 1. Falso. 2. Falso. 3. Falso. 4. Falso. 5. Cierto.

2 Answers will vary.

3 1. foto 2. profesor 3. diccionarios 4. computadora 5. cuadernos

4 1. Son las nueve y veinte de la noche. 2. es a las once de la mañana. 3. es a las tres menos cuarto/quince de la tarde. 4. es a las cuatro y media/treinta de la tarde. 5. Es a las diez de la noche.

5 1. días 2. llamas 3. me 4. tú 5. Mucho 6. gusto 7. Eres 8. soy 9. A 10. vemos

6 Answers will vary.

7 1. El nombre del chico es Javier. 2. El chico es de Costa Rica. 3. En la maleta hay un diccionario, un mapa, una computadora y dos cuadernos. 4. El número de teléfono de Sarah es el treinta y cuatro, veintinueve, cero seis.

8 Answers will vary.

Test C

1 Answers will vary.

2 1. La clase de biología es a las ocho de la mañana. 2. La clase de literatura es a las nueve y media/treinta de la mañana. 3. La clase de geografía es a las once menos cuarto/quince de la mañana. 4. El laboratorio es a las doce y cuarto/quince de la tarde. 5. La clase de matemáticas es a la una y media/treinta de la tarde.

3 1. El nombre del conductor es Armando. 2. En el autobús hay cinco maletas. 3. Las maletas son de los estudiantes de los Estados Unidos. 4. Es la una de la tarde. 5. El número de teléfono de Armando es el veinticuatro, treinta, doce.

4 Answers will vary.

Test D

1 Answers will vary.

2 1. La clase de biología es a las ocho y cuarto/quince de la mañana. 2. La clase de literatura es a las nueve y media/treinta de la mañana. 3. La clase de geografía es las once y cinco de la mañana. 4. El laboratorio es a las doce y cuarto/quince de la tarde. 5. La clase de matemáticas es a la una y media/treinta de la tarde.

3 1. Hay dos maletas en el autobús. 2. Hay cuatro libros en el autobús. 3. Las maletas son de los turistas de México. 4. Son las seis de la tarde. 5. El número de teléfono de Eduardo es el veintitrés, cero seis, quince.

4 Answers will vary.

Test E

1 1. c 2. a 3. c 4. a 5. c

2 1. e 2. c 3. d 4. b 5. a

3 a. 3 b. 5 c. 4 d. 2 e. 1

4 1. incorrecta 2. correcta 3. incorrecta 4. correcta 5. correcta

5 1. es 2. son 3. somos 4. Es 5. eres 6. soy

6 1. dos diccionarios 2. tres autobuses 3. una escuela 4. una maleta 5. dos fotos 6. un cuaderno

7 1. nuevo 2. Nada 3. estás 4. es 5. se 6. presento 7. gusto 8. soy 9. mío

8 1. Puerto Rico 2. Los Ángeles 3. estudiante 4. ocho y cuarto 5. dos 6. Mario

Test F

1 1. a 2. a 3. a 4. b 5. c

2 1. b 2. c 3. d 4. e 5. a

3 a. 4 b. 1 c. 5 d. 2 e. 3

4 1. correcta 2. incorrecta 3. correcta 4. correcta 5. incorrecta

5 1. es 2. es 3. soy 4. eres 5. son 6. somos

6 1. dos diccionarios 2. una maleta 3. dos fotos 4. cuatro maletas 5. una escuela 6. tres hombres

7 1. estás 2. bien 3. nuevo 4. es 5. llama 6. Hola 7. el 8. nombre 9. Gracias

8 1. Perú 2. Boston 3. estudiante 4. ocho y media/treinta 5. tres 6. José

Lección 2

Test A

1 1. Falso. 2. Falso. 3. Cierto. 4. Cierto. 5. Falso.

2 Answers will vary.

3 Answers may vary slightly. 1. dónde está el libro de literatura 2. Te gusta (estudiar) literatura 3. Por qué te gusta la literatura/la materia/el curso 4. Quién enseña la clase de literatura 5. Cuántas chicas hay en la clase

4 1. Hay mil quinientos estudiantes en total. 2. Hay cuatrocientos noventa y siete chicos y novecientas tres chicas. 3. Ochenta y seis estudiantes hablan español. 4. Setenta y dos estudiantes hablan otras lenguas. 5. Setecientos cincuenta estudiantes estudian español.

5 1. estoy 2. gusta 3. estudio 4. terminan 5. regreso 6. trabaja 7. enseña 8. hablamos 9. miramos 10. llegas

6 Answers will vary.

7 1. La cafetería está al lado de la biblioteca. 2. Hay nueve estudiantes en la cafetería. 3. Mira a los estudiantes (que caminan al gimnasio). 4. Estudia en la cafetería porque su hermana está en casa con unas chicas (y necesita estudiar mucho). 5. El examen es el jueves a las tres de la tarde.

8 Answers will vary.

Test B

1 1. Falso. 2. Falso. 3. Falso. 4. Cierto. 5. Cierto.

2 Answers will vary.

3 Answers may vary slightly. 1. dónde está el diccionario 2. Te gusta estudiar español/Te gusta el español 3. Por qué te gusta estudiar español/la materia/el curso 4. Quién enseña la clase de español/Quién es el profesor 5. Cuántos estudiantes hay en la clase

4 1. Hay dos mil seiscientos cincuenta estudiantes en la escuela en total. 2. Hay mil ciento treinta y cuatro chicos en la escuela. 3. Hay mil quinientas dieciséis chicas en la escuela. 4. Hay treinta y cinco especialidades. 5. Ciento cinco profesores enseñan en esta escuela.

5 1. estoy 2. gusta 3. está 4. estudio 5. descanso 6. enseño 7. preparamos 8. escuchamos 9. necesitamos 10. llegas

6 Answers will vary.

7 1. La biblioteca está al lado del gimnasio. 2. En la biblioteca hay once estudiantes. 3. (Juan Antonio/Él) Camina a la cafetería y toma un café. 4. (Juan Antonio/Él) Estudia en la biblioteca porque su hermano está en casa con unos chicos (y Juan Antonio necesita preparar el examen). 5. El examen es el viernes a las 10 de la mañana.

8 Answers will vary.

Test C

1 Answers will vary.

2 Answers will vary.

3 1. Estudia en la biblioteca de la escuela. 2. Está en la biblioteca porque no hay muchos estudiantes/porque necesita estudiar (para el examen de física)/porque su primo está en casa con diez amigos. 3. Mira a los estudiantes (que caminan a clase). 4. El examen es el martes a las 10 de la mañana. 5. Desea llegar a la residencia a las ocho (de la noche) para tomar algo y escuchar música.

4 Answers will vary.

Test D

1 Answers will vary.

2 Answers will vary.

3 1. Estudia en casa. 2. Porque necesita estudiar para el examen de historia. 3. No, no desea estudiar en la biblioteca porque siempre hay muchos estudiantes. 4. El examen es mañana, lunes, a las cuatro de la tarde. 5. Camina a la cafetería (que está muy cerca) y toma un café.

4 Answers will vary.

Test E

1 1. Falso. 2. Cierto. 3. Cierto. 4. Cierto. 5. Falso.

2 1. quinientos cuarenta y seis 2. doscientos cinco 3. treinta y ocho 4. mil ciento diesiséis 5. ochocientos nueve

3 1. horario 2. trimestre 3. química 4. lado 5. Caminamos

4 1. c 2. b 3. e 4. d 5. a

5 1. c 2. b 3. c 4. c 5. b 6. a

6 1. estamos 2. estoy 3. está 4. están 5. estás 6. están

7 1. compramos 2. cenan 3. desayuno 4. explica 5. dibujan 6. pregunto 7. contesta 8. regresan 9. necesitan

8 1. b 2. c 3. b 4. b 5. c 6. a

Test F

1 1. Cierto. 2. Cierto. 3. Cierto. 4. Falso. 5. Cierto.

2 1. trescientos veinticuatro 2. ciento once 3. cuatrocientos dieciocho 4. mil quinientos treinta y siete 5. ochocientos diecinueve

3 1. regresar 2. química 3. detrás 4. Caminamos 5. trimestre

4 1. e 2. c 3. a 4. b 5. d

5 1. a 2. c 3. b 4. a 5. b 6. c

6 1. están 2. está 3. estoy 4. estamos 5. está 6. estás

7 1. ceno 2. estudian 3. conversa 4. dibuja 5. preguntan 6. trabaja 7. explican 8. regresan 9. desayunas

8 1. a 2. a 3. c 4. b 5. c 6. b

Lección 3

Test A

1 1. Falso. 2. Falso. 3. Cierto. 4. Falso. 5. Falso.

2 Order of answers will vary. David es el abuelo de Graciela. Lupe es la tía de Graciela. María es la madre de Graciela. Ramón es el hermano de Graciela. Ernesto es el primo de Graciela. Descriptions of family members will vary.

3 1. Mis 2. nuestro 3. mi 4. tus 5. mi

4 1. vive 2. abre 3. son 4. tienen 5. asiste 6. comparten 7. escribe 8. recibe 9. comprenden 10. debe

5 Answers will vary.

6 1. Tiene veintitrés años. 2. Trabaja en la cafetería por las tardes. 3. Necesita estudiar química porque desea ser médico. 4. Su madre es médica. 5. Adrián vive con Vicente/un estudiante colombiano.

7 Answers will vary.

Test B

1 1. Cierto. 2. Falso. 3. Falso. 4. Falso. 5. Falso.

2 Order of answers will vary. José Antonio es el sobrino de Luis Miguel. Pilar es la hija de Luis Miguel. Raquel es la cuñada de Luis Miguel. Eduardo es el hermano de Luis Miguel. Juan Carlos es el padre de Luis Miguel. Descriptions of family members will vary.

3 1. mi 2. mi 3. tu 4. tu 5. su

4 1. vivimos 2. escribe 3. lee 4. asisto 5. corremos 6. bebemos 7. comemos 8. debo 9. viene 10. comprendo

5 Answers will vary.

6 1. Es argentina/de Argentina. 2. Vive con su amiga Rosana. 3. Prepara la tarea en la biblioteca o en la cafetería. 4. No, no trabaja los domingos. 5. No, es fácil vivir con Rosana porque es fácil compartir problemas con ella.

7 Answers will vary.

Test C

1 Answers will vary.

2 Order of answers will vary. Joaquín es el esposo de la prima de Manuela. Pilar es la prima de Manuela. Ana María es la tía de Manuela. Eduardo es el padre de Manuela. Juan Carlos es el abuelo de Manuela. Descriptions of family members will vary.

3 1. Tiene veinte años. 2. Trabaja en la biblioteca porque tiene tiempo para leer y estudiar. 3. Necesita estudiar inglés porque desea ser periodista. 4. Su madre es periodista. 5. Rosa comparte el cuarto de la residencia con Mónica.

4 Answers will vary.

Test D

1 Answers will vary.

2 Order of answers will vary. Luis Miguel es el cuñado de Eduardo. José Antonio es el hijo de Eduardo. Pilar es la sobrina de Eduardo. Raquel es la esposa de Eduardo. Sofía es la madre de Eduardo. Descriptions of family members will vary.

3 1. Es mexicano/de México. 2. Debe estudiar mucho porque también trabaja por las tardes. 3. Su padre es artista. 4. Comparte su/Vive en un apartamento con su viejo amigo, Peter. 5. Habla con Peter en español porque Peter desea estudiar un año en España (y necesita practicar).

4 Answers will vary.

Test E

1 1. Cierto. 2. Falso. 3. Falso. 4. Cierto. 5. Falso.

2 1. d 2. e 3. c 4. a 5. b

3 1. cuñada 2. prima 3. yerno 4. madrastra 5. suegra

4 1. vienen 2. debes 3. vengo 4. asisto 5. corro

5 1. a 2. d 3. e 4. c 5. b

6 1. viene 2. tengo 3. tienes 4. comprendo 5. asistes 6. Vienes 7. comemos

7 1. mi 2. Sus 3. Sus 4. nuestra 5. Mi 6. tu 7. Sus 8. tus 9. Mis

8 1. Cierto. 2. Falso. 3. Falso. 4. Falso. 5. Cierto. 6. Falso.

Test F

1 1. Cierto. 2. Falso. 3. Cierto. 4. Falso. 5. Falso.

2 1. d 2. e 3. b 4. c 5. a

3 1. abuelos 2. sobrinos 3. suegra 4. padre 5. tíos

4 1. estoy 2. es 3. vienen 4. corro 5. tienes

5 1. e 2. a 3. c 4. b 5. d

6 1. comprendo 2. creo 3. simpática 4. difícil 5. vives 6. Vienes 7. comemos

7 1. mi 2. Nuestros 3. Sus 4. mis 5. Su 6. tus 7. Su 8. su 9. Nuestra

8 1. Cierto. 2. Falso. 3. Cierto. 4. Cierto. 5. Falso. 6. Cierto.

Lección 4

Test A

1 1. c 2. b 3. a 4. a 5. a

2 Answers will vary.

3 1. Vemos 2. prefiero 3. quiero 4. Pienso 5. entiendes 6. vamos 7. podemos 8. comienza/empieza 9. supongo 10. volvemos

4 Answers will vary.

5 1. Porque tiene un poco de tiempo. 2. Sandra está en un parque de la ciudad. 3. Tiene ganas de descansar. 4. Sandra y Daniel piensan ir al museo. 5. Sandra quiere almorzar en un pequeño café que hay en la plaza Mayor. 6. Daniel piensa que las montañas son muy bonitas.

6 Answers will vary.

Test B

1 1. c 2. a 3. c 4. c 5. b

2 Answers will vary.

3 1. Quieres 2. prefiero 3. podemos 4. juega 5. entiendo 6. supongo 7. vamos 8. piensas 9. comienza/empieza 10. vuelves

4 Answers will vary.

5 1. Rubén está en la cafetería de la escuela. 2. Él y sus amigos quieren salir. 3. Prefiere pasar tiempo en el gimnasio y después leer una revista. 4. Van a ir al museo y después a comer en un bonito restaurante del centro. 5. Va a estudiar a la biblioteca. 6. Porque tiene un examen de historia.

6 Answers will vary.

Test C

1 Answers will vary.

2 Answers will vary.

3 1. Está en el parque del centro de la ciudad. 2. Hay partidos cada fin de semana. 3. Puedo/Puedes leer mi correo electrónico en el café. 4. Puedo/Puedes practicar la natación, el ciclismo, el tenis, el béisbol, el vóleibol y el baloncesto. 5. Answers will vary.

4 Answers will vary.

Answers to Tests

Test D

1 Answers will vary.

2 Answers will vary.

3 1. Está en el centro de la ciudad, al lado del Museo de Arte. 2. Puedo/Puedes practicar la natación, el baloncesto y el tenis. 3. Puedo/ Puedes leer el periódico en la biblioteca. 4. El número de teléfono es veinticuatro, noventa y ocho, cincuenta. 5. Answers will vary.

4 Answers will vary.

Test E

1 1. Cierto. 2. Falso. 3. Cierto. 4. Falso. 5. Cierto.

2 1. consigo 2. conseguimos 3. cuento 4. pierdo 5. mostramos

3 1. Patricia va a leer el periódico en los ratos libres. 2. Jorge va a visitar monumentos en el centro. 3. Yo voy a jugar videojuegos el fin de semana. 4. Nosotros vamos a nadar en el gimnasio. 5. Lola y Daniel van a ir al parque.

4 1. c 2. a 3. b 4. c 5. b

5 1. empieza 2. juegan 3. pide 4. oye 5. preferimos 6. sigues

6 1. salgo 2. Oigo 3. veo 4. Traigo 5. hago 6. digo

7 1. consiguen 2. juega 3. muestra 4. prefieren 5. empezamos 6. recuerda 7. trae 8. podemos 9. quieres

8 1. a 2. c 3. a 4. a 5. c 6. b

Test F

1 1. Cierto. 2. Cierto. 3. Falso. 4. Falso. 5. Falso.

2 1. digo 2. decimos 3. duermo 4. entendemos 5. volvemos

3 1. Yo voy a escribir una carta a las tres de la tarde. 2. Camilo y Natalia van a andar en patineta en el parque. 3. Nosotros vamos a jugar al tenis. 4. Paula va a pasear en bicicleta en el centro. 5. Daniel va a ir a la iglesia el domingo.

4 1. c 2. c 3. a 4. b 5. b

5 1. cierra 2. repites 3. ve 4. recordamos 5. consigue 6. comienzan

6 1. oigo 2. traigo 3. hago 4. pongo 5. veo 6. digo

7 1. quiere 2. vuelven 3. piensan 4. sigue 5. pide 6. almuerza 7. visitas 8. recuerda 9. traemos

8 1. b 2. a 3. c 4. c 5. b 6. a

Lección 5

Test A

1 1. c 2. a 3. a 4. b 5. a

2 Answers will vary.

3 1. La biblioteca está en el primer piso. 2. La habitación cuarenta y nueve está en el cuarto piso. 3. El restaurante Vistas está en el quinto piso. 4. El gimnasio está en el tercer piso. 5. La cafetería está en el segundo piso.

4 1. Toda la familia las hace. 2. Juan los pone en el automóvil. 3. Mariselis los lleva. 4. Su hijo, Emilio, las pide. 5. La abuela, Rosa, lo busca. 6. Juan los tiene. 7. Mariselis los va a comprar/ va a comprarlos. 8. La abuela y Mariselis/Ellas los quieren visitar/quieren visitarlos.

5 1. Está 2. es 3. está 4. Estás 5. es 6. está 7. son 8. está 9. somos 10. estoy

6 Answers will vary.

7 1. Puedes pasar unas buenas vacaciones viajando en barco por el Caribe y visitando las bonitas playas puertorriqueñas. 2. Las personas que prefieren las ciudades deben ir a San Juan. 3. El hotel El Gran Sol está abierto todo el año. 4. Los huéspedes del hotel pueden pasear por la (interesante) ciudad. 5. Las actividades del hotel son pescar, ir de excursión, montar a caballo y nadar.

8 Answers will vary.

Test B

1 1. b 2. a 3. a 4. b. 5. b

2 Answers will vary.

3 1. La biblioteca está en el segundo piso. 2. La habitación sesenta y dos está en el quinto piso. 3. El restaurante Vistas está en el cuarto piso. 4. El gimnasio está en el primer piso. 5. La agencia de viajes Sol está en el tercer piso.

4 1. Vicente las pone en el automóvil. 2. Isabel los lleva. 3. Su hijo, José Manuel, la tiene. 4. Su hija, Anabel, lo busca. 5. Vicente los tiene. 6. La abuela e Isabel quieren visitarlos/los quieren visitar. 7. Vicente e Isabel quieren escribirlas/las quieren escribir. 8. Todos quieren tomarlo/lo quieren tomar.

5 1. Está 2. es 3. está 4. Estás 5. está 6. está 7. son 8. somos 9. está 10. estoy

6 Answers will vary.

7 1. Las personas activas pueden nadar, bucear, viajar en barco y montar a caballo. 2. (Si estás cansado/a) Puedes tomar el sol y pescar. 3. Por la tarde puedes visitar la ciudad y por la noche puedes cenar en restaurantes y bailar en las discotecas. 4. Puedes visitar el hotel Mar Azul todos los meses; está abierto todo el año. 5. En el hotel hay excursiones en barco, excursiones a caballo y clases de salsa.

8 Answers will vary.

Test C

1 Answers will vary.

2 Answers will vary.

3 1. El restaurante Latino está en el cuarto piso. 2. La habitación veintidós está en el segundo piso. 3. La biblioteca está en el quinto piso. 4. La cafetería está en el primer piso. 5. El gimnasio está en el tercer piso.

4 1. Los huéspedes pueden ir en autobús a la playa. 2. En el Viejo San Juan hay cafés, monumentos y restaurantes. 3. El hotel Morro está abierto todo el año. 4. Los huéspedes del hotel pueden tomar el sol en la playa. 5. Las actividades del hotel son pescar, ir de excursión, montar a caballo y nadar.

5 Answers will vary.

Test D

1 Answers will vary.

2 Answers will vary.

3 1. El restaurante Tostones está en el sexto piso. 2. La habitación cuarenta y tres está en el cuarto piso. 3. La biblioteca está en el segundo piso. 4. La cafetería está en el primer piso. 5. La agencia de viajes Sol está en el tercer piso.

4 1. Los huéspedes del hotel Conquistador pueden ir a la playa en autobús. 2. En el Viejo San Juan hay museos, monumentos y muy buenos restaurantes. 3. Puedes visitar el hotel Coquí todos los meses del año porque está abierto todo el año. 4. Los huéspedes del hotel Coquí pueden nadar y bucear. 5. En el hotel Coquí hay clases de salsa, excursiones en bicicleta y excursiones a caballo.

5 Answers will vary.

Test E

1 1. Cierto. 2. Falso. 3. Cierto. 4. Falso. 5. Falso.

2 1. Llueve. 2. Hace buen tiempo. 3. Está nublado. 4. Hace mucho viento. 5. Nieva.

3 1. f 2. e 3. g 4. c 5. d

4 1. está leyendo 2. estamos jugando 3. estás comiendo 4. está oyendo 5. están durmiendo

5 1. La puerta está abierta. 2. Víctor y Carlos son de Puerto Rico. 3. La clase es a las doce. 4. Nosotros estamos lejos de la estación. 5. Tú eres muy inteligente. 6. Yo estoy haciendo windsurf.

6 1. c 2. a 3. c 4. b 5. b 6. a

7 1. estamos 2. Nos 3. son 4. viviendo 5. haciendo 6. lo 7. estoy 8. descansando 9. Me

8 1. b 2. a 3. c 4. c 5. a 6. b

Test F

1 1. Cierto. 2. Falso. 3. Cierto. 4. Falso. 5. Cierto.

2 1. Hace buen tiempo. 2. Está nublado. 3. Está lloviendo. 4. Está nevando. 5. Hace mucho viento.

3 1. a 2. d 3. f 4. g 5. c

4 1. está jugando 2. están leyendo 3. estás nadando 4. está comiendo 5. están estudiando

5 1. Carla y yo estamos en el museo. 2. La fiesta es a las diez. 3. Tú eres costarricense. 4. El café está cerrado. 5. Yo estoy montando a caballo. 6. José y Roberto son primos.

6 1. b 2. c 3. b 4. a 5. c 6. a

7 1. están 2. Los 3. estamos 4. Aburridos 5. las 6. enojado 7. haciendo 8. estoy 9. Es

8 1. a 2. b 3. a 4. c 5. b 6. c

Lección 6

Test A

1 1. c 2. b 3. a 4. b 5. a

2 Answers will vary.

3 1. éstas 2. Ésa 3. aquélla 4. Aquélla 5. Éstos 6. ésos 7. aquéllos

4 1. abrió 2. llegamos 3. tomamos 4. Visitamos 5. volvimos 6. compré 7. recibió 8. vi 9. gastó 10. salimos

5 Answers will vary.

6 1. La ropa para la temporada de primavera-verano tiene/viene en muchos colores y es muy cómoda. 2. Los vestidos tienen variedad de estilos y colores. 3. Los zapatos que cuestan ciento cincuenta y nueve pesos son marrones/de color marrón.

7 Answers will vary.

8 Answers will vary.

Test B

1 1. b 2. a 3. a 4. c 5. b

2 Answers will vary.

3 1. aquéllos 2. éstos 3. ésa 4. Ésa 5. aquélla 6. Aquélla 7. éste

4 1. llegamos 2. abrió 3. esperamos 4. empezamos 5. compró 6. mostró 7. encontré 8. vi 9. salimos 10. cerraron

5 Answers will vary.

6 1. La moda viene en muchos colores para darles alegría a los días fríos. 2. Las nuevas botas son de colores verde y rosado. 3. Es de color gris.

7 Answers will vary.

8 Answers will vary.

Test C

1 Answers will vary.

2 Answers will vary.

3 1. La ropa viene en colores marrón y anaranjado y es muy cómoda. 2. Pueden llevar trajes de pantalón y chaqueta. 3. El suéter morado es de lana. 4. El abrigo que cuesta cuatrocientos treinta pesos es rojo. 5. Pueden llevar los pantalones marrones para ir al trabajo.

4 Answers will vary.

Test D

1 Answers will vary.

2 Answers will vary.

3 1. La moda de primavera-verano viene en colores morado y rosado y en estilos muy cómodos, pero elegantes. 2. Pueden llevar zapatos y bolsas de muchos estilos. 3. Venden diferentes estilos de faldas largas y trajes de pantalón y chaqueta para ir al trabajo. 4. Venden pantalones cortos y sandalias de todos los colores. 5. Venden trajes elegantes en colores claros y camisetas cómodas.

4 Answers will vary.

Test E

1 1. Falso. 2. Cierto. 3. Cierto. 4. Falso. 5. Falso.

2 1. d 2. a 3. e 4. b 5. c

3 1. sé 2. conoces 3. sabe 4. conocemos 5. saben

4 1. buscaron 2. vendió 3. Escribimos 4. pagaste 5. llegó

5 1. f 2. c 3. e 4. a 5. b 6. d

6 1. Mario les presta dinero. 2. Ellos me escriben mensajes electrónicos. 3. Juana le vende una cartera. 4. La vendedora nos dice dónde comprar trajes de baño. 5. Lola te da los calcetines. 6. El vendedor les ofrece un descuento.

7 1. ofrecer 2. caras 3. tenis 4. efectivo 5. rebaja 6. número 7. traje 8. bolsa 9. esta

8 1. b 2. a 3. c 4. a 5. b 6. c

Test F

1 1. Cierto. 2. Falso. 3. Falso. 4. Cierto. 5. Falso.

2 1. a 2. d 3. c 4. e 5. b

3 1. sabe 2. conocen 3. sabes 4. conocemos 5. saben

4 1. compró 2. ofrecieron 3. busqué 4. pagamos 5. empezaste

5 1. d 2. f 3. c 4. e 5. a 6. b

6 1. Luis les paga con tarjeta de crédito. 2. Mariana les trae la ropa. 3. Félix me escribe un mensaje electrónico. 4. La vendedora te muestra los trajes de baño. 5. Elisabeth le compra calcetines. 6. Los padres nos dan dinero.

7 1. servirle 2. baratas 3. zapatos 4. efectivo 5. rebaja 6. calza 7. gafas 8. vestido 9. estos

8 1. b 2. c 3. a 4. a 5. b 6. b

Lección 7

Test A

1 1. Cierto. 2. Falso. 3. Cierto. 4. Falso. 5. Falso.

2 Answers will vary.

3 Answers will vary.

4 1. nada 2. algo 3. siempre 4. alguna 5. ninguno

5 Answers will vary.

6 1. Sí, le interesa el trabajo/le encanta la columna de los domingos del/de la periodista. 2. No. Le molesta/No le gusta levantarse temprano. 3. Necesita/Se viste/Se pone la ropa en diez minutos. 4. Al llegar a casa, se quita la ropa, se pone el pijama y se acuesta. 5. La rutina de Fernando León no le gusta a nadie.

7 Answers will vary.

Test B

1 1. Falso. 2. Falso. 3. Falso. 4. Cierto. 5. Cierto.

2 Answers will vary.

3 Answers will vary.

4 1. nada 2. algo 3. Siempre 4. algunos 5. ningún

5 Answers will vary.

6 1. Le molestan algunas cosas de/No siempre le gusta/No le gusta su estilo de vida/su horario/su rutina. 2. Se quita la ropa, se pone el pijama y se acuesta. 3. A sus hijos no les gusta la rutina de su padre. 4. Le fascina escribir novelas. 5. Quiere cambiar de trabajo porque puede/quiere trabajar en casa y estar cerca de su familia.

7 Answers will vary.

Test C

1 Answers will vary.

2 Answers will vary.

3 Answers will vary.

4 1. Pamela y su hermana fueron a Latinoamérica de vacaciones. 2. Primero fueron a Ecuador. 3. En México, Pamela fue sola a Acapulco, Mérida y Cancún. Su hermana fue sola a Monterrey, Guadalajara y Puebla. 4. Fueron a Puerto Rico y a Cuba antes de terminar su viaje. 5. El lugar favorito de Pamela fue La Habana. El lugar favorito de su hermana fue las islas Galápagos.

5 Answers will vary.

Test D

1 Answers will vary.

2 Answers will vary.

3 Answers will vary.

4 1. Enrique y su hermano fueron a España y a Latinoamérica de vacaciones. 2. En España, Enrique fue solo a Salamanca, Zaragoza y Barcelona. Su hermano fue solo a Ibiza, Mallorca y Menorca. 3. En Puerto Rico fueron a San Juan, Ponce, Arecibo y la isla de Vieques. 4. Fueron a Perú antes de terminar su viaje. 5. El lugar favorito de Enrique fue Machu Picchu. El lugar favorito de su hermano fue San Juan.

5 Answers will vary.

Test E

1 1. a 2. b 3. c 4. b 5. a

2 1. c 2. d 3. b 4. a 5. e

3 1. nos probamos 2. se va 3. se seca 4. te sientes 5. nos sentimos

4 1. c 2. a 3. b 4. c 5. a

5 1. fuimos; ir 2. fueron; ser 3. fue; ir 4. fuiste; ir 5. fui; ir 6. fueron; ir

6 1. despertador 2. pantuflas 3. se cepilla 4. se sienta 5. le molesta 6. Se cambia 7. nada 8. Entonces 9. se maquilla

7 1. le aburren 2. les encanta 3. me importa 4. te gustan 5. les faltan 6. nos molesta

8 1. b 2. a 3. a 4. c 5. b 6. b

Test F

1 1. a 2. b 3. b 4. c 5. c

2 1. b 2. c 3. e 4. a 5. d

3 1. te vas 2. nos vamos 3. se cepilla 4. se lava 5. nos quedamos

4 1. b 2. a 3. c 4. a 5. c

5 1. fueron; ir 2. fuimos; ser 3. fuiste; ir 4. fueron; ir 5. fue; ser 6. fui; ser

6 1. durante 2. Nunca 3. baño 4. champú 5. toalla 6. le encanta 7. se maquilla 8. o 9. le molesta

7 1. nos encantan 2. les molesta 3. le queda 4. me faltan 5. te aburres 6. les interesa

8 1. a 2. c 3. b 4. b 5. a 6. c

Lección 8

Test A

1 1. a 2. a 3. a 4. c 5. b

2 Answers will vary.

3 Answers will vary.

4 1. Se lo 2. Me los 3. Se los 4. se las 5. Se lo

5 1. se vistió 2. pidió 3. prefirió 4. sirvió 5. siguieron 6. se sintieron 7. pidieron 8. volvieron

6 Answers will vary.

7 1. Este estudio se hizo para saber más sobre los hábitos de los estudiantes universitarios. 2. Los estudiantes desean/A los estudiantes les interesa estar bien, practicar deportes y estar delgados. 3. Sí, les gusta el tipo de comida que les dan en las universidades. 4. Al mediodía, muchos estudiantes comen un sándwich y toman un refresco. 5. Los hábitos de los estudiantes no son buenos

8 Answers will vary.

Test B

1 1. b 2. b 3. a 4. a 5. b

2 Answers will vary.

3 Answers will vary.

4 1. se lo 2. se lo 3. Me la 4. se la 5. me la

5 1. nos vestimos 2. prefirió 3. consiguió 4. pedimos 5. sirvió 6. empezamos 7. nos sentimos 8. volvimos

6 Answers will vary.

7 1. Answers may vary. Possible answer: Le gusta mucho España y este verano quiere ir con Eduardo. 2. Answers may vary. Possible answer: Lo que más le gustó fue la comida, el aceite de oliva y las tapas. 3. Es natural y auténtica porque está preparada de una manera muy simple, con ajo, perejil y aceite de oliva. 4. Piensa que son una buena oportunidad para probar muchos platos diferentes/para conocer gente y conversar. 5. Possible answer: Pienso que Eduardo es el novio de Clara porque, en su carta, ella dice: "llevo la misma ropa de siempre, la que a ti te gusta" y "este verano vamos tú y yo".

8 Answers will vary.

Test C

1 Answers will vary.

2 Answers will vary.

3 1. Hicieron esta encuesta para saber qué almuerzan los estudiantes universitarios. 2. Los días de clases, los estudiantes normalmente almuerzan caminando y en muy poco tiempo/quince minutos. 3. Durante la semana, muchos estudiantes almuerzan un sándwich y toman un refresco. 4. Piensan que la comida de las cafeterías es buena para lo que necesitan. 5. Los fines de semana pasan más tiempo comiendo y prueban comidas nuevas/socializan comiendo.

4 Answers will vary.

Test D

1 Answers will vary.

2 Answers will vary.

3 1. El almuerzo estadounidense es más pequeño./Los estadounidenses almuerzan en poco tiempo/comen poco. 2. Toman dos o tres horas para comer y descansar. 3. La comida principal para los mexicanos es el almuerzo. 4. No es popular porque les gusta sentarse y comer sin prisa/descansar antes de regresar al trabajo. 5. No la llevan a casa. La comida se queda en el plato.

4 Answers will vary.

Test E

1 1. b 2. a 3. c 4. c 5. b

2 1. c 2. a 3. a 4. b 5. c

3 1. más 2. tantos 3. menos 4. mejor 5. menor

4 1. le serviste 2. dormí 3. pidieron 4. prefirieron 5. se vistió

5 1. f 2. c 3. b 4. a 5. e 6. d

6 1. b 2. b 3. a 4. b 5. a 6. a

7 1. pidieron 2. tinto 3. refrescos 4. leche 5. se los 6. hamburguesas 7. prefirió 8. más 9. Se las

8 1. b 2. a 3. b 4. c 5. a 6. a

Test F

1 1. c 2. b 3. a 4. c 5. c

2 1. b 2. c 3. a 4. c 5. b

3 1. tan 2. menos 3. mejores 4. más 5. mayor

4 1. se vistió 2. pedí 3. durmieron 4. repitieron 5. les sirvió

5 1. a 2. f 3. e 4. c 5. d 6. b

6 1. b 2. a 3. b 4. a 5. b 6. a

7 1. pidió 2. camarones 3. prefirieron 4. vino 5. jugo 6. más 7. Se la 8. entremeses 9. Se los

8 1. a 2. c 3. b 4. c 5. a 6. a

Lección 9

Test A

1 1. a 2. b 3. a 4. c 5. c

2 Answers will vary.

3 1. Qué 2. Qué 3. quiso 4. pudo 5. quiero 6. Sabes 7. pude 8. conozco 9. conocí 10. pudiste

4 1. se casaron 2. se comprometieron 3. celebraron 4. pudieron 5. dieron 6. conduje 7. se puso 8. dijo 9. tuvieron 10. trajo

5 1. Alejandro y Lucía se casaron. 2. Después de la iglesia, todos fueron a una fiesta en un restaurante. 3. Todos los amigos de la familia fueron a la fiesta. 4. Cenaron en el restaurante El Pardo. 5. Miguel Ángel y Carmen están casados/son esposos.

6 Answers will vary.

Test B

1 1. a 2. c 3. c 4. b 5. a

2 Answers will vary.

3 1. Qué 2. qué 3. pudimos 4. supo 5. quiso 6. cuál 7. cuál 8. conozco 9. conocí 10. sabes

4 1. estuve 2. quiso 3. Hubo 4. se puso 5. dieron 6. traje 7. dijo 8. nos reímos 9. nos divertimos 10. tuvimos

5 1. Los hijos de César y Estela invitaron a toda la familia y amigos de sus padres y los sorprendieron con una fiesta. 2. Después de la cena todos fueron a bailar a la Sala Conde Luna. 3. El bautizo fue en la catedral de Santa María. 4. Doña Esmeralda es la madre de Liliana Obregón y la abuela de María Esmeralda. 5. Elena Cárdenas es la tía de María Esmeralda./María Esmeralda es la sobrina de Elena Cárdenas.

6 Answers will vary.

Test C

1 Answers will vary.

2 Answers will vary.

3 1. Albeto Araneda está en la niñez. 2. Quieren compartir su alegría por el nacimiento de su hijo. 3. A la cena fueron invitados muchos periodistas y profesores. 4. Los invitados se divirtieron mucho. 5. Amalia Rodríguez es divorciada.

4 Answers will vary.

Test D

1 Answers will vary.

2 Answers will vary.

3 1. No. (Ésta) Es la segunda vez que Javier se casa. 2. Iván y Susana son los hijos de Javier con su primera esposa, Marta. Marta es la primera/ex esposa de Javier. 3. Doña Matilde está en la vejez. 4. Organizó una fiesta sorpresa para celebrar el cumpleaños/los noventa y un años de doña Matilde. 5. Nieves habló de la interesante y larga vida de su madre y también recordó la vida de su padre.

4 Answers will vary.

Test E

1 1. Falso. 2. Falso. 3. Falso. 4. Cierto. 5. Cierto.

2 1. e 2. d 3. c 4. b 5. a

3 1. Cuál 2. Qué 3. Cuáles 4. Qué 5. Cuál

4 1. tuve 2. dijeron 3. trajeron 4. supimos 5. estuviste 6. quisieron 7. pudiste 8. supo 9. conocieron 10. quiso 11. di

5 1. conmigo 2. para él 3. con usted 4. contigo 5. con ella 6. para ti

6 1. aniversario 2. para 3. pudieron 4. hizo 5. condujo 6. con 7. quiso 8. brindaron 9. trajo

7 1. a 2. c 3. a 4. c 5. a 6. a

Test F

1 1. Cierto. 2. Cierto. 3. Falso. 4. Falso. 5. Falso.

2 1. b 2. d 3. e 4. a 5. c

3 1. Qué 2. Cuál 3. Qué 4. Cuáles 5. Qué

4 1. hice 2. tradujo 3. pusieron 4. condujiste 5. quisimos 6. conocí 7. supieron 8. pudimos 9. quiso 10. supimos 11. diste

5 1. para ti 2. con él 3. conmigo 4. para mí 5. para ella 6. contigo

6 1. hicieron 2. celebrar 3. postres 4. botellas 5. quiso 6. alegría 7. estuvo 8. condujeron 9. con

7 1. c 2. b 3. c 4. a 5. b 6. a

ANSWERS TO EXAMS

Lecciones 1–4

Exam A

1 1. a 2. c 3. c 4. c 5. b

2 Answers will vary.

3 Some answers will vary. Sample answers: 1. Hay seis mochilas. 2. Hay cuatro relojes. 3. Son las dos menos diez./Son las diez y diez. 4. Las computadoras están encima de/en la mesa. 5. Hay cinco cuadernos.

4 1. Tienes hambre 2. tengo ganas 3. tengo sueño 4. tengo calor 5. Tienes razón

5 1. empiezan 2. pienso 3. quiero 4. vuelves 5. muestro

6 Some answers will vary. Sample answers: 1. Yo salgo de casa a las siete y cuarto de la mañana todos los días. 2. El gimnasio cierra a las once menos cuarto de la noche. 3. Mario va a visitar el museo el fin de semana. 4. Yo juego al futbol trescientos sesenta y cinco días al año. 5. Tú duermes siete horas todos los días.

7 Answers will vary.

8 Answers may vary. Possible answers: 1. Rafael va a tomar el sol en la playa. 2. Paola va a nadar en el mar. 3. El señor Barrera está esquiando. 4. Elena y José Fernando están patinando. 5. Francisco y José van a jugar al vóleibol.

9 Answers will vary.

10 Some answers will vary. Sample answers: 1. El club se llama Club Verano. 2. La biblioteca pública está en el centro de la ciudad, a la izquierda del Club Verano. 3. Hay un gimnasio para niños. 4. El club abre a las siete y media de la mañana y cierra a las once menos cuarto de la noche. 5. Answers will vary.

11 Answers will vary.

Exam B

1 1. b 2. a 3. a 4. c 5. b

2 Answers will vary.

3 Some answers will vary. Sample answers: 1. Hay cuatro computadoras. 2. Las mochilas están debajo de la mesa. 3. Son las dos menos diez./Son las diez y diez. 4. Hay cinco cuadernos. 5. Hay cuatro relojes.

4 1. Tengo frío 2. tengo ganas 3. tengo miedo 4. Tienes razón 5. tienes hambre

5 1. almuerzas 2. piensa 3. quiere 4. supongo 5. encontrar

6 Some answers will vary. Sample answers: 1. Yo veo el partido de baloncesto en la televisión a las ocho menos cuarto de la tarde/noche. 2. Nosotros jugamos al vóleibol los martes y los jueves. 3. María y su hermana van a cenar a un restaurante del/en el centro. 4. La biblioteca cierra a las siete y media de la tarde/noche. 5. Ellos duermen ocho horas todos los días.

7 Answers will vary.

8 1. José va a leer el periódico. 2. Angélica y Jessica van a jugar al fútbol. 3. Orlando va a pasear en bicicleta. 4. Mercedes va a visitar un monumento. 5. Pablo y Lucía van a caminar/ pasear (por el parque).

9 Answers will vary.

10 Some answers will vary. Sample answers: 1. El club se llama Club Diversión. 2. La escuela pública está en el centro de la ciudad, a la derecha del Club Diversión. 3. Hay dos piscinas. 4. El club abre a las ocho menos cuarto de la mañana y cierra a las nueve y media de la noche. 5. Answers will vary.

11 Answers will vary.

Lecciones 1–9

Exam A

1 1. Falso. 2. Cierto. 3. Falso. 4. Falso. 5. Cierto.

2 Answers will vary.

3 Answers will vary.

4 1. estás 2. estoy 3. estás 4. es 5. es 6. está 7. soy 8. Son 9. están 10. está

5 1. se lo 2. se lo 3. se la 4. Se las 5. me/te los

6 1. se vistieron 2. pidió 3. prefirió 4. sirvió 5. se despidieron 6. durmió 7. perdió

7 Answers will vary.

8 1. Cuestan dos mil trescientos quince pesos. 2. Cuestan mil cuatrocientos cincuenta pesos. 3. Cierra(n) a las nueve de la noche de lunes a viernes y cierra(n) a las ocho de la noche los sábados. 4. Tienen los números treinta y cinco a treinta y ocho.

9 Answers will vary.

10 1. Verónica Cortés es casada. 2. Decidieron casarse en abril de 2010. 3. La fiesta fue sólo para la familia./Casi todos los miembros de las dos familias fueron a la fiesta. 4. Sí, le gustó mucho. 5. Carmen no fue porque está de vacaciones en el Caribe.

11 Answers will vary.

Exam B

1 1. Cierto. 2. Falso. 3. Falso. 4. Cierto. 5. Falso.

2 Answers will vary.

3 Answers will vary.

4 1. estás 2. estoy 3. Estás 4. soy 5. es 6. es 7. es 8. es 9. estamos 10. es

5 1. se lo 2. se lo 3. te la 4. Me las 5. te lo

6 1. se vistió 2. prefirió 3. Pidieron 4. trajo 5. estuvo 6. salieron 7. dieron

7 Answers will vary.

8 1. Cuestan mil trescientos quince pesos. 2. Cuestan mil doscientos sesenta pesos. 3. Cierra(n) a las diez de la noche de lunes a viernes y cierra(n) a las ocho de la noche los sábados. 4. Tiene(n) los números treinta y seis a cuarenta.

9 Answers will vary.

10 1. Corina Bran es casada. 2. Ella tiene 40 años. 3. Pepe Cuevas es un artista español. Estuvo en la fiesta porque es el hijo del doctor Ignacio Cuevas. 4. Juana no bailó porque llevó al bebé a su habitación a/para dormir. 5. Piensa que son interesantes porque el esposo es mucho mayor que la esposa.

11 Answers will vary.

ANSWERS TO OPTIONAL TEST SECTIONS

Lección 1

Fotonovela Video Test Items

1 1. Marissa es de los Estados Unidos/de Wisconsin, Estados Unidos. 2. La señora Díaz es de Cuba. 3. El señor Díaz es de México/de Mérida, México. 4. Jimena y Felipe son de México.

Panorama Textbook Section Test Items

1 1. Cierto. 2. Falso. La Pequeña Habana es un barrio de Miami. 3. Falso. El desfile puertorriqueño se celebra en Nueva York. 4. Cierto. 5. Falso. Las enchiladas y las quesadillas son platos de México. 6. Cierto.

Panorama cultural Video Test Items

1 Answers will vary.

Flash cultura Video Test Items

1 1. Answers will vary. 2. Answers will vary.

Lección 2

Fotonovela Video Test Items

1 Order of items in the answers may vary. 1. Marissa: arqueología, español, geografía, historia, literatura 2. Felipe: administración, economía 3. Juan Carlos: ciencias ambientales, computación, química

Panorama Textbook Section Test Items

1 1. a 2. b 3. c 4. b 5. a 6. c

Panorama cultural Video Test Items

1 1. celebran 2. viajan 3. delante de 4. mañana 5. llevan 6. turistas

Flash cultura Video Test Items

1 1. Falso. 2. Cierto. 3. Falso. 5. Cierto. 6. Cierto.

Lección 3

Fotonovela Video Test Items

1 Answers will vary.

Panorama Textbook Section Test Items

1 1. Cierto. 2. Falso. Muchas personas van a las islas Galápagos por sus plantas y animales. 3. Falso. Charles Darwin estudió las especies de las islas Galápagos. 4. Cierto. 5. Falso. Oswaldo Guayasamín es un pintor ecuatoriano famoso. 6. Cierto. 7. Falso. En la Sierra los turistas practican deportes. 8. Cierto.

Panorama cultural Video Test Items

1 1. viven 2. tiene 3. tienen 4. cerca 5. turistas

Flash cultura Video Test Items

1 Answers will vary.

Lección 4

Fotonovela Video Test Items

1 Answers will vary.

Panorama Textbook Section Test Items

1 1. Falso. Los aztecas dominaron en México del siglo XIV al XVI. 2. Falso. Frida Kahlo era la esposa de Diego Rivera. 3. Cierto. 4. Cierto. 5. Falso. México es el mayor productor de plata en el mundo. 6. Cierto. 7. Falso. La Ciudad de México/México D.F. es el centro económico y cultural de México. 8. Cierto.

Panorama cultural Video Test Items

1 1. b 2. a 3. b 4. c 5. b

Flash cultura Video Test Items

1 Answers will vary.

Lección 5

Fotonovela Video Test Items

1 Answers will vary.

Panorama Textbook Section Test Items

1 1. e 2. h 3. d 4. c 5. a 6. g 7. f 8. b

Panorama cultural Video Test Items

1 Answers will vary.

Flash cultura Video Test Items

1 Answers will vary.

Lección 6

Fotonovela Video Test Items

1 Answers will vary.

Panorama Textbook Section Test Items

1 1. José Martí 2. colibrí abeja 3. europeos 4. Alicia Alonso 5. El tabaco 6. *Buena Vista Social Club*

Panorama cultural Video Test Items

1 1. c 2. c 3. b 4. b 5. a 6. a

Flash cultura Video Test Items

1 Answers will vary.

Lección 7

Fotonovela Video Test Items

1 Answers will vary.

Panorama Textbook Section Test Items

1 1. e 2. g 3. d 4. h 5. b 6. a

Panorama cultural Video Test Items

1 1. pasear en bicicleta 2. *sandboard* 3. ir de excursión 4. caminar con llamas 5. el Camino Inca 6. la pesca

Flash cultura Video Test Items

1 Answers will vary.

Lección 8

Fotonovela Video Test Items

1 Answers will vary.

Panorama Textbook Section Test Items

1 1. Falso. En Guatemala hablan español, lenguas mayas, xinca y garífuna. 2. Cierto. 3. Cierto. 4. Cierto. 5. Falso. La capital de Guatemala es la Ciudad de Guatemala. 6. Cierto. 7. Cierto. 8. Cierto.

Panorama cultural Video Test Items

1 1. Falso. Esta ciudad fue la capital de Guatemala (hasta 1773). 2. Cierto. 3. Cierto. 4. Falso. Chichicastenango es una ciudad más pequeña que Antigua. 5. Falso. Todos los jueves y domingos hay un mercado al aire libre en las calles y plazas de la ciudad. 6. Falso. Ningún producto tiene un precio fijo y los clientes tienen que regatear al hacer sus compras.

Flash cultura Video Test Items

1 Answers will vary.

Lección 9

Fotonovela Video Test Items

1 Answers will vary.

Panorama Textbook Section Test Items

1 1. d 2. c 3. b 4. e 5. a

Panorama cultural Video Test Items

1 Answers will vary.

Flash cultura Video Test Items

1 Answers will vary.

Lección 1–4

Fotonovela Video Test Items

1 Answers will vary.

Panorama Textbook Section Test Items

1 1. d 2. b 3. c 4. a 5. e

Panorama cultural Video Test Items

1 Answers will vary. Possible answers: 1. Los dominicanos celebran en agosto el día de la independencia de su país. 2. El canal de televisión Telelatino, la revista *Picante* y el periódico *El correo canadiense* ofrecen servicios en español. 3. Los encierros son la actividad central del Festival de San Fermín. 4. Las islas Galápagos están en el océano Pacífico, cerca de la costa de Ecuador. 5. Teotihuacán es uno de los lugares arqueológicos más importantes de Latinoamérica .

Flash cultura Video Test Items

1 Answers will vary.

Lección 1–9

Fotonovela Video Test Items

1 Answers will vary.

Panorama Textbook Section Test Items

1 1. f 2. a 3. h 4. b 5. e 6. d 7. i 8. c 9. j 10. g

Panorama cultural Video Test Items

1 1. Cierto. 2. Cierto. 3. Cierto. 4. Falso. En cuatro de las islas Galápagos viven personas. 5. Falso. El Castillo de San Felipe del Morro es un sitio histórico nacional de Puerto Rico. 6. Falso. Regla es una ciudad cubana donde se practica la santería. 7. Falso. En la isla de Pascua siempre hace mucho calor y también mucho viento.

Flash cultura Video Test Items

1 Answers will vary.

Credits

Every effort has been made to trace the copyright holders of the works published herein. If proper copyright acknowledgment has not been made, please contact the publisher and we will correct the information in future printings.

Photography and Art Credits

All images © Vista Higher Learning unless otherwise noted.

Testing Program: 141: (all) Martín Bernetti; **145:** (l, r) Martín Bernetti; (m) Media Bakery; **147:** Noam Armonn/Shutterstock; **151:** Anne Loubet; **155:** Martín Bernetti; **157:** Piranka/iStockphoto; **169:** Martín Bernetti; **173:** Martín Bernetti; **176:** Martín Bernetti; **178:** Martín Bernetti; **209:** Janet Dracksdorf; **213:** Janet Dracksdorf; **216:** José Blanco; **218:** José Blanco; **229:** Martín Bernetti; **233:** Martín Bernetti; **236:** Martín Bernetti; **238:** Martín Bernetti; **248:** Martín Bernetti; **252:** Martín Bernetti; **269:** Monkey Business Images/Shutterstock; **273:** Martín Bernetti; **275:** Big Cheese/AGE Fotostock; **277:** Andersen Ross/Blend Images/Corbis; **278:** VHL; **307:** Martín Bernetti; **313:** Martín Bernetti; **319:** Martín Bernetti; **322:** (all) VHL; **325:** Martín Bernetti; **326:** (all) Martín Bernetti; **328:** (all) VHL.